MW00772601

HIMALAYAN BLUNDER

The curtain-raiser to the Sino-Indian War of 1962

Brig. J.P. DALVI (Retd.)
INDIAN ARMY

FOREWORD
FRANK MORAES

SPECIAL PREFACE
Lt. Gen. A.K. HANDOO PVSM (Retd.)
INDIAN ARMY

NATRAJ PUBLISHERS
DEHRA DUN

First published 1969
Reprint 1997, 2010

ISBN 978-81-8158-145-7

Published by Mrs. Veena Arora for Natraj Publishers, Publication Division, Dehra Dun and printed at Anubha Printers, Noida.

DEDICATED TO

THE MEMORY OF ALL RANKS OF 7 INFANTRY BRIGADE WHO LAID DOWN THEIR LIVES FOR INDIA IN THE BATTLE OF THE NAMKA CHU IN OCTOBER 1962.

"Men who had fallen from high command, whether for cause or as scapegoats . . . wrote their private justifications. As each account appeared, inevitably shifting responsibility or blame to someone else, another was provoked. Private feuds became public, public controversies expanded. Men who would otherwise have remained mute were stung to publish . . . Books proliferated. Whole schools of partisans . . . produced libraries of controversy. Through this forest of special pleading the historian gropes his way, trying to recapture the truth of past events and find out what really happened".

MRS. BARBARA TUCHMAN
"*The Guns Of August.*"

This book is one more tree in the inevitable forest which will grow around the Indian humiliation of 1962.

ACKNOWLEDGEMENTS

NO SERVING OFFICER has helped me in any way in the preparation of this book.

I am indebted to some civilian friends who helped me in producing this work, but who desire to remain anonymous.

My debt to my school friend, Lt.-Col. C. L. (Larry) Proudfoot (Retd.) is incalculable. No formal acknowledgement can convey my gratitude for his comprehensive assistance at every stage of the preparation and production of this book. I am also grateful for the kind and generous hospitality extended to me by Connie and Larry Proudfoot during my prolonged visits to Bombay in connection with the publication of the book.

I wish to thank my brother, Colonel Jai Dalvi (Retd.), for his criticisms, constructive suggestions and for helping me in the search for background material.

I am indebted to the following authors for background material and permission to quote from books of their copyright. Appropriate acknowledgement has been made in the text. I apologise in any case where such permission or acknowledgement has been overlooked.

1. *The Battle of NEFA* by G. S. Bhargava – Allied Publishers.
2. *China Invades India* edited by V. B. Karnik – Allied Publishers.
3. *After Nehru Who?* by Welles Hangen – Rupert Hart Davis.
4. *Chinese Invasion of NEFA* by Major S. R. Johori – Himalaya Publications.
5. *Guilty Men of 1962* by D. R. Mankekar – Tulsi Shah Enterprises.

6. *Forging The Shield* by Lt.-Gen. P. S. Bhagat, V.C. – The Statesmen Press.

7. *Cassino – Portrait of a Battle* by F. Majdalany – Longman Green & Co.

8. *The Desert Generals* by Corelli Barnett – The Viking Press.

9. "*Auchinleck*" by John Connell – Cassell & Co. Ltd.

10. "*The Donkeys*" by Allen Clark – William Morrow & Co.

11. *The Guns of August* by Mrs. Barbara Tuchman – The MacMillan Co. of New York.

12. *A History of Militarism* by Alfred Vagts – Meridian Books Inc.

13. *The Untold Story* by Lt.-Gen. B. M. Kaul – Allied Publishers.

14. *The Statesman Supplement* "Black November" of 20th November 1967.

15. Statement by the Hon'ble Y. B. Chavan, Defence Minister of the Union Cabinet of India, to the Lok Sabha, on 3rd September 1963.

16. "*Lost Victories*" by Field Marshal Eric von Manstein – Henry Regnery Company, Chicago, U.S.A.

Finally, I owe a debt to Mr. Derek Pinto who made the drawings from my clumsy memory sketches.

FOREWORD

I HAVE HAD occasion to read a number of books and other material on the Indian military debacle of October-November 1962 when the Chinese inflicted a humiliating reverse on our armed forces in NEFA and along the Himalayan border. These contributions have come from various sources, from soldiers, some of whom have participated in the fighting in various capacities, from bureaucrats, military correspondents, journalists and commentators.

Brigadier John Dalvi's account not only of the disastrous thirty days conflict but of the policies and attitudes of mind which led to it, as also of the lessons to be drawn from that tragic confrontation gives this book an unusual dimension. The author had the advantage of being a participant in the fighting when on the morning of 20th October 1962 massed Chinese artillery opened up a heavy concentration on the weak Indian garrison in a narrow sector of the Namka Chu valley of Kameng Frontier Division in the North-East Frontier Agency (NEFA). Dalvi was taken prisoner and held in captivity for seven months during which as he writes poignantly, "a wave of bitter shame" for this country overwhelmed him.

This book is partly the result of those seven months of brooding and thinking. It is remarkable not only for its sensitive writing but for its thinking in depth. No soldier who passed through that searing experience, however generous his nature, could be impervious to a deep embitterment of spirit and feeling. It is to Dalvi's credit that he does not allow this embitterment to cloud his judgement and thought.

He does not, however, spare those whom he believes were the guilty men. But neither his assessment of them nor his conclusions have the enveloping sweep of a flat vindictive indictment. Dalvi had evidently thought deeply over the military dangers inherent in the political policies of our omniscient know-alls in New Delhi long before the confrontation came. There is a dramatic but impressive picture of General Lentaigne, then commandant of the Defence Services Staff College in Wellington, boldly challenging a very senior official of the External Affairs Ministry who had given a talk on Sino-Tibetan relations justifying the policy of China's subjugation of Tibet. Lentaigne warned the complacent speaker – this was early in 1951 – of the military threat to India by the Chinese presence in Tibet.

Lentaigne, of course, was ignored, as were some others, by the all-seeing Pooh Bahs of New Delhi. Retribution came eleven years later. It is the great merit of Dalvi's book that while he evidently has sufficient dynamite to blow some political and military reputations sky-high, he refrains from doing so merely for the heck of doing so.

None-the-less his book throws new light on certain decisive periods notably on the vague borderland of September-October 1962. His objects and objectives are not so much concerned with the past as with the future. Major mistakes, like minor diseases, are often preventible. If so, why are they not prevented?

This is the question which Dalvi poses and asks. He is deeply concerned that these mistakes, exposed and analysed, should not be repeated, for it is obvious that he realises the basic reason why history repeats itself. History repeats itself because men repeat their mistakes.

I confess that I have never read an account of those tragic thirty days that has so stirred me cerebally or moved me so emotionally. I think it is because Dalvi's writing is an exercise in restraint, in the way he unfolds the evidence not merely to establish his case, but, going further, to suggest ways and means of improving our apparatus for the higher direction of war.

What is the use of the past if it has no lessons for the future? Experience, as Oscar Wilde observed, is the name men give to their mistakes.

Wise men and wise nations profit by their mistakes. Humility is the beginning of wisdom for progress starts with the thought that perhaps one might oneself be mistaken. I like Dalvi's courage, his conviction, his deep understanding of what he is writing about, his openness of mind. That is why I would do more than recommend this book. I would implore every Indian capable of arriving at an independent decision, to read it.

FRANK MORAES

New Delhi, 25th March, 1969.

PREFACE

THIS BOOK was born in a Prisoner of War Camp in Tibet on a cold bleak night.

On the night of 21st November 1962, I was woken up by the Chinese Major in charge of my solitary confinement with shouts of 'good news – good news'. He told me that the Sino-Indian War was over and that the Chinese Government had decided to withdraw from all the areas which they had overrun, in their lightning campaign. When I asked the reason for this decision he gave me this Peking inspired answer: "India and China have been friends for thousands of years and have never fought before. China does not want war. It is the reactionary (*sic*) Indian Government that was bent on war. So the Chinese counter-attacked in self-defence and liberated all our territories in NEFA and Ladakh, in just one month. Now we have decided to go back as we do not want to settle the border problem by force. We have proved that you are no match for mighty China". He concluded with this supercilious and patronising remark: "We hope that the Indian Government will now see sense and come to the conference table at once so that 1,200 million Chinese and Indians can get on with their national development plans and halt Western Imperialism".

This kindergarten homily was, and remains, the most humiliating moment of my 7-month captivity and indeed of my life. That night I experienced a wave of bitter shame for my country. In my grief I took a solemn vow that one day I would tell the truth about how we let ourselves reach such a sorry pass. With time heavy on my hands, as I had no radio, newspapers or books, I brooded over India's humiliation and the fate of my command.

I was repatriated, along with all the other officers of field rank, on 4th May 1963. We reached Barrackpore, the Military Airport at Calcutta at mid-day but could not land there and were diverted to Dum Dum.

We deplaned and were greeted with correct military protocol, tinged with a chill reserve. It was only later that I found out that we had to clear ourselves of the charge of having been brainwashed – a strange charge from a Government which had itself been brainwashed into championing China's cause for more than a decade.

Without a doubt the prisoners had been declared outcasts. Apparently we should have atoned for the past national sins of omission and commission with our lives. Our repatriation was embarrasing as the national spotlight had again been focused on the Sino-Indian Conflict.

From the tarmac we were herded straight to the Customs enclosure where a sprightly team of appraisers had assembled to 'examine' our luggage. They had been told that some Indians had arrived from Hong Kong and were waiting to confiscate transistors and opium! I knew then that there had been no material change in India and we were in the same old *groove*.

After a cursory and stereotyped de-briefing at Ranchi, I was ordered to meet the Chief of Army Staff, Gen. J. N. Chaudhuri at Delhi on 15th May. He asked me to write a report for the personal information of the Defence Minister and himself. The aim was, in Gen. Chaudhuri's words: "To teach ourselves how not to hand over a brigade on a plate to the Chinese in future". He added that we had become the laughing stock of even countries like . . . and . . . (I hesitate to name these countries!)

I welcomed the opportunity afforded by the Chief's instruction for a personal report as this would give me a chance to collect my thoughts. The basic facts had been branded into my memory. To make doubly sure, I had many sessions with Lt.-Col. Rikh, Commanding Officer of 2 Rajputs and Lt.-Col. B. S. Ahluwalia,

Commanding Officer of the 1/9 Gorkhas, Major R. O. Kharbanda and Captain T. K. Gupta of my Staff. We recounted, cross-checked and authenticated the facts which form the basis for this book. Rankling at our unfriendly reception and the many garbled versions I heard from friends, I wrote a forthright account which I handed over to the Chief personally. I do not know the fate of this report as I was never again asked to discuss or explain it. It may have touched some sensitive nerves.

It was soon apparent that the Army had become the centre of much controversy and that the blame for the 1962 fiasco had been cunningly shifted to its alleged 'shortcomings'. What was more alarming were the extravagant claims made by some senior Army Officers, who attained eminence only after the 1962 reshuffles, as to how brilliantly they would have handled the situation and defied the authority of Nehru, Menon and Kaul. This attitude made me despair of whether my countrymen and colleagues would ever learn any lessons from India's first attempt at conducting a modern war and strengthened my resolution to tell my story.

1962 was a National Failure of which every Indian is guilty. It was a failure in the Higher Direction of War, a failure of the Opposition, a failure of the General Staff (myself included); it was a failure of Responsible Public Opinion and the Press. For the Government of India, it was a Himalayan Blunder at all levels.

* * *

The people of India want to know the truth but have been denied it on the dubious grounds of national security. The result has been an unhealthy amalgam of inuendo, mythology, conjecture, outright calumny and sustained efforts to confuse and conceal the truth. Even the truncated 'NEFA' Enquiry has been withheld except for a few paraphrased extracts read out to the

Lok Sabha on 2nd September 1963. For some undisclosed reason, I was not asked to give evidence before this body nor (to the best of my knowledge) were my repatriated Commanding Officers.

It is thus vitally necessary to trace, without rancour and without malice, the overall causes which resulted in the reverses and which so seriously affected India's honour. Some of the things that happened in 1962 must never be allowed to happen again. There is a school of thought which advocates a moratorium on the NEFA Affair on the grounds that such 'patriotic reticence' is desirable in the context of the continuing Chinese (and Pakistani) military threats. I do not think that this theory is tenable. The main protagonists of this line played a part in the tragic drama, or belonged to the political party which provided the national leadership and their plea for silence does not spring entirely from a sense of patriotism.

There are others, mostly barren politicians, who use the Nehru legend to buttress their failures, or inveterate hero-worshippers, who express irritation at any adverse reference to Mr. Nehru's long spell as the Prime Minister of India. As was said of Lord Chatham, the British Prime Minister, 'His country men were so conscious of what they owed him that they did not want to hear about his faults'. But it is impossible to narrate a failure, which historically marked the end of the Nehru saga, without critical, often harsh comments on the principle *dramatis personae* who held high office and who were revered by the people. The magnitude of our defeat could not have been wrought without Himalayan Blunders at all levels. But this is not a "*J' Accuse*".

India has a near unbroken record of military failures through the ages. Our peasantry has always fought gallantly; but it is an indisputable fact that seldom has this bravery been utilised to win battlefield victories and thus to attain our political objectives, due to inept political or military leadership, or both. Need we follow this tragic path interminably?

It had fallen to my lot to be associated with the China problem for over 8 years from 1954 to 1962. I was first connected with the Higher Direction of War, in a modest capacity, as a Lt.-Colonel in Military Operations Directorate. Later, as Brigadier-in-Charge of Administration of the troops on Ladakh, I saw, at first hand, what passed for 'logistic support'. Finally as Commander of the key sector of Towang, North-East Frontier Agency, I was involved in our so-called operational planning to defend our borders. The years of higher responsibility were complementary and gave me a personal insight into our National Policy as well as our half-hearted military response to the Chinese challenge.

I have tried to tell the story as I saw it unfold, over the years, to add to our knowledge. I have included the politico-military background only because this had a direct bearing on our performance in the military field, in 1962.

This is a personal narrative – a narrative of what Infantry Brigade was ordered to do and what happened when they attempted to carry out those orders. In all humility I can claim that only I am in a position to explain many nagging questions that need explaining, facts that are necessary.

The theme of the book is the steadfastness of the Indian soldier in the midst of political wavering and a military leadership which was influenced more by political than military considerations. The book records their valour, resolution and loyalty – qualities which are generally forgotten in the mass of political post-mortems which have been served up to the Indian people.

This is a record of the destruction of a Brigade without a formal declaration of war – another central fact that is often overlooked – and which coloured the actions of all the principal participants.

I have made every effort not to view things in a retrospective light or with the clarity of hindsight. I have recorded experiences, ideas and feelings as they appeared at the time. I have tried to give an objective account of all that happened, of the people involved and of the decisions they took. My opinions as a participant in the climatic *finale* of September-October 1962 must be subjective. The main essential is to know how the principal participants thought and reacted.

As Lord Avon (Sir Anthony Eden) says in the Preface to his Memoirs, *The Full Circle:* "This book will expose many wounds; by doing so it may help to heal them".

By this book I express my undying gratitude to my Commanding Officers for their trust and loyalty; to the men of all classes and from all units under my command for their selfless devotion to duty; and to my staff whose dedication sustained me in those harrowing days.

This book is the fulfilment of my promises to my friends, in all walks of life, to vindicate the reputation of the men I had the honour to command. I hope that I shall have discharged my responsibility to all those who gave their lives in the line of duty and whose sacrifice deserves a permanent, printed memorial.

61, St. Patrick's Town,
Sholapur Road,
Poona-1

1st March 1969.

J P Dalvi
Brig

SPECIAL PREFACE

To loosely paraphrase an old dictum - "Victory has many disciples, defeat few votaries". Himalayan Blunder authored by the late Brigadier (Retired) J.P. Dalvi is a seminal work ; an authentic, wholly objective account of the decimation of a formation in the initial phase of the Sino Indian Conflict of 1962. The trauma of this event, which scarred the national psyche, was the outcome of a deeply flawed national policy; the articulation of this policy was limited to cliche ridden rhetoric; its implementation violated the cannons of the higher direction of war.

The author has set out the tragic sequence of events on a broad canvas; he has lucidly analysed the political compulsions which led to the ill conceived "Forward Policy", and then examined its impact on the deployment of 4 Infantry Division, essentially comprising 7 Infantry Brigade, in the Kameng Sector. The circumstances leading to adhoc decision making, wholly unrelated to resource constraints which severely limited our war waging capability, have been enumerated in convincing detail. The author has established with damning impact the prevailing dichotomy between ill advised professions of intent at the strategic level, and the utter lack of resources at the tactical level to stake out or contest territorial claims in the mountains. This situation was compounded by a ill-defined yet highly personalised command structure, supported by fragile staff framework incapable of responding to critical conflict situations. To this explosive brew must be added, as brought out by the author with a high degree of credibility, the fear psychosis which paralysed elements of the higher command structure. The author examines this theme, which is central to this work, in all its complexities and nuances with great clarity and conviction.

Brig. Dalvi has recreated the ambience of 1962 with layer on layer of structured observation aimed at determining limitations in the formation and execution of defence policy at the national level. The topicality and relevance of his analysis, extrapolated to the current geo-strategic environment, demonstrates that we have not fully absorbed the lessons of 1962. A listing of the unfinished agenda derived from the author's analysis would include : Item : The Infantry soldier is currently committed to combating insurgency with a rifle of 1964 vintage; according to media reports, Pay Commission has equated his status to that of a peon. Item : The Defence Ministry has not been integrated with Service Headquarters and continues to function in a parasitical mode with no accountability to the Defence Services. Item : The National Security Council conceived as an organ for formulating national defence policy has not been institutionalised. This is why I consider Himalayan Blunder a compelling read in this our 50th anniversary of Independence : our yet to be accomplished "tryst with destiny".

July 11, 1997

Dehra Dun.

Lt. Gen. (Retd) A.K. Handoo, PVSM

CONTENTS

Page

PART I

THE YEARS OF CREDULITY AND NEGLIGENCE

I. Introduction 1
II. The Annexation of Tibet and India's China Policy 6
III. The Uneasy Lull, 1950/55 18
IV. The Twilight Years, 1955/59 30
V. The Army Mans The Border, 1959/60 ... 55
VI. Half-Hearted Preparations, 1961 76

PART II

THE FATEFUL YEAR - 1962

VII. The Defence of The McMahon Line - The Battle Zone; Strategy Unrelated to Means; Operation ONKAR; Wishful Thinking ... 107
VIII. The Line-Up On The Eve of Battle — 7th September 1962 - China Prepares for the *Coup de Grace*; China's Deception Plans; India Unprepared for War 146

PART III

"ON TO THE NAMKA CHU"

IX. China Crosses The McMahon Line - 8th September 1962 165
X. The Trap is Baited 184
XI. "Evict The Chinese" 221

Page

XII. The Final Appreciation, 23rd/29th September 1962 231

Part IV

THE END OF MAKE-BELIEVE

XIII. Nehru Takes Over – 2nd October 1962 ... 245
XIV. A Soldier Uninhibited 255
XV. The Clash At Tseng Jong, 10th October 1962... 292

Part V

THE BATTLE AT THE NAMKA CHU RIVER

XVI. "Defend Your Present Positions" 307
XVII. Feverish Activity 314
XVIII. Occupation and Build-Up of Tsangle ... 325
XIX. The Blinkered Command 330
XX. The Vain Fight For Decisions 336
XXI. 7 Brigade Without Higher Leadership ... 344
XXII. The Ethics of Resigning a Field Command ... 357
XXIII. The Trap Is Set 360
XXIV. The Day of Reckoning, 20th October 1962 ... 364
XXV. Captive of The Chinese Army ... 381

Part VI

THE REASON WHY

XXVI. Faulty Higher Direction of War – The Ministry of Defence; The Chiefs of Staff Committee;

The Cabinet Secretariat (Military Wing); The Chief of Army Staff; Army Headquarters; The Penalty for Hustling 397

Page

XXVII. India's Defence Ministers from 1947 to 1962 400

EPILOGUE

XXVIII. The Political and Economic Aftermath ... 478

Appendix I. Letter from Sardar Vallabhbhai Patel to Pandit Jawaharlal Nehru on the implications of the Chinese occupation of Tibet 501

Appendix II. Author's Career and Credentials ... 499

SKETCHES

Sketch I. Kameng Frontier Division of NEFA – the route from the Brahmaputra Valley to the McMahon Line ... ... opp. 109

Sketch II. The Thagla Ridge-Namka Chu Valley Battle-zone and maintenance routes ... ... End

Sketch III. The Massive Chinese Assaults on 20th October 1962 against 7 Brigade ... ... End

Part I

Credulous and Negligent

CHAPTER I

Introduction

AT 5 on the morning of 20th October 1962 massed Chinese artillery opened up a heavy concentration on the weak Indian garrison, in a narrow sector of the Namka Chu Valley, of Kameng Frontier Division, in the North East Frontier Agency (NEFA). Massive infantry assaults followed, and within three hours the unequal contest was over. The route to the plains of Assam lay wide open. The Chinese exploited their initial successes and advanced 160 miles into Indian territory down the southern slopes of the Himalayas, reaching the Brahmaputra Valley by 20th November. They swept aside the so-called impregnable defences at Sela Pass; Bomdilla was literally overrun; the monastery town of Towang fell without a fight. India's panicky reaction included the scrambling of ill-equipped, ill-trained for mountain warfare and unacclimatised military formations from the Punjab – over 1,600 miles away. They were merely funnelled into the Chinese bag, as there were no pre-planned and prepared defended zones in depth. The Chinese were amazed at this grave military blunder, as they had assembled a huge army opposite NEFA (estimates vary between 30,000 and 50,000) without alerting the Indian Government, much less provoking the Indian Army into undertaking the minimum necessary strategic counter-measures. The Chinese had lit the fuse on 8th September 1962 by intruding into the Thagla Ridge area; but this was not treated as a prelude to a full-scale invasion; it was dismissed as yet another minor border incident which could be "localised and dealt with firmly".

The NEFA Reverse, as this short war has since been named, rocked the political and military foundations of India and bred a defeatist mentality. The people lost faith in the higher leadership.

Prior to the Chinese invasion the prevalent political and military thinking was that there would be no war with China. The Chinese were our friends, and the only combustible issue was the undemarcated Indo-Tibetan border. We accepted the possibility of some misunderstanding about the actual alignment of these remote areas, and were prepared for incursions and border clashes; but rejected the probability of a major military conflict.

India was therefore taken by complete surprise politically, diplomatically and strategically. There was no overall political objective; no National Policy; no grand strategy and total unreadiness for military operations in the awesome Himalayan mountains, against a first-class land power. The Government had not prepared the nation for war.

The initial reaction to the Chinese invasion and our reverses was one of shock, disbelief and indignation. India's distinguished President, Dr. S. Radhakrishnan summed up the feeling of the nation succintly when he exclaimed, "We have been negligent and credulous". From the highest constitutional authority in the country, this was unqualified censure against our political and military hierarchies.

The Prime Minister of India, Mr. Jawaharlal Nehru expressed the view that the Chinese had treacherously stabbed India in the back. He was shocked and dismayed by the sudden, unforeseen developments. In a radio talk at that time, he said, "I am grieved at the setbacks to our troops that have occurred on the frontier, and the reverses we have had. They were overwhelmed by vast numbers and big artillery, mountain guns and heavy mortars which the Chinese have brought with them". This was a courageous but sad admission of failure by the executive head of Government.

The Indian Defence Minister, Mr. Vengalil Krishnan Krishna Menon said, "The Chinese have very considerable superiority in numbers and fire-power. We have been heavily out-numbered and out-weaponed". This was another admission of culpability by the Minister directly responsible for the defence of India.

It was clear that the country and the Army found themselves in this predicament largely because of Government's failure to anticipate the possibility of war with China.

India lay prostrate, her foreign policy in disarray; her developing economy halted and her political and military leadership discredited. A wave of bewilderment and anger swept the country. Over the years, half-truths and rash promises had been made to reassure the Indian people that the country was prepared for a military showdown with China. Even at the height of the crisis, in September-October 1962, important personalities were issuing confident and bellicose statements and talking glibly of "evicting" the Chinese in one short, sharp engagement.

When detailed news of the disasters percolated to the people, indignation mounted. The decisiveness and completeness of our defeat made it painfully clear that we were caught napping and had tried to bluff our way out of a crisis that was partly of our own making. Despite the relatively heavy military expenditure of the preceding years our men were ill-equipped, we had built no worthwhile road communications and had not reorganised and trained the Army for a war with China. The Army came in for a good deal of uninformed criticism and even ridicule. The magnificent traditional heroism of the Indian jawan was overlooked amidst the debris of mutual recrimination that followed our battlefield defeat.

National indignation was accompanied by national despondency. There were reports of confusion and even chaos in the border state of Assam, which was threatened by the Chinese advance. Mr. Kuldip Nayar, the Press Officer to Mr. Lal Bahadur Shastri, the Home Minister in 1962, who had visited Assam in those black days, disclosed that there was utter confusion and demoralisation at Tezpur and a wild exodus. There were plans to blow up the installations at Tezpur airfield and the famous Digboi oilfields of Assam. He reported complaints by the civil population against Government officials who allegedly bungled the evacuation of Tezpur. He heard that "suddenly one evening at about 8 p.m. an announcement was made over loudspeakers that the Government was no longer responsible for citizens' lives and property". The Deputy Commissioner is reported to have fled after releasing prisoners, burning files and destroying currency notes from the local treasury. One shudders to think of what would have happened if the Chinese had entered the Assam Plains. Clearly the people were not prepared for war and its horrors.

In the wake of our defeats many heads had to fall. Mr. Menon, the controversial Defence Minister resigned on 7th November, as a result of strong and implacable Parliamentary and Party wrath with his stewardship of the Defence portfolio, during the critical years of 1957 to 1962. His mentor, Mr. Nehru tried desperately to retain him in the Government by designating him Minister for Defence Production, but this was unacceptable to a furious and disgusted House. Mr. Nehru had to bow to the will of the people for the first time in his overlordship of India, a development that was to have far-reaching effects on the Indian political scene. Nehru's supreme authority over the Indian people had been eroded by the errors and omissions of his China Policy. With a sure touch for survival at all costs, he sacrificed Mr. Menon.

The Chief of Army Staff, General Pran Nath Thapar resigned on "grounds of health" – the hackneyed euphemism for what the British call "the bowler hat". He was rewarded with the Ambassadorship to Afghanistan. Lt.-General B. M. Kaul, the Commander of the ill-conceived and ill-fated IV Corps, was compelled to seek premature retirement – a bitter pill for Mr. Nehru to swallow – as Kaul was widely believed to have been his *protegé* and military confidant.

There were many errant civil servants and military officers who had not achieved enough publicity to get involved in the post-mortems, and who went on to higher ranks. Time and superannuation have taken care of the others.

The Chinese announced their intention to withdraw from the areas which they had occupied in thirty lightning days; and this gave India a chance to take stock of the political and economic damage. It was soon evident that the Chinese had dealt near-mortal blows to India's international standing and had altered the national political scene. There were major inroads into our development plans and economic progress. India's achievements over the past decade were to be nullified as a result of one short, sharp military campaign.

Chapter II

The Annexation of Tibet and India's China Policy

It is axiomatic that all international disputes which end in war have a historical background and the Sino-Indian-Tibetan problem was no exception. It was the function of Government and of the appropriate desk in the Ministry of External Affairs to constantly review the points of dispute with neighbouring countries, seeking to resolve them amicably if suitable opportunities present themselves, or can be created. Failing this the nation must be alerted for the possibility of war. Inaction or wishful thinking are inexcusable.

The Sino-Indian border dispute, which resulted in the clash of 1962, had its genesis in 1950, when China and India faced each other across a common frontier, for the first time in centuries. On 7th October 1950 the Chinese Liberation Army entered Tibet, although China was preparing to take an active part in the Korean War. The Chinese move apparently took India by surprise. Tibet appealed for help but we refused, and advised the Tibetans to negotiate a peaceful settlement.

India was in a quandary. The entry of Chinese troops into Tibet had potentially ominous long-term consequences. Tibet had been a buffer zone, and had been vital to British India's strategic defence. The abrupt removal of this buffer would alter the geo-political balance, and henceforth India would have a live northern border to reckon with. There was a definite possibility that Tibet could be used as a spring-board for aggression against India whenever this suited the Communist regime in China. Professor N. G. Ranga asked, in 1950, "Whether the Prime Minister could be indifferent to the gathering clouds of threats to our safety". Mr. Shyama Prasad Mookerjee had a premonition that India would one day have to fight China in Tibet. Many others expressed similar views and misgivings. Sardar Vallabhbhai Patel, popularly called India's strong man, wanted a showdown and a tough line with China, but he did not live long enough to convert his remarkable vision into positive action. The only plausible excuse for direct intervention would have been to defend the rights which we had inherited from the British. Many years later, in 1954, Mr. Nehru revealed his mind when he said, "What right does India have to keep a part of its Army in Tibet, whether Tibet is independent or part of China?"

Sardar K. M. Panikkar, India's first Ambassador to China, is reported to have advised Mr. Nehru not to oppose the annexation of Tibet. There was considerable confused thinking and hair-splitting about China's 'suzerainty' and 'sovereignty' over Tibet. It appeared that we were trying to find some face-saving device for the policy that we had decided to adopt, viz. to allow the Chinese to make Tibet a province of China. We exchanged a few diplomatic notes with China, and expressed our "concern, surprise and regret" at the Chinese move, and ended with the pious hope that China would respect Tibet's autonomy and settle this problem peacefully. The Chinese promised to be good boys and we let the matter rest at that.

At that time, except for a few far-sighted men, the rest of India failed to connect the happenings with their own future and destiny. In fact the average Indian, basking in his newly won freedom, could not pin-point Tibet on a world map. The officials of the Ministry of External Affairs were preoccupied with the establishment of diplomatic relations with the rest of the world; dealing with the diplomatic problem of steering our Kashmir case in the United Nations; and preparing briefs for Mr. Nehru's increasing participation in world affairs. Mr. Nehru was then gradually consolidating his position as the elder statesman of the world, and was being looked upon as the leading Afro-Asian spokesman against colonialism. He was busy with Indonesia, and some African countries. The country's legislators were busy working the Constitution which had been adopted on 26th January 1950. It was obvious that little thought had been spared for China and any possible hostile move by her. It seemed inconceivable that a nation that had itself suffered grievously at the hands of foreign powers, should start trouble for a neighbouring ex-colonial nation.

Cold war considerations inevitably intruded into this problem. The Chinese justified their action by raising the bogey of Western plots to turn Tibet into an American base. On 25th October 1950 the New China News Agency announced that "The Chinese Army had been ordered to advance into Tibet to liberate the people of Tibet; to complete the unification of China; *to prevent Imperialism from invading an inch of the territory of the Fatherland*, and to safeguard and build up the frontier regions of the country".

One school of Indian thought was that a clash over Tibet might trigger off a larger conflagration, as the Korean War was on and India could not be responsible for starting a third World War and therefore had to act with circumspection. Domestic politics also helped to confuse such Government thinking as there was. The Communists tended to whitewash China's action, while the Rightists demanded a showdown. Mr. Nehru was placed in a most embarrassing position, as he was not prepared for an international issue so soon after gaining independence. He had not anticipated any drastic Chinese move despite her oft-repeated claims to Tibet. The Chinese Communist Party had not concealed its intentions and aspirations with regard to Tibet, for, as early as 1922 the Party had announced that it would liberate Tibet and unify her with the Motherland. On 4th August 1950, General Lio Po-Chang said, "The Army must launch an attack on Tibet . . . to enable the Tibetan peoples to return to the great family of the Chinese Peoples Republic, while consolidating the defence of South-West China".

A word about Sino-Tibetan relations in the 20th Century would be useful to clarify the background to our doubts and hesitancy in dealing with the Chinese annexation of Tibet. In 1904, the British Indian Government of Lord Curzon organised a military expedition, under Colonel Younghusband, against Tibet, with the aim of "forestalling any likely collusion between the Dalai Lama and Russian agents". It will be recalled that Czarist Russia was the bogey-man of the early part of the 20th Century. Younghusband successfully reached Lhasa, and the Dalai Lama was forced to agree to terms. The resultant Anglo-Tibetan Treaty of 1904 secured Britain certain trading rights, and a guarantee against concessions to foreign Powers. The British thereafter had a direct influence over the foreign policy of Tibet. This was a thinly-disguised arrangement to create and maintain a buffer zone to protect the northern borders of British India.

The Treaty was confirmed by the Anglo-Chinese Treaty of 1906. Lord Curzon urged the British Government to secure *de-jure* international recognition of Tibet as a sovereign state, but he was overruled by the Home Government as the rather vague concept of Chinese suzerainty was considered to be a harmless fiction. Britain was then at the zenith of her world power and China was weak and dominated by various European Powers. There was little point in making an issue of a trifling matter with a harmless neighbour.

Chinese suzerainty over Tibet was always nebulous and nominal. Tibet had been independent for long periods up to the 18th Century. In 1720 Chinese Forces entered Tibet "to forestall a suspected Tibetan-Mongol alliance against China". They occupied Lhasa and two Chinese Ambans, or Residents, were introduced. In 1792, Emperor Chien Lung exacted a formal recognition of Chinese suzerainty and the administration of Tibet was brought more under the control of the Ambans. During the latter half of the 19th Century Chinese control weakened. The Tibetans chose a Dalai Lama without informing China, as they were required to do. The Chinese had little option but to condone the irregularity, as they were too weak to enforce their agreement by force of arms.

The Chinese Imperial Government of the Manchus tried to exercise greater control over Tibet and in 1910 they invaded Tibet forcing the Dalai Lama to flee to India. He was deposed by an Imperial decree. After the overthrow of the Manchu Dynasty by the Chinese Revolution of 1911, the authority of China as the suzerain Power was speedily challenged and overthrown. The Dalai Lama was restored to power, returned to Lhasa in 1912, and drove out the Chinese garrisons.

The Chinese Government tried to recapture Tibet but were prevented from doing so by the British Government. This time the British Government claimed that any attempt to capture Tibet would be a violation of the Anglo-Chinese Treaty of 1906. While Chinese suzerainty was not disputed, "the British Government could not consent to the forcible assertion of full sovereignty over a state which had established independent treaty relations with the British Government".

In 1913 the Tibetans proclaimed their independence. In the same year the British Government held a Tripartite Conference of Tibet, China and Britain, in Simla (India). The Conference concluded its deliberations by April 1914. Briefly, the main provisions which concern our study, were that Tibet was divided into two regions, i.e. Inner and Outer Tibet. China agreed to abstain from all interference in the administration of Outer Tibet, which was to be fully autonomous. A Chinese Resident was to be re-established.

China agreed not to convert Tibet into a Chinese Province or send troops to Outer Tibet. Agreement was also reached on the boundary between India and Tibet, from Bhutan eastwards to Burma, which was then under the British Indian Government. This boundary later became known as the McMahon Line, which has figured so largely in the recent Sino-Indian dispute. The question of Chinese "suzerainty" was settled bilaterally between the Governments of Tibet and British India. Mr. Hugh Richardson, CIE, OBE, former Officer-in-Charge of the Indian Mission in Lhasa, has made this authoritative statement in a letter entitled "The Myth of 'Suzerainty'": "A term that was bandied about in the past and a little today is 'suzerainty'. We hear that somehow or other Tibet has always been under the suzerainty of China and that various Governments, our own and the Indian Government, have recognised that. The facts are quite the opposite. In 1914 by the Simla Convention, the British Government signed a declaration directly with Tibet by which it undertook not to recognise the suzerainty of China over Tibet unless the Chinese gave a substantial *quid pro quo* by admitting the autonomy of Tibet and fixing a frontier. The *quid pro quo* was never given and consequently to this day, or rather till we handed over our responsibility in 1947 to the Indian Government, the British Government did not recognise the suzerainty of China over Tibet. I am aware that certain Ministers of the Crown have made statements that might give you another impression. But whatever a Minister may say in Parliament cannot affect the terms of a mutually signed declaration with another Government".

China did not ratify the Simla Agreement on the grounds that they *could not accept the proposed boundaries between Inner and Outer Tibet.* The British and the Tibetans went ahead and signed a Convention almost identical to that agreed at Simla. Now the Chinese claim that they have never accepted the McMahon

Line because they were not signatories to the Simla Convention.

After the Simla Convention Tibet remained in effect independent. In 1921 the British Government informed China that they did not feel justified in withholding any longer recognition of the status of Tibet as an autonomous State, under the suzerainty of China, and intended to deal on this basis with Tibet in future. China was too weak to challenge this position.

During World War II Tibet opened its own Foreign Affairs Bureau. She did not join China which was directly involved in the war. Tibet claimed neutrality and resisted Chinese pressure for opening up communications through Tibet. If Tibet had been under China, she could not have been neutral or denied facilities to the Central authority. In 1947, a Tibetan trade mission travelled abroad on Tibetan and not Chinese passports.

Tibet was thus never a full-fledged Chinese province. Chinese suzerainty was nominal and was challenged by the Tibetans whenever they were strong, or the Central Chinese Government was weak. China never had any direct control over Tibet except by conquest. Except for two short periods of direct Chinese rule, Tibet had been independent for years. British officials who ought to know, have proclaimed Tibet's independence. The last British officer in Lhasa, Mr. H. Richardsons has said, "There was not a trace of Chinese authority in Tibet after 1912".

Mr. Jayaprakash Narayan, the revered, revolutionary leader of the 1942 freedom movement, cited the historical record in 1959. He said, "China has not exercised suzerainty, sovereignty or any other form of control over Tibet at any time from 1912 to 1950 when Chinese Communist Forces invaded the country and compelled the Dalai Lama to accept the so-called Seventeen-Point Agreement. After Peking broke its pledge to respect Tibet's autonomy, the Dalai

Lama's Government repudiated this Agreement on 11th March 1959, thereby provoking the full-scale Chinese assault". He then called Mr. Nehru, "The worldly-wise, who by their lack of courage and faith, block the progress of the human race not towards the moon but towards humanity itself. These persons have a myopic view and forget that nothing stands, or can stand still in history — not even the Chinese Empire".

These irrefutable historical facts could have provided us with the opportunity to engage in a dialogue with China, and adduce legal arguments for mobilising world opinion to prevent China's annexation of Tibet. Our most fundamental national interests demanded such a move. Instead we adopted a policy of appeasement and surrender to China. We acquiesced meekly and accepted the change in the *status quo*. We went out of our way to defend China's annexation and found historical justification. We accepted Chinese assertions that they would respect Tibet's autonomy, and their promises that they would not resort to violence.

We even went so far as to oppose discussion of Tibet's appeal to the United Nations. When the Tibetan appeal came up for discussion in the U.N. General Assembly on 23rd November 1950, the Indian Delegate opposed the inclusion of the question on the agenda saying that "in the latest note received by my Government, the Peking Government was certain that the Tibet question could still be settled by peaceful means, and that such a settlement could safeguard the autonomy which Tibet has enjoyed for several decades while maintaining its historical association with China". The matter was dropped: If India was satisfied no other country was prepared to stick its neck out.

By the end of 1950 the Tibetan question was "solved by India". Our action was typical of a weak nation faced by a superior power. We could not, or did not, want to face China alone. We were non-aligned and peaceful so we could not enlist the help of allies. We believed in China's professions of eternal friendship. Henceforth our National Policy was to cultivate China's friendship in every way, and thereby we hoped to buy her off. We advocated her cause in the U.N. and hoped that China's initial revolutionary zeal would mellow and she would behave in a civilised manner. Meanwhile, we would concentrate on developing our economy.

China began patrolling Ladakh in 1951, at the time when she was involved in Korea and weak. She might have then accepted a compromise on the border. Nehru did nothing and did not even bother to inform Parliament. He later admitted in Parliament that, "I saw no reason to discuss the frontier with the Chinese Government because, foolishly if you like, I thought there was nothing to discuss".

We failed to recognise two important and overwhelming facts. A strong China has always been an expansionist China. Tibet had exercised ecclesiastical authority over a large portion of NEFA, Bhutan, Sikkim and parts of Nepal, and political privileges often accompanied religious jurisdiction. If China was allowed to exercise the legal powers and prerogatives of Tibet she could lay claims to large tracts of land on our northern frontiers, and she had the will and means to enforce her claims. The boundary issue could be activated. For centuries India and Tibet had lived by custom, usage, tradition and without a surveyed boundary. Such customary and *de-facto* delineation could be rendered invalid by a hostile neighbour. A ruthless and expansionist China could be tempted to use the boundary question to create tension.

The second fact was that we would sooner or later have to be prepared to defend our sovereignty and territorial integrity in the northern regions, a contingency that would place a great strain on the national exchequer of a poor, developing nation.

We should either have prepared ourselves to resist China or to make concessions, including border adjustments. We did neither. After 1956 we would not concede China's territorial claims and therefore accepted the possibility of a clash. Unfortunately we did not build up militarily to thwart China if she chose to use force to sustain her claims. Instead we based our policy on hopes that by befriending her we would stave off the evil day of reckoning. The evil day came on 20th October 1962, barely 15 years after Independence, and 12 years after China's annexation of Tibet.

I would like to add an interesting footnote. In October 1950 I was a student at the Defence Services Staff College in Wellington, South India. Soon after the news of the Chinese entry into Tibet reached us, the Commandant, General W. D. A. ('Joe') Lentaigne, strode into the main lecture hall, interrupted the lecturer and proceeded to denounce our leaders for their short-sightedness and inaction, in the face of the Chinese action. Speaking purely as a soldier and strategist, he said that India's back door had been opened, and the Himalayas had become the boundary with a large, powerful and expansionist China. He dwelt on the vulnerability of our eastern regions due to the concentration of industry and sources of raw materials, and said that these would be within range of bombers operating from bases in Tibet. He forecast that the defence of this mountainous frontier would cost India more than she could afford. Roads would have to be built; and large, specially equipped forces would have to be raised and stationed in accommodation which we would have to construct at great expense. If the Kashmir issue was not solved then India would have an unmanageable defence burden. He reminded us that the Indian Air Force and Navy would have to be modernised at considerable cost. He predicted that India would have to pay dearly for failure to act before China became stronger and was free of her commitment in Korea. His last prophetic remark was that some of the students present in the hall would be fighting the Chinese before retirement. How right he was! Lt.-Col. 'Baij' Mehta was killed in 1962, I was taken prisoner, and another officer who was the senior staff officer to the Corps Commander.

General Lentaigne was a distinguished British General with an impressive war record. He had commanded a Gorkha battalion in the withdrawal from Burma in 1942, and later a brigade. He was given command of the second Chindit Operation after the tragic death of General Orde Wingate in 1944. He also commanded a division. He was extremely well read, and a keen student of war and history. He was loved by the students. His outburst against our leaders outraged us. We felt that he had no right to criticise our Government, and classified him as an old imperialist *koi-hai* and a Blimp. Now I realise that Joe was a true friend of India, and he was deeply grieved at the prospect of a military confrontation with China. Joe loved India and had volunteered to stay on after the departure of the British, to start the Staff College, which till today is a monument to his professional skill and dedicated work.

Soon after this, in early 1951, a very senior official of the External Affairs Ministry gave us a talk on the history of Sino-Tibetan relations over the centuries. He naturally held a brief for Government to justify the policy of allowing China to subjugate Tibet. He harped on the influence of Buddhism and told us fairy tales of beautiful princesses who won the hearts of sundry rulers and introduced Buddhism into Tibet – blah, blah, blah. His final summing up was that China might be behaving crudely but legally she was exercising her traditional rights and jurisdiction. I must admit that I was very impressed by the facts that he had marshalled, and in my ignorance was satisfied that there was nothing that we could do about this affair.

General Lentaigne who was skilled at heckling and pestering guest speakers, promptly rose to his feet and asked the learned speaker whether India intended to accept the rape of Tibet whatever the historical background. He asked him if history bore any relation to the facts as known in the 20th Century. He then asked searching questions about the strategic implications of the Chinese presence in Tibet, and whether India would countenance the exercise of full sovereignty in Tibet, including the stationing of troops along our northern borders. Pat came the answer, "General, I thought that you had asked me to give a talk on history and not strategy – strategy I leave to you soldiers". New India's bureaucrats and thinkers were obviously attempting to separate history, politics and strategy into three unrelated compartments.

Sardar Patel died in December 1950 and there was no one to question the China Policy adopted by India. He wrote a prophetic letter to Mr. Nehru on 7th November 1950, a month before his death. Patel's predictions have proved to be remarkably percipient. We have not only been subjected to a Chinese invasion but have been saddled with a restive north-eastern border population. The Sardar's letter deserves a place in every analysis of Sino-Indian relations between 1950 and 1962 and is reproduced in full in Appendix I.

Chapter III

The Uneasy Lull — 1950 to 1955

The Chinese began to consolidate their hold on Tibet with customary thoroughness. On 9th September 1951 they entered Lhasa "peacefully". In political matters they were patient, and did not force the pace of change. They used the existing political system and the immense authority of the Dalai Lama to implement the famous Seventeen-Point Agreement.

In the early years, their primary aim appeared to be to build strategic roads and airfields, and set up their communications to Sinkiang Province *via* Rudok, in Tibet. They had to swallow a large chunk of Indian territory in the Aksai Chin area to build this vital highway. They increased the number of their garrisons and began to "set up their national defences". They were also preparing to crush any armed revolt that may be started by what they termed feudal reactionaries. The tough sturdy Khampas of Eastern Tibet had not been reconciled to subservience to Chinese rule. By 1953 all the important towns were connected by telegraph.

By 1954 China had been linked by two major roads with Tibet, capable of carrying heavy traffic. As there were no other heavy vehicles except Army lorries, these roads were clearly for military use. Opposite NEFA they built a 3-ton road just north of the McMahon Line, and many feeders to their border detachments.

A railway line to Lhasa was contemplated and detailed survey operations had commenced.

On the political side, the Chinese took hundreds of young, bright Tibetans, many of the serf class, for higher education and indoctrination, to Mainland China. They returned to occupy key positions in the local administration. I met one of these officials during my imprisonment, and he was more rabidly anti-feudal than the Chinese themselves. These young men were ideal for China's long-term purposes, as their families had suffered for generations at the hands of rapacious landlords and monks.

During this period China did not want to agitate the Indo-Tibetan border areas, as they needed time, and India's help. Besides, they were fully occupied by the Korean War between 1950 and 1953; and later in helping the Viet-Minh in the latter's war with the French in Indo-China between 1953 and 1954. China talked of eternal peace and friendship between India and China. The era of "Hindi-Chini bhai bhai" (Brotherliness), cultural delegations, missions and mutual visits was thus born.

China's early restraint and outward manifestations of peaceful behaviour paid them handsome dividends. The Indo-Tibetan crisis of 1950 was dismissed. We announced our firm resolve to remove India's woeful poverty and accorded priority to development. The First Five-Year Plan was launched with great *elan* and hopes. Mild doses of socialism were prescribed in a basically capitalist economy mainly to silence the Communists and the Left Socialists, and to isolate them from the restive masses. Soon after Independence the Congress Socialists had left the parent organisation, and some of the best brains of the Congress severed their long connection with the giant political Party. India had also received a shock by the agrarian revolt in Warangal and Telengana (South India) where the peasantry rose against the Government. This was a dangerous portent for a Government ostensibly wedded to progress by democratic methods.

In the prevailing atmosphere of cordiality and peace, China and India signed the Sino-Indian Agreement on Trade and Intercourse between the Tibetan Region of China and India on 29th April 1954. The preamble to this Agreement enunciated the now infamous "Panch Sheel" or Five Principles to govern relations between the two countries. These were:

(*a*) Mutual respect for each other's territorial integrity and sovereignty.

(*b*) Mutual non-aggression.

(*c*) Mutual non-interference in each other's internal affairs.

(*d*) Equal and mutual benefit.

(*e*) Peaceful co-existence.

China was the main beneficiary of this Agreement. India had formally recognised China's complete control over Tibet. We had written off Tibet in return for Chinese guarantees of good behaviour, as embodied in the Five Principles. We sought security by a written treaty, and believed that we were guaranteed against an invasion. We failed to demand any reciprocal benefit, especially in insisting on a final border agreement, which at that time was the only possible source of friction.

We voluntarily gave up the military, communication and postal rights in Tibet which we had inherited from the British as a result of the Anglo-Tibetan Treaty of 1904, and agreed to withdraw completely, within six months, the military detachments stationed at Yatung and Gyantse; we offered to hand over to China, the postal and telegraph services together with their equipment.

Defending the Agreement Mr. Nehru said, "It was recognition of the existing situation there. Historical and practical considerations necessitated the step". This was the only approach of a man who desired peace and who wanted to avoid conflict. He hoped to cement China's friendship and thought that he could solve any differences that may arise, peacefully. Illogically, he did not keep his powder dry and completely ignored the military problems posed by our northern Himalayan Border. The slogan coined was "There will be no war with China in Mr. Nehru's life-time". This was the guide-line for Government, the Civil Service, the Financial experts, the Services, the Press and the Public. It also became the corner-stone of our National Aims and National Policy. This approach dominated our actions during the next eight years and was responsible for Mr. Nehru's anguished cry of having been stabbed in the back.

Mr. Nehru introduced Mr. Chou-en Lai to the Afro-Asian world at Bandung in 1955. We continued to champion China's cause in the U.N. and advocated her admission to the world body. The era of Indo-China friendship and brotherhood had begun to gather momentum. This facade of friendship suited China as this gave her more time to build up her economy and military strength. India was then an honoured and influential member of the world community, the moral leader of the newly independent nations, and thus a powerful advocate of China's cause. China sedulously propounded the theory that China and India had never been at war, and had no cause in the future to resort to arms.

This period closed with some faint warning murmurs, which might have been heeded, but were not. In August 1954 the Chinese created a border incident at a place called Bara-Hoti on the Uttar-Pradesh-Tibet Border, when the ink had hardly dried on Panch Sheel. The Chinese claimed that Bara-Hoti (called Wuje by them) was Chinese territory.

In Bandung Mr. Chou-en Lai said, "We have not yet fixed our border line with some countries". We were again warned, but not alerted.

Mr. Nehru visited China in 1954 and was given a royal reception, returning charmed and impressed. He thought that China's leaders did not want war. In a lesser being it might have been alleged that he was brain-washed.

Let us see what the views of the Army General Staff were, as the Chinese threat was a matter of concern to any live and alert Army. What action did the Army take to assess the potential Chinese threat and what was done to project the General Staff appreciation to the Government? In 1952 General Kulwant Singh, a very able and distinguished field commander, who had exercised high command in Kashmir in 1947-48, headed a committee to study the military threat to our Northern borders, and to assess the requirements in the event of a clash with China in the Himalayan region. He submitted a lengthy and comprehensive report. Unfortunately, like many other reports to Government, it was shelved. All that emerged was the raising of a small Indo-Tibetan Border Force, under the Home Ministry, mainly to establish our administration in a few selected places. Militarily the Force was useless and ineffective.

The Kulwant Singh report gave Government an opportunity to consider the purely military aspects, and the counter-measures required to challenge the Chinese in the Himalayas if ever this unpleasant situation arose. Government's orders were clear. It was decided at the highest level, presumably the Cabinet, that no military preparations against China were necessary, and there was little the Army could do in the face of this direct and unequivocal order. It was clear even before the 1954 Agreement, that we would not attempt to challenge the Chinese militarily. So, literally nothing was done about our Northern Defences. We built no roads; we did not strengthen our intelligence arrangements (assuming we had any) and did not even carry out any reconnaissance of likely trouble spots in our own areas.

We did not carry out staff studies for the reorganisation of our field formations. We did not study the pattern of weapons and communications equipments that we may require. Army Schools of Instruction were orientated towards open warfare. There was little emphasis on mountain warfare despite the Army's deployment in Kashmir from 1947.

Up to 1954 China was not allowed to figure in the thinking at Army HQ, Pakistan then posed the main threat. For historical and religious reasons, Pakistan and India were natural enemies and only statesmanship of the highest order could avert war. The two nations were carved out of the great Indian Peninsula, Partition being based on religious majority. Partition and Independence in 1947 were preceded by mass killings, riots and atrocities that made every decent Pakistani and Indian hang his head in shame. The aftermath of Partition was even worse, when we witnessed the wholesale murders of the Punjab and the reprisals in Bihar and elsewhere. The hatred and revengeful feelings of 1947 have yet to be removed. Time has not healed the scars of mutual distrust and loss of property.

Hardly had sanity returned when Pakistan unleashed her tribals against Kashmir in October 1947. The Indian Army rushed to the rescue of the Kashmiris who had belatedly acceded to India under the Instrument of Accession that governed the political relations and future of the erstwhile Indian States. Soon the Regular Pakistan Army was thrown in, and in less than a year after Partition, Pakistan and India were at war.

When the tide had turned in India's favour and the military situation could have enabled us to achieve a battlefield decision, Mr. Nehru decided to refer the issue to the U.N. and a cease-fire was accepted on 1st January 1949, leaving one-third of Kashmir under Pakistan's control. The so-called Kashmir deadlock remains unsolved despite interminable talks, U.N. debates and the intervention of U.N. mediators. History will demand an answer to the question as to why a cease-fire was sought by us when the involvement of Pakistan was not even proved. We have saddled ourselves with a problem that has bedevilled relations between India and Pakistan for two decades. Only a computer can assess the cost in terms of money, loss of life, alienation of other countries and the resultant hardships to the Indian people. The manning of the Cease-Fire Line costs money and ties down troops. The recurring border incidents vitiate the atmosphere between the two countries.

The Kashmir War was a strange war. The two sides were led by British Commanders-in-Chief, General Boucher of the Indian Army and General Gracey of the Pakistan Army. They had access to each other and were reported to have held talks every evening to discuss the day's events.

Partition left many problems in its wake, viz. the demarcation of the boundaries between the two countries; division of assets; the canal waters dispute; religious minorities on the wrong side of the border and many others. Any of these could cause a major military clash. In 1951 the armies of the two countries faced each other across the border in the Punjab, but fortunately wisdom prevailed and war was averted.

The confrontation of 1951 taught the Pakistan Government a major lesson. They knew that they had to do something urgently to achieve near military parity with India. As they saw it, they had to free themselves from the constant threat and intimidatory tactics of India. They also foresaw an inevitable clash of arms with India over Kashmir or any of the other outstanding issues. The Kashmir issue was crystallising into a set pattern, with India refusing to budge from her position that there was nothing to discuss. Only victory in war would give Pakistan what she considered her dues and rights.

In 1953 Pakistan signed a Mutual-Aid Treaty with the U.S.A., and joined the US-sponsored security pacts of CENTO and SEATO. They traded bases in Pakistan for massive military aid and were fully in the Western camp. This was a dangerous portent for India. On 13th November Mr. Nehru issued a clear warning that India would regard U.S. Military Aid to Pakistan as an unfriendly act. He also denounced the pact in Parliament as endangering peace and tending towards colonialism. In January 1954 he thought, "it will certainly bring world war nearer in the matter of time as also nearer India's frontier". Mr. John Foster Dulles, the U.S. Secretary of State, was not impressed with Nehru's verbal views and proceeded to do what he thought was best for his country. Mr. Dulles was the prime architect of the theory of containing Communism by building a ring of collective security pacts. Pakistan on the southern boundaries of Russia was an invaluable base. It is now known that American U-2 spy aeroplanes have operated from Peshawar airfield in Pakistan. We were satisfied, after indulging in another futile gesture of recording our displeasure.

Mr. Eisenhower, the U.S. President, is reported to have offered India similar aid but without strings. Mr. Nehru disdainfully declined the offer. We were a peace-loving country and did not wish to align ourselves with any Power. We also had to give the impression of being self-reliant and independent.

1954 was a critical year for India. American Aid in the form of money, construction of military accommodation, Patton Tanks, F-86 fighter aircraft, radar equipment, medium and heavy artillery guns and the latest family of infantry weapons flowed to rejuvenate Pakistan's World War II type Army. Pakistan was gifted sufficient military hardware to raise a modern, powerful strike force to threaten the security of the Punjab and even Delhi itself. In any case, India could no longer conquer Pakistan, and there would be no more one-sided military confrontations.

Politically Kashmir could no longer be solved in the U.N. as the Western Powers would have to side with their new ally, Pakistan. This was a possibility that was not foreseen by us. We did not evaluate the long-term implications of this, and continued to rely on Western impartiality and U.N. fairplay. The exaggerated international respect paid to India and her non-aligned policy gave us the totally erroneous impression that we could count on being free of power-politics.

Our appreciation was that Pakistan would need about three years to absorb aid, reorganise her Army and train on the U.S. Army patterns and procedures. It was well known that hundreds of Pakistani Army and Air Force officers were being trained in U.S. Schools of Instruction. Knowing that India, under Mr. Nehru would never commit aggression, the regular Pakistan Army was concentrated for re-equipment and training, and her borders were handed over to para-military forces. The large influx of modern U.S. arms enabled Pakistan to re-equip her irregular forces with the World War II arms shed by the American-aided Divisions. The so-called Azad Kashmir Forces, manning the Cease-Fire Line on the Pakistan-occupied side of Jammu and Kashmir, became a more effective fighting force, and one that could no longer be treated contemptuously by the regular Indian Army.

The military balance of power had been altered to India's disadvantage. India now faced the possibility of war along the entire Western and Northern borders of the Indian sub-continent, compelling the Indian General Staff to review defence plans. Detailed appreciations were made and the minimum inescapable requirements projected to Government. After many delays, procrastinations and conferences Government were prevailed upon to sanction a modest reorganisation programme; permit a few new raisings and the purchase of essential equipment. It was fortunate that this was done as we would otherwise have been in dire straits in the 1965 conflict with Pakistan.

In granting these small additions to the strength of the Army, Government made it clear that we were not to think in terms of an arms race with Pakistan. Our main reliance was to be placed on the assurances given by the U.S. President to Mr. Nehru, that the U.S. would never permit Pakistan to use American arms against India. This assurance had been given to pacify India when there was alarm at Pakistan's military build-up. We did not pause to ask ourselves where Pakistan hopes to use Patton Tanks and short-range supersonic aircraft against any Communist nation, except the snow-bound, inhospitable Gilgit region of occupied Kashmir, where there is a frontier with China.

We also hoped that the cold war would give us additional security, as the U.S.S.R. would not stand by idly, while an American-aided and equipped army invaded India. In other words, vague diplomatic promises and hopes would be our safeguard to ward off the Pakistani danger. Once again India trusted her defences to others, as she has done so often in her history. This was the official National Aim and the National Policy, in so far as Pakistan was concerned, in 1954.

Government and the Congress majority in Parliament blindly and unwisely accepted Mr. Eisenhower's word. Pakistan used her American aircraft and armour against us in the Rann of Kutch, in April 1965; in the Chhamb Sector in Jammu and Kashmir and in the Punjab in September 1965. President Johnson of the U.S.A. was unable to prevent Pakistan from breaking her pledge to the U.S.A. The recent (1968) Soviet-Pakistan Arms Deal has agitated the public, responsible leaders and alert organisations. We have been treated to the same doses of soothing promises, assurances and barely plausible explanations from Russian and Indian leaders. Is it conceivable that India will allow herself to be duped twice in one generation?

During 1954-55 Mr. Nehru was extolling the 2,000 years of Sino-Indian friendship. China was, at that time, surveying various routes through Aksai Chin, while India remained apparently ignorant of this. India did not even know that a route was being built till the Chinese announced, in September 1957, that they would open the route for traffic within a month. We sent reconnaissance parties to the area and one was "arrested" by the Chinese. Mr. Nehru did not deem it fit to inform Parliament of this humiliating experience. When questioned, Mr. Nehru gave his classic reply. He said, "No particular occasion arose to bring the matter to the House because we thought we might make progress by correspondence, and when the time was ripe for it we would inform the House".

This then was the political climate in 1954 and early 1955. Defence was relegated to the lowest priority in the national effort. The role given to the Army was "to be prepared to defend ourselves against a second-class power" – obviously Pakistan. Was Pakistan going to remain a second-class power after her reorganisation? What is the definition of a second-class power in the context of the formulation of the size and constitution of the Indian Armed Forces?

Minor border incidents were the only military problems that we were called upon to deal with. The Indian Corps in the Punjab was capable of repelling any attack by the Pakistani Army, and in any case, such an attack was impossible until Pakistan had re-organised and re-equipped her forces, sometime by mid-July 1957. China was a friend. The Indian Government, which has been accused of working on a day-to-day basis, felt it had been reprieved for the next few years anyway.

The Army was forgotten; its equipment allowed to become obsolete, certainly obsolescent; and its training academic and outdated. We merely tried to maintain what we had inherited in 1947, at Independence.

The years between 1947 and 1955 must go down in our history as wasted years, in our defence thinking and military preparedness. The political assumptions for our defence policies were invalid and dangerous. Friendship with China was a variable factor and could be changed at short notice. While friendly gestures are to be welcomed, they cannot be used as an excuse for improvident hopes, military inaction and neglect. American assurances regarding Pakistan's good behaviour could not be enforced short of war.

Even if the political assumptions were valid, it would still have been prudent on our part to embark on a phased programme of modernisation of military equipment and reorientating our planning and training. We should have reorganised the Army which was still on the World War II pattern. There was a good deal that should have been done but was not done. During this period we did not have the required ministerial talent, and if one is honest, the professional ability, to keep a watching brief on the activities of our neighbours and take far-sighted and timely decisions. Lacking firm higher directions, the Armed Forces merely coasted along, and began to lose the professional efficiency gained during World War II and in the Kashmir Operations.

Later, after 1959 we embarked on various crash programmes, but by then it was too late. Crash programmes have no place in long-term planning for possible war. This has now been admitted by the Government, when Mr. Chavan the Defence Minister said that an Army requires not only money but also time to prepare for war.

Chapter IV

The Twilight Years — 1955 to 1959

Our Military affairs continued to drift. Our Policy was based on wishful thinking, reliance on foreign assurances, indifference to the mounting threats, and misconceived financial stringency. Military problems were handled on a day-to-day basis and no effort was made to evolve a rational long-term policy consistent with our foreign policy. The Armed Forces were not designed to implement our National Aims or to guard our vital national interests. No serious consideration whatsoever was given to the safeguarding of the political frontiers of India. Mr. Nehru followed the same path of most previous rulers. He relegated the frontier problem to the status of a petty issue and ignored the serious consequences to India. It is an astonishing historical fact that most invaders have been allowed to enter undefended borders and battles have invariably been fought well inside our frontiers.

U.N. mediation efforts and fruitless Security Council debates had failed to find an acceptable solution to the Kashmir deadlock. Many Army officers felt that Pakistan would try to force a settlement by war, as soon as she felt secure in West Pakistan. This security would be assured by her American-aided Corps. During this period Pakistan provoked major border clashes at Chhad Bet in the Rann of Kutch area, later to be the scene of bitter fighting in April 1965; at Husseiniwala on the Ferozepore border in Punjab where there was a pitched battle with artillery and heavy mortars; in the Patharia Reserve Forest area in Assam and many others. The tempo and intensity of border and cease-fire violations in Jammu and Kashmir was stepped up, raising tempers on both sides to boiling point. The aim of these frequent and widely-separated incidents was undoubtedly to test our will to resist. In each case we reacted sharply and rapidly and localised the dispute. We were satisfied that we could contain and deal firmly with Pakistan, and nothing more was required to handle the Pakistani threat.

From 1956 onwards China gradually began to shed her cloak of friendship and started a clever campaign to claim and assert her rights to vast areas in Ladakh and NEFA, while retaining an outward façade of reasonableness and readiness to engage in talks. In 1958 China published maps showing large tracts of Indian territory as Chinese. When questioned, Mr. Chou-en Lai said that they were reproductions of old maps and the new Chinese Government had no time to rectify them. He said, ominously, "The area would have to be surveyed properly".

News of the Chinese Highway through our territory in Aksai Chin in Ladakh began to leak out. A leading Chinese pictorial magazine showed pictures of this road. The era of "Hindi-Chini bhai bhai" was drawing to an end. Despite odd meetings between the Indian and Chinese Premiers, no final settlement was reached. China continued to enjoy the financial and commercial benefits of the 1954 Trade Agreement.

It has been argued that by 1957 Mr. Nehru belatedly began to appreciate the dangers to our northern borders as well as the threat from Pakistan, but could not quite decide on the necessary counter-measures. The wasted years from 1950 to 1957 and the radically altered international situation made a choice neither easy nor palatable. With the benefit of hindsight it may be said that he left himself with only two alternatives. The first was to shelve our much-publicised development plans and revoke all promises of quickly industrialising India, thereby diverting all our resources to rearmament and preparation for a military showdown with China and Pakistan. Indian progress, already painfully slow, would be retarded, perhaps for decades. Even total concentration on defence would not have ensured complete re-equipment and certain readiness for war. We would still require large-scale arms aid to equip the Army to fight two potential enemies, on two completely different types of terrain, viz. plains/deserts and the Himalayan mountains. Mr. Nehru was impatient with the squalor and poverty of India and it was against all that he stood for and all his ambitions to adopt this course.

Even if he had decided to give priority to defence, it would have been extremely difficult to find an assured source of arms supply, specially ammunition and spares. In 1965 the Western arms embargo (including spares) was a serious embarrassment in the short war with Pakistan. Our traditional suppliers had been the Western countries, especially the U.K. and U.S.A., largely because the Indian Army had inherited arms from these countries at the time of Independence and we had substantial sterling balances to pay for our modest military requirements. It would have been impossible to diversify the equipment of the Army without serious operational repercussions in the matter of ammunition, repair facilities and tactical doctrines which are so closely tied up with equipment. The U.K. and U.S.A. would have been hesitant to supply large quantities, without strings, as the international political environment in 1957 was vastly different to the situation prevailing in 1954. These countries could not supply or gift us arms in case we used these to fight Pakistan and settle outstanding issues on the battlefield, once and for all. They had created Pakistan and were committed to maintaining a balance of military capability between the two nations. Pakistan was wholly in the Western camp, and a member of two U.S.-sponsored security organisations. On the other hand, India was at the zenith of her influence in the world, and had increasingly clashed with the West on major world issues, notably the Suez crisis and the Hungarian episode of 1956. An independent India could not be given the arms to back her political postures with military power. We would certainly have been forced to make political concessions and thereby deviate from our chosen, independent foreign policy.

In 1957 we did not have enough convertible currency to buy our total requirements from open suppliers like France and Sweden. We had already embarked on a large borrowing programme, had incurred heavy debts, particularly with the U.S.A. and U.K., and had exhausted our sterling reserves. The Western Powers could hardly be expected to loan us more money for development while we utilised our own resources on arms purchases from their competitors, to fight their *protegé* – Pakistan. This would have been a ludicrous situation. A sudden halt in economic aid would have been disastrous at that time, as we were in the midst of the Second Five-Year Plan.

A Kashmir settlement would have been a prerequisite for any substantial Western arms sales or aid. We would also have probably been asked to nominate China as a potential adversary and thereby abandon, or partially modify, our non-aligned policy in world affairs, and our desire to befriend China. We might have been called upon to evolve some sort of joint defence plans with Pakistan, for the security of the Indian sub-continent against Communist China. There was inspired talk of the alleged benefits of such an arrangement, in those days. These concessions were unthinkable in the mid-1950's.

Moreover, we could not afford to antagonise Russia with whom we had begun to develop close and friendly relations, after the much-publicised visit of Mr. Khrushchev and Marshal Bulganin, in 1955. They had championed our Kashmir stand in the Security Council, even to the extent of using the veto. They were beginning to give us substantial aid and technical know-how, particularly in developing heavy industries and in financing oil—projects which the Western countries had been reluctant to finance and undertake.

Russia and the other Communist countries could not supply us with arms for practical and ideological reasons. China and Russia were allies and had not come to the parting of the ways at that time. Russia was helping China to build up her industrial and military potential. It would have been both unreasonable and imprudent to rely on Russia and her allies for help.

An all-out military rearmament programme would have destroyed Mr. Nehru's hopes and aspirations for India, and would have demolished her image in the international sphere, where India had always advocated a peaceful settlement of disputes and even disarmament. A belligerent India, or an India which was a satellite of any power bloc, was an impossibility in the first decade of her independence.

Mr. Nehru was left with the second alternative, that of continuing the policy of cultivating China's friendship and relying on the U.S.A. to restrain Pakistan. The main Indian national effort would be focused on the development of the industrial foundations of the country. He constantly stressed that the strength of a country was not only its armed forces, but also the industrial potential and the morale of the people.

Having been forced to take this decision Mr. Nehru failed to follow it up to its logical conclusion. It should have been obvious that India could not afford a perpetual confrontation against two neighbours, each of whom posed different military problems of terrain and equipment. Even major powers cannot afford to fight on two fronts; for a poor developing country it was suicidal to divert inadequate or "available funds" for defence. In the event we got neither security from invasion nor progress. Government would have been better advised to study the possible causes of war with China and eliminate them by negotiation or compromise, once it was decided that we did not have the resources for full-scale defence preparedness. We could have taken advantage of the favourable climate of friendship with China, as any solution found in the prevailing atmosphere of cordiality between 1954 and 1957 would have been accepted by the people. As we had chosen to concentrate on progress and had eschewed war as the means of settling our disputes, we might have negotiated for a mutually acceptable formula for delineating the Indo-Tibetan border. In those early days, few Indians had even heard of Ladakh or NEFA, and it might have been easy to gain advantages for ourselves and accommodate China in the process. Instead we allowed the border issue to become an emotional one, and the defence of this inhospitable region (in the words of Mr. Nehru) became associated with India's honour and manhood, and no concessions were possible under the threat of superior military force. In 1962 an allegedly inflamed public opinion is credited with having forced the Government to take hasty, imprudent and disastrous measures.

By letting matters drift, the border poser became a convenient stick to beat Mr. Nehru's Congress Government. Mr. Nehru, in defending his policies was compelled to make bombastic and reassuring statements, knowing fully well that he could not back his words with guns. Once the Chinese began nibbling at our territory, any concessions made would have been looked upon as appeasement and surrender. Government thus lost the initiative and had no alternative but to proclaim a tough and uncompromising posture. The border problem became the test of Government's will and determination, and was heatedly debated at every session of the Lok Sabha. It was easy to accuse Government of being neglectful of India's pride and independence; and of a willingness to surrender Indian territory. Emotion is the arch-enemy of reason and precludes the possibility of sober consideration of the military implications of any given situation.

While Nehru was beset by doubts in formulating a firm National Policy, China demonstrated her belligerence by the increased frequency and intensity of border encroachments and incidents. It was also displayed at meetings and conferences where the Chinese representatives took an inflexible and intransigent attitude. They seldom agreed to see our point of view or to study our documentary evidence. Our documents were summarily dismissed as being the views of imperialist bureaucrats or mere travellers. Agreements arrived at during the British period were abrogated on the grounds that they had been imposed by a superior military power against weaker Asian nations. They took the stand that the whole question would have to be studied *de novo*. They were successful in making history stand still, and in wiping out the British Era in Asia.

Initially the main focus was on the Indo-Tibetan border in Ladakh where China was bent on establishing her claim to, and keeping the Aksai Chin plateau through which she had built the Tibet-Sinkiang Highway. There was only one major incursion in the Walong sector of NEFA, in 1957. One of the strangest episodes of this period was the "visit" of a high-powered Chinese military, naval and air force delegation, consisting of Marshals and Generals. To the utter amazement and consternation of the Indian Army, the delegation was sent on a sight-seeing visit to every major military establishment in India, with orders to "show them everything"!

1959 was the turning point in Sino-Indian relations, and there was no longer any room for vacillation or procrastination. There was no place for hopes, empty boasts or equivocation. On 10th March news of pitched battles between the Chinese Army and Tibetan patriots reached Delhi. Lhasa was the scene of a major clash. The first cautious reaction of the Government was expressed by Mr. Nehru in Parliament, when he said that he did not wish to express any view on the situation in Tibet since, apart from being embarrassing it might make a difficult position more difficult. "I do not say", he added, "that there has been any large-scale violence; the situation there at present is more a clash of wills than a clash of arms of physical bodies". Later he said that "We have no intention of interfering in the internal affairs of China with whom we have friendly relations".

The rebellion was inevitably and inexorably crushed. The Dalai Lama was forced to flee from Lhasa for the second time in fifty years. On 3rd April Mr. Nehru confirmed that the Dalai Lama had crossed into Indian territory on 31st March and had been granted political asylum, at his own request.

The Dalai Lama was met by high Indian officials and given a reception befitting his high ecclesiastical and political status. After the protocol preliminaries India had to do some hard thinking, and take unequivocal decisions as a result of this sudden development. Government appeared to have been taken by surprise, as it did not give the impression of having an answer to the radically new political situation. Mr. Nehru confirmed his dilemma on 27th April when he affirmed "our desire to maintain friendly relations with China and our deep sympathy with the Tibetan people". Asylum to the Dalai Lama was an unfriendly act in the eyes of the Chinese, and it would be difficult to reconcile friendship with China and sympathy with the Tibetans. On 14th May 1959, Mr. Nehru conceded that "the presence of the Dalai Lama does involve a certain strain on the relations between China and India".

In the event we adopted a compromise policy in that we granted asylum but forbade the Dalai Lama any political activity, thereby alienating the Chinese without reaping any benefit from his presence in India and his animosity to the Chinese Communist regime.

It is interesting to note that Burma and Ceylon, two Buddhist countries, refused to allow the Dalai Lama even to visit their, countries. They had decided that they were not going to walk a tight-rope.

Predictably, China soon launched a tirade against India and her leaders, who were labelled "expansionist elements inheriting the British legacy". The pressure was now really on. 1959 was probably the year that China decided to teach India a lesson, steadily built up for an invasion and awaited a pretext for overt military action that would not be too obviously a display of naked power. The men and material for the massive attacks of October-November 1962 were concentrated over at least three stocking seasons. Little did the Chinese hope that India, with her feeble and ill-conceived 'Forward Policy' would provide the convenient and plausible *casus belli* for her evil designs.

In April 1959 China gave another clear warning that the border question with India was still not settled. Speaking in the National People's Congress, Chou-en Lai said, "The boundaries between China and certain neighbouring south-eastern countries remain undetermined and they could reasonably be solved through peaceful negotiations". This hint went unnoticed and did little to stimulate us into some positive action.

China then proceeded to hot up the pace of the sullen border confrontation and created three serious border incidents between August and October 1959, which could no longer hide the seriousness of the Sino-India border conundrum. The August incidents are best recounted in the words of the Prime Minister as he narrated the dismal failure of forbearance, and admitted the virtual lack of any kind of military preparations for retaliation. On 28th August 1959 he informed the House about these incidents. He first admitted that the Chinese had built a highway across our territory in Aksai Chin and disclosed that an Indian police party sent to reconnoitre the area was "apprehended" by the Chinese on 28th July. He also admitted that the Chinese had established a camp near a place called Spanggur, well within our territory. These startling disclosures evoked more questions forcing the Prime Minister to concede that two or three other places had also had frontier trouble.

Mr. Nehru first dealt with the Khenzemane clash of arms. He said: "On 7th August about 200 Chinese violated our border at Khenzemane, north of Chutangmu, in Kameng Frontier Division. When *requested* to withdraw they pushed back—actually pushed back—our greatly out-numbered patrol to the Bridge at Drokung Samba. Our people consisted of ten or a dozen . . . there was no firing. Later on the Chinese detachment withdrew and our forces established themselves. All this was over a question of about two miles. I might say that *according to us there is an international border*. Two miles on this side is the Bridge and two miles on that side is our picket or small force. So our patrol was pushed back to the Bridge and two miles away *they stood facing each other*. Then both retired. Whatever it was, *later on the Chinese withdrew* and our picket went back to the frontier and established a small picket there. The Chinese party later arrived and demanded immediate withdrawal of our picket and lowering of our flag there. This *request* was refused. There was an attempt by the Chinese forces to outflank our people, but as far as we know our people remained there and *nothing further happened*; that is on the border itself. This was one instance which happened two weeks ago".

The second incident was at Longju. The Prime Minister said, "The present incident I am talking about is a very recent one and in fact a continuing one. On the 25th a strong Chinese detachment crossed into our territory, in the Subansiri Frontier Division, at a place south of Migyitun and *opened fire* at a forward post of ours. Honourable Members will remember I just

---

Author's italics.

mentioned Migyitun in connection with the Chinese protest that we had violated their territory, and were in collusion with some Tibetan rebels. That was the protest in June last and *there the matter ended.* Now round about that area, and a little further away, but not far from it, this Chinese detachment came and met our forward picket of about a dozen persons. It is said that they fired at our forward picket. They were in much larger numbers, it is difficult to say in what numbers but they were in some hundreds – 200, 300 or even more. *They surrounded the picket . . . they apparently apprehended this lot. . . .* The outpost is at a place called Longju . . . Longju is about 3 to 4 miles from *our frontier between India and Tibet as we conceive it. Longju is 5 days' march from another post of ours,* in the interior, a bigger post called Limeking. *Limeking is about 12 days' march from the next place behind it.* So in this way *Longju is about 3 weeks from a roadhead.* I merely mention this to give the House some idea of the communication, transport, distance and time taken. . . . The Chinese came again on the 26th and opened fire and practically *encircled the picket and post* . . . and although there was firing for a considerable time, we had no account of any casualties. Our people apparently fired back too. When the people were more or less surrounded at Longju they left the place and withdrew under overwhelming pressure".

The Prime Minister then gave an indication of the action taken by the Government in the face of this explosive situation. He told the House "The moment this information came *we immediately protested to the Chinese Government* about it and took certain other steps in that area to strengthen our various posts — Limeking and others as we thought necessary and *feasible*".

He then disclosed that, "We have in fact placed this border area of NEFA directly under the military authorities. That is to say it was being dealt with by the Assam Rifles, under the Assam Rifles Directorate, which was functioning under the Governor of Assam, and the Governor is the agent of the Government of India, in the External Affairs Ministry. The Assam Rifles will of course remain there and such other forces as will be necessary will be sent, but they will function now under the Army Authorities and their Headquarters".

Incredible as it seems now in retrospect, Parliament and the Press were satisfied with the Prime Minister's "arrangements" to defend the borders. There were no probing questions, and no one asked where the additional forces were to come from. Surely the Army did not have surplus troops standing by for just such a contingency? The Army had always been restricted both in its man-power and its budget to ceilings fixed by the Cabinet. Were troops to be withdrawn from the Pakistan borders? If so what diplomatic action was proposed to ensure that we did not get involved with Pakistan while we were undertaking this additional commitment? Did Government seriously mean to take on both China and Pakistan simultaneously? Would the Government need more money to meet this extra commitment? If so what were the Government's supplementary budget proposals? Was there to be an increase in the strength of the Army? Had the Army the necessary mountain warfare equipment?

I have merely indicated the type of questions that should have agitated Members of Parliament and spurred the Press to editorial comment to keep Government on its toes, and not get away with "paper preparations".

The Prime Minister spoke for the first time of defending our border, and using the Army to do so, but there was no long-term appreciation of the Chinese threat and possible Chinese reactions. Mr. Nehru did not link border incidents with aggressive Chinese intentions. Right up to 1962, the Prime Minister treated recurring Chinese aggression as isolated incidents, and no serious military response was contemplated or ordered. He did not link them with the overall boundary dispute, China's territorial claims or her ideological differences with India. In the circumstances he could not formulate any National Policy worth the name.

In September 1959 China laid formal claim to some 50,000 square miles of Indian territory in Ladakh and NEFA. It was only in 1961 that the Government considered it necessary to take "limited defence measures to contain Chinese incursions into Indian territory" (*Chinese Aggression in War and Peace*, Government of India Publication, 1962).

All along he stressed the remoteness of these areas and admitted, "There is no actual demarcation (in Ladakh)". Once when questioned about Chinese intentions, he said, "I cannot imagine that all this is a precursor of anything more serious. I do not think they will attack".

Mr. Menon has since confirmed this approach to the China problem. He is reported to have said, "We were all the time, either because of lack of knowledge of these matters, or because the regions concerned were far away, or for other reasons, trying not to look upon it as a major conflict but as something we could resolve ultimately. From 1958 onwards we tried to reassert ourselves in these areas". At another time a Government spokesman minimised the whole border question and dismissed the entire area as "wasteland where not even a blade of grass grows".

Parliamentary thinking remained clouded over the Sino-Indian border problem. The problem continued to get mixed up with domestic politics. Defence debates were used to air their own ideological beliefs and personal feuds, and the national interests got lost in the verbiage.

The powerful Congress ruling Party was made up of heterogenous elements from princes to paupers;

extreme Right to extreme Left. Welles Hangen has aptly summed up the Party as "Huge, amorphous coalition of conflicting interests united in little but their self-interest". Such a party could not tackle the Chinese problem. No attempt at a non-party foreign policy was made. In any case Mr. Nehru had never permitted foreign affairs to be decided by anyone but himself, advised by Mr. Menon and a few External Affairs Ministry officials.

Without meaningful debates, with a compliant Parliament and an adoring public, Mr. Nehru was left to his own judgement and he continued to drift along, living in fond hopes of a peaceful settlement of the Sino-Indian Border dispute. Later, in 1961-62 he succumbed to taunts from Right Opposition Parties and tried to simulate a posture of resolute determination to guard India's frontiers. He may have quietened his critics but he did not dissuade the Chinese from over-running our pitiful military outposts.

Despite the clear lessons of Khenzemane and Longju our political and military thinking continued to be beset by doubts, inertia and lethargy. We learnt no lessons.

Let us take the Khenzemane incident first. Khenzemane is at the eastern end of the Thagla Ridge, which was to be the scene of the opening round of the 1962 War with China. As is well known, the Chinese do not officially accept the McMahon Line as the boundary between India and Tibet, as they contend that they were not signatory to the Simla Convention of 1913-14. In so far as the alignment of the McMahon Line, in the Thagla Ridge-Khenzemane sector is concerned, they claim that the Line runs through the Drokung Samba Bridge, some two miles inside our territory. That is why they pushed our men back to this Bridge. Even Mr. Nehru said vaguely, "According to us there is an international boundary". In the 1960 talks with Chinese officials, the Chinese delegation raised many probing questions about the exact alignment of the boundary in this area. The matter was not settled amicably, and this area remained disputed on a matter of detail, without prejudice to the larger issue of the legality of the McMahon Line. As we shall see later, it was an unwise act to set up a post (Dhola), in May-June 1962, in the same area, without the military force to sustain our interpretation of the Line, by force if necessary. This was the first major mistake in the tragic events of 1962.

In both incidents it will be noted that the Chinese considerably out-numbered us. Our posts were always a dozen or so men, with no reinforcements at hand, isolated and dependent on air-supply. When confronted by superior Chinese forces they could offer no worthwhile resistance. Despite the known difficulties, more similar posts were opened up, in 1961-62, under the ill-conceived "Forward Policy". Dhola which was one such post had only 40 men and could offer no resistance. All the commander could do was to raise an alarm. Dhola was used as a bait by the Chinese to lure us to the Namka Chu, denude our defences at Towang and open the road to the plains of Assam.

We were taken in neatly by the Chinese tactics. The Prime Minister talked about "Requesting the Chinese to withdraw . . . there was no firing . . . they pushed us back—actually pushed us back . . . they stood facing each other, then retired . . . the Chinese withdrew . . . the Chinese came back and demanded our withdrawal . . . we refused . . . and there the matter ended". We accepted this as the *modus operandi* of the Chinese. There would be no escalation and no war. This kind of fallacious thinking and reasoning led us to accept battle in a remote death-trap in the Dhola area post, in 1962. When the Chinese used maximum force we were surprised.

In Longju, "the Chinese fired . . . there were no casualties . . . they surrounded our post-picket . . .

they apprehended our men (this was a more ominous development than just pushing our men) . . . our picket ultimately withdrew under pressure". So we deduced anew that the Chinese were still playing parlour games and did not intend to fight.

Mr. Nehru himself admitted the vast distances and the difficult logistics problem in the Himalayan border areas. Longju was three weeks from a road-head, but then so was Dhola post. The difficulties of Dhola were conveniently ignored when we decided and announced, that we were going to evict the Chinese. The Longju incident gave us a foretaste of the difficulties in store for us in NEFA. The defenders ran out of ammunition, and air-supply was not possible due to bad weather (as August and September are monsoon months). Possibly the Air Force was short of aircraft or there was no supply-dropping equipment. The sorties that did get through missed the dropping zone. All this was to be repeated in 1962. We learnt nothing nor, apparently, did we wish to learn anything. In 1962 we relied entirely on air-drops involving thousands of tons and under worse conditions. Air-drops became an end in themselves; what the forward troops could collect was secondary.

Predictably, after both incidents, we sent protest notes about the Chinese misbehaviour. The Chinese misbehaviour was only one of pushing, prodding, and protest notes!

Handing over the borders to the Army was a meaningless gesture, without the additional resources required. In fact, we made a bad situation worse by dragging in the Army and allowing the Chinese to claim that the Indians were bent on war. The Chinese went to great lengths to tell the world they only used "Frontier Guards". We did not increase our vigilance or our preparedness, and only misled our friends who were stunned by our defeats, when we had claimed that we had started preparations as early as 1959. The

Army was again embroiled in a thankless task without the tools to carry out the job. In the next chapter we shall trace the deployment of the Army, and see how the moves actually took place.

The last major incident of 1959 took place in Ladakh on 20th October. The Chinese ambushed a police party, under Havildar Karam Singh, about 40 miles inside our own territory, while it was on a routine patrol in the Chang Chenmo Valley, south of Kongka Pass. The Chinese later claimed that our party had intruded into Chinese territory. We lost 9 killed and 10 were taken prisoners. This incident really inflamed public opinion, as our Army always seemed to be at the receiving end of Chinese acts of aggression.

By the end of 1959 there was no longer any room for doubts or complacency. Even Mr. Menon has since asserted that from that time onwards Government was not "inactive". A clash of arms was a near certainty if the border problem was not negotiated across a table; and it was no longer a question of minor adjustments and delineating boundaries by consulting old documents, but the prospect of war over a vast area of our inhospitable northern regions. The Chinese had given us clear warning that they were serious, and were not averse to a fight if this was unavoidable. They had used force, and come what may they were going to sustain their rights and claims with Mao Tse Tung's famous "barrel of the gun".

The Army did not share the complacency of the country and were wary of the Chinese. The facile optimism of Parliamentary statements obviously could not remove the harsh realities of terrain and our inadequacies. General Thimayya, the Army Chief, had always warned Government about the Chinese threat. As early as 1959 he had informed Government of what would be required in men and material to contain the Chinese. He was dubbed pro-West by Mr. Menon and an alarmist by officialdom. Anyway with civil supremacy Government would tell him when and what to do about the Chinese. General Thimayya returned Mr. Menon's compliment and labelled him a Communist. Mr. Menon still kept harping on Pakistan being the Number One Enemy of India to divert the Indian people from the real and imminent Chinese danger. General Thimayya did not subscribe to the theory of numbering our likely enemies.

General Thimayya had for some years before becoming the Chief, been aware that the Army was overstretched, with commitments far in excess of its resources. The additional commitment of the North-East Frontier Agency and Ladakh could not be fulfilled without increasing its strength and organising an assured supply system. New weapons, new organisations, roads and accommodation were prerequisites before we could contemplate major operations in the Himalayas.

A month after the incidents at Khenzemane and Longju we witnessed the unfortunate clash between the Defence Minister and the Army Chief. A great deal of inspired publicity was given to Menon's alleged interference with senior Army promotions and other petty procedural matters.

General Thimayya submitted his resignation to Nehru. Mr. Nehru handled the impasse like a seasoned politician, used his immense authority and his personal charm on the straightforward soldier and persuaded him to withdraw his resignation. He promised to consider the General's requests personally and intervene with the Defence Minister. Later Nehru publicly stated that he thought that Thimayya was making an issue over trivial matters. He defended Menon against bitter criticism and said that Thimayya's resignation was due to "temperamental differences" with Menon. He dismissed the General's charges of interference as "rather trivial and of no consequence". He publicly chided the General and reproached him for "wanting to quit in the midst of the Sino-Indian border crisis". He also made a statement deprecating soldiers coercing the Civil Authority which must remain supreme in a democracy. Nehru won his Pyrrhic victory but lived to regret it. In 1962 he was compelled to replace those he had publicly defended and was forced to recall General Thimayya, after the NEFA Reverses, to lend respectability to the National Defence Council which was set up to assure the people against further military adventures.

I cannot resist an aside. Here we see Mr. Nehru using the so-called Sino-Indian border crisis to subdue General Thimayya. We know that the same crisis has been used to extract taxes from a reluctant Parliament. If he sincerely believed in the existence of a real crisis why was he guilty of neglecting the defences of the nation? How is it possible to reconcile his appreciation of a Chinese threat with his subsequent statement that China was too weak and preoccupied to start a war with India? To an Indian it is always distressing to find evidence that Mr. Nehru was a human politician. His subsequent actions are irreconcilable with his assertion that there was a Sino-Indian border crisis at the time of the Thimayya-Menon episode.

The more likely probability is that Menon and Thimayya fell out over the Government's China Policy. General Thimayya was a seasoned, disciplined soldier who needed no lessons in elementary patriotism. He would hardly have made an issue over trifles. Only over-riding national interests would have provoked him to the extreme step of resignation; and later withdraw the resignation in dutiful obedience to his Prime Minister. If he was unbalanced and prone to make issues over trifles, Mr. Nehru should not have appointed him Chief of the Army – the choice was entirely his and his alone. Thimayya had always harboured misgivings about Chinese motives and intentions. In one of his rare public statements (in June 1960) he said, "Reports so far indicate that the Chinese had certainly made heavy concentrations along some of our border areas, and what worries me is the motive of the build-up. China had the advantage of an early start in developing border communications . . . Indian border posts had to encounter tremendous natural obstacles".

The General's worries were brushed aside as the Government's thinking, at the time, was that there was nothing sinister in the quantum of Chinese forces in Tibet. It was accepted that the Army divisions were located there to suppress the rebellious Khampas and to maintain law and order. Their presence did not signify any war preparations against India.

Mr. Nehru's biographers will have a difficult time explaining his inexplicable descent to ordinary norms of behaviour to save a colleague at the expense of jeopardising the defence of his country. Pettiness and selfishness are not qualities that one would wish to associate with a man of the stature of Mr. Nehru.

General Thimayya was the ablest of India's generals and easily the best-loved – a rare combination. He was popularly known as 'Timmy'. He was the most outstanding field commander in the Indian Army and was the first and only Indian to command a fighting brigade in battle, in the Arakan, in World War II. He won the British Distinguished Service Order on the battlefield. North Indian soldiers, the bulk of the Army, loved him as much as the rest. This is a rare tribute.

In 1947 he commanded the Punjab Boundary Force, during the critical post-Partition days, when murder, massacre and madness were the order of the day. He was a big man in every way and when most people had lost their heads, he remained calm, scrupulously fair and absolutely honest in his dealings with Hindus and Muslims alike. He did an outstanding job of this difficult and thankless assignment.

In 1948, soon after the Punjab disturbances, he commanded the Indian Forces in the Kashmir Valley, where he won some notable successes and military victories in areas where no modern armies had ever operated. He had cleared the Kashmir Valley of the enemy and was poised to free the Pakistan-held portion of Kashmir when the war was called off by Nehru, for reasons that have never been revealed.

He later served as a Principal Staff Officer at Army HQ and Army Commander. His military background was impeccable and he had not lost years on quasi-military assignments at the behest of politicians.

His personal qualities matched his military talents and experience. As a commander he had a magic touch with both officers and men. In all my service of over 25 years I have never heard an ill-word spoken against him; or had an unwise military decision attributed to him. This is the highest praise and tribute that can be paid to an officer, a gallant gentleman and an outstanding soldier.

He achieved international fame as a result of his work on the International Commission in Korea, in 1953-54. He was one of the few Indians who was nationally famous and who was a potential rival to the *prima donna* of the Indian stage – Mr. Nehru. He could not be brow-beaten, bullied or summarily dismissed as Mr. Nehru was wont to do with some other more pliable and submissive Chiefs. His war record made his professional advice meaningful and difficult to ignore. No wonder the *Times of India* wrote at the time of his assumption of office, in March 1957: "A thrill has just passed through the Army. The signal has gone out that Timmy is on". The Army had waited hopefully for the day when Timmy would be the Chief.

For some years prior to becoming Chief, General Thimayya had smarted at the neglect of the Army. The Army in turn knew that he was the only General who knew what had to be done and who had the authority to put things right.

I had the great pleasure and invaluable experience of serving closely with this great man, in operational and organisational matters, during my tenure in Military Operations Directorate. I knew with what energy and enthusiasm he started trying to repair the damage done to the Army, and I saw his confidence being gradually eroded because he could make little headway against an indifferent and often hostile (and ignorant) Ministry of Defence, under Mr. Menon. He retired a sad and disillusioned man, his advice regarding China ignored and the Army in the same state of unreadiness for its ordained tasks. In one of his farewell speeches before relinquishing command, he told his audience: "I hope that I am not leaving you as cannon-fodder for the Chinese. God bless you all".

As a disciplined officer he had accepted the advice and assurances of his Prime Minister and had withdrawn his resignation. Resignation is the last constitutional resort of a Service Chief in a democratic set-up, to focus national attention on a fundamental issue to give the Nation an opportunity to debate the points of disagreement between the Civil and Military authorities. In a democracy, this is the only safeguard against incompetent, unscrupulous or ambitious politicians. He bravely bore the humiliations heaped on him by Nehru in Parliament, but he was never again the same man. He had only one ambition left and that was to preside over the Centenary celebrations of his beloved Kumaonis, while still the Chief. It was a sad end to the most distinguished soldier India is likely to have in decades.

In his last days of office he undoubtedly lost some of his personal hold on the officers and the other Services who resented the withdrawal of his resignation. Something drastic was necessary to move Government to face the realities of a conflict with China or Pakistan, and only Timmy had the necessary stature. Many felt that he should have resigned a second time, after

Nehru's injudicious Parliamentary statement. I am firmly of the opinion that had he done so, Mr. Menon would not have emerged the all-powerful figure who contributed so much to India's humiliation in September and October 1962. A second resignation, with the additional disclosure of differences, would have put the pressure on Nehru. Powerful enemies, many within the Congress Party; a hostile Press and others were waiting to destroy Menon and only General Thimayya could have given them the excuse and the opportunity. Mr. Nehru would have had to face the awkward dilemma of having to sack either Menon or Thimayya. Had he been forced to sack Menon under strong pressure from Parliament and the Press, he would have been a chastened man. Such a reverse would also have had a salutary effect on his own ego and would have demolished the aura of infallibility and indispensability that was built around him, in spite of the democratic system that was given to us in the Constitution.

As it was, Menon emerged the victor and Timmy's advice was no longer decisive. Mr. Nehru also came out of this unsavoury episode the unquestioned master, and now there was no one in the Army to oppose his wrong military policy *vis-a-vis* China. He now received advice only from Mr. Menon and the latter's chosen coterie of soldiers and officials who were willing to play at war with China without expecting to wound or to be wounded. A game of chess with posts instead of pawns!

History is replete with 'ifs'. If only General Thimayya had stuck to his guns, would India have been saved the ignominy of 1962 and the subsequent political upheavals, financial distress, the suffering of the people and the international humiliation?

Government did not offer him a Governorship or Ambassadorship, when lesser generals were rewarded with such high positions. Employment after retirement

General K. S. Thimayya, Chief of Army Staff (1960) arriving to take the salute at the Passing Out Parade of the Indian Military Academy, escorted by the author.

"*The most distinguished soldier India is likely to have in decades.*" (pg. 51)

Khenzamane Post which was overwhelmed by the Chinese in a few hours on 20th October 1962.

"It would be wrong to call them Check Posts and they are in fact military outposts" – NEHRU (pg. 74)

Members of a Parliamentary Delegation which inspected the Indian Military Academy in April 1960 when the author was Deputy Commandant.

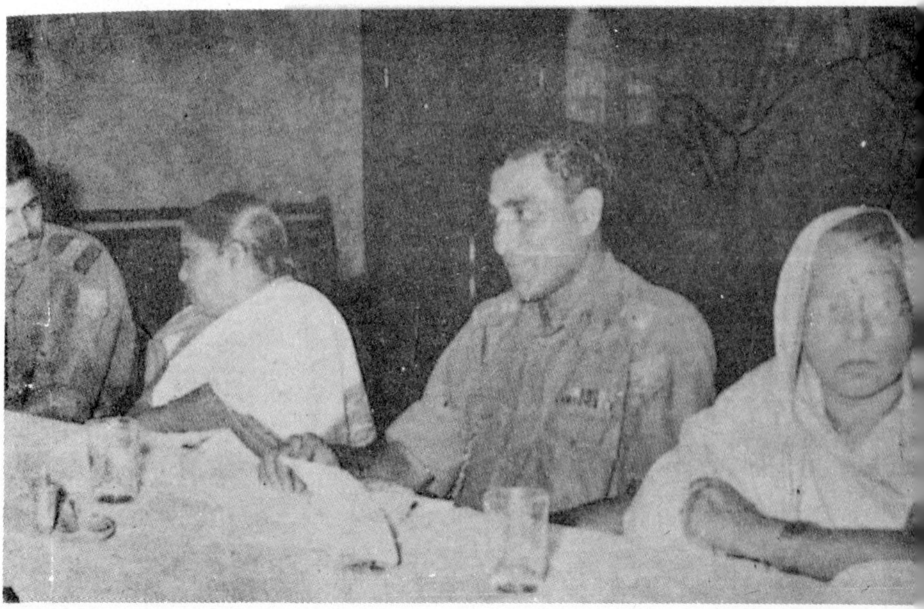

Lt.-Col. (now Brigadier) Maha Singh Rikh, gallant Commanding Officer of 2nd Rajputs in the battle of the Namka Chu in October 1962.

The author (1952) as Commanding Officer of 4th Battalion, The Guards, in regimental mess kit.

was a powerful weapon used by Government to keep Service Brass in tow. I have not read of one instance where an Ambassadorial appointment was questioned by the Press. General Timmy was rescued from the obscurity of the South Indian Coffee Board and appointed Chief of the U.N. Force in Cyprus where he died in December 1965, in the saddle. One of India's greatest post-Independence figures died in the international arena, but no thanks are due to the Indian Government for this.

During the years 1954-59 there were serious shortcomings in our National Policy. We did not build up the nation's will to fight and to accept the sacrifices without which no country can ensure its security. We gave the impression of not knowing what we wanted, appeared confused and wavered between the implacable will to fight and a desire to appease the Chinese.

We relied on untenable diplomatic assurances to ward off the Pakistan and Chinese threats. We did not initiate diplomatic measures to ensure that we were not isolated in a war with either Pakistan or China.

We accepted a situation where we would be perpetually in a state of armed readiness, a suicidal policy for a developing country. We allowed ourselves to be lulled into complacency by the outward manifestations of friendship with China. When the Chinese threat became unmistakable, we had no ready answer.

To sum up, we did not plan for war nor did we have diplomatic ties which would ensure timely aid in the event of war. We frittered away a large portion of our meagre resources without ensuring our security. In 1959, India lacked a firm, unequivocal policy, had no declared friends to assist her against China and no military power to challenge China.

Major-General B. M. Kaul was promoted Lt.-General and brought to Delhi in July 1959 as the Quarter Master General of the Army. It was widely believed at the time that this was done by Mr. Menon against the recommendation or advice of the Army Chief, General Thimayya. Welles Hangen suggests that Mr. Menon chose Kaul because he (Menon) felt that Kaul was far to the Left of the other conservative generals in Delhi. Whatever the reasons, the Menon-Kaul era began and these two began to have an increasingly decisive voice in policy matters. The harmony and cohesion of Army HQ were inevitably affected due to the barely concealed antagonism between the Chief and one of his Principal Staff Officers, especially as it was believed that Kaul had the backing of Menon and had access to the Prime Minister. This was a dangerous development, as Army HQ had to speak with one voice in the crucial years that lay ahead.

I served in Army HQ from 1954 to July 1959 and saw at first hand, the way we handled the Chinese problem, as well as the changing military situation *vis-a-vis* Pakistan. I left with some misgivings about the future and wondered what was in store for us. The negligence and damage of the years could not easily be repaired. General Thimayya was at the fag-end of his career and with his retirement in April 1961, we would lose the last hope of highlighting the Army's requirements; and maintaining the balance between the hopes of the country and the minimum military preparedness.

Chapter V

The Army Mans the Border — 1959 / 60

Although the Prime Minister had announced in August 1959, to the Lok Sabha, that the Army had taken over the NEFA border, it was only in November of that year that the actual moves of regular troops could take place. The gap of three months in implementing the Prime Minister's order is most revealing and can be explained by the Army's reluctance to get implicated precipitously in the Himalayas. The final prod may well have been provided by the Karam Singh episode of October 1959.

The Chinese incidents of August and October 1959 were beautifully timed. There was some discord and heart-burning in the relations between the Ministry of Defence and Army HQ as a result of the Menon-Thimayya clash; the weather in the Himalayas would soon close and we would have little time to move, quarter troops and organise proper administrative arrangements. There was bound to be more than a little dissatisfaction among the troops deployed and their morale would be affected. This did happen and the operation started with a lot of heart-burning and mutual recrimination. The Indian jawan does not understand high politics and he blames his officers if things appear to be senseless, pointless and wrong.

Having provoked us and baited us into an unplanned and hasty action, the Chinese retreated to the warmth and comparative comfort of their winter quarters — generally requisitioned monasteries. On our side troops suffered unspeakable hardships in their first winter, without achieving any worthwhile object. We learnt one more wrong lesson, viz. that a military problem is solved by the mere despatch of regular troops to the scene of trouble.

The world-renowned 4 Indian Division was rushed from the plains of the Punjab to Assam for deployment in the North East Frontier Agency. This Division was organised, equipped and trained for warfare in the plains – i.e. open country. Its transport and artillery were unsuitable for mountain warfare. In fact much heavy equipment was left behind in the foothills and useful man-power was wasted in maintaining this impedimenta. The officers and men were not acclimatised for high altitudes. As usual, compelling political pressure forced the deployment of the wrong troops, at the wrong place and at the wrong time.

The actual move was a compulsive reaction to events. To illustrate, I will recount the move of 1/9 Gorkha Rifles from the Simla Hills to NEFA, and the course of their induction into Towang. The battalion was stationed in the beautiful hill cantonment of Dagshai. One evening in November 1959 the officers had assembled in the Officers' Mess prior to proceeding to the unit lines of a sister battalion, 2 Jats, to attend the celebrations of the latter's Raising Day. Before the officers had embussed a despatch rider from Brigade HQ arrived with an important message for the Officiating Commanding Officer. This officer did not disclose the contents of the message till the officers returned from 2 Jats, late at night. He then informed everyone that 4 Division, less a few units, had been ordered to move to NEFA in the next fortnight.

The battalion entrained on 22nd November and reached Misamari on the 29th. The rest of the Brigade concentrated in the following week. The snows had set in and any further advance into the heights of NEFA was ruled out in the prevailing conditions. To keep the troops occupied a jungle training camp was established at the Foothills camp, about 14 miles from Misamari.

4 Division was given the task of defending the entire McMahon Line from the Bhutan Tri-junction to the Burma border, a distance of over 360 miles. There were no roads and no laterals; access to each sector being from the Brahmaputra Valley. There were no shelters for the troops and no animal transport. This precipitate deployment was of no military value, especially as incidents were unlikely in the winter.

However there was complete satisfaction in Delhi where maps of NEFA sprouted in the offices of the big Brass, with little pins showing our defence preparations. A little blue pin-head can be very satisfying and re-assuring in Delhi. Politicians can get up in the Lok Sabha and assert that Government had initiated military counter-measures to prevent any further incursions by the Chinese.

The deployment and quantum of troops were dictated solely and entirely by the administrative capacity, which was in turn dependent on the available air-lift and supply dropping equipment. There was no question of deploying units or formations to fulfil any assessed task. Indeed I doubt whether we had any policy or task other than to "defend our borders". The induction of the maximum numbers that could be maintained became the end and not the means for implementing operational plans. If we had any National Policy and National Aim we would have appreciated the futility of sending our men into the wilderness of NEFA, without a purpose and without a military task.

The move of the Brigade was not co-ordinated with the civil authorities, i.e. the NEFA Administration which was under the Ministry of External Affairs. The move of the Army appeared to be an *ad-hoc* decision and not as the result of the deliberations of the Defence Committee of the Cabinet. I have heard that the NEFA officials and the Assam Rifles (also under the Ministry of External Affairs) did not relish the idea of the Army poaching in their territory and private domain. One responsible civil official is reported to have said, in January 1960, that Government was considering the withdrawal of the Army. Apparently he did not seem to understand the need for regular troops as he was satisfied that the Assam Rifles were perfectly capable of ensuring the "defence" of the region, since there was no serious threat from our great neighbour. This attitude prevailed for a long time and was displayed whenever the Army approached the Civil Authority for help in the way of accommodation, porters, ponies and so on. They showed apathy and indifference if not actual hostility.

In January 1960, one company of the Gorkhas was sent to establish a camp at Bomdilla. In February a second company was ordered to move to Towang and establish a base. After undergoing incredible hardships they reached in March. The whole battalion eventually concentrated in Towang by August 1960 – almost one year after the Prime Minister had "handed over the border" to the Army. At this time one battalion was located in Dirang and one at Tenga. The Brigade HQ was at Bomdilla. In 1961 one company was sent to Pankentang on the Bumla-Towang axis, and one company to Shakti on the Khenzemane-Towang route.

In the initial stages the Regular Army was driven to scrounge some life-saving shelters from the Assam Rifles and the Administration – a ridiculous state of affairs. The first Gorkha company to reach Towang was lucky to be given one hutment and the Inspection Bungalow. Other administrative arrangements were equally unsatisfactory. There was an amusing story circulating in the Army in those days. A Lieut.-Colonel known for his pungent wit and sense of humour, got so fed up with the lack of any sort of supply system that he decided to use some heavy sarcasm and act in a facetious manner. He is reported to have sent one of his monthly routine reports on a "chappatti" (a flat unleavened bread). This caused some consternation in the rear. He was asked to forward his "explanation". He sent the now classic retort, "I regret the unorthodox nature of my stationery, but atta (flour) is the only commodity I have for fighting, for feeding and for futile correspondence". (The quotation is obviously not verbatim.)

One of the main problems faced by the Army was the selection of sites for building accommodation for the troops. As usual there was no co-ordinating agency and these details were left to local initiative. The Civilians were averse to the location of the Army in Towang proper, although it was the only suitable place both tactically and for receiving air-drops on which the garrison relied for survival. There were the usual conferences to settle this vexed question. At these meetings the Civil would spell out their grandiose plans for developing Towang into a health and holiday resort and brought blue-prints indicating the future location of colleges, parks and housing projects. The Army was invited to find some other place away from Towang and Pankentang, at 14,000 feet, was magnanimously offered to the soldiers. Eventually the matter was settled by some strong-arm tactics by the Commander, Brigadier Ranbir Singh, a tough, blunt Rajput. Exasperated by the comic deliberations of the "siting boards" he decided to enforce a unilateral settlement. One morning he planted his Commander's pennant, the proud Red Eagle of 4 Division and staked his claim to that particular piece of ground as the Command Post. He then sited the other elements of the Brigade and allotted unit lines without further ado. The "Civil" bowed to the will of this fine soldier and despite some desultory murmurings and threats they accepted the *fait accompli*. General Officer Commanding (GOC) 4 Division later endorsed the action of his Brigade Commander and a potentially ugly situation was finally resolved amicably.

Soon after the induction of regular troops into NEFA, General S. P. P. Thorat, General Officer Commanding-in-Chief, Eastern Command wrote an appreciation of the military situation facing us in NEFA, bringing out lucidly and thoroughly the terrain, communications, routes, vital ground and administration. He then enunciated the correct strategy to be employed in defending NEFA. I heard that this paper was seen by Mr. Chavan when he took over in November 1962 and he was aghast that we had ignored the advice of this capable General.

From the outset General Thorat appreciated that the operative principle was the need to advance from secure bases. He correctly appreciated that the key to the defence of the Assam plains was around Bomdilla. He had also anticipated the only three routes that the Chinese used in 1962. (The Chinese spent two months in Kameng after their victory in 1962 and would undoubtedly have made copious notes of this fact!) The importance of Bomdilla was confirmed by three successive brigadiers who commanded in NEFA. Everyone agreed that any forward move should be undertaken only after consolidating Bomdilla. To put it simply, it was necessary to move from firm base to firm base, and not backward from the political boundaries of the country. Political and military boundaries seldom coincide.

The McMahon Line cannot be defended by sitting on it. This self-evident fact cannot be altered by Parliamentary baiting or pressure of public opinion. Once Government decided to employ the Army to a possible war with China then the only aim should have been the destruction of the intruding Chinese. The Army cannot have its main aim diverted by such tasks as defending every inch of territory, ensuring the security of our territory, ensuring the security of every pass or crossing place and not allowing a single intruder to enter our territory. The strategic deployment and dispositions of regular troops is dictated solely by the ground and administrative factors. This is even more applicable where the enemy has the political and strategic initiative, as in the case of the Chinese.

As we have seen, General Thorat initially deployed only one infantry company in Towang, leaving the rest of the battalion in Bomdilla; and the Brigade further back. In the context of the border problem with China it may be necessary to set up check-posts, border-posts or flag-posts to establish our claims by physical possession, and to provide day-to-day protection to the civil administration. They must not, however be treated as defended zones or tactical positions, to be defended to the last man and last round.

General Thorat's plan was made when NEFA had not been developed and the Border Roads Organisation had not begun operations. In 1960 the Chinese already had a network of good roads opposite NEFA. The General's plan might have entailed the initial trading of space for time to rush fresh troops forward, establish communications, set up the administrative arrangements and above all, ascertain the main thrust of the enemy before committing his reserves. General Thorat's plan, approved by his Chief, was not acceptable to Government. Government was dominated by the belief that a war with China was unlikely; and were pressed by the political necessity of appearing to defend the entire McMahon Line. Mr. Menon has recently (November 1967) set out the Government's dilemma. In an interview with Mr. Inder Malhotra of the *Statesman* he has made the following observations: "It might have been useful to let them come into Indian territory in depth before giving them a fight. But this is a kind of thing which we were unable to persuade our public opinion to accept then and perhaps would be equally difficult to do so today or for some time to come". He goes on to say, "So inflamed was public opinion that if any Defence Minister or Prime Minister had wanted to let the Chinese take our territory in the hope that we would take it back soon – which is something quite necessary to do from the military point of view – he could not have done so". He concludes, "Public opinion was built up by various parties sometimes under the influence of foreign propaganda that we were never able to look at things objectively". This statement clearly indicates that Menon had imbibed the advice of his military experts. His statement is a courageous admission, but does raise the point of whether the nation's leaders are expected to lead the nation or to dispense with military principles and prudence under pressure from so nebulous a factor as public opinion, especially in India where such an opinion is difficult to assess. The justifiable dissatisfaction of a few alert Opposition members cannot be used as an excuse for rashness in a moment of crisis.

Mr. Menon understood this aspect of strategy when he was quoted by the *Press Trust of India* as saying (on 23rd April 1960), "India does not want to fight over the Himalayan ranges, but if China has any intention of coming down the Himalayan slopes and entering the plains, then we are prepared to give her a warm reception – warmer than she might expect". Then why did he not educate his Opposition colleagues?

The second pertinent point is why was public opinion not educated to appreciate the realities of the confrontation with China? And lastly were our leaders not to blame for making reassuring statements about our defence preparedness? My own reading is that the public have learnt a lesson and the present Government has conducted its affairs with commendable courage and restraint. The reader will recall our dignified and calm reaction to the Chinese threats in the middle of the 1965 Indo-Pak War. We did not panic when the Chinese were reported to have crossed the McMahon Line in the Thagla Ridge area and reached Hathungla Pass in 1964. The last and most notable example was the conduct of the major battle at Nathu La Pass in September 1967. After exchanging blow for blow we offered a cease-fire as evidence of our strength and restraint. The Indian public, having faith in their present leadership, was content to leave the matter to Government and made no attempt to hustle the issue. Public opinion is an unsatisfactory reason for abandoning the basic canons of war.

Prior to 1962, Government's solution to the military problem of defending the border was to locate a string of small, weak outposts backed by company strength detachments of regular troops, all along the border. Parliament and the public could then be told that our borders were being adequately guarded.

Our politicians had not studied military history, nor did they have the humility to listen to the advice of capable generals who had. Indian politicians are the only ones in the world who have had no experience of war. According to the Military Correspondent of the *Statesman*, "They know nothing of military affairs and are not prepared to learn. This applies equally to the nabobs of the Ministries of External Affairs and Defence. Hence the gap between the Civilian and soldier".

In difficult terrain, be it mountain, jungle or snow-covered steppe, it is sometimes militarily unavoidable to trade space for time. This is a stark military fact. Military history affords many examples to prove this. In war the primary aim is the destruction of enemy forces. It is not the holding of impossible ground for political reasons or the undertaking of operations to appease an aroused public opinion.

Both in 1812, when Napoleon invaded Russia and in 1941 when Hitler launched an invasion, the Russians drew the advancing armies deep into Russian territory. They relied on their most formidable weapons – snow in winter and the dreaded spring thaw (facetiously known as Generals January and February) which turns Russia into a vast sea of mud, that brings armies to a grinding halt. In both cases the Russians sapped the vitality of the advancing enemy; and on both occasions mighty Russian counter-offensives regained all lost territories and destroyed or ejected the invaders.

In 1944, Field-Marshal Sir William Slim, Commander of the British/Indian 14 Army, faced a major Japanese offensive from Burma into India, aimed at capturing the base at Dimapur. Slim had the option of fighting from his positions or falling back to Kohima. After careful deliberation, he opted for the latter course despite strong political pressure not to abandon any Indian territory and give the Indians the impression that the Allies were losing. He stood firm and based his plans entirely on military considerations. Had he fought from his forward positions on the Chindwin River, his Lines of Communication would have been long and tenuous. A defeat would open the way to the plains of Assam. His decision to fall back and shorten his lines, and to a better killing ground at Kohima, forced the Japanese Commander, General Mutaguchi, to extend his lines. By standing fast at Kohima despite being invested, till the outbreak of the monsoons, victory was assured. The Japanese could not maintain their forces and had to retreat. The defeat was so overwhelming that Field-Marshal Slim followed up his Kohima victory with the classic pursuit operation to Rangoon itself, which fell in May 1945.

The strategic considerations applicable to the Himalayas were well enunciated by Brigadier Thompson, the Military Correspondent of the *Daily Telegraph.* Writing on 12th November 1962, at the height of the Chinese invasion, he said, "The Chinese have better land access as they have been building frontier roads and airfields since they annexed Tibet. In the vicinity of the Tibetan frontier of NEFA there are passes up to 16,000 feet. On the Indian side the precipitation is great. The mountains are covered in dense forest and thick snow in winter. Land communications with the area from India are exceptionally difficult. On the Tibetan side, the high plateau, over which the Chinese have built approach roads and airfields is extremely cold but snowfall is light. The military problem is not the relative size of the Indian or Chinese armies but how many troops each side can maintain in the frontier areas. India can only match China's ability by means of air transport and the dropping of supplies by parachutes. Even so, in establishing a favourable air situation for the use of her air transport she may find herself at a disadvantage with regard to the accessibility of airfields". Brigadier Thompson might well have added the difficulty of finding dropping zones for parachute drops, which were few and far between and very rarely within convenient distance of forward troops. Operations are often dictated by the availability of dropping zones.

The moral of Brigadier Thompson's comment is that it might have been militarily sounder to give the Chinese the problems of the southern slopes of the Himalayas, in 1962, as our own communications had not been developed and we had no forward administrative bases and animal transport to support the troops. A delaying action through Towang and Sela Pass, instead of offering pitched battles on unequal terms, might have delayed the Chinese. Our own build-up then would have more closely approximated the Chinese build-up, as they would have lost the advantage of their well-developed road communications up to the NEFA border and their established forward bases. It was suicidal to fight them at a place which was three hours from a 7-ton roadhead, while our 3-ton roadhead at Misamari was 21 days and the 1-ton roadhead at Towang 6 days away. Even these roads were useless for the carry forward of Towang due to lack of porters, pack transport, tracks and bridges. We relied on air transport, but the scattered drops were of no use to the forward garrisons, apart from the dropping zones being 1 to 3 days carry from the front-line troops.

To complete this discourse on the strategic considerations applicable to NEFA, let us review the basic advantages enjoyed by the Chinese. Tibet was a sanctuary, as India could not attack Chinese bases there without going to war. Their bases at Le, Marmang and Tsona enjoyed immunity from both ground and air attack and did not need to be guarded, thus freeing combat troops for their offensive. They had the advantage both of 'economy of force' and 'concentration of effort' – two important principles of war. If they could have been forced to set up forward bases inside NEFA, these would have been vulnerable and would have diverted troops. Every additional mouth to feed becomes a liability in the mountains.

Since we decided to sit on the border i.e. the McMahon Line we could only manoeuvre backward unless we were prepared to invade Tibet, assuming that we had the necessary military strength to do so. On the other hand, the Chinese claimed the whole of NEFA and could plan on operations in this disputed area without risking immediate, adverse world opinion. In fact, in November 1961 and again on 3rd October 1962 Mr. Chou-en Lai made it clear that he would not respect the McMahon Line.

The public and our higher planners must learn these military facts of life. They cannot be ignored whatever the other imperatives. There is no point in getting hysterical and demanding immediate reprisals, every time the Chinese intrude into our territory. It takes time and military skill to create the necessary favourable conditions for mounting an offensive, to evict intruders.

It is to the credit of General Thimayya and General Thorat that we did not deploy in strength beyond Bomdilla, during their command. They were adamant. They advised against establishing any further forward posts without adequate military arrangements. It was only after they left that we adopted the ill-fated Forward Policy and gave the Chinese an excuse for the clash of 1962, and the subsequent lightning thrust to the plains.

Having faced stiff opposition from the older and more sober generals, Government now looked for some other general who would collaborate with their forward policy. Here I would quote Mr. G. S. Bhargava from his excellently documented book, *The Battle of NEFA*. He says, " . . . a new class of Army Officer who could collude with politicians to land the country in the straits in which it found itself in September-October 1962. Since qualities of heart and head ceased to be a passport to promotion for military officers . . . war and fighting having been ruled out, the more ambitious among them started currying favour with the politicians. . . . In such circumstances a general with an eye on the future need only tell Ministers that a network of border posts, plus half-hearted preparations for 'positional warfare' – General Kaul's pet phrase in those days—would contain the Chinese. Harassed policymakers would have jumped at it. . . . They would have calculated . . . (that this) without provoking the enemy would silence the critics at home".

The so-called 'Forward Policy' has been the subject of much controversy and debate. Even after six years it is not clear as to who was actually responsible for devising this policy and whether the policy itself was the sole reason for the military riposte from China. It therefore warrants a detailed study of the available information.

General Kaul attributes the decision to Mr. Nehru. According to him, Mr. Nehru was being subjected to mounting criticism for allowing Chinese incursions and was anxious to devise some *via media* and take action, short of war, in order to appease the people. Mr. Nehru is reported to have held a meeting in the autumn of 1961 in his room, at which Mr. Menon, General Thapar and General Kaul were present. Studying a map showing recent Chinese incursions, Mr. Nehru is reported to have said that whoever succeeded in establishing a post would establish a claim to that territory, as possession was nine-tenths of the law. He then asked if the Chinese could set up posts why couldn't we?

Kaul claims that, "He (Nehru) was told that owing to numerical and logistical difficulties, we could not keep up in this race with the Chinese. If we inducted more posts in retaliation, we would not be able to maintain them logistically. Also, China with her superior military resources could operationally make the position of our small posts untenable". Presumably this military advice was given by Thapar and Kaul.

After some discussion Mr. Nehru is alleged to have evolved a new policy for our border areas. Briefly the new policy was that, *as China was unlikely to wage war with India*, there was no reason why we should not play a game of chess and a battle of wits with them and maintain *a few of our posts in what we were convinced was our territory*. If the Chinese advanced in one place, we should advance in another. Mr. Nehru is reported to have been of the view that this defensive step on our part might irritate the Chinese but no more.

General Kaul's summing up is, "I think Nehru framed this policy principally for the benefit of the Parliament and the public and also perhaps as a strategy of beating the Chinese at their own game.... He saw in it one reply to his critics".

It would be unfair to Mr. Nehru to suggest that he embarked on such a course without tacit military approval from some general. It is inconceivable that such a major change could have been decreed in such a wholly impromptu manner, for such selfish reasons, and without consulting the Cabinet and the Defence Chiefs. The Defence Committee of the Cabinet does not appear to have had a hand in this decision.

Mr. Welles Hangen, in his book *After Nehru, Who?* says: "One significant issue on which I know Kaul outmanœuvred Menon is the 'forward' strategy adopted by the Indian Army in the summer of 1962 against the Chinese in Ladakh and on the North-East Frontier. Kaul went to Nehru and persuaded him to let the Army establish advance check posts to outflank Chinese posts set up on Indian territory".

Most Army officers will agree with Messrs. Bhargava and Hangen. In 1962, it was generally believed that Kaul was the man largely responsible for getting the Army committed to the northern borders before the required means were made available. With due respect to General Thapar it must be admitted that his advice counted for little in 1961/62, in these policy matters.

Kaul himself confesses the truth about his part in forcing the Forward Policy on a reluctant Army. I quote: "In connection with some difficulties which GOC XXXIII Corps had raised, I went to Gauhati in February 1962 and held a conference attended by senior civil and military officials who were dealing with this question in NEFA. I told them why it was important for us to establish posts all along our border and that failure on our part to do so would result in the Chinese establishing these posts instead. In view of the extreme shortage of man-power, labour, supply-dropping equipment and the inaccessibility of certain areas, many of which were not easy to identify, and unreliable maps, Lt.-General K. Umrao Singh, Commander, XXXIII Corps, apprehended it might be difficult to fully implement this policy. After some discussion, *it was agreed by all present that it was imperative* *in the national interests of defence to establish as many posts along our border in NEFA as possible, despite our difficulties.** . . . The Chinese must have resented being forestalled and in frustration and anger provoked a combustible situation in October 1962".

An analysis of General Kaul's version of his visit to Gauhati raises many interesting and controversial issues. The first relevant point is the propriety of the Chief of the General Staff dealing directly, on a major policy matter, with a Corps HQ and by-passing Command HQ which was the correct channel of command. Unfortunately, this sort of impromptu order group, presided over by Kaul, had become the accepted procedure and was resorted to whenever he felt that the forward commanders were not acting with the speed and determination which he demanded.

Having claimed that the Forward Policy was the brain-child of Mr. Nehru he states that the Gauhati meeting took a major decision. He says, "It was agreed by all present that it was imperative in the national interests of defence to establish as many posts along our borders in NEFA as possible, despite our difficulties". The vital issue is whether a gathering of assorted officials is empowered to take decisions on matters concerning the national interests – a matter that is solely the duty and prerogative of the Defence Committee of the Cabinet. The unavoidable deduction is that Kaul has tried to build up a case to prove that this controversial decision was taken by Nehru and was later unanimously "determined" by many officials. In other words, he tries to absolve himself of the widely-held belief that it was Kaul himself who was the architect and prime mover of the Forward Policy.

In the same passage he goes on to say, "It was in pursuance of this effort that the Commander of the 4 Infantry Division sent out various Assam Rifles parties, each accompanied by a regular army officer, to ensure that these posts were correctly established.

* *Authors italics.*

One such party went under the guidance of Captain Mahabir Prasad, MC, of 1 Sikh and established a post at Dhola in NEFA near the area of Tri-junction". The word "effort" is misleading. This passage does not enlighten us as to who selected Dhola as one of the posts under the Forward Policy; a crucial matter that cannot be side-tracked by clever verbiage. Even if we accept that Mr. Nehru advised the Forward Policy, his alleged "instructions" were that we should establish these forward posts *in what we were convinced was our territory.* Now who disobeyed this order and set up a post in a sensitive, disputed remote area and one which the Chinese had more than once refused to concede as Indian territory? Kaul says that in setting up the posts he was given "invaluable data and assistance" by Mr. B. N. Mullick and Mr. Hooja of the Intelligence Bureau, thus dragging them into the dismal picture. Was Dhola set up on their advice? Was the Ministry of External Affairs consulted, or was it the decision of GOC 4 Division? Was it Kaul who gave the list of forward posts to Command HQ's or was it the unanimous decision of the February 1962 conference of Gauhati? Whoever is responsible was guilty of an error of judgement, an error that provided the Chinese with the detonator for which they were looking.

There is one last comment that must be made. General Kaul was a senior Army General and it is strange, to say the least, that he should have ordered a military venture with the vague administrative injunction of "despite our difficulties". Such vagueness does not represent the orthodox way of issuing military orders.

There is something unconvincing about the alleged proceedings of the conference at Gauhati. To my knowledge, Kaul had gone there to brow-beat and bully the doubtful generals who had misgivings about the whole idea of setting up forward posts. I know that from the Corps Commander down to myself as the Brigade Commander we had grave reservations about the wisdom of this new policy.

General Kaul visited HQ 4 Division in July 1962 to speed up the establishment of one of the posts that we were having difficulty in setting up due to administrative problems. We see that he now came directly to the level of a division to do the "chasing". At this meeting he made his famous speech about there being some officers "who can and some who can't" after the Eno's Fruit Salt advertisement. All those who did not get a move on with the establishment of forward posts were classified as "can'ts" and would be severely dealt with. I was on my way down from Towang to Tezpur to attend an operational conference that I shall be referring to later. I was stopped by the GSO I of the Division at Bomdilla on 3rd July 1962, and was told that I would be "personally" responsible for organising the move to a certain forward post. When I pointed out that these posts were being established under the administrative arrangements of the Assam Rifles and the NEFA Administration, I was told to liase with them and hurry the move as General Kaul was furious at the delay and would not accept any excuses. As Commander I was personally to blame. I was dumbfounded.

General Kaul has tried to use two *alibis:* the first is blaming Mr. Nehru and the second the meeting at Gauhati. He has carefully avoided indicating his own views on the Forward Policy other than the administrative problems that he claims were put up to Mr. Nehru. Was he loyally implementing the orders of his Prime Minister in February and again in July 1962, or was he hounding the local commanders and by-passing the normal chain of command in the process, in pursuance of his own idea of combating the Chinese?

The Military Correspondent of the *Statesman*, writing in a special supplement in November 1967, has summed up the contributory responsibility of

Generals Thapar and Kaul neatly and comprehensively. He writes, "The two Generals did not say that they could not assume responsibility for the Forward Policy and its consequences with the means at their disposal. They thus made themselves party to a dangerous decision. At various times they represented, implored and complained that they faced 'logistical difficulties'. But they did not say at any time that because of these difficulties the execution of the Forward Policy, at that time, was impossible or dangerous. They only questioned the means to implement the policy and not the policy itself". He aptly concluded, "To wake up civilians, generals must protest against a policy which they know to be beyond India's military capacity, to the point of resignation. Instead Kaul and Thapar did not even make a written protest. It is the duty of soldiers to obey; it is equally the duty of senior soldiers on rare occasions, to say that certain orders cannot be obeyed. It is the duty of responsible military men not to take on an impossible assignment from their civilian masters without at least firm written protest and at best submitting their resignations". Far from doing this, General Kaul took it upon himself to visit lower formation HQ; brush aside difficulties and threaten disciplinary action against those officers who were stalling the establishment of posts.

The advice of capable generals who counselled caution, restraint and adherence to the basic principles of war was ignored and the principles of war violated. Such generals were labelled pro-West, alarmists or over-cautious. With the eclipse of General Thimayya, General Thorat's claims to be the Chief were waived aside and General Thapar's seniority was invoked to promote him, in April 1961. General S. D. Verma, who was commanding Ladakh and who held similar views to General Thorat, was superseded, his seniority being ignored. The truth is that officers who opposed the indiscriminate opening of posts were ear-marked for elimination. There was no room for practical, professional views in Mr. Nehru's quest for political survival in the face of a militant Opposition.

In April 1961 General Thimayya was retired, General Thorat was pensioned off and General Verma, a man of principle, resigned immediately he was superseded. The stage was set for the Forward Policy.

We established a number of additional forward posts. Mr. Nehru said, "It would be wrong to call them check-posts and that they were in fact military outposts". The Chinese were later to seize this inaccurate, off-the-cuff remark with glee. In 1962, after their military successes, they announced to the world that we had built 43 'strong points' as evidence of our intention to launch an attack against China. They quoted Mr. Nehru's own words. Actually these posts were militarily useless, and were brushed aside by the advancing Chinese. No sane military officer treated them as anything but flag-posts.

The complacency and confused thinking in the Government unfortunately infected some senior officers and military planners. Mr. G. S. Bhargava writes in *The Battle of NEFA*: "The prevalent political views bred a new type of military strategist, typified by Lt.-General B. M. Kaul. He developed the theory of positional warfare".

Mr. A. M. Rosenthal of the *New York Times* quotes an Indian Army officer as saying: "We thought it would be a sort of game. They would stick up a post and we would set up a post. We did not think it would come to much more". This disclosure of the "grand strategy" of the Sino-Indian border is quite fantastic, and could only be accepted by politically-tainted officers. We made brave statements of challenging China, and in occasional outbursts of enthusiasm, even spoke of "recovering our sacred soil". We had neither the equipment nor the money to organise a proper theatre of war and a task force. We did not prepare for a big battle as we did not believe the battle was a reality that we might have to face. We hoped for a non-violent bloodless war.

We created a separate Border Roads Organisation in 1960. Its policy was laid down by a separate Board and the Army was not the ultimate authority for deciding priorities. General Kaul was a permanent member of this Board, apparently in his personal capacity. When he moved to the Chief of the General Staff's chair from the Quarter Master General's chair, he remained a member of this Board. Road building was carried out in leisurely fashion and little progress was made as late as September 1962, despite some phoney stage-managed opening ceremonies.

Mr. Menon and his aides continued to make a big play of the expansion of our ordnance factories, assembly of aircraft and other impressive projects. We were still searching for aircraft and helicopters on rupee payments and Mr. Menon still deliberately kept the Private Sector out of defence production. We were critically short of most essential items of equipment.

This sad bubble was pricked on 20th October 1962 when all our so-called posts were overrun in a few hours and all we could do was to shout "FOUL!" "HELP!"

Chapter VI

Half-hearted Preparations 1960/61

> "*The situation has broadly changed in our favour*"
> —Nehru 1961.

The years 1960/61 were the years of half-hearted preparations and continued hopes of containing China by cultivating her friendship, while pursuing talks to settle the border issue. In the words of Government, "Limited defence measures to contain the Chinese incursions into Indian territory" were ordained. The Chinese and Indian Premiers met; and this meeting was followed by a meeting of officials, raising hopes of some accord and delaying military measures for a possible war.

Government orders were too vague for any real and effective war preparations. The word "limited" can mean many things to many people; it is an ambiguous word that gave the parsimonious financial experts a chance to hinder, delay and block proposals for re-organising the Army. As far as the Army was concerned the Government direction did not require any steps to counter an invasion, but merely to prevent further incursions. This also left room for dissent and argument among the Army planners.

Although the Army had been ordered to Ladakh and NEFA in 1959, little was achieved in the following months to provide the means for the defence of this long border area, even against incursions. Piecemeal raisings and *ad-hoc* appointments were sought and sanctioned from time to time – sometimes after bitter wrangling and haggling. Financial and man-power ceilings laid down by the Cabinet, and apparently not sufficiently modified after the handing over of the northern borders to the Army, hampered the development of the necessary military power. Border formations were compelled to rely on indigenous production of arms, equipment and clothing for operations in the mountains even where these were patently useless and obsolescent. The funds made available were residual amounts after allowing for our Third Five-Year Plan, which remained supreme.

The basis of operational planning was a series of leisurely "induction" plans based on the available airlift, and on the untenable assumption that the Chinese would watch idly while we gradually built up our Himalayan defences. Numerous small posts were established even though their military effectiveness was poor due to indifferent arms, lack of administrative cover and wide dispersion.

In April 1960 Mr. Chou-en Lai visited India for talks with Mr. Nehru. They agreed that the border problem should be re-examined by expert officials, who later met in Peking, Delhi and Rangoon between July and November 1960. At these meetings the Chinese raised many questions, and were particularly inquisitive about the alignment of the McMahon Line in the Thagla Ridge area. It is said that they were not convinced of the validity of our interpretation of the Line in this particular sector. As we shall see later, they reacted sharply to the establishment of a post within the disputed two-mile belt.

In October 1960 I was promoted Brigadier and posted as Brigadier-In-Charge Administration of XV Corps which was responsible for the Ladakh Sector. I seemed destined to continue my direct involvement with the Chinese problem. Now I would have the opportunity of assessing for myself the administrative arrangements for our border garrisons. Administration is at all times an important principle of war; in the mountains it is often the key one.

The Tibet-Ladakh border had also been handed over to the Army in October 1959, and there had been the same scramble to move and locate troops, before the onset of winter, as in NEFA. I was at that time commanding an infantry battalion in Kashmir and had read about the Karam Singh episode in the papers. I soon felt the impact of this incident when I was ordered to surrender a "percentage" of my unit snow-clothing as this was required for the troops being rushed to Ladakh, although we were ourselves located in a bitterly cold place and had troops at over 9,500 feet. The Cabinet had decided to hand over the border to the Army in August 1959, and here we were in October without any snow-clothing, having to resort to begging, borrowing and reducing scales – the normal procedures for dealing with unforeseen developments. Actually there should have been a General Staff Reserve to meet just this sort of contingency but as we had no Operational Plans, there were no administrative or mobilisation arrangements.

When I took over as Brigadier-In-Charge Administration in October 1960, we were at the fag-end of our so-called "stocking" programme. It was astonishing to find that even after one year we had practically no administrative backing and that we lived from air-drop to air-drop. The daily stock position of each post became the main preoccupation and was scrutinised even by the Army Commander. I once got an almighty rocket from Command HQ because one of my platoon posts had only four issues of matches, and was hard put to explain that this represented one month's supply as matches were issued once a week; and in any case I did not control the Air Force or the weather. This was a very strange situation. We had deployed troops which we could barely maintain and then the top commanders wasted their time keeping track of the stock position instead of dealing with matters more appropriate to their high office. I have recounted this little story to illustrate my belief that the sending and maintenance of troops was the end of the exercise. I was never once questioned about why we had no guns or machine-guns, or what were my administrative plans in the event of a war.

There were hardly any roads, as the newly created Border Roads Organisation had not been able to get firmly established and were still awaiting vital road-building equipment from abroad. We relied entirely on air-lifts and air-drops. Airfields had to be improved and some new ones had to be built. The Air Force were short of aircraft and were living in fond hopes of getting more transport aircraft from somewhere. There was a critical shortage of supply dropping equipment and some confusion as to who was responsible for placing the necessary indents and ensuring adequate production. We were still wrangling about procedural matters, after one year of experience. At about this time Mr. Nehru said that "Necessary preparations have been made for the defence of Indian territory, and in *about a year or two* arrangements would be complete for developing communications to enable the Indian Defence Forces to move easily into difficult mountainous terrain of the northern border".

There was little accommodation in the barren Ladakh region and everything except mud bricks (or trees in NEFA) had to be air-lifted or air-dropped. Troops were mainly used to make bricks, fetch logs or collect air-drops. No one seemed to bother about their training. Progress in construction was a more important routine requirement than the training report.

The intense cold required the supply of vast quantities of kerosene oil and oil-burning stoves. After allowing for the supply of rations there was little left for war-like stores. Survival was more important than readiness for war.

The troops were still on the normal Army ration provided in the plains. The Indian soldier's ration is the most awkward and complicated in the world, as numerous items are required for one meal and if anything is lost in air-drops the meal is either tasteless or lacking in essential food value. For years we had followed the British custom of not interfering with the eating habits of the jawan. This suited the Imperial Army but was useless in the mountains. India had begun to produce delicious tinned food, but of course these were too expensive for the simple, humble, volunteer jawan.

There was always a chronic deficiency of tinned milk, due to lack of foreign exchange. Dhal (lentils), the staple food of the jawan, could not be cooked at high altitudes, and as there was a shortage of pressure cookers the problem bedevilled the local commanders and the administrative staffs. There was also a major battle with Finance to "authorise" these new items. Finance were keen on ensuring that the special issues for the mountains would not be treated as a precedent. Finance lived in fear of precedents and the erring official who allowed a departure from past practice was likely to blot his copy-book. Oil-cookers too were in short supply. Since there are no trees in Ladakh all cooking was done on these antiquated, unreliable and frustrating contraptions.

Medical facilities could not be provided as the troops were so widely dispersed and treatment was possible only if patients were evacuated by helicopters to base hospitals. There was a critical shortage of "choppers" and some deaths occurred because evacuation was not possible due to inclement weather. These deaths did not seem to bother anyone and were accepted as occupational hazards. The scale of doctors remained at one per battalion, although some battalions were dispersed over hundreds of miles and had as many as 13 outposts each.

There was a shortage of administrative and service units to despatch, hold and issue stores. This responsibility devolved on the forward troops and was a clear breach of the principles of logistics. HQ XV Corps was responsible for calculating the requirements of each forward post – an extraordinary arrangement.

I had hardly settled down to my new job when we started planning the "induction" programme for 1961/62. I was amused to find the Army and the Air Force playing the oldest game in the world, viz. the chicken and the egg. We asked the Air Force to give us the maximum tonnage that they could lift and drop during 1961. They immediately countered by asking us to indicate the maximum tonnages we required so that they could project the Army's requirements to Government and get Government sanction for the additional aircraft and crews required. To confound the issue there were major imponderable factors on both sides. The Air Force could not predict the number of flying days as we had had no experience of the weather conditions in Ladakh. Our Engineers could not predict the number of days required for routine maintenance and the days the airfields would be closed for improvements as they wanted to know the programme of air sorties to calculate their dumping programme.

I make no apology for raising this question as I consider it is a vital one for the future. These paper games could not have been played if there was any attempt at co-ordinating the efforts of the Army and Air Force. In the absence of a permanent Chief of Defence Staff the responsibility devolved on the Defence Minister. It is an open secret that Mr. Menon forced the Air Force to exaggerate their capacity to give the impression that our build-up was proceeding apace. It is also well known that he was the final authority for deciding on what aircraft would be purchased and from where. The delivery dates were known only to him, whereas the Air Force was forced to commit themselves to a target without the assurance that they would have the required time and capacity to absorb the new planes.

The General Staff was not concerned with the mundane question of air-lift capacity and blithely insisted that they had been ordered to open so many posts, induct so many troops and send so many guns and weapons, and the Administrative Staff and the Air Force could sort out the petty matter of air-lifts with the help of hopes and guesswork.

In the end, three or four alternative induction plans would be drawn up, the plan nearest to the available air-lift being adopted. Officers and clerks worked for many days and nights calculating tonnages itemwise, for each post. Armed with these figures, General Staff and Administrative Branch Officers of Command HQ, Corps HQ and Army HQ met at Army HQ in Delhi on 5th February 1961, in the office of the Chief of the General Staff, Lt.-General L. P. Sen. General Sen was later to command Eastern Command during the fateful days of September-November 1962. The aim of the conference was to "co-ordinate" the induction plans and the maintenance plans for 1961/62.

General Kaul was the Quarter - Master General (QMG) of the Army and the one most intimately connected with the maintenance of troops. He arrived a few minutes late and did not even bother to apologise to the chair, merely announcing that he had been held up. We were all duly impressed with this important and busy man, and his immense stature.

Without further ado, he announced that whatever our bids for tonnages he could only make available "X" tons, and we would have to "make do" with this. He added with supreme confidence that he did not want to hear any "belly-aches" from anyone. He then left the meeting pleading another engagement. I had heard a lot about General Kaul but this was the first time I had seen him officially. He had not bothered to greet the senior officers who had come many miles to attend this conference, which was the normal Army custom. He did not bother to discuss the operational situation.

The Chief of the General Staff was really responsible for co-ordinating the induction plans. We waited for his reaction, as it was his branch that had ordered the induction of additional troops and fire-power during 1961/62. Fantastically, General Sen smiled, shrugged his shoulders and said, "Well gentlemen, you have heard the QMG; you can all go back and recast your plans accordingly. There is little more that I can do".

General Verma, my Corps Commander, looked at me aghast at the casual approach of Army HQ to the vital issue of what we could induct and maintain in Ladakh; and what was required to fulfil the operational tasks allotted to us. He had been Chief of the General Staff and Master General of Ordnance and knew the workings of Army HQ as well as any officer in the Army. There appeared to be something sinister and radically wrong in the way the QMG dominated such a vital meeting, and ignored the administrative implications of operational requirements.

General Verma demanded clear orders on what we were expected to achieve in the way of operational readiness. Operational plans cannot be based solely on the availability of air-lifts. This was not a case of fitting in the maximum number of children in the available buses for the annual school picnic.

General Verma protested to the CGS and tried to highlight the need for co-ordination between the General Staff and the QMG's Branch. With the tonnages allotted by the QMG it would barely be possible to maintain existing garrisons, improve airfields and send essential construction stores and therefore no war-like stores could be sent. He asked if this was acceptable to the General Staff, and if so a revised operation order should be issued.

I have recounted the conduct of this conference in some detail to illustrate the type of glib talk that passed for operational planning and the increasing dominance of General Kaul. As already mentioned, with the vague Government order, it was easy to sow the seeds of discord among key officers of the Army. Looking back on events, it is clear that there was no overall Operational Plan, no urgency and no anticipation of war in 1961 or 1962.

I attended a similar meeting in January 1962, my last act as Brigadier-In-Charge Administration XV Corps, before I left to command a brigade in NEFA. Now, it was General Kaul who was the CGS presiding over the co-ordination conference. The meeting was held in the main conference room of Army H.Q. and the setting was beautifully stage-managed.

There were many unusual characters and I wondered how they had come to be invited to a Top-Secret meeting. Before long I did not know whether to laugh or cry. I could hardly believe my ears when one person got up and bid for some air-drops. He was from the Ministry of Food and his Ministry had been instructed to try and grow vegetables in hot-houses in Ladakh. This gentleman constantly reiterated the need for very careful drops as he had some precious equipment which could not be replaced, and had been bought with even more precious foreign exchange.

The next gentleman came up with a scheme for breeding ponies, using wild pony stallions and local mares. For some months HQ XV Corps had been pestered with injunctions to catch a wild stallion but with no luck. We had tried everything from deep pits to mares on heat. The sturdy, independent stallions just would not co-operate and withstood all our snares and blandishments. I was astounded to hear of the famous breeding scheme at this august meeting.

The Survey of India put in a bid for large tonnages for their survey operations. The last bids were from the Kashmir Government, who wanted to know if we could help them by lifting "pilgrims" to Leh, and if so, what quota could they expect.

Let us revert to the first conference of February 1961. We returned to HQ XV Corps and began the tedious task of paring down our bids. After allowing for survival loads there was almost nothing left for weapons and additional troops. Airfield and construction stores absorbed a major portion of the lift promised. When the General Staff were confronted with this unpleasant arithmetical fact their reaction was why worry, the Chinese were not likely to start a war. We kept our fingers crossed and hoped that the Chinese would give us more time to find and buy aircraft; build airfields; complete our roads and organise our Lines of Communication.

In the circumstances there could be no overall strategic or tactical operational plans. We were really playing a game of opening as many lightly armed posts as we could maintain. As the senior administrative head of Ladakh my sole preoccupation was to ensure that no one starved or died of exposure.

Our main airfield at Chusul was strategically useless as the Chinese overlooked it and it could be neutralised in a matter of hours in the event of war, as in fact it was in 1962. Yet we continued to develop it to carry survival loads during the cold war phase.

The land route to Leh, the capital of Ladakh, was almost ready but no plans for organising a proper Line of Communication had been drawn up. A mountain Line of Communication cannot be used without transit camps, provost arrangements, staging posts, recovery detachments, medical facilities, supply and petrol dumps and a network of wireless communications to control one-way traffic. Reconnaissances to assess these requirements were carried out only in June 1961. Our bids would now have to face the gauntlet of man-power shortages and financial stringency. This is what did happen in September 1961. At a meeting at Staff Duties Directorate in Army HQ, we were told that our demands were extravagant and that "Finance would never look at it". The operational aspect was not the determining factor. This was the verdict of the General Staff. We were ordained "limited defence measures" and here was the final proof of how officials, defence and civil, can confuse and confound the main aim.

In February 1961, soon after the co-ordinating conference in Delhi, the Prime Minister made a statement in the Lok Sabha implying that our defences in Ladakh were in good fettle and that we were ready to take on the Chinese. Mr. Nehru said, "The situation has broadly changed in our favour, not as much as we want it, but it is a fact that in areas which they have occupied progressively, the situation has been changing from the military point of view and other points of view, in our favour". General Verma, who read this astounding assertion in the papers, immediately wrote a strongly worded letter to his immediate superior, General Thapar (Western Army Commander and Chief-designate). Briefly, he said that the Prime Minister's remarks were optimistic, misleading and bore little relation to the facts on the ground. General Verma then reminded Thapar that he (Verma) had repeatedly represented our weaknesses and shortages, and the unbridged gap between our wishes and our capability. The limited air-lift which was being made available by the QMG for the 1961/62 season would not permit any substantial improvement in our defence preparations. In conclusion General Verma requested that his military opinion be forwarded to Army HQ, for the record, as he did not wish to be associated with the optimistic view of our so-called operational readiness nor be a party to the misleading remarks of the Prime Minister. General Thapar tried (telephonically) to persuade Verma to withdraw this letter saying that the true position in Ladakh was well known, and that the Prime Minister's remarks were only for public consumption. Verma was adamant and refused to comply with this unreasonable request. Thapar was then an aspirant for the post of Chief and understandably did not want to antagonise the Prime Minister or

Defence Minister. Although General Thimayya, the outgoing Chief, was due to retire in early April 1961, for some time General Thapar had been based in Delhi understudying him. In the past, the outgoing and incoming Chiefs never met in Delhi and there was never any personal "handing and taking over". The new Chief was supposed to be briefed by his Principal Staff Officers, as the Chief of the Army Staff was expected to deal with very high policy matters.

A few days later, General Verma was superseded for promotion by Lt.-General L. P. Sen and Lt.-General Daulet Singh. He resigned within 24 hours of the confirmation of the news. He was harassed and hounded even after his retirement, and his pension was withheld for some time. There was open talk that some flimsy charges were being framed against him. Finally, in sheer desperation, he exiled himself to the United Kingdom leaving behind his home, aged parents and his beloved India, as he could no longer bear these humiliations. He was an extremely kind and sensitive man reputed for his integrity and had never harmed anyone in his life. He had had a brilliant military record and in simple honesty could not cope with the sort of situation that prevailed in early 1961. He had always felt that the proper course for a gentleman was to resign as soon as he was superseded. It had been customary for superseded officers to hang on in the Army, for as long as possible, meandering from one mediocre appointment to another. Many became disgruntled and made indiscreet remarks and irresponsible accusations against the Army and its promotion policies. Some hung on in the hope that their fortunes would improve with the next change in the Army hierarchy. There are many generals in the Army, even today, who had been superseded for years and who were promoted as soon as a new Chief or Army Commander took over. This was an unhealthy state of affairs and gave rise to favouritism and nepotism. Such officers could not command the loyalty and confidence of their subordinates. General Verma preferred to follow the dictates of his conscience. In all honesty he felt that he could not serve under officers junior to him and less qualified, and the only honourable course open to him was to leave gracefully. Unfortunately his supersession was seized upon by some members of the Lok Sabha to settle their own scores with Mr. Menon. Menon was accused of favouring his *protegés*, disregarding the recommendations of promotion boards and jeopardising the military preparations of the nation. A simple Army injustice became a national issue. There were bitter exchanges between Mr. Kripalani and Government spokesmen. Some newspapers soon joined battle. Mr. Nehru felt impelled to intervene and justify Menon's policy of supersessions in the Army, and he regally assumed personal responsibility for each case of promotion, supersession or appointment. In the process he eulogised General Kaul and praised his Service record in extravagant terms. He openly asserted that General Kaul was one of the best Infantry officers in the Army. Refuting charges that Kaul was only an Army Service Corps officer who had had no combat experience and whose sole achievement was the house-building undertaking in Ambala (Punjab), Nehru told the Lok Sabha that "Kaul was an officer who had been in Infantry for 25 years out of his 28 years of service. I can say with complete confidence and knowledge that he is one of our brightest and best officers in the Army". Menon later added, for good measure, that "His period in the Army Service Corps, during British times amounted to somewhere around 8 to 10 years out of 28 years of service".

General Kaul was not an Infantryman or indeed a combat soldier, in the accepted sense, as he had never commanded an infantry company or battalion, in war or peace. Temporary command during the absence of the permanent incumbent, while one is a junior subaltern, does not count. General Thimayya is reported to have remarked, "Every sepoy in the Army knows that Kaul has never been a combat soldier. You can't hide that sort of thing in the Army. The officers do not respect Kaul". Timmy certainly had free access to Kaul's Service dossier, and should know. He was not given to catty remarks and full consideration must be accorded to his forthright judgement. In his memoirs, General Kaul has explained the circumstances which prevented him from commanding – the ultimate goal of all infantrymen. He makes the astonishing claim that "national priority" was the reason! It is barely credible that any junior officer should merit any national importance.

General Kaul had voluntarily left the Infantry for personal, domestic reasons, which must be respected. It is a tragedy that he did not (or was not allowed to) return to the Infantry to which he had been commissioned, when circumstances permitted.

During the immediate post-war years, when he should have been learning his profession in the obscurity of an infantry battalion, he apparently moved in prime-ministerial circles and gained tremendous political pull. It was widely known that he had political contacts; but I must confess that I did not realise how close these were till I read his autobiography.

It is said that *"he was picked by his powerful relative, Mr. Nehru, in 1947 to serve as the Military Attache in Washington, as India's first free military representative". He was then already serving on the quasi-political Nationalisation of the Armed Forces Committee. In 1948, Mr. Nehru is said to have selected him to be the Military Adviser to the Indian Delegation to the Security Council on the Kashmir case. After this he was appointed to command the para-military Jammu and Kashmir Militia in 1948. He served in this post till he had to quit "due to some differences with Sheikh Abdullah, the Kashmir Premier". Kaul had therefore become a "political general and a

*Welles Hangen's *After Nehru, Who?*

quasi-military figure in the Army from the earliest post-war days". In 1953 Nehru is credited with the decision to send Kaul to Srinagar to oversee the arrest of Sheikh Abdullah, when the latter was playing a dangerous political game. It is fantastic that at every turn Mr. Nehru should have found it necessary to consult or use Kaul, or send him on delicate national assignments. Little wonder, then, that Kaul in later years became the all-powerful figure who played the vital role in India's China Policy. It is easy to find excuses for Mr. Nehru, as he was new to the duties of Prime Minister of a democratic country, and probably did not realise the serious erosion to the authority of the Army Command set-up by his direct dealings with a junior officer. Living himself on a high moral plane, he did not appreciate that such unconstitutional methods could be misused.

This early taste of politics gave Kaul illusions of a greater role in India's future. Mr. Welles Hangen quotes an old schoolmate of Kaul's as saying, "Kaul probably thinks that he could be Prime Minister of India". He also quotes a Western military officer as saying, "Kaul's ambitions certainly do not stop short of being Defence Minister, probably Prime Minister". Hangen adds that, "Kaul's family ties with Nehru gave him an early taste of politics on a high level. He met most of the important politicians and Government officials long before he would have done in the line of duty".

Before the Nehru era, Kaul seems to have been singularly unfortunate in the variety of military assignments which came his way during a major World War. The clever but devious defence of Kaul's career by the Prime Minister and the Defence Minister would have appeared plausible to a House and public that had virtually no knowledge of the various stages in the build-up of Service careers, and the kind of appointments that are considered essential for aspirants to the highest military commands. Service in the Army is divided into three categories, viz. regimental, staff and extra-regimental employment. For purposes of selection or promotion regimental service in an officer's parent arm or service is the vital criterion. General Kaul's many assorted staff and other appointments cannot be counted as service in his parent corps, be it Infantry or the Army Service Corps. To suggest that such service should be added to his allegedly Infantry parent arm, on the grounds that he had been commissioned into this arm, is a distortion of facts that borders on the immoral.

Kaul was a pre-war regular officer and World War II had lasted for six years giving every professional an opportunity to practise his profession. Had he wanted to serve again in the Infantry, he could surely have arranged to do so. I must emphasise that it is not a liability or disgrace to belong to other arms or services. All branches of the Army have important and complementary roles to play in battle.

It is however wrong to claim to be something that one is not, particularly that one is an Infantryman when one has not served in the usual appointments in an infantry battalion. Command of infantry brigades and divisions is open to officers of all arms. By the time officers reach these senior positions, they are known as "General Officers" and do not "belong" to any arm.

It would be pertinent to tell the story of a fine Indian General, who is still serving, and who faced much the same problem as General Kaul. Lt.-Gen. G. G. Bewoor and I served in the same battalion during the war. His brother was killed in the Arakan Campaign in 1943. They were sons of a very distinguished and highly placed member of the war-time Viceroy's Council – Sir Gurunath Bewoor. To obviate the possibility of General Bewoor's death, orders were issued that he was not to be sent to the front and that he was to be employed in a rear area "safe job". He was duly posted to a newly raised propaganda cell created to indoctrinate the Indian National Army of Mr. Subhas Chandra Bose. General Bewoor had joined the Army to fight and that too with his own Baluchis. He moved everybody and pulled every string to get out of this position. To our delight, he soon showed up in the battalion again and resumed command of 'D' company. He campaigned with the battalion throughout, commanding many vanguard actions and fought in the famous battle of the Irrawady Crossing in January-February 1945, where the entire Japanese Army seemed to be pitted against his boys. This story illustrates that it is impossible to deny an officer his right to fight with his battalion.

I have laboured this point because I sincerely believe that had Mr. Nehru not chosen to be misled as to General Kaul's military record and ability, he might not have placed such implicit faith in his military advice, in preference to more experienced Generals. General Kaul had held an assortment of Staff and Extra Regimental Employment during the crucial and formative years when he should have been honing his professional knowledge and gaining practical experience of all the ramifications of handling troops of all arms in battle.

Even as a Brigadier, General Kaul failed to hold important Staff appointments. He was Director of Organisation and Director of the Territorial Army. The latter appointment is not one for a bright prospective Chief. If he was being groomed for big things, he would surely have had his career planned differently. Officers destined for high rank generally serve as Grade I Staff Officers in key appointments, after command. Later, they are expected to follow their Brigade command tenure as a Brigadier General Staff in a fighting Command or Corps HQ or in a key Directorate in the Army HQ such as Military Operations or Staff Duties. Kaul had apparently been selected as Brigadier General Staff Southern Command in 1954. Southern Command was a non-operational command. Even so, Kaul did not take up this appointment to help General Moti Sagar (whom he was to replace) who wished "to continue serving in Poona to enable his son to receive proper medical attention".

A proper system of selection for high Command must be based on certain inalterable criteria. It is bad luck if an officer has not been given the chance to serve in the many key appointments which are considered essential for exercising high Command. Performance is the only yard-stick to measure an officer's potential. Whatever the reasons for Kaul's inability to command and hold high-grade Staff jobs, the fact remains that by 1959, he did not have the qualifications that would be required to be adjudged "outstanding". I say this with no malice or animus. Kaul was an average officer, having regard to the standards of his contemporaries, but he was not the outstanding officer that he was made out to be. In fairness, I must record that Kaul had many admirable qualities. He was dynamic and a go-getter. He had a clear brain and was dedicated to his work. His personal conduct was above criticism. He had a warm heart and was generous. Had he not been infected by the virus of politics, he would have made an outstanding QMG. He was not trained to be CGS or to command a Corps.

His meteoric advancement was clearly not based entirely on merit or on the basis of his Service dossier. Kaul superseded at least six officers to be the Chief of the General Staff. Competent observers were of the opinion that Menon's aim was to clear the way for him to succeed Thapar as the Army Chief. No one doubted that it was Kaul who would run the Army, with Thapar as the amiable, nominal Chief. General Kaul's career would not ordinarily merit a detailed analysis. However, his rise in the Army and the open championship of his cause by the Prime Minister of the nation had a vital bearing on the events of 1961/62. The Prime Minister selected General Kaul in preference to more competent military generals for reasons best known to himself. He allowed (unwillingly perhaps) his name to be used by General Kaul in the latter's attempt to enhance his stature and consolidate his position. Everyone in the Army was petrified of him as he was supposed to have the backing of the Prime Minister. Mr. Nehru was no mere Prime Minister; to the peasantry of India he was a demi-god and infallible. No one could question his action. Few men in history had been given such voluntary, plenipotentiary powers. Anyone who had his ear and confidence wielded immense power.

Kaul's advancement was symptomatic of India's half-hearted and limited preparations for war with China. Had India seriously anticipated war then it is inconceivable that Government would have eliminated the best military talent. The Prime Minister in a democracy has the absolute right to select and appoint senior generals. He is equally responsible for harnessing the best available talent in the interests of the nation. It is his duty to study and understand the qualities and qualifications required for the highest military posts. Mr. Nehru made many unfortunate choices and took many questionable decisions, but none more disastrous than the championship of Kaul and his appointment as Commander of the so-called task force to evict the Chinese from NEFA in October 1962.

It is extremely distressing to write in this vein about Mr. Nehru. To Indians of my generation, he has been both hero and idol since childhood. In the Independence struggle, he was the *epitomé* of the Indian who could tilt lances with the British on equal terms. He was the aristocrat who had voluntarily given up wealth and position to fight for the down-trodden, and spent over 10 years in British jails to give us self-respect and freedom. It was said that he refused British honours and privileges. Mr. Nehru was a man whom no Indian would criticise lightly. I have often regretted the fact that I became involved in a situation that revealed his shortcomings.

Nehru had become indispensable to the Indian people. His personal and emotional appeal held the people together. He had often proclaimed that he drew immense strength from the Indian people's love and affection, but it is true that, given his aristocratic background, wealth, Harrow and Cambridge educational and cultural background, he had nothing in common with the Indian peasant or his Congress colleagues. He found it impossible to communicate with most of his Cabinet, State Party bosses and the average Indian. He gradually withdrew into a shell and reserved all major policy decisions for himself. This trend became more noticeable after the death of Sardar Vallabhbhai Patel (in 1950) who was of equal stature and wielded the same power and influence in the country and Party. Gradually Nehru dwarfed or subdued everyone. He had been described by a colleague as "the banyan tree under whose shade not a blade of grass grows". He became and was meekly accepted as the "benevolent moghul" who took the final decision on all major and even trivial matters, till he became convinced of his own omniscience and infallibility. Nehru was a mortal and he could not but succumb to the adulation of the people and the sycophancy of the Congress and Government officials. The people are equally to blame for placing him on an unnatural pedestal. To oppose him was political suicide; to express contrary views was the termination of even the most brilliant official career. In the circumstances the Indian China Policy was his and his alone.

Mr. Nehru's China and Defence policies were found wanting in 1962. His declared China Policy was to confront China and not to surrender to force, and yet inwardly he hoped for a peaceful settlement. However his subsequent political actions were not designed to implement this policy. He did not prepare for a military decision. He ordered only limited preparations, misled the nation in various statements which he made from time to time and contributed more than his fair share to the euphoria and equivocation, prior to the Chinese invasion. The following statement made after the major clash in Ladakh, in October 1959 is just one example. He said, "I can tell the House that at no time since our Independence have our defences been in better condition and finer fettle and backed by greater industrial production. . . . Our defence forces are well capable of looking after our security". Mr. Nehru was either wrongly advised or he deliberately chose to make an optimistic statement to mollify an irate House. He did not give the right leadership to the Defence Committee of the Cabinet, and allowed the Finance and Defence Ministries to work at cross-purposes.

He did not seek allies to maintain the military balance of power in the event of a military clash. He was party to the neglect of the Armed Forces and starved them of essential weapons and equipment in the name of "development needs". Had he feared or anticipated war, he would not have allowed Generals of the calibre of Chaudhuri and Manekshaw to remain in the wilderness from 1959 onwards. He would not have permitted Generals Thorat and Verma to be pensioned off. It is fantastic that India, which did not have surplus military talent, should have dispensed with the services of these capable men. After 1962, he was forced to rehabilitate Generals Chaudhuri and Manekshaw. Can his most ardent admirers absolve Mr. Nehru of responsibility for this outrageous state of affairs? He was omnipotent for over fifteen years and in 1962 he is solely responsible for these miscalculations and omissions.

By April 1961 the new Command set-up had General Thapar as Chief and General Kaul as CGS.

The stage was set for our Forward Policy. We embarked on a policy of bluff, until it was called in 1962. The induction of troops into the Indo-Tibetan border areas was openly publicised and Parliament was repeatedly assured that military arrangements were adequate. This was not so. There was much that had to be done before we could make such a claim. Perhaps because we had given ourselves a limited National Aim, very little was actually done to reorganise and re-equip the Army.

Our standard divisions had to be converted to mountain divisions before they were fit to operate in the Himalayas. Our divisions were organised for the Burma Campaign in World War II. Piece-meal changes had been made from time to time, but there had been no attempt at making the radical changes that were dictated by the terrain and operational requirements of the Himalayas and the Chinese Army.

Most of our weapons and equipment were of World War II vintage and had long since been discarded by most respectable armies. In most cases they were of unsuitable design and pattern. Closely linked with this was the chronic shortages that bedevilled the Army in those days. Even obsolescent arms and ammunition were in short supply. Basic items were never available to full scales.

We should have developed, produced and issued suitable and adequate quantities of snow-clothing, regimental necessaries, specialist equipment, packed rations, wireless sets and charging engines. There was sometimes not enough equipment to issue to newly raised units. Sometimes recruits could not even be provided with boots.

There was a crying need for improving the mobility of forward formations. We had no proper means of carrying loads in the mountains, as motor transport was utterly useless and was left in rear areas. There were no porter companies and insufficient pack animals.

The old Army mule was of limited value in the mountains, as the tracks and fragile bamboo bridges would not take the fat well-fed brutes. Formations totally dependent on air supply found these animals an embarrassment, as the requirements of fodder absorbed a substantial proportion of the available lift.

The building of tracks and bridges was a prerequisite to ensure mobility, and yet this was undertaken at a leisurely pace. The main engineering effort was always allotted to construction of living accommodation and airfields. We paid a heavy price for this neglect in 1962. The concentration of troops from Towang to the Namka Chu was carried out under crippling handicaps, in the foulest weather, and yet it was criticised by the very same gentlemen who had failed to provide the means for mobility before operations commenced. For lack of tracks, bridges, ponies and porters, units were moved without their first-line equipment and heavy weapons. On arrival their military utility was comparable to that of a *possé* of policemen rushed to deal with an unruly crowd. We coined the slogan of moving on "hard scales and pouch ammunition", to cover up our inability to move and concentrate troops with their minimum fire-power.

Complete reliance was placed on air transport despite uncertain weather, limited flying days and lack of forward dropping zones. Of course there was no question of finding and developing forward landing grounds, in the Himalayan Valleys. It is a principle that, at best, air supply is a bonus, and no operational plans should have been based on maintaining a large force by air-drops at indifferent dropping zones. To add to our problems we could never provide enough supply-dropping equipment to meet all our commitments, forcing us to resort to the foolish policy of trying to retrieve and repair old equipment. There were frequent crises when we could barely stave off starvation, let alone build up for a major operation. These facts were well known to the high planners long before 1962. We did not import our requirements or gear up domestic production to meet the unprecedented demand for parachutes and other dropping gear.

The system of demanding and despatching the Army's requirements was totally inadequte. Man-power and financial restrictions precluded the creation of the necessary organisation to ensure stocking, despatch and issue to forward troops. While a few Rear Airfield Supply Organisations were raised, there were no HQs Army Air Transport Organisations (AATO), or Forward Airfield Supply Organisations (FASO) to handle stores at forward landing grounds or dropping zones. This burden was super-imposed on the forward troops themselves. This system could hardly cope with the day-to-day requirements, let alone the crisis of September-October 1962. My own formation, 7 Infantry Brigade, was maintained from Gauhati Airfield and yet there was no proper system to control air-drops. There were no forward dumps to hold reserves for a major operation. Stores were being rushed frantically from Army Base Depots. Here again we paid for neglecting to raise the required units. There was utter confusion in rear areas, and the hurriedly assembled troops were not kitted-up in time.

Perhaps the most serious omission was the lack of a joint commander to co-ordinate the overall deployment of the Army and the provision and control of the air transport requirements. Here I speak with full authority as the Brigadier-In-Charge of Administration. At Army/Air HQ level this co-ordination was attempted by holding periodic conferences. At lower levels there were further futile meetings to work out the details and check progress of air-lifts. Liaison and "old boy" methods had to be resorted to. The Air Force was under constant pressure to over-estimate their capacity to please some VIP in Delhi. They were seldom able to meet their commitments and targets. The constant shortfalls which were inevitable, resulted in the size of forward garrisons being dictated solely by the quantum of tonnages actually lifted or dropped, and not by the operational requirement. The troops were often put to considerable hardships. Had we seriously anticipated war, Government would have given this matter fresh thought.

Ever since Independence we have been reluctant to create a joint command and staff despite the clear lessons of World War II. In the Himalayas air transport replaces motor and animal transport. It is the key to the planning of maintenance and operations, and a commander must have absolute authority over such administrative units. Stemming from the loose Chiefs of Staffs arrangements in Delhi, we devised the system of "liaison officers", co-ordinating conferences and other procedures to achieve the desired co-operation. Only a joint operational plan, which is binding on both Services, will achieve the aim of inducting and maintaining troops in the mountains. Sooner or later we shall have to think in terms of Army Aviation units for purely Army needs such as air transport, casualty evacuation, air observation etc. It is improper for a senior Army officer to have to beg for a helicopter to evacuate a dying man. Sometimes I have been asked to certify that a man would die unless he was evacuated by air at once. I do not see how I, an infantryman, could give such a gloomy forecast.

Medical facilities and living conditions were always primitive. Planners became complacent and assumed that troops could live and fight in the Himalayas without the basic items of necessaries and medical cover. In 1961/62 it was a crime to represent difficulties to visiting commanders and staff officers. The stock answer was "There is a general shortage in the country", or "The troops will have to rough it out", or "You will have to improvise under your own arrangements". This latter substitute for administrative planning came to be known as working on the "Jai Hind" basis. It was this frame of mind that made commanders commit troops to the Namka Chu battle without the minimum basic fire-support and administrative backing.

As no immediate threat was expected from the Chinese this unhappy state of affairs was readily accepted by all. The funds for all these improvements and changes could not be found, despite repeated appeals from the Army. The stock answer was that war with China was unlikely. This then was the position as the fateful year of 1962 dawned. The day of reckoning was at hand and India would now have to pay for her negligence, credulity and half-hearted military preparations.

The many casual remarks of our political leaders revealed the lack of a carefully formulated National Policy, and the failure of the Defence Committee of the Cabinet to lay down a rational and feasible National Aim, consistent with our means and aspirations.

To hide our military weakness and lack of preparations, which was inconsistent with our tough and seemingly inflexible political postures, we used various, devious methods. We mouthed brave words. We emphasised the Pakistani threat as being the more dangerous one. We advertised grandiose schemes for building tanks and aircraft. At every opportunity we talked of nearing self-sufficiency in the production of war-like stores. We allowed our people, and our friends, to assume that a country on the threshold of manufacturing complicated and sophisticated military hardware must surely have a surfeit of the more mundane items such as boots, tinned rations, snow-clothing, parachutes and infantry weapons. In October 1962 Indians were shocked beyond words to discover that we had no modern rifle, although we were supposed to be ready to 'manufacture' an aircraft; and had the know-how to make an atom-bomb!

The year ended with a grim warning from the Chinese. According to a non-official publication –

Chinese Betrayal of India—"the Chinese Government in their Note of 30th November 1961 warned that the Chinese Government would have every reason to send troops across the McMahon Line and enter the vast area between the crest of the Himalayas and their southern foot".

In December 1961 I was granted 60 days' annual leave which I badly needed as I had had a harrowing time since General Verma left us in April 1961. The establishment of new posts in Ladakh was taken up in right earnest, despite the administrative limitations; I had to deal with frequent breakdowns in supplies and attend to numerous, frantic calls for evacuating dying jawans. Whenever anything went wrong the blame was pin-pointed to the local formation, although we did not have the resources, the man-power or control over the weather or the Air Force. I was tired of the endless planning conferences and co-ordinating meetings with the Air Force, which was itself woefully handicapped, by lack of aircraft and transport pilots. I had reached the end of my endurance. The only bright spot in those dismal days was Air Vice-Marshal Erhlich Pinto, who died so tragically in a helicopter crash in November 1963. He was the Air Officer Commanding-In-Chief, Western Air Command, and was responsible for air transport support operations.

A. V. M. Pinto was one of the few truly outstanding Service officers, and a fine gentleman. His death was an incalculable loss to India, as he would surely have reached the very top. He was always co-operative and strained himself and his Command to the utmost to maintain the Army outposts. He was faced with insurmountable odds but never lost his charm, urbanity and spirit of co-operation. His pilots faced daily hazards with remarkable courage and determination. They had worked long hours and flew cheerfully over the worst flying country in the world all the year round. Their unsung saga of courage should be known; when the American C-130 pilots first landed in Leh and Chusul in Ladakh, they were flabbergasted at the primitive navigational conditions under which the Air Force had been operating.

A. V. M. Pinto was fearless and gave his command, leadership of the front rank. He was always the first to blaze a new trail, and never asked his pilots to do anything that he was not prepared to do himself. He had an outstanding brain and unsurpassed experience of air operations. It was an honour and a pleasure to work under him.

After each unrealistic and optimistic Delhi co-ordinating conference, he would take us aside and tell us to plan on a lower overall figure despite the official bullying at the highest level. His forecasts were uncannily accurate. He maintained cordial relations with the Army despite the constant tension which could otherwise have broken out into open feuds.

I spent my leave in Delhi. While attending the MCC-India Cricket Test Match at the Ferozeshah Kotla ground in mid-December, I accidentally met the Military Secretary, Major-General (now Lt.-General) Moti Sagar. He told me that Commander 7 Brigade was being evacuated sick, as he had asthma and could not stand the cold damp climate of Towang. He enquired whether I would be willing to replace him. I jumped at the chance as a heaven-sent opportunity to leave the Staff, and said that I was prepared to move immediately. Although this posting meant that I would be transferred from one forward area to another and normally I could have raised an objection, I was delighted. Had I known what was in store for me I wonder if I would have accepted this assignment as readily.

Part II

The Fateful Year—1962

Chapter VII

The Defence of The McMahon Line

The Battle Zone

In January 1962 formal posting orders appointing me Commander of 7 Infantry Brigade were received. My Corps Commander, the late Lt.-Gen. Bikram Singh agreed to release me, although he was at first reluctant to do so, as we were all working under pressure planning the induction programme for 1962/63, and he was loath to change senior staff officers in mid-stream. He insisted that I attend the final induction conference in Delhi, as the Corps representative, which I gladly agreed to do as this would give me an opportunity to consult the Director of Military Operations (DMO), Brigadier (now Maj.-Gen.) D. K. Palit, who had commanded 7 Brigade and knew the area. I had been so engrossed with the Western Sector (Ladakh) that I had no idea of what was happening in the Eastern Sector.

I have already mentioned this bizarre conference and the comic bids for stallions, hot-houses and pilgrims.

The DMO was very kind and briefed me personally. He was calm and assured. There was no apprehension of any hot war in the immediate future. He raised the question of the induction of 9 Punjab of 7 Brigade into Towang, during the height of winter in December 1961. He was puzzled by this move which had stretched the slender air-lift resources without achieving any operational purpose. He recommended that I send them back to the plains unless I had a definite role for them, as the air-lift for the current induction season (1962) would be very tight and he did not want any more cries of starving garrisons. I promised to speak to my General Officer Commanding immediately on arrival. DMO then told me to keep an eye on the

Bhutan border area; otherwise there was nothing to worry about.

I left Delhi on 27th February, reaching Rangiya Station on 1st March, where I was met by Lt.-Col. Byram Master, Commanding Officer of 9 Punjab and officiating Brigade Commander. He was later promoted Brigadier and was killed in August 1965, in the Akhnur Sector of Jammu and Kashmir during the Pakistan military action against this State.

I was shocked to see the plight of the soldiers at Rangiya Junction. The station was littered with dishevelled men who were waiting for connecting trains to their final destinations. There were no rest-houses, no feeding arrangements and no bathing facilities. No one seemed to be concerned at this inexcusable waste of man-power which would have been more useful in forward areas and which often interfered with a unit's leave programme. After 1962, General Chaudhuri and his energetic Quarter Master Lt. Gen., General Paintal, rapidly put things right and established transit camps at all major junctions with canteens and bathing cubicles. He also arranged for a larger quota of military rail accommodation to cut down the wait at junctions.

I stayed at my rear HQ at Misamari. I made my first call on the General Officer Commanding (GOC) 4 Infantry Division, Major-General Amrik Singh, M.C. When I raised the question of the induction of the Punjabis, he claimed that he was ordered to do so by higher HQ and did not know the reasons nor had he deemed it necessary or proper to question orders. When I told him of the DMO's views he advised me to confine myself to orders from him. If the DMO had any comments to offer he should take up the matter with HQ Eastern Command. That was that.

I had worked under General Amrik at Army HQ when he was my DMO and I was disappointed to find

The Commander's hut in Towang, March 1962. "... a cold, draughty and altogether miserable dwelling place." (pg. 114)

A Monpa belle in typical working dress. Many of these sturdy women worked as porters. (pg. 115)

The author calls on the Khempo of Towang and performs the traditional exchanging of scarves. (pg. 110)

The Khempo honours the author by blessing his new hut, August 1962. (pg. 116)

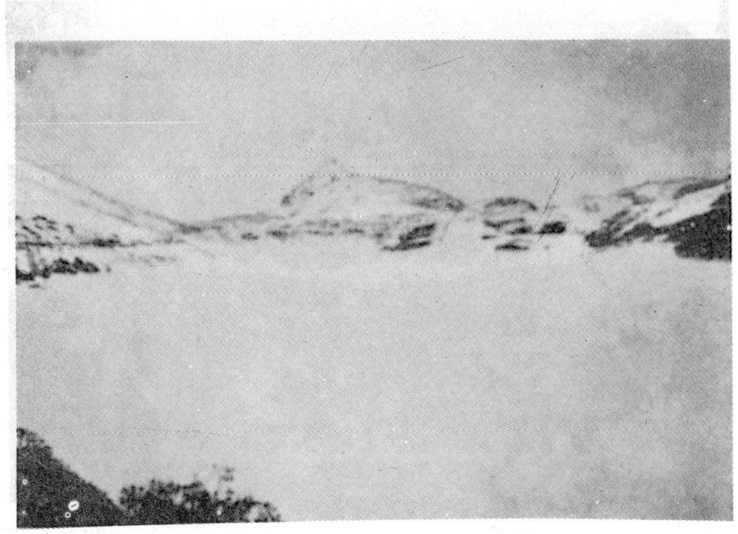

Two views of Sela Pass – the mighty feature in the Kameng Frontier Division of NEFA that attained international prominence in November 1962 (pg. 111).

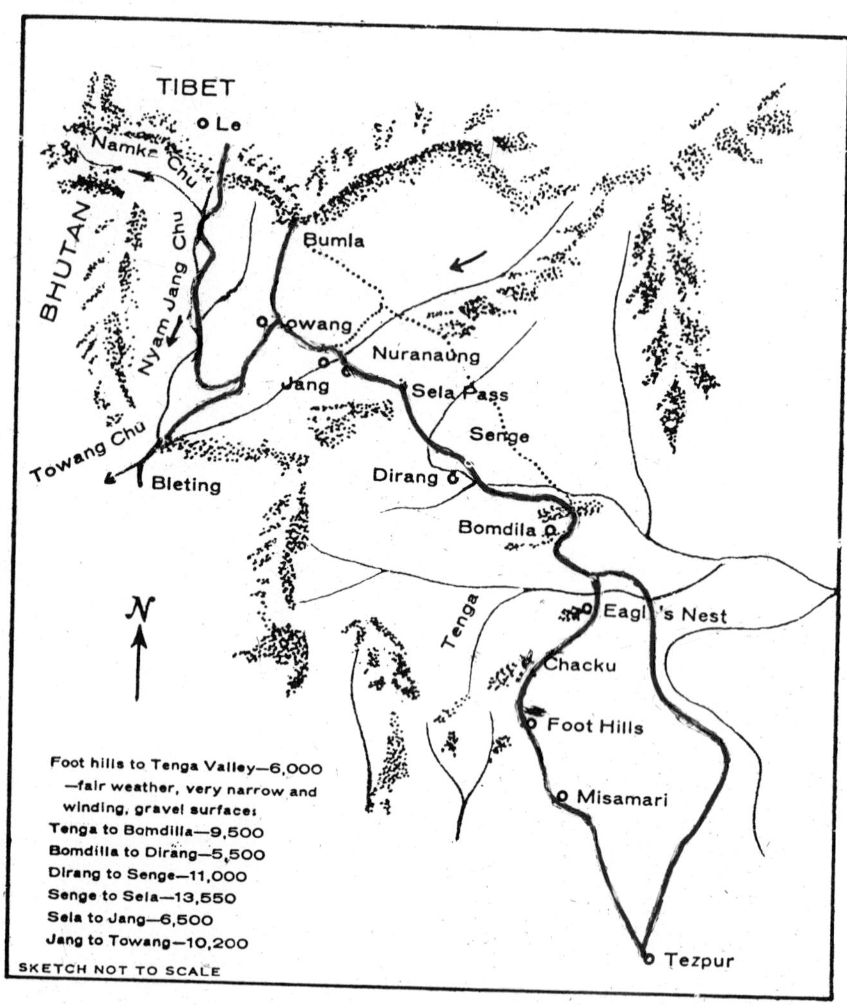

Sketch 1

Kameng Frontier Division of NEFA–the route from the Brahmaputra Valley to the McMahon Line.

Red lines: Roads/Tracks
Blue lines: Rivers.
Black hachures: Mountain Ranges.

him so irritable. He was normally a placid, quiet officer, who never raised his voice and seldom spoke unless forced to do so. Noticing the change in his behaviour, I was certain that the strain of 'inducting' troops into NEFA and the subsequent muddle had begun to take its toll.

After welcoming me to the 4th Division, he sent me to the General Staff Officer Grade I (GSO I), Lt.-Col. Manohar Singh for detailed briefing. After scanning through the Divisional Operation Order, Manohar told me that my main problem in the coming months would be the setting up of new posts under the Forward Policy, commencing from April under the code-name 'Operation Onkar'. It will be recalled that General Kaul had visited Gauhati in February and issued orders for establishing these posts. Manohar also told me that the Divisional Operation Order was being revised and as such there was no point in wasting time on the old one.

After this chat I went to see the Assistant Adjutant and Quarter Master General (AA&QMG), the senior administrative officer of the Division. After giving me the administrative layout, he emphasised the imperative and urgent necessity of returning supply-dropping equipment which was lying with forward posts. His main injunction was that I should personally go into this matter as higher HQ were complaining about the tardiness of 7 Brigade and I might get into trouble.

My first reaction to such casualness in a forward formation HQ was that we were playing the same game in NEFA as we were in Ladakh. There was no operational urgency. The lackadaisical approach of Army HQ, which itself stemmed from the lack of a firm, clear National Policy, had eventually infected everyone down the line.

The next two days I spent visiting my units in Misamari. I found a large number of detachments, rear parties and vehicles which had been left behind as the men could not be fed by air, in Towang.

Colonel Master and I left Misamari for Towang in a jeep. I was glad to have the opportunity of travelling over my Line of Communication, as the state of the road was a critical factor in my operational readiness and capability.

We halted for a cup of tea at Chacko at an altitude of 7,000 feet, having climbed steadily from the Foothills. I found a cluster of shabby huts, cheerfully accepted as a 'rest-camp' by the simple Indian jawan. The formation had been in Kameng for nearly two years and if this was the best that we were able to achieve then I shuddered to think of what the position in Towang would be like.

The first day's drive took us to Dirang at 5,500 feet, where I spent two days with 1 Sikhs. The next day the CO, Lt.-Col. 'Baij' Mehta, who was with me at the Staff College in 1950, briefed me on his role. I was more than a little surprised when he told me that he was 'responsible' for the operational commitments of 11 Infantry Brigade – the third Brigade of the Division, which had been 'loaned' to Nagaland. After some cross-examination I found that there were no plans to cater for the probability of 7 Brigade being committed before the arrival of 11 Brigade. This would have to be sorted out with Division, as I could not have two aims, the tasks of two brigades and operate over more than 200 miles.

The next day I visited the Border Roads HQ at Dirang. The Commanding Officer of the Task Force, a capable Engineer officer, Lt.-Col. Sandhu, gave me a lucid résumé of his plans and progress. The Border Roads Organisation commenced survey operations in 1960. It had taken some months to reconnoitre and select the final alignment; assess the task and position the necessary men, stores and equipment. It was not till 1962 that a fair-weather one-ton road was opened for traffic in the dry months. Sandhu had achieved remarkable results during the short period with the resources allotted to him and in the face of the enormous difficulties posed by the southern slopes of the Himalayas. He told me that his major problem was to find stones, with which to lay a metal foundation for the road, at convenient distances. This was retarding the project. He said that the roads in this region would take many years to settle down to the standards of an all-weather hill road. The excavated hill-sides would take anything up to 10 years to bed down to their final angle of repose; and until then we would have to learn to live with frequent, major land-slides. These facts were known to the planners at Delhi. In fact, Mr. Menon has since admitted that "Government was trying to build roads that would normally take 12 years, in a matter of 2 years".

We left Dirang for Towang *via* Senge and Sela Pass. The road in this sector was barely fit for a jeep. There were numerous landslips and slushy patches where the hill-sides had been cut to widen the track. We had to abandon the jeep twice and proceed in vehicles positioned on the far side of these slips. After a brief halt at Senge where I met a detachment of the Sikhs, manning the transit arrangements with their own resources, we left for Sela – the mighty feature that achieved international prominence in November 1962. At Sela we had to abandon hope of completing the journey in a vehicle, as the Pass was impassable due to heavy snow-piles. The Engineers tried their best to clear a track but failed as it snowed steadily and heavily throughout. Their superhuman efforts, at a height of over 13,000 feet, were of no avail. I decided to continue on foot as there were no shelters at Sela and I did not fancy a night in the open, on the wind-swept Pass.

We reached Nuranaung and halted. I had had my first experience of marching at heights over 12,000 feet, in biting cold. My feet were frozen as Army boots are not designed to keep one's feet warm in the snow. Nuranaung is reputed to be the coldest place in NEFA. Due to the steepness of the mountains surrounding the narrow valley, it gets a maximum of two hours of sunlight a day. At Nuranaung I inspected another makeshift transit point for the Animal Transport Company men who ply daily, in relays, carrying mail. I did not envy these dedicated mule-drivers having to spend nights under a tarpaulin with open sides. Despite these hardships they were cheerful and proud of their humble contribution to the welfare of the Towang Garrison. But for their grit and hardiness we would be cut off from our homes. I would like to record my tribute to these fine men, whose saga of toughness and devotion to duty does not receive due recognition. They ask nothing but that they are remembered when small amenities are handed out, reasonable transit facilities, a warm bed and a hot meal after tramping over the most incredible terrain in the world.

After a restless night due to lack of oxygen we resumed the journey on foot to Towang *via* Jang. The going was now all downhill through a leech-infested forest. We were received at Jang by the *ad hoc* 9 Punjab detachment in charge of the transit point. We carried on in a jeep which had been sent from Towang to pick us up. Just as I was having visions of making a triumphal drive into my HQ, we got bogged down in deep mud, some five miles short of Towang and had to complete the final lap on foot through more mud and dirt. I reached my HQ at 6.30 p.m. dishevelled, tired and depressed.

During the last minutes before reaching my camp, I thought about the so-called Line of Communication from the Foothills to Towang. I was horrified at the prospect of being dependent on such a devilish route over which to maintain and concentrate my force, in the event of hostilities with China. As I was the Commander, all the "resources" of the Brigade and the Border Roads had been placed at my disposal. If this was my experience, then what would be the fate of the men who would be scrambled from Misamari?

The route from the Foothills to Towang was incredible. There was a steep climb to a place called Eagle's Nest (9,000 feet); a further climb to Bomdilla at 10,000 feet; a drop to Dirang (5,500 feet); the ascent to Sela Pass (13,500 feet); the vertical drop to Jang (5,000 feet); and the final climb to Towang at 10,000 feet. The whole road had been aligned across the grain of the southern slopes of the Himalayas and was subject to frequent landslides. I doubted if a vehicle could do more than two trips before requiring a major overhaul.

To recapitulate, there were no trooping arrangements and there could be no certain time-table for any concentration from the plains. This was obviously the critical factor as a sizeable portion of my Brigade was at Misamari. All the arrangements I had seen were makeshift, improvised and inadequate. In fact we were working on the good old 'Jai Hind' basis, as the entire stretch was manned by my own men, with borrowed pots and pans and wireless sets. There were no supply or petrol dumps *en route.* All this was inexplicable as General Thapar, the Chief, and his CGS, General Kaul, had visited Towang in November 1961, and had traversed the same route. Surely, they could not have been satisfied with what they had seen with their own eyes! Kaul, surprisingly, omits mention of this November visit in his memoirs.

The next morning I had my first view of Towang and the Brigade camp. After two years we were still living under primitive conditions. The Commander's hut was a cold, draughty and an altogether miserable dwelling place from where to plan the defence of half of NEFA. Towang was a family station for the Assam Rifles and the NEFA Administration, and as such they were provided with comfortable accommodation – an invidious distinction that caused some heart-burning.

The accommodation for the men was even worse, as they were living in flimsy basha-type hutments with bamboo matting walls – a type of living quarters that was totally unsuitable for the damp cold of Towang. Initially the responsibility for building troop accommodation had been given to the Civil Central Public Works Department, but they were unable to keep pace with the induction of units. Eventually the local garrison was ordered to build its own accommodation using troop labour, assisted by Engineer supervisors.

The only satisfactory feature was the peace-time medical set-up in Towang. This is a factor that has a vital bearing on the morale of troops marooned in the mountains. Without a helipad, with uncertain weather conditions and an uncompleted road, a man would die of even a simple bout of pneumonia or of an inflamed appendix. This is a frightening thought. In 1960 a Mobile Surgical Unit (MSU) and a Field Ambulance had been moved to Towang. The move was carried out during the monsoon using porters and ponies as there was no road. Within a week of their arrival Major Jayaraman, the OC, a brilliant surgeon, performed a life-saving abdominal surgery using petromax lamps and hurricane lights. Thereafter everything possible was done to house and look after this invaluable unit. By 1961 a 25-bedded dieted hospital was established. Gradually a cement floor was provided and annexes built to protect medical stores and provide recreational centres. An X-Ray plant was installed in due course. The plant was carried over Sela Pass by 16 porters. The Army 'hospital' became extremely popular with the civilians and the locals, who had not previously enjoyed the blessings of modern medicine and surgery. Great credit is due to Colonel A. K. Maitra, the Senior Medical Officer of the Division; to Major V. Jayaraman, the Surgeon, Lt.-Col. K. B. Sen of the field ambulance and Major Mallick the anesthetist. I did have one nagging doubt. How would this static set-up function in the event of war?

The first view of Towang is breath-taking. It is a beautiful habitation, with some eight villages grouped round rich grazing grounds. Towang actually means a grazing ground. The place is dominated by the Monastery, one of the most famous in Lamaist Buddhism. The sturdy, healthy people of Mongoloid origin, wore a picturesque dress of red hand-woven wool, topped by a distinctive five-tasselled skull cap. Wherever I saw them they appeared to be carrying heavy loads cheerfully and exchanging bawdy jokes and gossip. Their life was changing fast with the arrival of the Army and the Border Roads. Large numbers were employed in road gangs and as porters. I was soon to find out that they were the prime source of mobility of my Brigade. Truly democratic, despite the dominance of monks, they were not afraid to look anyone in the eye. Simple, hospitable and generous, the Monpas, as they are known, were among the finest people that it has been my pleasure to come across during 25 years of service in many parts of the world. Like many a traveller before me I wondered whether we were really so far advanced that we should label them "backward tribes". They could teach us a thing or two about manners and culture. As farmers they were doing an excellent job of looking after themselves in one of the most difficult farming areas in the world.

My first formal call was on the Political Officer, a delightful gentleman named Mr. W. Shaiza. I met his staff, including the official interpreters, in their picturesque uniforms. I was to see a lot of these gentlemen as they always accompanied me on my tours and visits. They were very useful in establishing contact with the Monpas with whom we could not otherwise communicate.

My next call was to pay my respects to the Head Lama of the Towang Monastery – known as the Khempo. I was very impressed with the transparent holiness and dignity of this remarkable man. He was accepted as an Incarnation of the first rank and had received his theological training in Tibet. He was revered by the Monpas. Fortunately he took to me and permitted me the honour of becoming a personal friend. He went out of his way to demonstrate his regard for me. His patronage was of practical benefit to us. He visited my hut accompanied by his full *entourage* and with the full ceremonial pomp and grandeur befitting an Incarnation. When a new hut was built for me, he insisted on performing the opening ceremony and blessing the premises. He told me that it was essential to do this, on an auspicious day, to safeguard me from evil, as I was at that time under evil influences. Looking back, I am certain that he enjoyed clairvoyant faculties. In time I came to love and revere this good, holy man. He carried his immense knowledge of Buddhism and his vast powers lightly and with great humility.

Towang, birth-place of the Sixth Dalai Lama, beautiful and an idyllic spot, was to be the scene of the most frustrating months of my entire military career. I spent the loneliest and most agonising days of my life brooding over the casualness of our planning and official indifference to the hardships of my men. There were no daily papers or books to relieve the monotony of life. For a Commander there was no companionship or diversion. In such circumstances only a saint can combat fits of depression and foreboding. I often pondered at my continuous involvement with the China issue. It might have been easier if I had not been an eye-witness of our tepid military response to the Chinese threat. I might have at least enjoyed the proverbial bliss of the ignorant. The months in Towang were easily the most fruitless, frustrating and frightening of my life.

However, there was little time for introspection or regrets. I had to tackle the operational matters in hand. I had entered the fateful year of 1962 with the rather light-hearted stocking conference in Delhi; with calm assurances from Army HQ; Division's preoccupation with opening posts and slow progress on road-building. I wondered if we were really serious about the possibility of war. I feared that the air of unreality might infect the rank and file. The Junior Commissioned Officers had all been through World War II and had practical experience of what makes for war preparations and what measures indicate seriousness and the imminence of war. They would never believe that the Towang Garrison was based there for any war-like activity.

My most urgent priorities were to review operational plans with special reference to the concentration plan, in the event of war; and to prevent the men from going to seed if we did not have to fight.

Strategy Unrelated to Means

I immediately plunged into a series of conferences with my COs and my staff. I asked my Commanding Officers (COs) to give me their frank opinion about what they thought of their tasks and whether their battalions were capable of carrying out these tasks. The CO of an Indian infantry battalion is the most important individual in our military set-up. He is the only one who knows the true state of his unit's readiness for war. The denigration of this vital appointment in the years preceding the Sino-Indian War of 1962 played a major part in much that went wrong in those days. Yes-men, masquerading as commanding Officers, will land the Army in the same straits in which we found ourselves in 1962. I have deliberately included this aside to bring out that the true state of affairs pertaining to the shortcomings of the Towang Garrison was well known to the COs. I gave them full freedom to express their opinions and I based my own judgement on their advice. I worked on the old Army principle that no CO would lightly admit that his unit is not ready for the ordained military task. When he does admit this unpleasant fact, he should be admired and not damned. In 1962 forthright COs were not easy to come by. I was fortunate as both Lt.-Col. B. S. Ahluwalia and Lt.-Col. Master were not yes-men.

After consulting my COs, I studied the Divisional Operation Order and the appreciations of my predecessors. This is not only sensible but courteous to boot, as only fools try to imply that they have to undo the work of all those who preceded them. I got an invaluable insight into the problems of Kameng Frontier Division by studying the views of Brigadiers Palit and Ranbir Singh, both experienced and decorated commanders. Brigadier Palit is the well-known Indian military author and critic whose books have been widely read throughout the world.

The tasks given to 7 Infantry Brigade were to:

(*a*) defend Towang – the primary role;
(*b*) prevent any penetration of the McMahon Line;
(*c*) establish Assam Rifles post; and
(*d*) assist Assam Rifles posts.

It was at once obvious that the planning seemed to be a little haywire and was based on invalid assumptions. The area of responsibility was abnormal for a brigade. The plans were vague and academic. There were convenient gaps in the administrative paragraphs of the Divisional Operation Order that could hamstring operational aspirations.

The best operational plans can only be implemented by infantry units who are equipped and trained for their roles. For a new Brigade Commander the battle-worthiness of his battalions becomes the first and foremost item for investigation.

The advice of my COs and an impartial assessment of the factual position revealed that there were insurmountable obstacles in the fulfilment of our operational tasks. I shall go into these in some detail as they will explain what went wrong in September-October 1962.

I found that my men were employed in building a helipad; collecting logs of wood for the construction of shelters and manning the dropping zone. The helipad absorbed 1,200 men a day for over three months — a job which two or three bulldozers could have completed in a few days. Moreover, there was a good helipad in Towang proper, but this was not acceptable to the Air Force who demanded a helipad at an elevation under 7,000 feet. In those days the system was that "if the bloody Army want helicopters, they can bloody well produce a helipad". The Air Force was doing the Army a "favour". It is interesting that after the Chinese intruded into our territory in September 1962 and when all this inter-service bickering was shed, the Air Force used the same helipad that they had rejected on "technical grounds". In the event, 1,200 men a day were used to clear an entire hill. They had to go down 2,500 feet, work the whole day and climb back to their unit lines. This senseless and wasteful effort could have been sorted out by a joint commander, who would have been serving the Nation and not the Army or Air Force.

The Border Roads Organisation could not help with the loan of earth-moving equipment due to "accounting and other procedural difficulties". They belonged to another Ministry and sundry preliminary sanctions would have to be obtained. One day the Indian Government is going to be asphyxiated by its own procedures! The Commander of the Border Roads was an old Staff College colleague of mine. I appealed for his help when I saw this waste of first-class Infantrymen, as labourers on an improper task, at the expense of training. The trade union of staff officers in the Army is very strong, and Brigadier Mani ordered up some earth-moving equipment. He requested me not to disclose the fact, as he was "wangling" the expenditure on some other task. This was an inexcusable state of affairs. An expensive Border Roads Organisation for "developing border communications" was operating in the area and the commander was willing to help, provided the procedural difficulties were sorted out. Helipads are covered by the term "communications", and should logically have been accorded priority in the Border Roads programme.

The remainder of the garrison was sent to collect wooden beams from Pankentang, at a height of 14,000 feet, for constructing shelters. This project was accorded operational immediate priority, as the work had to be completed by a given day to avoid audit objections and the lapse of funds. The training of units was secondary. I found that units had not trained for some time; 1/9 Gorkhas not since they were inducted in 1960. No annual classification or field firing had been possible due to lack of ranges. The mortar crews had not fired a bomb for a long time. The Civil authorities were finding it difficult to "acquire" a range as the locals were not agreeable to handing over the sites selected by us to meet technical and safety standards.

All units were under-posted. They had been heavily milked of NCOs and JCOs for new raisings in their groups. There was a constant shortage of officers, which was unacceptable in forward formations where the demand for extraneous duties is heavy e.g. to man the Line of Communication, for rear parties, long-range reconnaissances, for the establishment of Assam Rifles posts under Operation ONKAR and so on.

1/9 Gorkha Rifles was a first-class infantry battalion with an impressive war record. They had distinguished themselves in Italy in the battle of Cassino in 1943. They had fought gallantly at Poonch in the Kashmir War in 1948. In March 1962 they were a tired and listless unit which had suffered incredible hardships for two years. They were due to be relieved in June 1962 and were looking forward to a spell of peace and to rejoin their families.

9 Punjab (my second battalion) was another first-rate unit. It was to fight with great *élan* and determination in the war of September-October 1962. It too had had a gruelling time, being inducted at the height of winter, without adequate shelters in Towang. No one to this day knows who ordered their move.

My third battalion, 1 Sikhs, was, as we know, at Dirang Dzong as it could not be maintained in Towang.

In spite of the operational tasks, the garrison at Towang was subject to a man-power ceiling of 1,700 up to November 1961 and 2,400 from November 1961 to September 1962; the remainder being located at Misamari. The full fighting complement of an Infantry Brigade exceeds 3,500 men, but the size and constitution of 7 Infantry Brigade was dictated entirely by the availability of air effort and supply-dropping equipment; the operational requirement was secondary. The composition of the garrison at Towang was laid down by HQ 4 Division, and catered for the requirements of large numbers of Pioneers and Construction Companies to assist in building accommodation, and two Animal Transport Companies to return the supply-dropping equipment retrieved by forward troops.

These animals used up most of the air-drops allotted to the Brigade for their own bulky rations.

There were serious shortcomings in our ability to fulfil the operational tasks laid down by Division. The first was that although a sizeable portion of 7 Brigade could not be located in Towang, no warning period had been laid down for the concentration of the remainder, before the Brigade was committed to battle. There were no clear-cut concentration plans or arrangements for organising and controlling moves. Although Border Roads had built a fair-weather one-ton road to Towang, no staging facilities had been provided on grounds of economy, and this burden too devolved on 7 Brigade. This Brigade was also responsible for manning Gauhati Airfield (for non-ASC) despatches and the entire Line of Communcation from Misamari to Towang. This system inevitably broke down during the emergency of September-October 1962. Further *ad hoc* measures were resorted to, in that the CO of 4 Division's Medium Machine-Gun Battalion was given this task. As anticipated, the concentration of troops was haphazard, slow and uncertain. The troops were put to avoidable hardships and reached the battlefield exhausted. One battalion had to abandon their vehicles at Dirang and walk over the Sela Pass, as there were no petrol dumps at Dirang to fill up the vehicles. Planners sitting in Lucknow and Delhi did not appreciate the administrative problem and entertained rash hopes of quickly concentrating large forces.

The second major factor was that there were no reserve stocks at Towang to issue to troops that would have to be inducted in an emergency. Even the laid down, normal stocking policy had not been achieved. My appeals to locate stocks in Towang were not heeded. I was called a dreamer. How could India, a poor country, afford to tie up stocks for an emergency, when it was barely possible to maintain existing garrisons? I had failed both as a staff officer and as a commander to convince my superiors of the imperative need to build up reserves close to possible areas of operations.

7 Infantry Brigade troops left behind in rear areas, would not be acclimatised for operations at altitudes over 15,000 feet. A minimum of six weeks had been laid down by the medical authorities. There would have to be a guarantee of a long enough warning period to move and acclimatise troops.

Units were poorly trained and equipped. They had a strength of only 400 bayonets per battalion instead of 800, the remainder being on leave, training courses, or left behind in Misamari. The two battalions in Towang had the battle strength of only one!

The road to Towang was only a fair-weather one-ton road. Its capacity was limited even under ideal conditions, and was negligible during and after the monsoons.

There were other operational considerations which had a major bearing on our plans. I was not satisfied with some of the assumptions made, as they appeared to be based on invalid factors. All our plans were based on the assumption, presumably an Intelligence appreciation, that the maximum strength that the Chinese would deploy was one regiment which is equivalent to our brigade. In the event, the Chinese used two divisions in 1962. Now what was the basis for the categorical assumption that the Chinese were limited to just one regiment? The answer is very simple. Since our air-lift would not permit us to deploy more than one brigade, then it was axiomatic that the Chinese also should not exceed our strength, or how else would senior commanders answer awkward questions from forward troops and commanders? Most average generals plan to counter the worst the enemy can do. We believed in planning for the best case, and limited the enemy's potential to suit us.

7 Brigade was required to guard three approaches, with no laterals. In fact nothing more than a string

of outposts, with regular troops at intervals could be deployed.

Assam Rifles posts were deployed non-tactically and they were ill-armed and even worse equipped than the Regular Army. At best, they could only function as border check-posts and yet their task was "to fight to the last man and the last round" – a high-sounding slogan coined by someone far in the rear, and one that is more easy to issue than to obey. Although they were under the operational command of 7 Infantry Brigade, their administration was under the Inspector General of the Assam Rifles in Shillong. This system cut across all accepted canons of military organisation.

There were no inter-communication facilities/arrangements between Assam Rifles' posts and the nearest Army sub-unit. This was in spite of the fact that the Army was "responsible for assisting" these posts in the event of trouble. The standard explanation was that there was "a general shortage of wireless sets in the country".

The Assam Rifles were a separate private army of the External Affairs Ministry. And who would dare to bell the cat about this extraordinary command system?

The last major deficiency that was transparent was the lack of any worthwhile Intelligence. There was no overall appreciation of Chinese intentions and preparations. We were totally dependent on the local civilian Intelligence Bureau representative and information given was useless for rational planning purposes. Not one Intelligence appreciation was received from Army HQ. I do not know if Army HQ ever got any assessment from the Joint Intelligence Committee. If they did, they certainly never considered it worthwhile passing on any information to commanders in the front line. Lacking Intelligence, we kept on basing our actions on what we were able to do, and not to counter the worst the Chinese could do. We were like bad chess players who make moves without anticipating the opponent's moves, or expecting him to counter our moves.

I decided to carry out a personal reconnaissance of the main areas of my responsibility before making any representation to Divisional HQ. My first destination was Khenzemane on the McMahon Line, in the Thagla Ridge area. I left within 20 days of reaching Towang, although it is normally wiser to allow a longer period for acclimatisation. The urgency was necessitated by the impending establishment of Dhola Post in the area.

The aims of the reconnaissance were to study the state of the tracks and bridges; as well as the stages required to move troops to "assist" the Assam Rifles posts located on this axis. I would also have the opportunity to gain first-hand knowledge of the main tactical features, availability of dropping zones and availability of porters.

In mountainous terrain it is important for commanders at all levels to have a clear idea of the ground over which their troops may have to operate; as it is otherwise impossible to appreciate the problems of mobility in terms of time and space. In the Indian Army of 1962, the need was even greater. Many key officers had served only in the plains of the Punjab or on static picquet duty in Kashmir. Many senior commanders and staff officers had not commanded in an operational area and practically none in mountain formations. This is not a criticism but a statement of a well-known fact. After the Chinese incursion in September 1962, these officers suddenly found themselves ordering the moves of units over steep paths and severe gradients, in appalling weather conditions. Everybody kept yelling at everybody else to "get a move on". Instead of pre-planning, harmony and mutual understanding, we had the sad spectacle of junior officers cursing their seniors and saying "why the hell don't these staff and backroom experts come and see what it is like out here". Senior officers cannot always walk over every piece of ground in their area of responsibility. They are at least expected to fly over the country to get an idea of what their troops are facing and to issue realistic orders. It is a tragic fact that no one of importance had visited, or flown over the Nyamjang Chu Valley. Some had not even seen Towang. These officers made rash promises of concentrating forces by given dates that could not be implemented. Orders, counter-orders and frequent postponement of promised dates resulted in recriminations and accusations and threats of sacking those who were not achieving the miracles that were being ordained from above.

I was accompanied by Lt.-Col. Ahluwalia of the Gorkhas, who was responsible for this sector and who knew the area well. The Political Officer at Towang very kindly deputed an officer from his department to assist us. I was also given an interpreter. Unfortunately I was also given the sturdiest pony in Towang, owned by an even sturdier Tibetan woman. This was extremely embarrassing as I could not very well ride while a lady led my riding pony. I decided to forego the comfort of the ride and walk the whole way. There was little rumpus after the first day's march, when the lady complained that I had insulted her and her pony by refusing to ride. Her deduction was simple – that I considered the pony unworthy to carry a brigadier. To please her I was forced to sit on the sure-footed beast for at least the last 200 yards before entering the main village. Everybody was satisfied with this solution. I saved pride in my manhood and she kept her pride in her horse.

The first stage was an easy one of about 10 miles, to a large village called Thonglen. The idea was to meet the Headman (Gaonbura) and the villagers; as well as get acclimatised in easy stages. In the hill areas, it is an important function of commanders to gain the good-will of the local inhabitants, as this has a vital bearing on porterage and thus the mobility of the force. Indeed, day-to-day maintenance would be very difficult without the help of the lovable and simple Monpas of Kameng Frontier Division. We were greeted by the whole village who had obviously taken a day off from their arduous daily chores. I went through the usual ceremony of exchanging scarves with the headman and drinking the local brew – a rice beer which was surprisingly tasty and nourishing. The villagers were extremely friendly and hospitable. They are always happy to receive visitors.

Throughout my tour of the villages along the Nyamjang Chu, I found the Monpas an intelligent people with a well organised agricultural system. Despite the harshness of nature they have terraced fields and grow a variety of cereals, vegetables and fruits. They are incredibly hardy and both men and women can carry heavy loads over long marches. They work long hours in their fields or in the jungles collecting wood.

They have a fast indigenous dye and produce simple but attractive paintings on woodwork. They are adept at weaving. They love dressing up in colourful clothes and wear a variety of beads and exquisite jewellery. A Monpa village turned out in ceremonial dress is an unforgettable sight. Even their headgear and footwear flaunt diverse colours.

The advent of the Army, Border Roads and the Civil Administration had upset their traditional life and suddenly they found themselves earning and spending large sums of money, in place of the traditional barter system. I was told that at first they did not know what to do with this strange means of payment for labour, services and goods, and just stuffed their notes in bamboo containers. Later when the Administration opened stores they shopped enthusiastically for the things that we are pleased to call the blessings of science and civilisation. They love coloured rain-capes and plastic buckets. Bhutanese traders soon learnt to cater to their tastes and reaped a rich harvest at the monthly bazaar in Towang.

I found that the Army was very popular and all the credit for the excellent relations with the Monpas was due to the 1/9 Gorkhas. Gorkha troops are the best ambassadors of the Indian Army. They love children and endear themselves to the local population wherever they go. They never cheat and spend freely. The high regard in which the Army was held in the outlying villages was invaluable; it was an asset for which I am grateful to the Gorkhas, for without the all-out, spontaneous help of the Monpas in September 1962, we would have been in dire straits.

I decided to do my bit to improve relations with the headmen of the villages which I had visited on this first reconnaissance. I invited them to visit me whenever they had occasion to come to Towang. At first the response was extremely poor and they seemed diffident and shy to call on an important man. But when I explained that Towang was my "village" and I was the headman and as such it was my duty, pleasure and privilege to entertain them and reciprocate their hospitality, they readily fell in with my wishes. Thereafter they would call without any inhibitions. After a few rounds of rum we would all sit round a fire and be on the friendliest terms, arguing on equal basis. Our hill people are very democratic and proud.

The next stage from Thonglen was to Lumla, about 12 miles away, where we had the HQ of an Assam Rifles Wing. I inspected the Wing besides noting the availability of a dropping zone for use in an emergency.

Shakti village was the next halting place. We had a detachment of the Gorkhas stationed here. On the way we had lunch at a big village called Gyspu, famous for its lush apples and peaches. We had the same friendly reception and a repetition of the scarf ceremony.

I was received by Captain P. K. Hazra, the Regimental Medical Officer of the Gorkhas, who was the *de facto* infantry company commander. Capt. Hazra was the ideal type of medical officer. He had been with the Battalion since its induction, and had shared the hardships of the unit. At Shakti he was the only officer and yet he was cheerful and kept himself busy with his hobbies of reading and photography. He was the father-confessor of the villagers and was loved by them. They came to him for all sorts of minor ailments. He did much to help curb the incidence of goitre, which is endemic in Kameng.

The Headman of Shakti appeared to be somewhat reserved and I could not get him to unbend and tell me what was bothering him. I thought that he may have had some trouble with the soldiers and was reluctant to talk in front of the CO. After a little coaxing he admitted that he was very annoyed with the Army, because we owed him a large sum of money for the past two years, and he had been unable to obtain payment despite numerous trips to Towang. He had apparently supplied some timber and labour to the Army in 1960 and held a receipt from a major. Lt.-Col. Ahluwalia confirmed the correctness of the claim and told me that payment had been withheld due to some audit queries about who had ordered the wood; why it was ordered and was the person authorised to place such a large order and so on *ad nauseam.* The emergency of 1959, when the Army had rushed to NEFA on orders from the Prime Minister was aparently not known to, or was forgotten, by these custodians of the exchequer. I rushed a signal to my General and said that I wanted the amount sent by the fastest means, failing which I was at liberty to represent the matter to higher authority. It was outrageous that these simple, honest men should be kept waiting all these years, while we were sorting out and adjusting our book-keeping. The General, who had not been told of this, was even more angry than I was. He sent the amount and I was able to hand over the cash to the headman on my return journey. The villagers of Shakti rendered immense help in the crisis of September-October 1962.

Ahluwalia and I spent some-time studying the tactical importance of the Shakti defile, which I found was easily defensible and difficult to bypass. It was obviously a vital layback position. It was a pity that it was not held in 1962, as everyone was rushed to the border to contain the Chinese incursion and there were no strategic dispositions in the rear. Since no important planner had seen Shakti, except Brigadier Palit the DMO, the lack of appreciation of the defile was inevitable.

The last leg of the reconnaissance was to the Assam Rifles post at Ziminthaung. This was the biggest and probably the richest village in the area. The people were pastoral and lived on the produce of their cattle wealth in addition to good farmlands. They produced enormous quantities of butter for the monasteries. Ziminthaung was their winter location, and Lumpu their summer headquarters from where their herds were taken to the high Thagla Pastures. They owned all the herders' huts and maintained the so-called "log bridges" that we shall be hearing about soon.

Basing ourselves at Ziminthaung we visited Khenzemane and Lumpu, over the next three days. It was an exciting experience to visit a remote place which had achieved national importance in 1959, after the serious clash with the Chinese. On the way I passed the famous Drokung Samba Bridge, which achieved prominence when the Chinese pushed our men back to this point claiming that the Indian boundary, according to the McMahon Line, ended at this bridge. If destroyed, the water gap at the bridge site would become a formidable obstacle. The bridge was high over the water line, with steep rocky abutments. It is a pity that there were no demolition plans to blow up this obstacle on 20th October 1962. The bridge was captured intact, enabling the Chinese Forces to carry out an immediate, uninterrupted pursuit operation. Here again our anxiety to rush everything to the border caused us to neglect the principle of security.

Khenzemane was tactically useless and was merely a check-post. It could not be defended without holding the Thagla Heights. The post certainly could not fight to the last man and the last round.

I studied the alignment of the McMahon Line, with the help of the civil official who had accompanied me.

The next day I visited Lumpu where we had another Assam Rifles post. Lumpu had an excellent dropping zone with good approaches. From the high ground at Lumpu I had a clear view of the Choksen Ridge across the Ziminthaung Valley. Lumpu-Choksen was vital for the security of the Lumpu dropping zone, and was also not held in 1962.

The return journey was uneventful. The main conclusions of my reconnaissance were that mobility to the Nyamjang Chu Valley was severely restricted due to narrow paths, which would not take Army mules: weak bamboo bridges: steep gradients which hampered speed; troops would require full acclimatisation before they could be employed; and lastly limitations in the availability of porters as with the best intentions, the population could not provide more than a few hundreds.

The ground factor revealed that Shakti and the Lumpu-Choksen line were vital to the defence of the only dropping zone in this sector and must be held to ensure the administrative security of any force despatched to this area.

Within a week of my return I went on my second reconnaissance, to the Bumla-Towang axis. This was the old direct trade route to Tibet, stretching only 14 miles from Towang to the border. Bumla was at a height of 14,000 feet and bitterly cold even in the first week of April. The area is barren and rocky, after the tree-line at Pankentang. On the way I studied the various tactical positions relevant to the inner defences of Towang – which was my primary task. I concurred with the appreciations of my predecessors with regard to the number of battalions required to defend Towang, though I made minor alterations in the dispositions of the battalions to ensure the security of this vital objective.

The appreciation for the defence of Towang and the number of battalions required had been projected to the Chief of Army Staff, General Thapar and the Chief of the General Staff, General Kaul, when they visited Towang in November 1961. They accepted the recommendations of Brigadier Ranbir Singh, but deferred implementation due to paucity of troops and shortage of air effort. It was an appalling error of judgement to leave only one battalion to defend Towang in September 1962, under an *ad hoc* sector commander. Worse still, this battalion was taken from the Order of Battle of 7 Brigade, leaving me with only one battalion for the task of containing the Chinese incursion into Thagla Ridge. The Towang battalion was overrun and Towang fell without a fight. Here again we did not make the vital strategic dispositions required BEFORE the Chinese launched their invasion, which was a criminal breach of military principles.

As a result of my personal ground reconnaissance I took some immediate steps to get troops familiar with their possible operational roles, and ordered various readjustments. 9 Punjab who were new to the area had to be given a chance to familiarise themselves with the surrounding topography. Reconnaissance parties down to platoon commander level were sent. The inner defences were improved and re-sited where necessary. Artillery fire plans were made out and forward dumping of ammunition was carried out. I established a few more localities of regular troops around Towang. This was all that was possible within the limitations of our operational plans. However, even these limited precautions were nullified, for when the Thagla flap started all these troops were sent to another sector and fresh troops inducted into Towang.

Operation Onkar

Apart from my reconnaissances, the month of April 1962 was dominated by Operation ONKAR, the code-name given to the establishment of additional forward posts on or near the McMahon Line. Dhola was one such post.

I have already dealt with the major policy implications of this so-called Forward Policy and have analysed the background to trace its author. Let us now look at the problem from the viewpoint of a local commander who was called upon to implement the policy on the ground.

From the outset it should have been appreciated that a move into the Dhola area would attract Chinese attention, if not a severe reaction. The area of the Tri-junction was extremely sensitive, as the exact alignment of the McMahon Line had been made the subject of open dispute by China. Apart from the incident of August 1959, which brought the Army into NEFA, we knew (or should have known) that Chinese officials in the 1960 discussions had not conceded our version of the Line in this particular area. I was naturally doubtful about activating a sensitive area, specially after I had seen for myself the difficulties of moving and maintaining a force there. The Thagla

Ridge had a tactical significance for the Chinese as it overlooked their forward base at Le. Chinese countermeasures would place us at a grave disadvantage, both tactically and administratively. The Chinese were known to have improved their roads while we had no road beyond Towang – and this too had not been opened for traffic in April 1962. We were hoping to have our first convoy by the end of April, carrying supplies, in one-ton vehicles.

When these awkward questions were raised, I was told categorically to "lay off" as this was a "matter of national policy" and was being implemented by the Assam Rifles. We were only required to render assistance in the way of officers. Our inability to organise a clear command and control set-up is revealed in the manner in which we approached Operation Onkar. The Assam Rifles were directly under the Ministry of External Affairs and had to work closely with the NEFA Administration. Their administration was NOT the responsibility of the Army. The Army had only operational control over them. For many purposes they were under the Inspector-General of the Assam Rifles, with Headquarters in Shillong. We were in those days proficient in creating private armies, with the most nebulous command arrangements and allocation of responsibilities. It is a fundamental principle of the organisation of forces that a commander cannot exercise operational responsibility without controlling the administrative backing. The two functions are inseparable.

I have emphasised this point because it is the one crucial factor creating doubts as to how the Dhola Post came into existence. We seemed to have ventured most casually into a potentially explosive commitment. Instead of working in water-tight compartments we should have alerted the whole Army and prepared for a clash. Once the decision to locate a post in a disputed area was taken by the Civil Authority, then the necessary force should have been positioned within striking distance. Civil Supremacy cannot be invoked after 40,000 Chinamen appear on the scene to challenge the presence of 40 ill-armed men, in an area of disagreement.

Let us now examine the question of what is termed Civil Supremacy, in the context of the establishment of Dhola Post. Even as late as November 1967, Mr. Menon casts doubts on whether the so-called Forward Policy was responsible for the armed conflict of 1962. In an interview given to Mr. Inder Malhotra of *The Statesman*, Mr. Menon has this to say: "I know that some people have said that what has come to be known as India's forward policy, the policy of establishing forward posts, was at least partly responsible for converting the situation from one of confrontation to that of an armed conflict. I think this is an entirely wrong view. We never followed any forward policy. A forward policy means our trying to get into someone else's territory, like Lord Curzon tried to do. There has been at no time an attempt by us to take anything that was not our territory. Establishing posts in an area which belongs to us cannot be called a forward policy. . . . It was China that was following a forward policy in our territory".

On the question of political leadership he said: "But whether we should defend a particular area, whether we should pursue a policy of this kind or that . . . or whether we should repel the Chinese invasion of our territories are political decisions and on political issues the Government must decide. . . . It is the Government which tells the Military Command the objectives that it must try to achieve, and it is the Military Command which decides upon operational matters. The Government can only say you must hold this or you can give up that".

This erudite exposition of the constitutional responsibilities of the Civil *vis-a-vis* the Military still does not enlighten us on the selection of Dhola as the site for one of the posts under the Forward Policy. The pertinent question is who selected this particular area. We know that Mr. Nehru is supposed to have said that we should only operate in areas which we were convinced was our territory. Mr. Menon had one leg in the Ministry of External Affairs and the other in Defence. Did he order this post? Did he in fact know the background to the dispute? The officials of the Ministry of External Affairs ran the Assam Rifles. Did they order Dhola? The Intelligence Bureau of the Home Ministry were co-opted for advice. Did they suggest Dhola?

The Chief of the General Staff, General Kaul too must have been aware of the background to the Dhola area, and the possible military repercussions of treading on dangerous ground. Was Dhola established under Government orders; or was it established by the Army Command purely as 'an operational matter'? Did the Government say that we must hold Dhola?

The Chinese had raised a dispute about the exact alignment of the McMahon Line in the Thagla Ridge area. Therefore the Thagla-Dhola area was not strictly territory that "we should have been convinced was ours" as directed by the Prime Minister, Mr. Nehru, and someone is guilty of exceeding the limits prescribed by him. The unilateral definition of the border by individual Ministers, or sundry officials, is of no use unless the Cabinet authorises the use of force to sustain such claims.

The next point is whether Government wished to make an issue of the alignment of the McMahon Line in the Thagla area. If so what were the actual directions to the Armed Forces? These are vital questions, as Dhola was the detonator that allegedly sparked off the NEFA incident and the subsequent war. This is an issue which cannot remain clouded in discoursive discussions of the relative questions of civil and military supremacies or buried under a heap of verbal platitudes.

"The sturdiest pony in Towang owned by an even sturdier Tibetan woman. . . . " (pg. 126)

The author passing through a village in NEFA where journeys are measured in days and not in miles calculated from a map.

NEFA LANDSCAPE

This is a typical landscape in NEFA, ranging from 10,000 to 18,000 feet. It is gaunt, rugged, pitiless – as harsh as the face of the moon. It was over terrain like this that the concentration and maintenance of troops was ordained to meet political deadlines.

"*If 7 Infantry Brigade do not get a move on, you know what to expect!*" (pg. 228)

A cheerful group of Monpa porters, the sole means of maintenance and mobility for 7 Brigade in September-October 1962. They were sturdy and willing but limited under battle conditions to a payload of 15-20 lbs, infinitely more than the Indian Pioneer was able to deliver! This was the type of logistic support with which 7 Brigade was expected to "evict the Chinese", whilst our planners were shopping for modern means of mobility on "rupee payment".

It is known that many generals, including General Umrao Singh, opposed the indiscriminate opening up of more posts. Who forced him to open Dhola? Surely India was not landed in the straits of 1962 by an unplanned and thoughtless drift into a disputed area because of an archaic map?

The opening up of posts in undisputed areas cannot be questioned. The setting up of posts in disputed territory is a different matter. It is an act of rashness, whoever decreed it and with whatever authority, unless we had the means to settle the resultant dispute on the battlefield.

Dhola was established in June 1962 by Captain Mahabir Prasad of 1 Sikh, who had been "loaned" for this task, with one platoon of Assam Rifles. After setting up the post it was to be left in charge of a Junior Commissioned Officer of the Assam Rifles.

In view of the special significance of Dhola and the likely repercussions, I briefed Prasad myself in general and sent him to Ahluwalia for detailed briefing. He was told what to do in the event of encountering the Chinese. I asked him to send me regular situation reports as I feared that an incident may develop and I needed the earliest possible information to render the help that I was required to give by the terms of my operational tasks. This arrangement was objected to by higher HQ, and my instructions were overruled. I was curtly told that reports would be sent through the normal channels of the Assam Rifles. This was amazing as I was operationally responsible for this sector.

Prasad's party was deficient of certain stores and these were provided by me. For this too I was criticised on the ground that administration was an Assam Rifles' responsibility.

Captain Prasad was de-briefed by Divisional HQ on his return from Dhola. It now seems fantastic that I was not given the opportunity to talk to him;

and I was the commander responsible for doing something if the Chinese got tough.

Later I found out that the post was established on the south bank of the Namka Chu as this was the only place which was snow-free and for other administrative reasons, such as the availability of water and easier accessibility for re-supply parties. Dhola was tactically unsound and a certain death-trap in the event of a serious clash of arms. The obvious tactical location was either on Thagla Ridge itself, or further back on the Hathungla Pass/Tsangdhar. There was no immediate reaction to the site of the post. Since war with China had been ruled out there was no call to get involved in the tactical trivia of setting up a post. Administration had been brushed aside as a minor issue and the troops had no alternative but to ensure their survival by sitting near water and where porters could bring in their monthly rations.

Sometime in July or August 1962 GOC 4 Division represented the unsoundness of the location of Dhola to his superior, but had not received a reply up to 8th September when the Chinese debouched across Thagla Ridge and threatened the post.

The name of the person who did not give an answer, or failed to take a decision on this vital issue for over two months, will have to be made known as his was a major contribution to the events of September 1962.

Dhola was the worst possible place to get involved with the Chinese. Having set up the post everybody promptly forgot about it till the Chinese gave us a rude awakening on the morning of 8th September 1962. The Chinese suddenly, and without warning, reminded us that those who want to settle a dispute must be prepared to fight; and they were prepared to fight for Thagla as a matter of principle. We reacted with anticipated bravado and declared that we too would fight if necessary.

Was this too a political decision as averred by Menon? Can a Government decision stem out of an earlier miscalculation on the part of some politician or erring official? Was such a decision forced on the Government by a clamorous public?

The persons who set up Dhola without the necessary military might to slug it out with the Chinese are guilty of providing the Chinese with the excuse they wanted; and of placing the Indian Army in a shameful and invidious position.

Wishful Thinking

From April onwards I represented to Division the *lacunæ* in our current operational plans and gave my reasons. I also said that Assam Rifles posts could not be given timely help due to poor communications and difficulty of organising timely moves, over a widespread area. The command and control set-up between the Assam Rifles and the Army was defective. The roles of assisting the Assam Rifles and defending Towang were *prima facie* contradictory. To achieve the first I would have to disperse my command; to achieve the second I would need to concentrate the whole Brigade at Towang.

There was no reaction from Division initially as Gen. Amrik Singh had been posted out and the new commander was due to arrive only in early May. The outgoing GOC had visited Towang, but was reluctant to discuss operations. He was obviously glad to be out of the mess with which he had had to deal for over two and a half years. He advised me to discuss my problems with the new GOC.

The new GOC, Major-General Niranjan Prasad, visited me in May. I put forward my doubts and asked for various clarifications especially with regard to the assessment of the Chinese threat on which we had based our plans. We did not really have any high level intelligence assessment of the Chinese capability, intentions or likely actions. The task of stopping further incursions is too vague for purposeful planning. He promised to go into the matter fully and then jointly formulate new plans, after he had had time to acquaint himself with operations.

Instead of getting any formal replies to my queries, I was ordered to "revise" the existing plans and issue a fresh operation order instead of an operation instruction, in spite of my representation that I could not carry out the existing plan. It should have been obvious that it is impossible to write an operation order with numerous imponderables such as time, enemy strength, direction of main thrust, warning period, staging arrangements, leave policy and a host of other administrative factors without which no precise orders can be issued. Instead of coming to grips with the real problem of defending the McMahon Line and Towang, in the light of the many difficulties we faced, we were playing a staff college game of writing paper plans, which were impracticable and based on fallacious reasoning. I doubt if any plans had been properly worked out at Army HQ, and accepted by Command and Corps. If Army HQ are not clear about the tasks facing the Army then lower formations cannot function on a realistic basis.

We wasted more time in April and May 1962; planning to hold a full-scale exercise with troops, with the aim of "testing 7 Brigade's operational plans". Although there were no telephone communications, the exercise was to be held with wireless silence. I could not conceive of anything more foolish than this impractical idea. Any large-scale movement of troops on the border would surely attract Chinese attention and we would need clearance from Government. Political acceptance was essential as the Chinese might misunderstand our motives in swanning about a sensitive border area.

There were other practical difficulties in that we did not have sufficient rations, porters, animal transport and so on. My troops had an active operational rolè, so they would need to be relieved of their responsibility during the exercise; and yet it was laid down that 7 Brigade would continue to be responsible for the border. Eventually the exercise was cancelled but not before much infructuous correspondence and many acrimonious letters flew between Division and Brigade HQs and several futile reconnaissances carried out. A brigade cannot be tested without a minimum period of three months' collective training, the test exercise being the climax to a proper training season. Units had not even carried out individual training; nor had the Brigade practised the units before submitting to a Divisional test exercise.

In those days the Indian Army had developed a flair for stage-managing training exercises. There would have been many well-got-up files passed around. The area would have been swarming with umpires, 'observers' and VIPs. The main aim would have been buried in the spate of opening and closing addresses, comments from the Chief Guest and so on. A note would be made in the dossier of the General 'conducting' the exercise and everybody would go back happy that the Army was being trained and gingered up.

Operational plans were 'reviewed' and 'discussed' between May and August 1962, after General Prasad took over and after Operation Onkar had been launched. Eventually an operational conference was held in Tezpur, to tie up final details, in July 1962. Meanwhile matters continued to drift and we were still on the old plans. The monsoon set in by the first week of June and air-supply was reduced to a mere trickle, due to poor flying conditions. The ration was now extremely poor; the only vegetables provided were tinned carrots and peas. Local purchase was not possible (nor desirable) as there was little to spare in the villages. The troops were on a restricted diet.

By August 1962 some sort of plan was finalised. The Director of Military Operations from Army HQ had visited Divisional HQ and had given the latest appreciation of the Government and Army HQ. He is reported to have confirmed that *there was no question of a 'hot war' for the next few years.* In any case the Chinese were incapable of mounting any serious offensive till the railway line to Lhasa was completed, sometime in 1964.

The DMO works directly under the Chief of the General Staff and is the Director who lays down the Army's overall operational policy. Normally he would not make such a categorical assertion without the tacit approval of the CGS. The CGS, General Kaul, apparently did not share the views of DMO. He has written about a meeting he had with Mr. Chester Bowles (the present U.S. Ambassador to India) who visited India as the Special Representative of U.S. President Kennedy, in March 1962.

Chester Bowles had asked Kaul how serious in Kaul's opinion China was in its dispute with India. Kaul replied, "I had thought at first that the Chinese incursions into our territory had only a political significance and that our relations with China could perhaps be normalised by negotiation, but was now convinced by their pattern of behaviour recently, specially in Ladakh, that they seemed determined to establish their claims on some of our territory, if necessary by force".

In reply to a second query, Kaul claims that he told Bowles, "The Chinese were likely to provoke a clash with us in the summer or autumn of 1962 and this raised many problems for us".

This disclosure makes very sad reading indeed. There is no reason to doubt the credibility of this conversation, but it condemns Kaul. If this was his belief, then why were his actions in 1962 based on the diametrically opposite view?

The following questions are pertinent:

(*a*) Why did he allow the sensitive area of Dhola to be disturbed?

(*b*) Why did he not back-pedal on the Forward Policy?

(*c*) Why did he proceed on leave in the autumn of 1962, if he forecast that the Chinese would provoke a clash at this time?

(*d*) Why did he not alert the Army, particularly forward formation commanders, by sending his gloomy forecast as an Intelligence appreciation?

(*e*) Why did he not even brief his own Directors, one of whom mouthed exactly the opposite view of Chinese intentions, to GOC 4 Division?

(*f*) Why did he in October 1962 lightly accept the Thagla commitment?

(*g*) Why did he not make strategic dispositions or locate reserves, both as CGS and as Commander?

In August 1962, 4 Division issued orders for the implementation of a limited policy of re-siting of regular troops locations, and the establishment of additional company localities forward of Towang. The aim was to locate them nearer the McMahon Line to be more readily at hand to assist Assam Rifles posts. There was no plan to counter a full-scale invasion. As there was no immediate threat, and for various administrative reasons, this re-deployment was to be phased over two working seasons; the first phase to be completed by 30th November 1962, and the second during 1963. It now seems incredible that this was our operational thinking as late as August 1962, barely a fortnight before the Chinese incursion. At that time we were still indulging in the inexcusable game of guessing China's intentions and capability, while she was massing a huge army only a few miles from our border.

On 8th September, both 1 Sikh (who had relieved 1/9 Gorkhas) and 9 Punjab were in the process of establishing these new localities. This was fortuitous as detachments of 9 Punjab were in Lumpu and Shakti and were available for making early contact with Dhola Post.

The July operational conference did discuss the points that I had represented earlier. My anxieties with regard to the manning of the Line of Communication were met by the promise that Division would make the necessary arrangements to Towang, but that I would be responsible forward of this place. The problems of stocking reserves in Towang and the question of acclimatisation were accepted but conveniently brushed under the carpet, as there was no immediate threat.

7 Brigade continued to be responsible for the operational tasks of 11 Infantry Brigade, East of Sela Pass, as this formation was still in Nagaland. This role was in addition to the existing tasks of the Brigade and the new deployment arrangements that had been freshly ordered. As no additional administrative cover or troops could be given to me it was a mere "paper" responsibility. Its only use was to ensure that each corner of Kameng Frontier Division was "under" somebody, even if he could not exercise effective command. It also had the advantage of covering some senior HQ. In those days it had become the fashion to allot geographical responsibility, on the lines of the police practice. It was impossible to carry out all the tasks given to 7 Brigade concurrently. The absence of 11 Brigade proved disastrous. 4 Division had no depth and no balance. The vacuum was met by rushing in fresh troops who did not know the area.

Had 11 Brigade been in Bomdilla they would have studied the routes and vital features and Bomdilla would not have fallen so easily if 11 Brigade was where it should have been. Why was this Brigade not given to 4 Division as soon as the Chinese entered our territory?

Why was it later employed in Walong? The answer is the same. There was "no danger of a hot war" and thus there was no need for any strategic deployment.

The time and space factor was thoroughly thrashed out and the need for a warning period accepted. Unfortunately, only a few days later this was forgotten under pressure from Delhi and Lucknow. Once the political clarion call was given, the slogan was "On to the Namka Chu". The Army Commander ordered the move of 7 Brigade having made the rash promise of "concentrating a brigade in the requisite area".

Thus ended the process of operational planning for the year 1962. We were all exhorted to prepare our "revised" operation orders in time. We were also given a preview of the manner in which it was hoped to celebrate Sidi Barrani Day which commemorates the great battle victory in the desert war of 1940 in which 4 Division achieved international fame.

The leave programme of the senior commanders was discussed and I was granted leave from the first week of September, provided I had issued my new orders and had re-deployed my infantry companies.

Chapter VIII

The Line-up on 7th September 1962

China Prepares for the Coup de Grace

It would be well to summarise the relative political and military positions of India and China on the eve of battle. The anger and dismay of the Indian people at the poor performance of the Indian Army stemmed mainly from lack of knowledge of the facts about our so-called preparedness, and the very thorough Chinese war measures.

Let us first recapitulate the long-term Chinese preparations in the context of the political situation which gradually developed from 1950 to 1962. They always had the politico-strategic initiative. By surreptitiously usurping large portions of Indian territory, they placed the burden of recovery on India. Presented with a *fait accompli* India had the unenviable choice of fighting or acquiescing. No clear choice was made by those responsible for formulating the National Aim, and India fluctuated between the policy of outwardly confronting China and inwardly hoping to settle the differences by negotiations. National Policy, the duty and prerogative of the Civil Authority, cannot be based on dual aims. Inevitably India, in 1962, was neither prepared for war nor for a peaceful settlement short of the return of the Aksai Chin plateau. This was China's first major advantage.

The usurped territories in Ladakh were of vital importance to China and she would never give up her claims to them. Knowing this we continued to announce that we would recover "every inch" of our soil. Such remarks could not but alert China, as mature nations are not expected to indulge in empty boasts. Chinese defence preparations in Tibet commenced as early as 1950. Initially these may have been dictated by the needs of internal security, or by genuine fears of Western aggression. After the subjugation of Tibet, especially after 1959, the continued preparations were clearly aimed at India and yet we failed to heed all the transparent evidence of the massive Chinese build-up. They built strategic roads; set up a network of communications and stationed large garrisons along our borders.

On the political front, China appreciated our patronage and professed to be our friend. This gave her a head start of ten years in preparing to defend her interests in Tibet. To silence alert domestic critics we pretended to carry out defence preparations to meet the Chinese threat and promised to evict her from all the annexed territories.

When China gave unmistakable evidence and warnings that she had no intention of obliging us and withdrawing from any portion of occupied Ladakh, and was prepared to fight if necessary, we began a limited campaign of military preparations to silence a now more aroused and influential public opinion. We did not fool the Chinese.

We sought to deal with the Chinese threat by opening up more posts, building trunk border roads at a leisurely pace and locating regular troops in inadequate strength, with poor equipment and without the minimum administrative support. These feverish activities were not designed for a fight; they were merely a sop to an agitated public. Our ultimate hope was that we would be able to settle the border dispute by an exchange of copious, lengthy, erudite and well-documented notes; and finally negotiate our differences across a table. It must be remembered that our politicians were bred on the efficacy and magic of interminable talks and on non-violence. The methods used to drive away the British and liquidate the Empire on which the sun never sets must surely succeed against the friendly, civilised and Asian Chinese!

The Chinese deceived us by the pattern of their border activities. By not actually attacking us in disputed areas, and confining themselves to bloodless provocations, we were led to believe that they would not go to war over border disagreements. Khenzemane and Longju in 1959, and Galwan in 1962 were the most effective of China's deception tactics.

For many years China had concentrated on building up her armed forces, in readiness for an invasion by the Taiwan (Formosa) Government, backed by U.S. naval power. By 1962 she had a first-class land army with excellent modern small-arms and other conventional weapons. On our side, we did not deem it necessary to introduce modern weapons and relied on our World War II family of obsolete infantry and artillery pieces. We pleaded shortage of funds as an excuse for not modernising the Army. No country fearing war would fail to keep her armed forces in good shape, whatever the cost.

From 1959 onwards China intensified her war preparations and plans for an invasion of India. They had positioned the necessary superiority of men and fire-power. We remained blissfully ignorant of these moves.

China's Deception Plans

Let us now examine what the Chinese were doing on the politico-strategic plane in the first half of 1962, while we were formulating our 'plans'. There was greatly increased activity culminating in the climax of September. On the political front China re-stated her position and determination to fight, if necessary, over the border issue. Mr. Chou-en Lai said, "If India sets up posts in the Galwan Valley, Chinese troops would cross the McMahon Line".

In August 1962 there was a major clash in the Pangong Lake area in Ladakh. After this incident China opened thirty more posts, intensified patrolling and stepped up her offensive activity. China had already occupied 12,000 square miles of Ladakh, and later swallowed another 2,000 square miles.

In July-August India offered to hold talks on the border issue but the Chinese refused. On our side we continued to ignore the Chinese build-up to suit our ostrich policy. We persisted in living in a world of self-deception. There was little else that we could do now that the moment for paying for our negligence had come. We were now in the position of the sweating gambler who hopes to bluff his way out of an impossible position. Public opinion in India had become inflamed at the Government which made brave statements but appeared to take no action when the Chinese made an overt move.

The Chinese, in 1962 had prepared both for war and for talks, if India appreciated the futility of fighting for her rights. India was prepared neither for fighting nor for talking. Her military preparations were pathetic. Although the Border Roads Organisation was set up in 1960 there were still no usable roads. There was no urgency in anything connected with the possibility of war. We persisted in the hopes of a peaceful settlement of our disputes. We had developed a network of useless border posts, of a few ill-armed men. These were mere cannon-fodder in the event of a Chinese attack, especially when China had both political and strategical initiative. She could choose the time and place for the opening rounds of a war she may have decided upon.

The opening salvo of the 1962 war was fired at the peaceful town of neutral and friendly Geneva, in Switzerland. There was a story circulating in Delhi when I returned from China in May 1963. It may be apocryphal but could be true. The story ran as follows: Mr. Khrushchev, the Russian Premier, got the Chinese Foreign Minister, Marshal Chen Yi and Mr. Krishna Menon to meet and discuss the Sino-Indian border dispute. Both were present in Geneva at the time in connection with the meeting called by the Geneva Conference on Laos. He is alleged to have harangued them about the stupidity of their confrontation and its serious consequences to the international socialist movement. He is further supposed to have said that the only beneficiaries of this foolish and wasteful military effort would be the Imperialist Powers. He finally demanded to know what were the ultimate intentions of the Chinese and Indian Governments.

Marshal Chen Yi is believed to have given an assurance that China wanted a peaceful settlement of the border dispute and said that whatever happened China would never resort to war to settle this issue. This assurance was duly conveyed to Mr. Nehru by Mr. Menon and happily coincided with and confirmed his inner disbelief in the likelihood of war. We deduced anew that we could safely indulge in border brinkmanship without attracting full military retaliation from the huge Chinese Army stationed in Tibet. This was a golden opportunity for those who wanted to use the border dispute for their own political ends.

The next salvo in the Chinese deception plans was beautifully timed and placed. They selected the disputed Galwan Valley to create the next incident. Galwan is in Ladakh and was the perfect decoy to make their point without alerting NEFA. On 10th July 1962, some 300 Chinese troops surrounded our Galwan post of about 40 Gorkhas. We ordered the post to hold fast, and despite Chinese threats of interference, re-supplied the men but did not attempt to reinforce them. The Chinese tried every trick short of a direct assault, to intimidate, cajole and isolate the post. They made a special effort to suborn the Gorkhas by broadcasting that Indians and Nepalis were not friends and that Gorkhas should not fight as mercenaries for India. The Chinese advanced to within a few yards of our men in the hope that they would capitulate.

The Galwan garrison, under a brave Junior Commissioned Officer, held out. He was decorated and much was made of the bravery and steadfastness of the 1/8 Gorkhas detachment. It is true that our men behaved gallantly and fearlessly, and they deserved all the praise heaped on them; but unfortunately Government and the General Staff drew the wrong lessons.

The Galwan incident was the most explosive provocation to date. The Chinese showed restraint when they had us cornered; and their failure to physically assault the heavily outnumbered post, seemed to confirm Marshal Chen Yi's assurance. It was the perfect ruse. Our External Affairs Ministry duly "warned" the Chinese, since that was about all we could do. The Chinese did not lift the siege. The post was overrun in October 1962.

Galwan was undoubtedly part of the overall Chinese deception plan. It is not clear as to when they had taken the decision to humiliate us militarily; perhaps it was after the Dalai Lama's asylum in 1959. From that time they embarked on a well-thought-out plan to lull us into believing that whatever turn the border dispute took, it would never escalate into a shooting war. They had acted reasonably after the Khenzemane and Longju incidents in August 1959. These incidents were followed by the visit of the Chinese Premier to Delhi in April 1960. He gave the impression of being reasonable and made reassuring statements. The officials' talks also helped to calm frayed tempers generated by the clashes. After every border incident the Chinese would talk of concessions and the necessity for moderation and the avoidance of armed clashes. Sometimes they withdrew after a show of force, and permitted our post to be re-established.

This pattern of behaviour gave birth to the pernicious theory that all we had to do was to stand fast whenever surrounded or threatened by the Chinese; this theory was the major reason for the headlong dash to the Thagla Ridge, the subsequent bravado and the tactics attempted by Gen. Kaul to "sit" behind the Chinese.

The Chinese battle preparations were both thorough and impressive. From my own observations before the Thagla Battle and my findings subsequently as a prisoner of war, I was able to gather the following facts:

(*a*) The Chinese preparations began in earnest from May 1962. Prior to this they had infiltrated agents and had organised informers from among the Tibetan road gangs working in NEFA. They knew all our movements and dispositions.

(*b*) They moved a famous General of Korea fame, to command the Chinese Forces in Tibet.

(*c*) Interpreters in all major Indian languages and dialects were moved to Lhasa between March and May. They were acclimatised and trained in Indian customs, attitudes and characteristics of the various classes recruited in the Indian Army. Some were clearly Indian-born Chinamen who had been taken to China for use against us. I met some of them, but they were reluctant to admit that they had even been to India. The Intelligence set-up was under an ex-military attaché in Delhi.

(*d*) They moved scores of photographers and movie-cameramen to Tibet. I saw many in the Namka Chu Valley before 20th October and again after I was captured.

(*e*) They employed hundreds of sturdy Tibetan ponies for carrying supplies and ammunition. I myself passed at least 1,500 on my way back to the Chinese roadhead at Marmang. I was told that the Chinese had started their breeding farms as early as 1952, as they did not want to antagonise the Tibetans who had always smarted at the feudal system which required them to provide ponies and their own services to their landlords, each year.

(*f*) They had recruited thousands of Tibetan porters, both men and women. They had been organised into proper labour battalions. Later, in the village where I was imprisoned I saw many wearing odd items of Indian Army uniform and equipment.

(*g*) They had established forward dumps at Le, Marmang and Tsona Dzong. These dumps were not guarded as the Chinese had immunity from both ground and air attack. They had an assured system of carriage and delivery. The Chinese Commander was master of his own administration and could base his plans on realities and actuals. In the mountains, administration is the critical principle of war. Dependence on an uncertain source of supply and vague assurances is disastrous.

(*h*) The Chinese dumps were well stocked as September-November are the most advantageous months to the Chinese. The Tibetan plateau is dry during the monsoon months of May to August and the passes from China are snow-free. The Chinese thus had the whole of summer for intensive stock-piling and the concentration of troops.

(*i*) They had organised prisoner-of-war camps to hold 3,000 men. In these they had positioned blue-padded suits, bedding and essential clothing. The General Staff is responsible for forecasting the number of prisoners likely to be captured, as they are in the best position to know the scope of battle envisaged. The size of the camps is a clear indication that they were anticipating a big war.

(*j*) They had built a 7-ton road to Marmang, which was only a few hours from Thagla Ridge. They had moved at least two divisions and 150 artillery pieces to the Thagla area and opposite Towang.

(*k*) They had thoroughly indoctrinated their troops on their version of the border dispute. They knew what they were fighting for and the issues for which they had been sent to the border. They were made to believe that India was bent on nibbling at Chinese territory and had to be stopped. Everyone that I met parroted the same arguments.

(*l*) They had perfect communications and had laid telephone lines right up to the border. They were adept at laying line and were usually through on the phone within hours of capturing a position.

(*m*) They had a unified command and clear military and political objectives.

These eye-witness observations should silence all the critics of India who have said that it was India that started the Sino-Indian War of 1962. The seemingly minor points which I have enumerated give a more forceful indication of the thoroughness of the Chinese preparations and their intentions. The war was not an accident and was certainly not decided after 8th September 1962. It was coldly and calculatingly planned by the Chinese. It is ludicrous to suggest that India attacked, forcing the Chinese to launch "self-defence counter-attacks". When we go through the Indian state of readiness as on 7th September, it will be evident that no such possibility was envisaged, let alone planned for.

India Unprepared for War -- 7th September 1962

In contrast with the thoroughness of the Chinese preparations, India was completely unprepared in every way for hostilities. In fact, there was an air of unreality and complacency that would have damned any Government. The possibility of a Chinese attack having been ignored, we did not have an organised war plan.

We have already laboured the point about India's defective National and Strategic Aims. The corner-stone of our planning was that there would be no war with China in Mr. Nehru's lifetime. We were prepared only for Galwan type border incidents and to counter limited Chinese incursions. The broad strategy was that troops would be ordered to stand fast, despite being invested, and supplies and reinforcements would be sent. Thereafter brave words would be mouthed by everyone. The Chinese would be warned to desist from further aggressive activities; protest notes would be exchanged; and the Indian Cabinet could settle down to sorting out the next crisis on its agenda.

We had no allies, as our non-aligned policy did not permit us to get involved militarily. Our known weaknesses and lack of allies tempted the Chinese to teach us a lesson without inviting retaliation.

There were no strategic dispositions. Neither XXXIII Corps nor Eastern Command had any reserve formations to deploy in an emergency. The nearest troops were in the west, in the Punjab. This was a grave error on the part of the General Staff. Presumably because we did not expect to fight and capture any prisoners, there were no interpreters in Chinese anywhere in Assam.

It is well to remember some startling facts about the absence of most of the key persons responsible for conducting operations against the Chinese. This fact has not received the attention it merits. Mr. Nehru was attending the Commonwealth Prime Ministers' Conference in London when the Chinese first intruded into the Thagla area. He did not deem it necessary to return and take charge of the situation as the head of the Defence Committee of the Cabinet. Presumably he was not advised correctly by our Intelligence, who did not appear to have any idea of the nature and scope of the Chinese threat. It has been said that Mr. Menon, who was dealing with the situation and taking far-reaching decisions from the outset, minimised the seriousness of the developments and did not think it worthwhile to advise the Prime Minister to cut short his foreign tour. With his known conceit, and possibly having faith in Marshal Chen Yi's assurance, he probably thought that he could handle the Chinese incursion on his own and add another martial achievement to his Goa success. Mr. Nehru's absence was a grave handicap in the sphere of the Higher Direction of War. Mr. Nehru proceeded to Lagos, Nigeria, from London and returned home only on 2nd October. By then the decision to evict the Chinese had already been taken, and there was little that he could do to reverse the trend of events, as public opinion had been allowed to get out of hand. After taking the unfortunate decision to appoint Kaul to command a non-existent task force, Nehru gaily left for Colombo, Ceylon, on 12th October, returning on the 15th. This second trip at the height of the crisis proves that he was not unduly perturbed over the border situation. In fact before emplaning he grandiloquently informed the Press that he had ordered the Army to evict the Chinese intruders. In retrospect it seems to have been an amazing dereliction of duty on the part of the executive head of Government, his advisers and the Intelligence set-up. Mr. Nehru's claim that he was stabbed in the back by the Chinese, or that he was surprised by events cannot be sustained by history. He chose to absent himself from the helm of affairs, where he should have been from the very beginning. The nation did not take kindly to his international peregrinations at a time when he should have been leading the country.

Mr. Krishna Menon was partly preoccupied with his forthcoming visit to the U.N. for the annual General Assembly Meeting, in mid-September. For years he had been the *de facto* Deputy Foreign Minister. He appeared to be anxious to dispose of this petty, irritating border situation and move to the larger international arena, which he loved so dearly. It has been said that he deliberately underplayed the whole Thagla Affair to avoid being asked to stay back in Delhi in the absence of the Prime Minister.

Mr. Morarji Desai, the Finance Minister, had accompanied the Prime Minister to the London Conference. He subsequently left for Washington to attend a World Bank meeting.

Let the Nation be told how the Defence Committee of the Cabinet functioned in the absence of the three key members of this body. How was Civil Supremacy exercised? Was the all-embracing authority of this Committee delegated to the Ministry of Defence?

The Army was equally guilty in the matter of absence from duty at a critical juncture. The Chief of the General Staff, General Kaul, was holidaying in Srinagar and did not return till 2nd October. The CGS is in charge of Intelligence. What was he doing on leave? Obviously he did not anticipate war despite his recent claim that he forecast a Chinese clash in the autumn of 1962. Chiefs of the General Staff do not normally take leave when war is impending. Even so, why did he not return to duty as soon as the Thagla incident started and his prediction was proved right? He should at least have been recalled when Government decided to stop further incursions and to evict the Chinese. Such a decision was taken as early as mid-September. All responsible officers are expected to be at their posts when serious operations are envisaged. Obviously Army HQ did not anticipate a major war.

HQ 4 Infantry Division was busy with the annual celebration of the famous Battle of Sidi Barrani. Since they had been told that there was no threat of war till the railway line to Lhasa was completed, preparations were in full swing for this great day. All units had sent their athletes and teams for the various tournaments. Large numbers of officers and men were on leave. There was an air of peace and calm and prospects of a quiet, normal winter where the main enemies would be the cold and boredom.

As Commander 7 Infantry Brigade, and the seniormost officer in direct command of Kameng, I was on leave on the fateful day of 8th September when the Chinese first intruded into our territory at Thagla. Fortunately I was still in Tezpur and had not left for my leave station. Now leave for brigadiers in command is strictly controlled by HQ Commands, and is personally approved by the Army Commander. There is a very sound reason for this arrangement, as HQ Commands are in the best position to know when a senior commander can be spared without detriment to operational commitments. The sanctioning of my leave, at this particular period, is the clearest possible proof that Command did not anticipate war in September 1962. The stipulated state of readiness is laid down by Army HQs General Staff Branch; Command was therefore not correctly advised or warned. This is mysterious as the CGS, Kaul, claims that he anticipated a clash.

Lt.-Col. Manohar Singh, the GSO I of 4 Division, and the senior staff officer was sent on the Senior Officers' Course at the Infantry School, Mhow. The nominations for this particular course are made directly by Army HQ subject to representations on operational grounds. The fact that Manohar was made available implies that Division had not been placed in a state of operational readiness. 4 Division did not expect a war. He was later recalled, after the Thagla Affair had got out of hand.

From the foregoing, it is evident that our deployment along the northern borders, since 1960, was designed to stake our claims and not to fight a major campaign against a first-class enemy, at short notice. The numerous limitations and shortcomings were well known, and accepted at all levels. Had they been remembered, as they should have been, the Nation might not have been committed to the resolute and irrevocable decision to drive out the Chinese, inviting retaliation all along the Sino-Indian border, to which we had no military response. If the odds had been calculated, then senior Cabinet members would surely have been at their posts.

With the advantage of hind-sight, Mr. Menon is reported to have said in 1967, that "Yet the time had come when there was nothing else to do but fight. A war which is avoidable at one stage becomes unavoidable at another stage". He adds, "The war with China became unavoidable as we could not refrain from defending ourselves. In undertaking defensive operations a country can never consider the odds. If we are attacked we have to defend ourselves, even if we are defeated". The time had been coming for many years, and yet risks were taken in not organising and administering our forward troops, on the untenable assumption that the Chinese would not take military counter-measures, whatever our own publicised actions may be. This theory was strongly propounded and lulled everyone into a false sense of security.

The overall situation was ripe for a military disaster. In classic conformation to military principles, the Chinese High Command selected the remote and disputed Thagla Ridge area to provide the *casus belli* for a war on which they were bent, and for which they had made perfect preparations. As the aggressor, China had the added advantages of choosing the time and place for their feint. They were able to achieve maximum surprise and concentration of forces. They knew that fatal Indian weakness of wide dispersion along the entire border, in small detachments. Knowing the Indian penchant for hasty, ill-advised and rash reactions to border incidents, they selected a place away from our main defences thereby further stretching our Line of Communication and denuding the defences of Towang. A disputed area also gave them the opportunity to stall for time by pretending to want talks, and to restrict our military response to the low key of a border dispute. (That is why there were no strategic arrangements in the rear of Thagla.)

We fell for the trap; and without a pause for clear thinking, despatched the nearest available troops to "forestall the Chinese at Thagla". We accepted a possible war in an area for which we had made no preparations. It is criminal to fight *ad-hoc* battles. Man-pack columns, without heavy weapons and ammunition, were rushed to confront the Chinese with pouch ammunition. Imagine trying to fight the largest and one of the most powerful land forces in the world, with only pouch ammunition. Disaster was inevitable and should have surprised no one who had been dealing with the China problem from the beginning. The most deplorable part was the subsequent attempt to shift the blame to the Army. Individual politicians are expendable, but a country's Army is a permanent institution. The good name of the Army and its tested formations are infinitely more important than the political reputation of any individual, whatever his temporary stature and importance.

In one fateful month our Government tried to make up for its tardiness and wrong policies by embarking on a last desperate gamble which did not come off. Then to save the skins of those who had been forced to redeem their boastful pledges of fighting the Chinese, it became fashionable to blame pressure of political events and public opinion. As we shall see, the Thagla Affair was given undue prominence and importance even before the first commander reached the spot to assess the situation. Public opinion was allowed to get out of hand instead of being moulded to face harsh military realities. Even if we concede Menon's claim that war had become inevitable by September 1962, was it necessary to fight on the worse possible terms? Was it necessary to ignore all the principles of war? Is the word fight synonymous with suicide?

Instead of gracefully accepting responsibility for erroneous policies, the guilty men sought *alibis* and scapegoats. In any developed democracy the Government would have been replaced, instead of being allowed to continue in office and sit in judgement on their subordinates.

The moral of all this is that never again must the fate and destiny of India be placed in the hands of any one or two men. We must also learn that a democracy has no room for proven failures. This is not a matter of sentiment. Mr. Chamberlain was removed after Hitler invaded France in May 1940 with Cromwell's classic plea, "For God's sake, go". Mr. Anthony Eden was forced out of office after the disastrous Suez adventure of 1956. History records many instances where heads of elected Governments had the courage to resign, or who were forced to resign by public indignation and angry legislators.

We shall now follow the tragic events from 8th September to 20th October 1962. The basically faulty National Policy was rendered even more disastrous by faulty decisions, taken on a day-to-day basis. We moved inexorably and inevitably to a major military defeat; and there was no one with insight or force of character to stem the tide; or save us from the plunge into certain disaster.

Part III

"On To The Namka Chu"

Chapter IX

China Crosses McMahon Line — 8th September 1962

On 8th September 1962, I was at Tezpur *en route* to my leave station. GOC 4 Division and I spent the morning with 1/9 Gorkhas who were at Misamari ready to entrain for Yol, in the Punjab, after completing three gruelling years in NEFA.

General Niranjan Prasad addressed the assembled battalion, and thanked them for their excellent pioneering work in opening up and guarding Towang. He praised them for their devotion to duty, hardiness and cheerfulness despite the difficulties and hardships which they had had to encounter and surmount. Finally he wished them a happy and pleasant tenure in their new peace location, and hoped that they would be able to celebrate Dussehra (the great Gorkha festival due in early October), with their usual gusto and spirit. This was the first time in three years that the battalion would be re-united with their families.

The Gorkhas were understandably tired and over-due a spell in congenial surroundings.

When I left the battalion after a sumptuous lunch, I scarcely imagined that I would be seeing them again shortly under war conditions. Instead of proceeding to Yol they were rushed to the Thagla Ridge area. Brigadier D. K. Palit was then the Director of Military Operations, and the Colonel of the 9 Gorkhas. Palit had promised the Battalion that they would not be used in any operations, and that they would definitely spend Dussehra in Yol. He even promised to visit them and join in the festivities! Imagine their chagrin and dismay when they were ordered to return to Kameng. This decision did not endear the top brass to the simple Gorkha soldier.

In the afternoon I was invited by the GOC to play a round of golf at the newly laid course at Tezpur. After the game I went to my quarters at the Machine-Gun Unit, which was located near the airfield. As my plane was leaving at dawn I planned to turn-in after dinner and had declined the General's kind invitation to attend a cinema show at the local Planters' Club.

At exactly 6-30 p.m. the telephone rang while I was still in my bath. At first I was tempted to leave it alone. I was sick of telephone calls. Some extra-sensory intuition told me that I had better answer it as it was probably an emergency message. Very few people knew where I was staying and only someone who wanted me desperately would persist in contacting me. I was officially on leave from midday.

My Deputy Assistant Adjutant and Quarter Master General (DAA & QMG or D/Q), Major Bertie Pereira, spoke to me from Towang on Radio-Telephony and passed me this ominous message:

> "The Post Commander at Dhola has been sending frantic messages that about 600 Chinese soldiers crossed Thagla Ridge at 8 a.m. and had come down to Dhola Post. They had cut one of the log bridges on the supply route to the post, and they were threatening their water supply. The Post Commander wanted immediate help".

The message had been received only at 2-30 p.m. when the Assam Rifles Wing set at Lumpu had opened up under the informal arrangement we had made with them, and that is why the information had taken six hours to reach my HQ. I could get no further information from Pereira. I was particularly anxious to know if the Chinese had left or not.

I ordered Pereira to alert the Assam Rifles Wing at Lumla and the Assam Rifles Post at Lumpu, the nearest detachments to the scene of the Chinese incursion and two days' march away. I promised to return to Towang the next day. So, our Forward Policy was beginning to extract its price. Our day-dreams were coming to an end. A force of 600 intruders was not one that could be easily dealt with by the troops in Kameng Frontier Division, under my command.

I hastened to Division and tried to contact the GSO II, officiating for the GSO I who was away on a course. I also had a messenger sent to the Thakurbari Planters' Club to call the GOC. The Club is some 35 miles away and the GOC eventually arrived at about 9 p.m. The GSO II, who had the keys to the secret almirah and who held the secret maps in his own custody, could not be readily located. He was eventually tracked down and arrived at 8-45 p.m. The Air Force Liaison Officer, who was also required, was finally run down, somewhat the worse for wear. After all it was a Saturday night and we had inherited and nourished the Saturday night and week-end tradition bequeathed to us by our erstwhile British masters. The Anglo-Saxon and his followers are best tackled on a week-end. The Japanese attacked Pearl Harbour on a Sunday morning when the Americans were either recovering from the excesses of "Saturday night" or piously worshipping God in church! Who was left to man the guns against the approaching Japanese Armada?

I have no doubt that the Chinese selected Saturday to ignite the Thagla incident as they correctly reasoned that by the time information reached Delhi it would be late evening or early Sunday morning. It would take that long for the message to percolate down the line of peace stations and commanders to contact each other for orders. The Chinese must have known by 1962 that no Indian Commander had any initiative to act without consulting Government. This was the natural corollary to the lack of clear long-term orders and plans. Each border incident was handled according to the prevailing political pressures; and our response was tailored to these pressures.

At this stage it would be useful to consider the ponderous and cumbersome command set-up of the various HQs responsible for dealing with border incidents in NEFA, as this has a vital bearing not only on the conduct of operations but also on the mental attitude of the officers who control these operations. My Brigade HQ was at Towang, some five days' march from the scene of intrusion at Thagla Ridge. Towang is a field posting and a hardship station. Division was at Tezpur, 200 miles away. Although Tezpur is considered to be a field area, life is more or less normal, with planters' clubs, golf-courses and cinemas. Corps HQ was at Shillong, another 200 miles away. Shillong is a salubrious hill-station and a "peace posting". It is difficult to maintain a war-like atmosphere in this peaceful and picturesque town in the Khasi Hills. Command HQ was at Lucknow some 600 miles from Shillong. It is even more difficult to develop an operational outlook so far from the Sino-Indian border.

The last tier is the holy of holies at Delhi where we have Army HQ and "Government". Delhi is the most peaceful of the world's capitals and so far removed from military realities that political factors perforce dominate the formulation of national strategy. Over the years Army HQ had become a remote centre more concerned with politics, overall finance and administration than operations.

The peace stations of Shillong, Lucknow and Delhi give India's enemy a head start in war. These HQs were manned by officers who had earned the right of a "peace tenure". They worked standard office hours and lived normal family lives. After serving in hardship areas they were entitled to their rest, recreation and hobbies. Some were posted on medical grounds and others for compassionate reasons. A few would have requested postings to these places to 'rehabilitate' themselves prior to retirement. It is unreasonable to expect such HQs to "raise a gallop", particularly as border incidents with China and Pakistan had become a recurring commonplace, and an occupational hazard of the Indian Army. This was the inevitable outcome of placing a Regular Army on a semi-permanent war footing. Wars cannot be run efficiently by peace-time HQs. The direction of war is the business of HQs located, organised and manned for instant response. Staff officers have to be selected purely on merit and must be trained for operational appointments. Operational HQs must be freed from the distractions of life in major cities and family life.

To revert to the Thagla incident. The GOC held a conference on arrival, to decide on the immediate course of action. He informed the Brigadier General Staff (BGS) at XXXIII Corps HQ and asked for instructions. BGS instructed the GOC to be "prepared to relieve Dhola Post and ensure that its maintenance is not jeopardised. The Post must hold out at all costs, and not succumb to Chinese threats".

After some discussion, GOC gave the following preliminary orders:

(*a*) The Dhola Post Commander will be ordered to stay his ground and informed that a link-up party would be sent as soon as feasible. There was to be no withdrawal or shifting of the Post. The Assam Rifles Wing will be ordered to establish contact with, and send a re-supply column to Dhola to the beleaguered detachment. A Line of Communication to Dhola will be kept open.

(*b*) 9 Punjab detachments at Shakti and Lumpu will be warned to move to Dhola to open a Line of Communication. The remainder of the battalion, at Towang, will be prepared to move to Lumpu, to be within easy reach of Dhola.

(*c*) I was to cancel my leave and return to Towang the next day and prepare an appreciation of the military implications of moving to and operating in the Thagla area. The GOC promised to visit me to formulate concrete proposals for discussion with the Corps Commander.

(*d*) Leave parties were not to be recalled, but personnel in Misamari awaiting rail transportation were to be detained pending further orders.

At this conference I reiterated some well-known facts and requested the GOC to bring them to the notice of the Corps Commander, Lt.-Gen. Umrao Singh. The first was that any move forward of Towang would involve the abandonment of the defences of this "vital ground". I should, therefore, be given a clear alternative task and relieved of my responsibility East of Sela Pass.

The Thagla incursion should not be treated as a petty border incident. I reminded the GOC that we had all along been apprehensive of establishing a post in an area which the Chinese do not concede to be ours. The GOC had himself represented to Corps HQ, the tactical unsoundness of this post. We should cater for a sharp and massive Chinese reaction. I told the GOC that the Chinese had the advantage of time and space and logistic support, while we suffered from grave administrative handicaps.

That night, lying in bed, I had a premonition of disaster. I cursed myself for accepting the Military Secretary's offer to command 7 Brigade. The military problems in Kameng were formidable and would not be appreciated by those who did not know the area. A quarter-inch map of NEFA in Delhi does not convey the enormous logistic difficulties. We were short of everything.

I had attended many meetings in Delhi where "decisions" about border incidents had been taken. I knew that once political necessity is established the Army has no further say in the matter. We had got away with this in minor clashes with Pakistan. If someone should decide that the Chinese must be stopped "once and for all", then 7 Brigade would have no option but to make a headlong dash to Thagla, whatever the tactical or strategic disadvantages. The Thagla incident might be used to test Chinese intentions and designs. I cannot explain the reason for these thoughts; perhaps it was my training and experience in Operations Directorate. Anyway, I clearly remember telling my Brigade Major (BM), Major (now Brigadier) Rex Kharbanda, of these forebodings.

I left Tezpur the next morning (9th September) at 5-30 a.m. by helicopter. The BM met me at the helipad. I told him what had transpired at the GOC's conference and outlined the form of the "staff paper" that we had to make. I was very fortunate in that I had an excellent staff in Major Kharbanda and Major Pereira. They were competent and dedicated men. The Intelligence Officer, Captain (now Major) T. K. Gupta, was an extremely capable young man.

I immediately conferred with my Commanding Officers (COs), Lt.-Col. B. N. Mehta of the Sikhs and Lt.-Col. R. N. Misra. Misra had assumed command of 9 Punjab in June when Lt.-Col. Master, left to teach at the Infantry School. Misra had only just returned from the Thagla area, after carrying out an extensive reconnaissance and had visited Dhola. This was fortunate as we had the benefit of his first-hand knowledge of the ground, routes, timings and the going and most of the factors and deductions were based on his advice.

The salient points of the paper were as follows:

Ground Factor

(*a*) The main route to Thagla Ridge area was along the Nyamjang Chu Valley to Lumpu; thence to Hathungla Pass (13,400) and the Namka Chu River. The total distance was about 60 miles and required 4 or 5 forced marches. In the present weather conditions of rain and slush, 5 marches would be a more prudent planning figure.

(*b*) There was an alternative but more difficult route from Lumpu *via* Karpola I Pass (16,500) which had the advantage of being secure from Chinese interference.

Vital and Important Ground

(*a*) Tsangdhar and Hathungla were vital features and had to be held. Dhola itself was in a narrow valley and completely indefensible. At most, we could plant the Indian Tricolour there and stake our claims. We should not waste any further effort on this flag-post.

(*b*) Lumpu-Choksen was a suitable defensive line and should be held to secure Lumpu which was the only suitable dropping zone for the maintenance of the troops in the Namka Chu.

(*c*) Shakti was a key defile and must not be lost.

State of Routes

(*a*) The route from Towang to Thagla was fit only for man-pack columns. Civil porters were likely to be in short supply as the harvesting season was in full swing. The Political Officer whom I had consulted felt that he would not be justified in disrupting the normal life of the local population, unless he received special instructions from the NEFA Administration. (In fact, porters in the required numbers were not made available till after 24th September, when Chinese and Indian troops had already started exchanging fire, and the decision to evict the Chinese had been taken at Delhi.)

Relative Strengths/Relative Build-up

(*a*) Reports of the Chinese strength in Dhola varied between 60 and 1,200. The senior Indian military official at Dhola was a Junior Commissioned Officer (JCO) and he was not a reliable source, as he was liable to exaggerate the situation to get help. In any case, it would be prudent to assume that the Chinese had at least a battalion in the Thagla area and possibly the rest of the regiment (brigade) somewhere between Thagla and their base at Marmang. (Good armies operate in recognised units and formations.)

(*b*) 7 Brigade had only two battalions and a battery of mountain guns. The guns and artillery mules could not be moved forward of Towang and therefore the Brigade would have to confront the Chinese without artillery support. Each battalion had 350/400 bayonets, i.e. the total strength of only one full battalion. The Engineer element consisted of about half a field company, with no earth-moving plant, explosives or bridging equipment. Only elements of 7 Brigade were in Towang and the Brigade could not be committed until it was fully concentrated and its order of battle completed.

(*c*) The primary task of 7 Brigade was the defence of Towang, which had been declared vital ground. Its fall would have serious repercussions. Any diversion of troops to Thagla would leave Towang at the mercy of the Chinese. There were no plans to cater for a major confrontation forward of Towang. The diversion of 7 Brigade, from its primary role and its despatch to the Namka Chu would create complete imbalance. It should be understood that such a task would be an *ad hoc* one, on ground and time of Chinese choosing and under crippling administrative handicaps. (For many years the role of the Army has been orientated towards defence and this had eventually gnawed at its offensive spirit and developed a defence neurosis.) It is not a simple matter to suddenly order offensive action without the necessary training and mental conditioning.

(*d*) The additional role East of Sela Pass would have to be given to some other formation. (This was to suggest the recall of 11 Brigade from Nagaland.)

(*e*) In the absence of a three-ton road, from the Foothills to Towang, it would take some 10 to 12 days to concentrate fresh troops, leave parties and others who were left in the plains. It would take another 4 to 5 days to move them to Thagla. Troops would arrive tired and should not be expected to operate without a rest, and the minimum period of acclimatisation. The road from Foothills to Towang had suffered the ravages of a full Himalayan monsoon, and would require extensive repairs.

(*f*) Time and space favoured the Chinese as they had a roadhead only a few miles (and a few hours) from Thagla, while our one-ton head was at Towang. They had the advantage of a full summer's stocking and stock-piling.

The relative build-up capabilities was a critical factor. "Anything we could do they could do better".

(*g*) The Chinese could deploy heavier weapons than us due to their better communications. Unless we air-dropped heavy weapons we would be out-gunned in a serious fire-fight.

Administration

(*a*) Before troops were committed to battle, it would be necessary to drop, collect and ferry forward snow-clothing, ammunition of all types, rations (including a reasonable reserve), wireless equipment which was dangerously short; defence stores to secure firm bases which are vital in the mountains. (Detailed tonnages were worked out and included as appendices.)

(*b*) Lumpu was the only dropping zone which was suitable and which had been tested and approved by the Air Force. It must be commissioned at once.

(*c*) Porterage was a serious bottleneck. Details of the number required for the concentration and subsequent maintenance were worked out. The employment of army pioneers, in large numbers, would require additional tonnages to feed and clothe them. The law of diminishing returns would operate in their case.

(*d*) There were no stocks in Towang to issue to units moving to Thagla due to the cessation of drops during the monsoons i.e. from June. General Staff reserves of rations had been consumed, under appropriate authority. It was necessary for air-drops to continue in Towang to feed the local garrison as well as the transients passing through. We would also need drops at Lumla (*en route* to Thagla) to save the carry from Towang to Lumla. (Later this was agreed to, and proved a boon.)

(*e*) There were no trooping arrangements or dumps anywhere between Misamari and Thagla – a distance of over 220 miles. Division must assume responsibility for the induction of stores and men.

Weather Conditions

(*a*) Weather was the third critical factor both for the concentration of troops and for any battle in the immediate future. Due to incessant rains movement was slow and back-breaking. The going was extremely difficult with slippery paths and steep gradients.

(*b*) There were no shelters *en route* and troops would have to bivouac in the open. Coupled with the lack of suitable warm clothing and waterproofs, this would prove a health hazard. Health is vital in the mountains where resistance to chills and other pulmonary ailments is essential to avoid depletion of the fighting strength of units. It is neither easy to move reinforcements nor to evacuate casualties. A minimum number of tents would have to be carried forward or dropped if the Brigade was not to be rendered ineffective through illness.

Surprise

It would be difficult to achieve surprise, one of the most important principles of war. We should not operate after the fashion of policemen who rush to the scene of occurrence without fear of detection or armed retaliation.

I have recounted the points of the first military appraisal in some detail because while the Indian people maintain a large standing Army they are perhaps unique in the world in that few of them have any understanding or experience of war. We are apt to panic or indulge in extreme emotionalism in a crisis. It is only by understanding the ramifications of war that we can resist hustling Government and the Army to undertake rash military ventures. However indignant we may be, we just cannot stop the rains or bulldoze mountain passes from our path. We cannot wish our enemies away. We cannot create dumps with a conjuror's flourish. Military operations are cool, calculated and deliberate actions. Haste is the enemy of military planning. These statements which are *clichés* in Europe and America where most adults have rendered national service, had to be learnt the hard way by us.

* * *

On this day 9 Punjab sent a detachment from Lumpu to Dhola, *via* Hathungla Pass, to ascertain the locations and strengths of the Chinese intruders; to link up with the Post and keep the Line of Communication open. I also sent an Assam Rifles party over the Karpola I Pass route to contact Dhola.

The remainder of 9 Punjab were placed on 4 hours' notice to be prepared to move to Lumpu to establish a firm base and man the dropping zone. I allotted them 100 pioneers and closed down all work on the construction of shelters. To hell with audit objections! By the afternoon 9 Punjab confirmed that they had prepared their loads; had shanghaied every available local porter, and were ready to leave as soon as ordered.

* * *

Gen. Prasad arrived by helicopter early the next day (10th September), and immediately plunged into a discussion of my appreciation. He also met my COs and the new Assistant Political Officer, Mr. V. V. Mongia, who had replaced Mr. Shaiza.

The General agreed with my appreciation and requirements. Later, this appreciation formed the basis for the letter which General Umrao Singh, the Corps Commander, wrote to HQ Eastern Command in which he stated that there were serious handicaps in mounting hasty operations against the Chinese in the Dhola area.

The GOC then briefed us on the latest situation and gave the following information/orders:

(*a*) HQ Eastern Command had ordered "7 Infantry Brigade to make preparations to move forward, within 48 hours, and deal with the Chinese investing Dhola".

(*b*) XXXIII Corps had asked permission to use 1/9 Gorkhas who had not yet left for Yol. 2 Rajputs were being sent to 7 Brigade immediately.

(*c*) Towang would not be denuded. 1 Sikh would remain deployed on the Bumla Axis (guarding the direct northern approach) and be responsible for the defence of this vital approach.

(*d*) 9 Punjab would move immediately to Lumpu. (In those days, there was no speed less than "immediate" and "as soon as possible" in the Indian Army. This sort of vague order, compounded of hope, pressure and unreadiness, saves the officer issuing it the bother of making a small movement appreciation to ascertain what time will be required to move from one place to another. This pernicious habit must be eradicated with the utmost vigour.)

(*e*) The Punjabi company and the Assam Riflee relief columns must move faster and make contact as "quickly as possible". (The required degree of acceleration was, of course, not specified.)

(*f*) Air-drops would be arranged wherever we wanted. I was somewhat sceptical about this promise. We relied entirely on air supply in uncertain weather conditions, and on indifferent dropping zones. There was a known shortage of carrying agencies, including helicopters, to supplement the air effort, or for the final carry from dropping zones to forward troops. As a commander I was naturally apprehensive about conducting operations with an erratic and haphazard supply system, particularly when the main agency (the Air Force) was not answerable for the failure of operations. The Air Force cannot control the weather, procure additional aircraft, train pilots or manufacture supply-dropping equipment in a matter of a few days. In the absence of a joint commander the best we could hope for was a promise from the Air Force that they would do their best to drop what we required, where and "as quickly as required". If they failed for reasons beyond their control, the Army would have "had it".

(*g*) Leave parties held up in Misamari would be ordered to rejoin their units at once. Personnel actually on leave would not be recalled.

(*h*) On a query from Lt.-Col. Misra, it was laid down that the following action would be taken in the event of encountering the Chinese:

(*i*) Persuade them to leave Indian territory and go back.

(*ii*) If the Chinese do not comply with our request and withdraw voluntarily, then troops will take up positions and dig-in opposite the intruders to prevent further incursions.

(*iii*) Fire was permitted only in self-defence; and minimum force would be used.

The Thagla Ridge Operation thus started with a very limited and modest aim. Such were the humble beginnings to the most disastrous military setback to Free India.

These orders revealed the naked truth that Army HQ had no strategic plans to deal with a major Chinese riposte to the establishment of forward posts, even in disputed areas like Dhola. The importance of long-range strategic forward planning cannot be disputed or brushed aside by blaming politicians. In Italy, in 1943/44 Field-Marshal Kesselring, the German C.-in-C. was faced with the problem of countering Allied landings along the extensive Italian coastline – a problem which is broadly analogous to countering border incursions, in that the enemy has the initiative to select the time and place for the landings or incursions. Marshal Kesselring had a defensive procedure for such a contingency. Mr. Majdalany in his book *Cassino – Portrait of a Battle* spells out the Marshal's arrangements. "Realising the futility of attempting to defend every beach on Italy's long coastline where the Allies might attempt a landing, the German High Command had issued a *comprehensive emergency plan to cover the whole country*. In it was laid down what troops should move against the possible landing points, as soon as the landing had occurred, on what roads and at what time they should move, and what tasks they should undertake. It was only necessary to issue a code-word to put these pre-arranged plans into operation". We had no pre-arranged plans.

When the other officers left the meeting I had a private talk with the GOC on the command and control arrangements, the location of my HQ and my own movements. In mountain operations this is a calculated arrangement, as once a commander leaves his HQ he may be on the move for long periods. Time in the mountains is reckoned in days and not hours, and a commander can neither retrace his steps nor be recalled easily. A brigade HQ is not designed to be split for more than a few hours as there are only two staff officers and they must meet the commander daily. As all movement is on foot, the location of HQs assumes critical importance if continuous effective command is to be exercised. In the early stages of an operation and before commanders at various levels have agreed upon a joint plan, the need for constant contact is self-evident.

Now commanders are appointed to command and not to man a fire-pump to extinguish a blaze. They are required "to perform the functions of Commanders not Corporals". I emphasise all these elementary facts because the Indian Army had got into the questionable habit of rushing senior officers to the "front" on every occasion. I knew from experience in Delhi, that everyone would start screaming "Where's the Brigade Commander!" I pointed out to the GOC that my command now consisted of only one battalion, 9 Punjab, which would be on the move for the next three days and would most probably be out of wireless touch most of the time, as the Brigade had only 62 sets with a range of about 22 miles (with wire aerials). If I was on the move as well, I would not only be out of touch with my battalion but also with my HQ and with Division at Tezpur. I asked the GOC if he would want me to meet him again after his Tezpur Conference with the Corps Commander on 12th September. I made it clear that I was not prepared to accept any criticism on the score that I did not charge to the scene of the incident with the leading company.

The GOC instructed me to remain at my HQ in Towang until the Punjabis reached Lumpu. He promised to send a helicopter to take me to Lumpu as soon as the Punjabis arrived there.

The rest of the day was spent in receiving further frantic and conflicting messages from Dhola Post. We were also trying to establish contact with the two relieving columns to ascertain their progress. The 9 Punjab patrol lost its way across Hathungla Pass, as it had moved without guides and porters.

That night I had a long chat with GOC. I could talk to him freely as I had served under Gen. Niranjan Prasad in 1949, when he was commanding the 5th Royal

Gorkha Rifles Regimental Centre and I was his second-in-command. We had become family friends and had maintained this friendship over the years. He was a fine gentleman and I was proud to claim him as a friend. I had implicit faith in his personal and professional integrity. My only doubt was whether as a disciplined soldier, he would raise enough moral courage to oppose plans which were impracticable and which could only commit us to an impossible situation.

I requested him to emphasise at the meeting of 12th September that the maximum force which could be deployed in the Namka Chu was one battalion; and the only role that this battalion could fulfil was to give heart to the Dhola Post Garrison and prevent further petty incursions into our territory. There was no question of conducting any formal operations of war against a large Chinese Force in the prevailing circumstances. I warned him that he would be subjected to political pressures relayed by the Army Command and coerced to undertake impossible tasks. I hoped he would resist improper orders. I myself would be too close to events, while he, in Tezpur, could view the military problems more objectively. He would not have to face the accusation of being a coward if he counselled caution or restraint. I could not afford to appear hesitant or over-cautious.

I raised these issues because my apprehensions had been aroused by the impracticable and unreasonable Eastern Command order "to concentrate 7 Infantry Brigade in the Thagla area". What was the order of battle of 7 Brigade? Did Eastern Command know the size and composition of the Towang Garrison? Had they worked out how a brigade was supposed to move and subsequently be maintained in the Dhola Area? Would the Army now try to cover up past omissions in preparing for a clash with the Chinese by flogging the troops and sacrificing their lives? Could Command HQ not wait for the considered views of the Brigade

Commander, the Divisional Commander and the Corps Commander before ordering a brigade to the scene of the Chinese incursion?

Some adverse factors which demanded consideration had obviously been overlooked and these were to prove disastrous later. The minimum warning period was not being adhered to. Failure to allow for the time factor misled planners at all levels above Division, resulting in the scrambling of troops into operations. 7 Brigade lacked tactical mobility; and was not armed, equipped, organised, clothed or stocked for a battle with a superior Chinese Force. It was prepared to defend Towang (however inadequately), where the ground was more suitable; was of our own choosing; was undisputed and where reconnaissances and dumping had taken place. The reckless ignoring of these factors was a major reason for the order to concentrate at the Namka Chu. To cover up our shortcomings, we coined the slogan of "moving on hard scales and pouch ammunition". This was patently not going to be enough against the Chinese, although it may have worked against Naga hotheads and Pathan tribesmen in Kashmir.

The order of battle of 7 Brigade was disturbed from the very inception. Of its normal grouping only 9 Punjab was retained. 1 Sikh was allotted to the "Towang Sector". The third battalion (4 Grenadiers) had not yet arrived from Delhi. (They did not join me till 12th October). The Corps Commander was trying to "find" some battalions to make up a "brigade".

The order to concentrate 7 Brigade at Thagla was the first of the many slogans that were issued during the September-October 1962 operations. According to accepted military teaching, formal orders should contain an Information paragraph; an Intention; a Method paragraph; Administrative arrangements and the Inter-Communications set-up. An Intention by itself is a mere slogan.

Chapter X

The Trap Is Baited

The NEFA War was played in three acts. Everything that I have narrated so far was the Prelude: Thagla Ridge was the Climax: everything that happened after Thagla, viz. Towang, Sela Pass and Bomdilla was the Anticlimax. The Thagla incursion was gradually allowed to become the battle for the survival of those responsible for India's China Policy including the Generals who had associated themselves with the tepid military response to the Chinese threat.

The story that I shall recount is the story of the curtain-raiser to the NEFA Campaign. To understand the Thagla Battle, which opened the short war, I have given the political and strategic background that produced it. The failure was essentially due to the tactical and administrative factors which proved insurmountable. The most dominating factor was the topography of the mighty Himalayan Ranges.

The most famous dictum in military history is von Clausewitz's "War is the continuation of State policy by other means". The Thagla Battle and the NEFA Campaign were NOT the continuation of the Indian State Policy by other means. It became an act of self-immolation brought on by political expediency in the face of uninformed public pressure; credulity in Chinese good behaviour and gross negligence in assessing and preparing for a military showdown.

The Thagla confrontation which began on 8th September and ended in the massive Chinese attack on 20th October can itself be divided into four phases. The first phase, from 8th September to 20th September, was the advance to contact, ending in the exchange of fire between regular battalions of India and China.

The second phase lasted from 20th September to 3rd October 1962, during which time a scratch force was hurriedly marshalled at Lumpu, some 15 miles from Thagla; Government and the Army High Command were insisting on the eviction of the Chinese intruders regardless of the consequences; and the forward commanders were trying to give military shape to the ordained tasks. This phase ended in a military deadlock, as there was no prospect of evicting the Chinese in the prevailing disparities between the two forces but Government would not bow to the harsh realities.

The third phase, from 3rd October to 10th October, marked the replacement of Lt.-Gen. Umrao Singh, XXXIII Corps Commander; the appointment of Lt.-Gen. B. M. Kaul to command, with the task of "speeding up operations"; and the move of 7 Brigade to the Namka Chu, culminating in the major skirmish of 10th October at Tseng Jong.

The fourth and final phase, from 10th to 20th October, witnessed 7 Brigade helplessly tethered to the Namka Chu Valley, until it was destroyed on the morning of the 20th.

* * *

On 11th September I was constantly prodded to give the "exact" location of the Assam Rifles and Punjab patrols which were moving post-haste to Dhola. My staff maintained a round-the-clock vigil by the wireless set but could not establish contact. There were cynical and sarcastic remarks about the standard of 7 Brigade's wireless proficiency, as if the Brigade signallers could redress the inadequacies of our antiquated equipment. (For years the Army had been waiting for Bharat Electronics to produce better sets indigenously. We spent many years drawing up qualitative requirements more to suit the capability of this Public Sector enterprise than to meet the Army's requirements in the mountains.) Everyone wanted to know why the columns had not yet relieved Dhola. On the current

¼-inch maps the distance appeared to be only six miles. All these nasty observations were from officers in the rear areas, who knew neither the terrain nor the timings involved. They could devise no better technique of command than by the issue of ceaseless exhortations to "hurry up". This is facetiously known as the "giddyap" system. In sheer disgust I had to point out that in the mountains troops could either keep moving or waste time halting and setting up special aerials to report progress. I recommended working on the old British Army slogan "No news is good news".

* * *

9 Punjab set off from Towang for Lumpu. I asked the CO to establish temporary, *ad hoc* transit camps at Lumla and Shakti. I milked everyone of pots and pans, tents and wireless sets, and allotted him some pioneers to collect air-drops at Lumla and Lumpu.

More frantic messages continued to be received from Dhola Post but there was nothing to be done till the relief parties reached the invested garrison.

GOC 4 Division left Towang on 12th September to meet the Army and Corps Commander.

* * *

I did not know at the time what was happening at Lucknow (Command HQ) or at Delhi. It is now known that on 11th September there was a meeting in the Defence Minister's office, attended by Lt.Gen. Sen. Sen is quoted as saying that there were some 600 Chinese in the vicinity of Dhola and that he would require a brigade to deal with them. He added that he had ordered "the brigade" on this mission and that it would take 10 days to concentrate.

In retrospect, I cannot understand the basis for General Sen's authoritative assessment of the Chinese strength, or his categorical guarantee of concentrating "a brigade" to deal with the Chinese, within 10 days. If he did make the statements attributed to him, he did so entirely on his own and without any assurance from the Corps, Divisional or Brigade Commanders. I had given no such undertaking, as indeed I was in no position to do so. I did not have a brigade to concentrate, nor did I have any idea of what my order of battle was to be. I did not control the administrative machine required to support operations.

Gen. Sen's statements, if true, are serious enough to warrant the closest study and could have been the fountain-head of many subsequent miscalculations – military and political. Who gave the firm figure of there being only 600 Chinese in the vicinity of the Dhola area? The area north of Dhola was dead ground and we did not know the strength of the Chinese Force. We could only do so if Government permitted tactical reconnaissance by aircraft, which was forbidden. Did he base his estimate on the latest message received from the Dhola Post Commander? The Commander was a Junior Commissioned Officer (JCO), and Army Commanders and Governments do not normally commit themselves irrevocably on the basis of such flimsy and uncorroborated information. Were the Intelligence Bureau and the Joint Intelligence Committee consulted? If so, what was their interpretation of the Chinese incursion? Did Gen. Sen have a guarantee that the Chinese would not, or could not, reinforce their troops in the Thagla area? Did he know that the Chinese ability to build up was infinitely greater than ours? Why was the Defence Committee of the Cabinet not summoned? Were the Chiefs of Staff consulted and alerted? Sovereign nations do not decide to "deal" with other sovereign nations in such a haphazard manner.

I have known Gen. Sen for some years and I can hardly believe that he would essay such a forthright opinion and commit himself and his country. He would surely have waited for a senior and responsible officer, of at least Lt.-Col. rank, to reach Dhola and send back a proper appreciation of the situation with all its military ramifications and repercussions. Decisions cannot be taken in Delhi by an *ad hoc* body, without a study of the military factors which shape national decisions. The meeting of 11th September could have been the source of many misplaced hopes and unfortunate postures.

What could Gen. Sen have meant by "the brigade"? The only Brigade within hundreds of miles was mine and it had only one battalion and no supporting arms. Could a decision on the threat and the quantum of troops required to deal with it not be postponed for a day or so till the Army Commander conferred with his subordinates? Had Sen waited he would have had a fuller picture of the immense problem of mounting operations in the Namka Chu Valley area, even against 600 Chinese soldiers. Having committed himself he later found the Corps Commander's "difficulties" unpalatable. War is not a mere question of disposing so many men against so many. Further, if he, as the Army Commander, had made a personal reconnaissance of this sensitive area in his command, he would have been better able to assess the situation.

* * *

In the meantime 9 Punjab completed their concentration at Lumpu with remarkable speed, in heavy monsoon weather and over high altitudes.

The Assam Rifles, under Officer Commanding Lumla Wing, established contact with Dhola Post as ordered. This Wing was under my operational command and the task given to them was a proper and legitimate one, as they were the closest to the Namka Chu, they knew the area and had the best organised porter and guide system. Considerable bitterness and recrimination arose from the fact that the Assam Rifles were the first to make contact and not regular troops. The Inspector General of the Assam Rifles (IGAR) was reported to have set up his "tactical

HQ" in or near Tezpur and was demanding direct reports from Lumpu. He appeared to be conducting his own private war. It is now possible to smile at the comedy that was being enacted then. When the Assam Rifles were being criticised for their slowness in reaching Dhola they were under 7 Brigade. Once they reached, they reverted to the Inspector General. The operation almost started with a confused and abrasive command and control set-up but fortunately was quickly put right when IGAR was told to keep off. In the abyss of recrimination and misunderstanding, the commendable effort of the Punjabis was forgotten. I exchanged some harsh words with my GOC on this issue. He later took up the matter with the Corps Commander to vindicate the professional honour of this fine Battalion.

* * *

On 13th September I went to the helipad at 5.30 a.m., to fly to Lumpu in the helicopter which the GOC had provided. The chopper came, with the Commander Artillery of 4 Division, Brigadier (now Major-General) Kalyan Singh. Unfortunately it developed propeller trouble and the pilot refused to risk a flight with a VIP, to an untested helipad. I was flattered to be classified as a VIP but disappointed that I would not be able to meet Lt.-Col Misra. The pilot promised to come back the next day with a better chopper. I rang up Divisional HQ and informed them of the mishap and the postponement of my flight.

I was surprised to see Kalyan. He told me that he had been sent to command "Towang Sector", as there was no task for the Commander Artillery in the forthcoming operations. He had also been made responsible for the administrative arrangements to, and forward of, Towang. Thus did someone higher up cover himself and pass on the responsibility for "defending" the Divisional vital ground. Now it could be claimed that Commander Artillery 4 Infantry

Division was "in charge of Towang". No one told him what he was in charge of; against what and with what.

Kalyan informed me that the Divisional Machine-Gun Battalion Commander had been placed in charge of the Line of Communication from the Foothills to Towang. I mention these points to highlight the fact that 4 Division never fought as a Division and thus did not sully its international fame. It had only two brigades stretched over 300 miles, the third, earmarked for Bomdilla and Sela Pass, was in Nagaland. The Division had no depth, no reserves and was unbalanced. It was never able to deploy its fire-power or administrative cover. The troops in NEFA could more appropriately have been named "Border Guards". This is the moment at which a résumé of 4 Indian Division's war record would be in order. I am indebted to Mr. F. Majdalany for this appreciation in his book, *Cassino – Portrait of a Battle.*

"The 4th (Indian) Division reached Egypt shortly before the outbreak of the war and at once began intensive training in desert warfare. In 1940 it carried out, with the 7th (British) Armoured Division, that defeat of the Italian Armies which is a classic of the rout of the many by a few. The following year it brought off the notable victory in Keren, in Eritrea. In 1942 and 1943 it played an important part in the final Desert Victory. Since then it had been resting and retraining in Africa".

In February 1944, 4 Division was moved from the Adriatic Front of Italy, to the Cassino front. "At that time", says Majdalany, "it was considered to be one of the finest and greatest fighting divisions of the War. It was able to claim a long record of success dating back to the earliest days of the War. In Italy, they brought an almost arrogant conviction of invincibility born of their great victories in the Western desert. An aura of glamour invested this Division".

It will always be a pity that the title of this great formation was given to the scattered troops, deployed on policing duty. The matchless, professional excellence of this formation was greatly admired by the Germans – no mean professionals themselves. It is said that General Von Arnim, Commander of the German Forces in Tunis in 1943, insisted on surrendering to the 4th. His caravan is today used by the GOC of 4 Division. No wonder the Chinese were aghast at the poor "performance" of this famous formation. It is ironic that the fame of this formation is more widely known and respected by foreigners than by the Indian people. Perhaps this is the price of segregating the Army from the public, except for the annual pat on the back during the debate on defence appropriations.

Mr. Chavan, while he was the Defence Minister, removed the slur on the prowess of 4 Division during his statement on the findings of the NEFA Enquiry, on 2nd September 1963. He told the Lok Sabha, "Before I end, I would like to add a word about the famous 'Fourth Division', which took part in these operations. It is indeed sad that this famous division had to sacrifice its good name in these series of reverses. It is still sadder that this division during the actual operations was only 'Fourth Division' in name, for it was not fighting with its original formations intact. Troops from different formations had to be rushed to the borders to fight under the banner of 'Fourth Division' while the original formations of the division themselves were deployed elsewhere".

Perhaps the most ironic fact of all is that 4th Division had been commanded by Generals Thapar, Sen and Kaul – the three Generals who led the Division to "these series of reverses".

* * *

The most astonishing arrangement was that I was to leave my staff in Towang to work under the Sector Commander to assist Kalyan in the arrangements for trooping. I was required to fight the Chinese single-handed and without the benefit of a staff. This was an unforgivable breach of military organisation and working procedures. These *ad-hoc* measures stemmed from our penchant for devising snap solutions to events that we never seem able to foresee. If we do anticipate them we get bogged down in a morass of financial considerations and other extraneous issues. At the last minute we created a sector at Towang, with a Commander Artillery in charge and gave him the staff of a Brigade Commander who was soon to be given the task of evicting the Chinese!

* * *

Gen. Umrao and Gen. Prasad conferred with the Army Commander at Tezpur on 12th September. Gen. Sen relayed Government's decision to expel the Chinese from our territory. This was the second slogan issued in three days.

Gen. Umrao Singh who had studied my appreciation and had heard the views of the Divisional Commander, confirmed our joint conclusions. He now informed Gen. Sen that the task of clearing the Chinese was beyond the capability of his troops in Kameng Frontier Division. Umrao said that, "Our ability to reinforce due to lack of troops and roads was limited. Our troops were on restricted scales of rations and had no reserves. Clothing was scanty for the extreme cold. We were short of ammunition and there were hardly any defence stores available. We did not have adequate fire support". Gen. Umrao then warned Eastern Command "that an attempt on our part to clear the Chinese south of Thagla Ridge would amount to an act of rashness. To produce even a semblance of the resources required for this purpose, he would have to completely uncover Towang and also withdraw troops from Nagaland. He pointed out that Towang was our vital ground and its fall into Chinese hands would have more disastrous consequences than the fall of Dhola"

These were sound, valid and cogent military reasons which presented a realistic appraisal of the military situation and which enjoined prudence on the Government.

Umrao's representation to Sen amply testifies to the fact that he, Prasad and I had no illusions about the odds against engaging the Chinese at Dhola, as early as 12th September.

Gen. Umrao confirmed his views in a formal letter to HQ Eastern Command. This letter is a vital document for future historians as it will reveal that the advice of those in direct touch with local events and conditions was turned down. It will turn the spotlight on the person or persons who ignored the military problems and got 7 Brigade embroiled without the semblance of a chance to put up a worthwhile resistance.

* * *

At about 5.30 on the evening of the 13th, I was briefing Brigadier Kalyan on the problems of defending Towang, when GOC 4 Division called me up on the wireless. Without any preamble he commenced to give me a sharp dressing down, and demanded to know why I had not gone "forward". I was at a loss to comprehend this stricture as he knew about the helicopter mishap, and had also agreed that I should not be on the move at the same time as the CO of 9 Punjab, to maintain uninterrupted command and control. The General then peremptorily ordered me to move "at once" without waiting for my explanation. His behaviour was so strange and out of character, that I suspected he was being goaded by someone. He seldom raised his voice and never at me. This was Kalyan's opinion too. Later Gen. Prasad told me that the Army Commander was pressing him to order me "forward". When the GOC ordered me to leave at once, I decided that someone had taken leave of his senses, so I pretended that I could not hear him and could not follow his orders due to heavy atmospherics. I asked the operator to tell the GOC to call me again when reception conditions improved. He did so after a few hours and asked me to leave the next day, on foot, and promised to explain the reasons later.

GOC ordered me, at the same time, to move 9 Punjab to the Namka Chu "forthwith", without halting at Lumpu. This had apparently been decreed by the Army Commander. I was astonished at this change of plans, specially as *no fresh aim or task was given.* This was the third slogan in three days. These two orders were most calamitous and set the pace for many subsequent unreasonable orders, improper haste and disregard for military principles. The unfortunate result was that the tactical and administrative problems were never thereafter fully weighed. Indian and Chinese regular forces came in contact, with the advantage in the Chinaman's favour. I do not know what the Delhi planners had in mind. Perhaps they may have hoped that the appearance of the Punjabis would cause the same consternation that is achieved by the police when raiding a gambling den or a bordello!

It will be recalled that the nature and scope of operations had not been decided, the relief of Dhola being the only immediate object. I was expecting another visit from the GOC, after his talks with the Army and Corps Commanders. I would serve no purpose by being on the march during the next three critical days; whereas I could fly to Lumpu in 20 minutes. What were the Punjabis to do in the Namka Chu, and who would give them orders in case they got involved with the Chinese? Contact with the Chinese was imminent. While on the move, I could neither send nor receive secret messages as high-grade ciphers are not carried by small parties for obvious reasons.

It was imperative to establish running and secure administrative arrangements before venturing into the Namka Chu Valley with a whole battalion. We can perceive the build-up of political pressure and how this pressure confuses commanders in the field.

To this day, I am firmly convinced that these two orders contributed materially to the tragic events leading to the defeat of 20th October. The advance to contact started in considerable confusion, with lack of planning and lack of confidence in the higher leadership. Relations between Sen and Umrao (already unhappy) worsened with this direct interference in Umrao's domain. Relations between forward and rear commanders were strained at the start line. Thereafter there was little mutual trust with disastrous consequences to the smooth conduct of operations.

In well regulated armies it is not the statutory function of superior commanders to order the moves of units, or to evict junior commanders from their HQs. A formation is given a task, and the formation commander executes it. If he fails, he should be removed. A task was given by GOC 4 Division and was being carried out competently by 9 Punjab. The move to the Namka Chu was not for the Army Commander to order, unless he did so as part of a full operation order, verbal or written, to his immediate subordinate – the Corps Commander. The tendency to issue verbal orders and to interfere with the actions of local commanders began as early as 13th September.

The entire chain of command was disrupted by two ill-conceived orders issued verbally, in temper or under duress. The head was severed and it was not till 25th September that the COs, the Brigade Commander and GOC 4 Division were able to communicate with each other readily. The result was lack of information, lack of direction, all-round uncertainty about what was happening, and frayed tempers – all during a vital phase. 9 Punjab was committed and pinned down at the Namka Chu without a firm base, without administrative cover, and with no commander to control or help them. As they were in contact they could not be used for mobile, offensive operations. Thus the only acclimatised battalion within 200 miles of Thagla was rendered ineffective. Instead of speeding up operations we had retarded them till fresh troops could be inducted. This haste set the pace for the next few days.

Darkness comes early in the mountains, the sun setting at about 2.30 p.m. in Towang. Movement is reckoned and organised in stages. One must move early enough to complete a stage by about 2 p.m. It was ridiculous and improper to order me to leave at once, as I would achieve no worthwhile distance. How could I organise porterage at that hour as a Brigade Commander's party requires at least 50 porters – 14 porters are required only for the Commander's Rover wireless set? What was I to do "forward?" Brigade Commanders are not appointed merely to rush to the "scene of occurrence"; they are expected to command and administer their brigades at a distance or they will only lose themselves in the confusion of combat and get a distorted picture of the tactical situation. They must of course visit the battlefield frequently to acquaint themselves with the ground and the battle situation and take personal charge when necessary. The decision is entirely theirs and not that of their superiors.

* * *

I left Towang at 5 a.m. on 14th September with my Intelligence Officer, Captain T. K. Gupta, and the usual commander's party, but without my senior staff officers. My staff had worked all night collecting porters and preparing loads for a long absence from HQ. My party had to be self-contained for our own administration and to carry charging sets, batteries and special fuel for charging sets. All these loads were bulky and heavy. I was reluctant to leave my staff behind. A Brigade Commander's staff has more to do than assist him in staff matters. The senior members are his confidants and companions and must be together in a crisis. For days while wandering in the Himalayas, I had no one to talk to or to share my thoughts and anxieties – a fate worse than solitary confinement.

It was raining heavily as we set out, with a gale-force wind. As usual, Towang was covered in a thick pall of mist, with visibility some 15 yards only – a miserable day on which to leave on a hopeless military venture. Little did I know that I would never see Towang again. I was feeling humiliated at the manner in which I had been ejected from my HQ. It should have been obvious that the senior field commander in Kameng should have had a helicopter on call to save time and energy.

After a gruelling march we reached Lumla after dark. I had tried to contact 9 Punjab throughout the march, but was unable to do so. I was pleased at covering 22 miles in the mountains in a few hours. The value of acclimatisation was amply demonstrated. Any normal fit man can survive and fight in the mountains, provided he is given a chance to adjust his lungs and blood count. I can say, in all humility, that I did not suffer a single day's indisposition. I kept fit and mentally alert throughout despite sharing all the hardships and privations of my men. The sudden illness of a commander can influence the whole course of events. The key to this is strict adherence to the laws of acclimatisation.

On the 15th we covered another march of 18 miles to Shakti. I was still out of touch with everyone. I cannot conceive of anything more frustrating (and dangerous) for a commander than to be away in the blue, and not know what was happening to his troops; or what was being plotted for him at higher levels.

On 16th September we made another early start from Shakti and reached Lumpu at about 3 p.m. The going was really hard due to incessant rain, cold, mud and slush. We wondered if we would ever get dry again and were very tired after three forced marches.

The base at Lumpu was organised by 9 Punjab, assisted by the Assam Rifles detachment. The Second-in-Command (2 1/C) 9 Punjab was in charge, and was responsible for collecting air-drops, the carry to the Namka Chu and for submitting indents to the rear. He was also responsible for maintaining wireless communication with Towang and Divisional HQ at Tezpur. All these duties were outside the scope of an infantry battalion; they were the responsibility of formation HQ. assisted by the necessary adminitrative and signal units.

The order to hasten the move of 9 Punjab to the Thagla area apparently came as a result of "decisions" taken in Delhi on 13th and 14th September. During the high-powered discussions held on the 13th, General Thapar, the Army Chief, is said to have informed the Defence Minister that there were now only 50 or 60 Chinese, and not 600, near Dhola. He had therefore ordered the Army Commander (Sen) to take action against them without waiting for the whole Brigade to concentrate. The Army Commander accordingly ordered 9 Punjab to be moved as fast as possible. How can history be kind to Chiefs and Army Commanders who set about their business in this way? It is wrong to be optimistic; and even more wrong to order units about, without hearing the local commander's views, fully assessing the relevant factors of the situation and the implications of such orders.

It is a notorious fact that the enemy strength and capability always appear more negligible at Army HQ and Government levels than to the unfortunate battalion and company commanders in direct contact with that enemy. Even allowing for this tendency, General Thapar's appreciation, if correctly reported, must surely take the prize as the most fantastic piece of wishful thinking and unwarranted assumption of the Thagla Battle. Ultimately the Chinese used over 20,000 men! One expects the Chief of an Army to have the latest Intelligence and air tactical reconnaissance reports.

I have harped on this point because I wish to emphasise that the Thagla operation was never looked upon as anything but a petty border dispute from the very start. Had it been otherwise, the entire approach might have been more circumspect.

To get back to the conference of 13th September, let us analyse the damage that was done by the casual approach to a potentially explosive situation. The comforting assessment of the Chinese strength (60 men) produced its own logical strategic deduction. For the arm-chair strategists and policy-framers at Delhi, it produced the delusion that this was the fleeting opportunity for a charge up the Thagla slopes regardless of all other factors. Such a charge, it was deduced, would cause panic and chaos in the Chinese ranks, after which the attackers would gallop on to the Thagla summits, with orders to build a helipad "at once". Sundry VIPs would then arrive with their favourite cameramen and the affair would be consigned to history.

This concept betrayed a lack of comprehension of the military problems involved. It was necessary to secure a firm base and organise an assured resupply route; as otherwise the enemy could cut off the Indian Force. We knew or should have known that the Chinese could easily rush reinforcements forward. The venture would surely have ended in disaster. No commander in the field could have ever issued such an order.

There was another meeting on 14th September. The Army Chief now seems to have arrived at a more realistic appraisal of the military factors. The previous day he was of the view that the small Chinese party could be evicted by one battalion. The Army Chief is also reported to have "reminded" Government of the many shortages and weaknesses of the Army and stated that it could not cope with large-scale reprisals in Ladakh and/or NEFA. Lieut.-General Daulet Singh, General Officer Commanding-in-Chief, Western Command, who was also present, forecast a complete military disaster in Ladakh. Gen. Sen stated that he could not counter the Chinese in NEFA, if they came in strength. Despite these warnings, Government thought that we must resist the Chinese, irrespective of the consequences. The time had come when "we should give – or appear to give – the Chinese a crack at least in one place, as we could no longer tolerate their encroachments into our territory". Obviously the military factors could have no place in such thinking. Chinese encroachments must be stopped: thus far and no further. However heroic the spirit of this determination, the Government "decision" was divorced from the realities – and the sudden switch to an offensive posture was ill-suited to an Army committed by the policy of non-violence, to a defensive role only and by Government parsimony to crippling shortages. When the enemy was the Peoples' Liberation Army of China the 'decision' was quixotic.

This Government "decision" which was obviously the datum line for the relentless and seemingly irrevocable determination to evict the Chinese, was taken at a meeting of the Defence Minister, the Army Chief and two Army Commanders with presumably one or two Ministry officials in attendance. The Prime Minister was abroad on this fateful day and so was the Finance Minister !

Did the Defence Minister give this order on his own initiative? Was it within his power to do so? Had he arrogated to himself the powers of Government and was it within his power to commit the nation to a clash of arms without consulting the Defence Committee of the Cabinet (DCC) and the Chiefs of Staff Committee? Mr. Lal Bahadur Shastri, the then Home Minister and a permanent member of the DCC, was present in Delhi; was he consulted? Where were all the various organs of Government, devised for planning and prosecuting war? Was the Prime Minister advised to return to India? Was public opinion really so inflamed on 13th/14th September, or was it allowed to become inflamed by subsequent ill-advised remarks by Government officials and inept public relations? Who whetted the public appetite for a confrontation with a first-class power? Whatever the compelling political reasons, no individual or group of individuals should have been allowed to take such far-reaching decisions, against expert military advice.

Having received and accepted this order from Government, the Chief of Army Staff should have recalled his Chief of the General Staff, Gen. Kaul from leave. He did so only on 2nd October after Nehru had returned from abroad. A major clash with China was more than probable and the General Staff could not function without its head. I have often wondered if Gen. Kaul would have accepted the task of evicting the Chinese so readily, if he had been in day-to-day touch with developments from 8th September. He had a reputation for being bold and active and he would surely have visited Towang and Tezpur and assessed the situation. He had visited Towang in November 1961 and had a fair idea of the logistical problems of this area. Had he kept in touch more recently, he might have been more inclined to 'bicker' at the difficulty of evicting the Chinese when offered this task. Looking back on events I believe Gen. Kaul's leave was ill-timed and the omission in not recalling him a blunder. His continuance on leave typified the casual air with which even the highest officials were approaching the task of "herding out the Chinese" from Dhola.

I might add here that the absence, on leave, of Senior Commanders and Staff Officers is a singular victory for the enemy's deception plans. I will illustrate this with just one of the many examples from World War II. Field-Marshal Alexander's cover plan before the fourth and last battle of Cassino was so successful that General Von Senger, Commander of the 14th Panzer Corps in Cassino was on leave in Germany, when the Allied assault commenced on 11th May 1944. Another German General, Von Vietinghoff, was planning to proceed on leave on this day. In September 1962, we were at the receiving end of Chinese ruses and stratagems. The Chinese deception and cover plans were well conceived and executed, and thus our key officials were on leave or abroad.

On this day a Government spokesman made this astonishing statement: "Government are satisfied that effective steps have been taken to keep the Chinese out of our territory". The Chinese were already *inside* our territory and 9 Punjab was stretched over 7 miles facing them at the so-called bridges. It would be interesting to find out who gave Government such a satisfying assurance. The Chinese could have encroached at any point they chose and at any time that suited them. These and subsequent facile pronouncements in official bulletins helped to inflame public opinion and not the other way round, as claimed by Government apologists. Had the Thagla incident been played down till the military implications were studied, public opinion would not have reacted as violently as it did.

* * *

I decided to rest at Lumpu for the day and make no apology for this decision. I felt it my duty and responsibility to the troops to husband my strength and not risk my health. It was not easy to find replacements for brigadiers in command of Himalayan formations. I had the advantage of being acclimatised. Some officers and men who were rushed to the Dhola area succumbed to the hazards of the mountains, fell ill and took no further part in the proceedings. It is foolish to ignore the problems of living and moving in the mountains, at heights above 9,000 feet. In this respect, we must emulate the local Monpas who move slowly, rest frequently and undertake short daily stages. Over the centuries they have developed the physique and the lungs for surviving in the Himalayas. Commanders who later ordered forced marches, day after day, and who otherwise drove troops beyond human endurance, only courted disaster.

The day's halt at Lumpu enabled me to establish contact with my staff at Towang and Division. I was informed that two more battalions from the plains were being made available to me to complete my order of battle, to enable me "to evict the Chinese". GOC sent a signal promising to visit the Dhola area as soon as possible, to discuss the next phase of operations. I told him to postpone his visit till I had had a chance to visit 9 Punjab, carry out a ground reconnaissance and make an appreciation. Without seeing the ground over which we had to operate it would have been sheer folly to plan any sort of military operation.

* * *

I watched the air-drops at Lumpu and found to my chagrin, but not surprise, that 30 to 40 per cent of the parachutes were not opening out and the drops were total losses. The reason for this waste of air effort was due to our policy of retrieving and re-using old parachutes. For years we had been wasting energy and resources on collecting used parachutes from forward posts. These would lie in the open for months and would then be transported on mules to the nearest road-head, sometimes a distance of over 100 miles. A repair team would then attempt to patch them up for re-use. In the crisis of September-October 1962 they proved wasteful and increased our administrative problems. No real planning could be carried out, as no one could predict the percentage of good drops. A little foreign exchange given in time, or a geared-up indigenous source, might have seen us a little better prepared for such emergencies. Air supply was the life-line of the troops sent to the Dhola area to fight the Chinese, as there was no land route for maintenance.

This was a glaring example of misplaced economy at the expense of operational readiness.

I was also amazed to find that there were no 4-gallon jerrycans and kerosene oil was being air-dropped in 44-gallon drums. The despatchers did not care to reason how such a large and heavy load could be retrieved up steep inclines; and how was precious kerosene to be delivered to the troops in the Namka Chu in large containers, over a 13,000 feet pass.

* * *

*I left Lumpu on 18th September for the Namka Chu, in torrential rain. There is not a single habitation between Lumpu and Thagla, a distance of about 15 miles; the area consisting of a number of grazing grounds, with occasional huts built by the local herders for shelter. The large flat pastures became quagmires in the monsoons. The locals use logs to make crossing places for individual herders and their cattle. When large bodies of troops moved across these logs they became submerged, and the only way to negotiate marshy patches was to wade across in knee-deep mud. There is nothing more depressing than to wade through a morass of cold mud and slush, burdened with a heavy load, at a height over 10,000 feet.

We camped in a herder's hut at Serkhim for the night.

After a very early start on 19th September, we made for Bridges I and II *via* Hathungla Pass (13,400 feet). The going was still bad and progress slow due to more mud, slush, marshes and numerous steep ascents. The climb from the base of Hathungla to the summit took over 2½ hours. Thereafter the descent was extremely treacherous, steep and strained knees and thighs to breaking point. A false step over slippery, lichen-covered boulders would result in a sprained ankle. It was extremely difficult to maintain one's balance, even with a staff. We marched through thick

*See Sketch II for route from Lumpu to the Namka Chu and description of the Thagla Ridge battle Zone.

jungles with numerous bamboo groves at 11,000 feet! I reached Bridge I exhausted and mentally depressed. I had seen for myself the maintenance route from Lumpu to the Namka Chu. On the map it appears to be a mere hop, but on the ground it was as devilish a Line of Communication as can be imagined.

The weather was bitterly cold and the scanty shelters could house but a handful of men. The turn-round time for loaded men, from Lumpu to the Namka Chu Valley, was a minimum of 4 days. Porters and pioneers would have to carry 4 days' rations and sufficient clothing and bedding to survive the bitterly cold nights. In the circumstances the effective pay-load of an average pioneer/porter would be negligible. Later, experience showed that not more than 10 lbs. per carrier were delivered to the Punjabis. The more unscrupulous pioneers delivered nothing, as they either dumped their loads or ate the rations meant for the troops manning the river line.

For the second time since 8th September I was assailed by doubts and misgivings. How was I to build up and maintain the Punjabis? They had moved on hard scales and pouch ammunition. They would require their heavy weapons, mortar ammunition, digging tools, defence stores, snow-clothing and cumbersome daily rations for 500 men. They had to man the Lumpu dropping zone, dig-in, carry out local patrolling and confront the Chinese wherever they showed themselves. They could not be expected to provide their own porterage as well. It was absolutely impossible to move artillery pieces, even if gun-sites could be found.

The Karpola I route over a precipitous 16,500-foot Pass would be even more difficult. It would be a herculean task to move a brigade to the Namka Chu and maintain it there. Even in my most pessimistic moments I had not imagined that we would have to face such insurmountable difficulties. Now I would have to convince Division. Above Division there was a likelihood that my representation would be labelled as "belly-aching". I am reminded of General Wolfe's famous saying: "People must be of the profession to understand the disadvantages and difficulties we labour under, arising from the uncommon natural strength of the country". The Indian Cabinet of 1962, with its civilian advisers was not the forum in which a detailed grasp of military practicalities could be expected to flourish. Very few, if any, had the slightest idea of the manifold ramifications of war. They were not "of the profession". Would those "of the profession" then summon the necessary courage to appreciate the disadvantages and difficulties? At such a time a cool head and a firm grasp of basic military principles was essential.

I was met at Bridge I by Colonel Misra. I first congratulated him on his truly remarkable feat in reaching the river so speedily and in good order. 9 Punjab had lived up to my assessment of them as a first-rate infantry battalion.

We sat within sight of Bridge I with a solitary field sketch spread out in front of us. This sketch was the only 'map' available as there were no accurate Survey maps of this area. The ¼-inch editions were very old and vaguely based on the details provided by the British Officer who was deputed to visit the area and align the McMahon Line, as agreed at the Simla Conference of 1913-14. It showed the Namka Chu flowing from North to South, whereas it actually flowed from West to East. There is a human story to explain this strange lapse. It is said that the British Survey Officer got infatuated with a Bhutanese beauty and spent more time in Bhutan than he had allowed for. To return on time, he by-passed the Namka Chu Valley and headed straight for the Nyamjang Chu. As the latter flowed from North to South from the Thagla Watershed, he deduced that the Namka Chu must do the same! I have often wondered if this map misled our planners into thinking that 9 Punjab were facing east instead of north!

The rough field sketch was made by a lance-naik of the Assam Rifles detachment which had first established Dhola Post in May 1962. He had drawn it on a foolscap sheet, marking the bridges as he went along, showing approximate distances, as accurate pacing was not possible due to mud, snow and frequent detours to avoid buffs and thick patches of jungle. The sketch had one major discrepancy which was later to cost us dearly. As the lance-naik was running out of the foolscap sheet he showed a hut, named Tsangle by the locals, at the extreme left-hand corner. On the sketch it appeared to be two or three miles from Dhola. In fact it was over two days' march away. I was hard put to make anyone believe this. The sketch had become an immutable, accurate document, guiding the decisions of the top brass, from the Government to the section commander. It was not meant to replace a Survey map and yet it misled higher formations and Army HQ. They could not, or deliberately did not want to allow for the formidable time and space problems of the area.

A word about the so-called bridges would be timely. The "bridges" on the Namka Chu achieved international fame during September-October 1962. There was a great deal of talk of bridges being destroyed or battles to gain possession of bridges and so on. In fact these bridges were just two or three logs, tied together, and slung across the fast flowing Namka Chu, to enable herders and their cattle to cross to the high Thagla pastures. It is important to remember this, as orders were issued to defend, or ensure the security of these "bridges". They had no significance, political, strategic or tactical, as by the first week of October it was possible to wade across the Namka Chu at any point. This was one more example of grandiloquent orders being issued from a remote controlling source profoundly ignorant of the ground factors.

The river Namka Chu was a very fast-flowing, boulder-strewn mountain stream. At the narrowest point it is some 24 feet and at its widest about 120 feet. It is a feeder to the main river the Nyamjang Chu which flows from Khenzemane in the north to the Bhutan border at Bleting. The Namka Chu forms the catchment area for the Thagla Massif and the Tsangdhar-Hathungla heights. Its source is a group of small lakes at a height of 14,000 feet. It drops 8,000 feet in about 16 miles. It was unfordable only after torrential rains or at the time of melting snows; it was not a military obstacle except for short periods.

* * *

Colonel Misra had a great deal to tell me as I had not seen him since 10th September. 9 Punjab had reached Bridge II at about 8·30 a.m. on the 15th of September and found a company of Chinese troops on both sides of the river. The Chinese party was accompanied by a Chinese civilian official. They shouted in Hindi that we should withdraw from the Namka Chu (Kachileng according to them) area as it was Chinese territory. They said that the Indian and Chinese peoples had an unbreakable friendship and this friendship should not be marred by petty border incidents. They asked our men why we had moved regular troops and claimed that they were only Chinese Frontier Guards and not soldiers of the People's Liberation Army of China. Finally they asked us to send our local civil officers to discuss the exact location of the border, with a view to an amicable settlement and to prevent firing and bloodshed.

I mentioned to Misra that the Chinese actions were true to their previous methods as they had behaved in a similar manner at Longju and Khenzemane in 1959 and on other occasions.

Colonel Misra said that as his orders were to fire only in self-defence and to sit in front of the Chinese if they refused to vacate Indian territory, he had left the battalion less a company at Bridges I and II, by-passed the Chinese blocking his path, and made for Bridges III and IV with one company. Dhola Post was at Bridge III. He had hacked his way across a thick bamboo jungle. The Chinese did not trail his party.

He had reached Dhola at about midday and found that the Chinese had previously destroyed the logs over the river at Bridge III. A Chinese detachment of some 50 men had taken up position, after our relieving Assam Rifles party had reached Dhola, on the 13th of September.

Misra had left the company at Bridge III to face the Chinese and sent one platoon to Tsangdhar which was the commanding feature dominating Bridges III and IV and which had earlier been nominated as vital to the defence of Dhola.

Misra and his gallant men had completed the first phase of the operation, namely the relief of Dhola Post, the re-opening of the supply route and taking up positions opposite the Chinese wherever they had dug-in.

The Namka Chu from Bridges I to IV had become the *de-facto* military boundary. The Chinese had control of the whole of Thagla Ridge, which was ours. Unfortunately the Punjabis were pinned down over 7 to 9 miles in small localities, manning flag-posts to prevent minor incursions. Their localities had no mutual support, limited fields of fire and no room for manœuvre. They had only pouch ammunition and two 3-inch mortars.

After this briefing and rest, we left for Bridge II. I went straight to the Chinese sentry post on our side of the river. The logs at this bridge were intact. I saw two red-faced Chinese soldiers with marked

Mongoloid features, who appeared to be in their late teens. Their uniforms were excellent and they had modern automatic weapons. When they saw me approaching them they made an attempt to increase their alertness, brought their weapons to the ready and trained the barrels at my solar plexus. The Chinese on the far bank were watching. When I attempted to speak to one of the sentries in Hindi, he merely grunted and waved me away with his rifle.

I must admit I was impressed with the Chinese soldiers. These were no scruffy Frontier Guards; they appeared to be healthy, well-clad, well-armed and determined troops. I later told my GOC of my favourable impression. For a long time there had been some loose talk in the Army that the Chinese in Tibet were ill-equipped and not as good as they had been made out to be. This view was allegedly expressed by Gen. Kaul, in his capacity as CGS, to the Infantry Commanders Conference held at Mhow, in mid-1962.

The Chinese later claimed that they knew of my arrival at the river bank on 19th September. While I was being taken back to my place of imprisonment, a Chinese staff officer came to see me and asked why I had deemed it necessary to intervene in a petty border situation. He claimed I was the Deputy Commander of 4 Infantry Division, and my presence at that early stage indicated our preparations and intention to attack. He blamed me for escalating a small border incident into a major battle! I was puzzled and wondered how this officer could have known of my arrival. Of course he may have obtained this information from other prisoners or he could have made an intelligent guess. However looking back, I realised that the information could have been passed on to the Chinese by an agent.

I recalled that the guide given to me for my trip to the river looked unusually alert and intelligent for a Monpa, and I remember mentioning this to my

Intelligence Officer. My suspicions were really aroused when I found that he had disappeared after our arrival at Bridge I. When questioned, my Intelligence Officer said that he had gone across to the Chinese-occupied Thagla Ridge to find his cattle, as well as to obtain information about the Chinese. Was he the classic spy working for both sides?

I believe that this same Monpa guide escorted Gen. Kaul and his party when they came to the Dhola area on 7th/8th October. I do not wish to malign anyone. I have recounted this incident merely to emphasise the necessity for vigilance in these matters. One doubtful guide can cause a great deal of harm. There must be greater co-ordination between the Army, Intelligence Staff and Civil Administration.

After my visit to the Chinese sentries we returned to the CO's command post. At this time, I was handed my copy of the most fantastic order issued between the 8th of September and the 20th of October 1962. The signal with a Military Operations Directorate file number (which I knew by heart after four years) was from the Chief of Army Staff to the entire chain of command. The gist of the order was:

> "*9 Punjab will capture Thagla, contain Yumtsola and Karpola II by 19th September*".

This was not a feasible order based on an estimate of the situation. It was another slogan sent as a result of political pressure. Apart from the gross impropriety of issuing orders directly to an infantry battalion, Gen. Thapar could have misled the Government into thinking that the operation could be carried out. Politicians do not expect their military chiefs to agree to undertake impossible tasks. A threat of resignation might have sobered the political bosses at that early stage. Gen. Thapar owed it to the nation to have done so.

The tasks given were beyond the scope of 9 Punjab. Later when Thapar was criticised for not evicting the Chinese as promised he is reported to have blamed the forward formation in words reminiscent of Marshal Joffre's famous: "Our troops have not shown in the field the offensive qualities expected of them!"

The Chief's signal created quite a mystery as it could not be traced, in Delhi, after the defeat in NEFA. The first question that I was asked by Gen. J. N. Chaudhuri, after my repatriation from China, was whether I had received any signal directly from the late Chief, to evict the Chinese. I promptly gave him a verbatim recitation of the extraordinary message. He shook his head in amazement at my ability to recite the signal by heart. I then told him that the message was so absurd that I would probably chant it on my death-bed.

This order was issued while the Prime Minister and Finance Minister were abroad and the Defence Minister was having his western clothes dry-cleaned for New York. The CGS of the Army was enjoying the salubrious climate of Kashmir. All the key desks in Delhi were empty.

How and why was this order issued? Gen. Kaul tells us that the Defence Minister held two meetings on 15th and 17th September in Delhi. On the 15th it was "decided" to contain the Chinese near Thagla and, if possible, to establish a post at Karpola and Yumtsola. Accordingly Army HQ issued this order to Eastern Command:

> "*9 Punjab will capture the Chinese position one thousand yards North-East of Dhola and contain them South of Thagla*".

On 17th September Gen. Sen said, "It would take more time for the Brigade to concentrate (his earlier estimate of 10 days being incorrect). It was decided to carry out defensive reconnaissance and capture any small Chinese pockets and dominate the area (south of Thagla)". This was another meaningless exercise in verbal gymnastics. The Chinese already held the whole of the Thagla Ridge and they had not obliged us with 'small pockets' to swallow. But one thing emerges clearly, that the seeds of Kaul's subsequent plan to sit behind the Chinese were planted at this meeting.

Gen. Thapar overlooked the following vital military factors at the time he issued his order. The Chinese had deployed more than two companies opposite us and a prudent estimate would indicate that the rest of the battalion would be near at hand. (Units always operate in recognised bodies and not in a count of heads.) 9 Punjab did not have the necessary superiority to dislodge the Chinese.

9 Punjab was pinned down opposite the Chinese posts and could not mount an attack without altering their positions and forsaking their original tasks. An attack cannot be mounted under enemy observation.

The terrain made it impossible for an attack to be mounted between Bridges I to IV. The precipitous slopes would have caused our troops to be massacred. On the far side of the fast-flowing Namka Chu the Punjabis would face not only prepared Chinese positions, but the great wall of mountains rising almost vertically immediately behind the river to the Thagla Massif. They would have to wade the roaring, boulder-strewn river as they had no bridging equipment before attacking the mountains head-on, while a comfortably entrenched enemy, watching them throughout from a vantage point, could pick them off as he pleased. On this battlefield Nature was as formidable an enemy as the Chinese.

The men had no rations and were short of ammunition and porters. They had come on hard scales and pouch ammunition. Every precious round had to be carried by the men for several miles over a 13,400-foot pass. For the defending Chinese there would be an abundance of everything.

We had no fire support except for the two mortars and a few bombs. A Chinese infantry battalion has a great deal more fire-power.

We had no digging tools or saws to cut logs for bunkers, or defence stores (mines and wire). If we attacked the Chinese and gained ground we could not consolidate and hold such ground against a counter-attack. There were no reinforcements within 15 days' march of the Namka Chu. If we precipitated a hasty, major skirmish and lost, the Chinese could advance to Hathungla or even to Lumpu and forestall our build-up. We had no firm base; any reckless advance or attack without securing a firm base to protect our line of communication would have been sheer madness and would certainly have resulted in the annihilation of the attacking force.*

I flatly refused to obey this order and informed Divisional HQ accordingly. GOC agreed with me and protested to XXXIII Corps, who in turn asked Eastern Command to have the order countermanded. I signalled GOC that I would not accept any further "orders" till I had completed my reconnaissance and had time to collect my thoughts for a detailed appreciation. I had not only to contend with a tactical battle at Brigade level but with the administrative problems of a major theatre of war.

I ordered Misra to ignore the signal and await orders from me. There was all-round relief. Indian troops are obedient and disciplined. They would have given their lives if ordered.

After a quick meal Misra and I discussed the various factors that had a bearing on the orders to evict the Chinese. It was at once apparent that it was not possible to do so with his battalion. We then visited the various company localities. At Bridge II I met the Company Second-in-command, Subedar Partap Singh. I was taken aback at seeing him at the front as I had attended his farewell party in Towang and had also met him at Misamari awaiting a berth

* These points remained valid on 25th September and were included in my Appreciation — *Author*.

on the train bound for Meerut, his Regimental Centre. He was proceeding on pension after completing 28 years of gallant service, mostly in the field in World War II and thereafter guarding India's extensive borders. When I asked him why he had not left for Meerut, he gave me this answer, "Sahib, is this the time to go on pension when the battalion is likely to be involved in an action?" He had voluntarily rejoined the unit and had walked many miles to the Namka Chu. He was later killed in action. This humble soldier had displayed more patriotism and sense of duty than many others who should have set an example.

At another platoon post I stopped to have tea with the men. I was offered a large mug of sweet tea. I knew that the battalion had been without sugar for some days and were drinking tea with salt. There were no grouses and no complaints. The Indian soldier asks for very little and does not worry if this little is not provided. Sometimes this sterling quality has been misused by incompetent staff officers to cover their lack of planning and organisation.

I also noted that the post was preparing a meal of rice, a cereal that is not relished by Sikhs and Dogras. North Indians prefer flour. When I asked why they had no flour I was told that they could not spare a man to carry the flat metal board (called a *tawa*) and preferred to carry an additional box of ammunition. The commander had parcelled out the rations to each individual to save man-power. Even a humble non-commissioned-officer had shown more sense of administration than some senior and more educated officers. God bless the Punjabis who cheerfully bore the hardships of the Himalayas in the cause of their country. They lived on rice and salt for the first five days – hard scales indeed!

* * *

To complete the story of the 18th let us return to Delhi. A senior Civil Servant was telling the Press that "The Army had been told to drive away the Chinese from our territory in NEFA". Ministers, Civil Servants and even the Army Chief were taking decisions regardless of the military situation and were blissfully unconcerned with the fact of whether the Army had the resources and capacity to develop a favourable military balance *vis-a-vis* China. No one seemed to require the services of senior officers who knew the ground and had appreciated the military factors.

The situation was explosive with regular troops of two big countries facing each other across a narrow river; an incident which could spark off a battle was inevitable sooner or later. The situation was unnatural, unprecedented and bordered on the eerie. This was the outcome of the ludicrous ideas of digging-in, in front of the Chinese wherever we found them.

Was this going to be another Longju or Khenzemane; or was it the prelude to something bigger? It would all depend on whether we kept our heads. Would we act in a mature and sensible manner? Would the top Army Brass ensure military sanity?

* * *

I started out on the last leg of my ground reconnaissance to Bridges III and IV on 20th September using the diversion made by the Punjabis. We trekked through more mud and slush. The gradients were not as steep as hitherto but were just as tiring to walk through, shin-deep in mud. It was as difficult to make progress on the down-slopes. To maintain one's balance with a load was a feat. The carry from Bridge I to Bridge III was another full day's march, making a total of three days from the dropping zone at Lumpu. The military problem was becoming increasingly one of porterage and delivery.

I met the Junior Commissioned Officer of Dhola Post and Major Chaudhry, Commander of the Punjab company that had been located there to bolster-up the morale of the Assam Rifles personnel. I questioned the JCO closely about the Chinese intrusion on the 8th of September and his frantic messages. He confessed that he might have inflated his original figure of Chinese intruders to ensure timely Army help. His reasons were sound and understandable. He said 600/1,200 Chinese troops would attract the immediate reaction of the Army. If he had reported 60 in the first instance he would have been told to deal with the situation himself. He also told me that he had been apprehensive for some days, as a week earlier a party from his post had been threatened by a Chinese patrol. His party was on its way to the main post at Khenzemane to draw pay for the men, when it was accosted by the Chinese. The Chinese officer in charge had asked our men to leave Chinese territory (Thagla) failing which they would be thrown out by force. With this incident fresh in his mind he thought that the Chinese had come to make good their threat and liquidate his post. I now do not blame the poor man as I would probably have felt and acted in the same way if I had been isolated, many miles away from help, and faced by a larger body of Chinese troops.

I studied the ground and realised that Dhola was militarily useless, indefensible and dominated by Chinese positions and located in a trap. It had poor approaches, no fields of fire and no mutual support. The Hathungla and Karpola I routes could not be defended by one battalion. A secure base for operations was an elementary precaution but could not be established as our Lines of Communication and the Lumpu dropping zone were vulnerable to a counter-thrust. It was impossible even for a brigade to provide its own firm base and assault troops. However since Dhola was a prestige post and the orders were that we were not to succumb to Chinese threats, there was no other option but to leave it as a symbol of our determination to retain the posts we had established under the Forward Policy.

The Dhola area was unsuitable as a forming-up place for mounting any form of attack against the intruding Chinese. I could see the three tiers of Chinese defence positions, the first was on the river bank opposite our own troops; the second half-way up the Thagla slopes on Paitsai Spur and the third on the crest of the Ridge. The northern slopes of Thagla were less wooded than the Namka Chu Valley, with reasonable fields of fire, and it would be suicidal to attempt a frontal assault. To silence the network of machine-guns on the forward slopes and the mortars on the reverse slopes, would require more artillery than we could ever hope to bring up. We did not have a single gun or heavy mortar.

I then studied the Tsangdhar feature, south of Dhola Post. It was some 3,000/4,000 yards south of Thagla and dominated both banks of the Namka Chu. It was the obvious feature on which to locate our main defended area once the "flag-waving" phase of operations was over. Tsangdhar had a flat top which provided the only possible gun positions. Colonel Misra told me that the Tsangdhar feature was a potential dropping zone for Dakota aircraft, as there was a suitable area approximately 120 yards by about 40/60 yards wide. He requested me to arrange for air-drops for his platoon to save him the long carry from Lumpu *via* the Bridges – a turn-round of some 7 days.

Little did I envisage that this innocent request would later mislead everyone, specially the inveterate optimists, and be the major plank on which they rested rash and ill-advised military and political decisions. Tsangdhar was later foisted on the Air Force as a full-fledged dropping zone, to drop the vast tonnages required, within 9 days, forcing them to use Fairchild Packets (C-119). They scattered their precious loads in deep ravines from where they could not be retrieved. They attempted to drop artillery guns and ammunition.

These feverish drops, under the noses of the Chinese, naturally gave the impression that we were 'building-up'. There is more to air-supply than wild drops into inaccessible ravines, and vague hopes that the troops will be able to salvage something.

We returned to Bridge I where I spent the night before returning to Lumpu. Colonel Misra finalised our notes for an appreciation of the ground, enemy dispositions, relative strengths (including fire-power), administration, build-up and weather factors.

* * *

At about 10.30 p.m. on 20th September the Chinese sentry on the south bank, near Bridge II threw a grenade at our sentry post which was a few yards away. Our post opened up and thereupon firing started from opposite sides of the Namka Chu. Two Chinese sentries were killed and two wounded. Our casualties were five wounded.

This firing marked the end of the first phase of the Thagla operations. The confrontation of regular troops of battalion strength could no longer be classified as a border incident which could be localised. It was evident that a major clash would develop. The Chinese could not be evicted, herded out or expelled from Thagla Ridge.

I set out on my return journey on 21st of September and reached Lumpu at 1.00 p.m. on 22nd September, where I met my friend Mr. Mongia, the Political Officer. He told me that he had come forward to meet the local Chinese Civil Official to discuss the Chinese incursion at Thagla. Due to the intransigent attitude of the Chinese, he had been ordered not to hold such talks.

Mr. Mongia was an ex-Army officer who had opted for the NEFA Frontier Service. He was a cadet when I was an Instructor at the Indian Military Academy in 1947-49, and normally we got on extremely well. He gave me the good news that he had been able to mobilise some 500 local porters, as the Army's needs were "now being accorded the highest priority".

Finally, we both discussed the employment of local porters and agreed that as firing had started at Bridge II, we would not use them beyond Serkhim. This was sensible and humane, but increased my administrative problem. Now it would be virtually impossible to achieve a build-up using Army pioneers only.

On my return journey, I met many casuals of 9 Punjab marching to rejoin the Battalion. These men had walked from Misamari in small parties on their own, and it will always be to their credit that not a single man shirked his duty. Many of the men were walking in torn canvas boots. The rubber soles and toe-caps had perished. However they bore this minor irritation cheerfully. When I jokingly remarked that Thagla was a poor substitute for leave, they promptly remarked that I too had cancelled my leave and preferred the delights of Thagla! Here was proof of the *esprit de corps* and sense of duty of our jawans.. It galled me to hear all the loose talk of how our jawans did not offer a fight, and other more vicious accusations.

* * *

On 20th September, the Army Commander is reported to have informed the Government that "a second battalion would reach Dhola area on 24th of September and the third battalion on the 29th, thus completing the concentration of a brigade in the 'requisite area'." I did not know of this promise at the time.

CHAPTER XI

"Evict The Chinese"

MY RETURN from the Thagla reconnaissance marks the beginning of the second phase of the Thagla Operation during which senior officers were "planning" and units were being inducted and equipped. I shall first recapitulate the circumstances under which plans had to be drawn up.

Dhola Post had been relieved and communications re-established.

9 Punjab had reached the Namka Chu and were deployed opposite Bridges I to IV to encourage the Dhola Garrison, prevent further minor incursions and stake a claim to what was left of our territory. The Namka Chu had become the *de facto* military boundary. Regular troops of India and China were facing each other across a narrow mountain stream.

After triggering off the Thagla incident, the Chinese used "every club in the bag" to sap our will to fight. They broadcast that talks between the two countries were imminent. They suggested talks at the petty local level to sort out the Thagla misunderstanding. The men began to wonder whether there would be war or talks. This is demoralising for troops in close contact with the enemy. We had no help from our own official organs and broadcasts thus placing the local commanders in a most awkward position. A while later, the phoney-war atmosphere was accentuated by the attendance of our senior Embassy officials at the National Day celebrations at Peking, on 1st October. Chinese and Indian troops had started exchanging fire from 20th September and there had been casualties on both sides. The troops were understandably indignant and confused. Enemies do not exchange diplomatic niceties and lethal fire on the same night. The civilian nabobs of the Ministries of External Affairs and Defence were no doubt still working on the Crimean War slogan of "Theirs but to do or die, theirs not to reason why". *Circa* 1962 we entertained some strange notions.

The Chinese stepped up their propaganda campaign. Loud-hailers proclaimed the eternal friendship between the Chinese and Indian peoples. Chinese announcers (speaking in the chastest Hindi) regaled our men with the information that as there would soon be talks, there should be no firing to foul up the required cordiality for settling this minor dispute. On occasion, they questioned our presence in the Namka Chu Valley and blared out their case, to substantiate their claim to the Thagla Ridge. In the absence of counter-propaganda they did some harm in planting the seeds of doubt in the minds of the simple jawans.

Sometimes the Chinese would magnanimously inform us that they were about to fell a tree, and that we should not get unduly perturbed if we heard loud crashing sounds. It was difficult to maintain a war-like atmosphere in the near-farcical setting. Never in the history of war could two regular armies have sat facing each other across a 40-foot water gap, exchanging fire and gossip; without a declaration of war; without a breach in diplomatic relations; and with vague possibilities of talks to settle the issues which had brough them face to face.

HQ Eastern Command and HQ XXXIII Corps who had been trying to cobble together a "brigade" had at last succeeded. They had been allowed by Army HQ to "use" 1/9 Gorkhas and 2 Rajput, who were being rushed post-haste to the "battlefield" by forced marches.

Miscellaneous sub-units were being directed to join 7 Brigade. Due to lack of porterage there was a serious bottle neck *en route* and sub-units were arriving without their equipment and weapons. Even by press-ganging Monpa women and children it was not possible for the Civil Administration to find enough load-carriers to meet the requirements of the ambitious build-up rashly promised by those who had no idea of local conditions. The men invariably arrived exhausted.

Thus was the name and title of 7 Infantry Brigade given to the miscellany of troops hurriedly marshalled for what was thought would be a limited show of force. Having been caught napping Army HQ sought to restore the position by collecting the first unfortunate units they could lay their hands on. The so-called 7 Brigade did not have any affiliation, no collective training and no time to get to know each other. It normally takes months of solid joint training as a formation to mould a team, develop mutual trust and confidence and to practice battle drills. Three battalions grouped together at the eleventh hour do not form a fighting brigade.

I mention this because in his memoirs Gen. Kaul has written that "If 7 Brigade was not up to the mark, then its own commander - Brigadier Dalvi—should be asked to explain". Since Kaul's own General Staff Branch "created" 7 Brigade after the Chinese incursion, the explanation, if any, is due from him. Everybody knows that brigadiers do not form their own commands. It is the first duty of a commander to ascertain the state of his command before launching them into battle. It is too late now to find out if the troops we sent to evict the Chinese were up to the mark or not. Kaul has been less than fair to the officers and men of 7 Brigade who never claimed that they were trained and ready to engage the superior Chinese force.

The Gorkhas and the Rajputs fetched up at Lumpu by about 26th September. I was supposed to give them further orders. I could not do so as I had received none myself (other than the unreasonable one of evicting the Chinese). When Lt.-Col. M. S. Rikh of the Rajputs asked me what I had in mind for his units I told him that there was no definite task for the immediate future and that I had first to collate my impressions for discussion with the GOC who was expected soon.

Both COs were personal friends and could talk to me more freely than they would have done had they been shackled by military protocol. They were disgusted with the arrangements made for their moves and had harrowing tales to tell about conditions on the improvised Line of Communication. The move of the 2nd Rajputs tells its own story.

The Rajputs had been concentrated at Charduar (Assam) in May 1962 after completing a three-year operational tenure at Walong in Lohit Frontier Division of NEFA. They were earmarked to move to the Lorried Brigade of the Armoured Division in Mathura, in Uttar Pradesh, in August 1962. In the intervening period the Battalion was to train for its new role in "open warfare". Before being relieved the Battalion had been ordered to hand over its wireless sets, serviceable digging tools, *dahs* and most other units stores to the relieving unit, 6 Kumaon.

Walong was to be the scene of a major Sino-Indian battle in November 1962 and the Rajputs knew every inch of ground in that area. Because we refused to countenance the possibility of an all-out war we did not think in strategic terms. Had we done so, the Rajputs would surely have been earmarked if not actually sent to Walong.

On 9th September the GOC had sent for Rikh and told him that his Battalion would be moving to Towang to "join 7 Brigade". GOC promised that the unit deficiencies would be made up on arrival there. At this time the unit could barely muster 550 all ranks.

The Battalion moved on 10th September in 70 one-tonners which were shed after three days as they could proceed no further due to the state of the road. The men had to march from Senge heavily loaded.

As they were not acclimatised to heights many of the men vomited blood while climbing Sela Pass and others contracted fever. To make matters worse it rained heavily throughout and the temperature dropped. Clothed in cotton, olive-green summer uniforms, the Battalion had to spend many nights in the open under improvised shelters made of tarpaulins and ground sheets.

After a day's rest at Towang the Battalion resumed the march to Lumpu where the last man finally clocked in on 24th September. It had taken them 15 days to reach. The men were exhausted and needed a rest before being committed to operations.

I must pay a tribute to this fine Battalion. Not one man fell out. Despite the hardships they were cheerful. When I spoke to the Subedar-Major and asked him if everything was all right, he gave me this proud answer: "Sahib, the Paltan is ready for any task that is required of it. The men will be fit in a day or so".

The story of the Gorkhas was much the same. They also had arrived exhausted and with major deficiencies as they too had been stripped of their equipment. Both the units were not "fit for war" in their present state. This then was the "brigade" being assembled in the "requisite area" to keep the rash promise made at Delhi.

I recalled the famous words of the Duke of Wellington: "I do not know how they will impress the enemy, but by God, they frighten me!" I wish the Chief or Army Commander had taken time off to inspect these units before agreeing to undertake an operation against the Chinese. They would have been less inclined to compromise or accept a gamble.

One morning I witnessed the unusual sight of Rajput squads doing weapon training in the same way as they would do in a peaceful cantonment in India. When I questioned the CO as to what he was doing he told me that he was giving his new recruits instruction in priming grenades as they had not been taught to do this at the Regimental Centre before being passed out. For years the Indian Army had been kept short of grenades and the men had not been able to train on this basic infantry weapon. These were the men who were soon to be ordered to evict the Chinese.

Commander Artillery 4 Division, Brigadier Kalyan Singh, had taken over responsibility for the "defence" of Towang (with the 1st Sikhs and one battery of Mountain Guns from the original order of battle of 7 Brigade). From the very outset there was a divided aim, i.e. to defend Towang as well as to challenge the Chinese intrusion into the Thagla area. In the event we were weak everywhere. There was "a certain woollyness of thought and indecision of purpose". Despite the mounting tension there was no strategic plans or dispositions throughout the September crisis.

The Machine-Gun unit commander was in charge of trooping arrangements on the Line of Communication from Misamari to Towang on an *ad-hoc* basis. He too was employed as a spare body as the poor man could not co-ordinate machine-gun fire over 300 miles!

Supplies for both 7 Brigade and the Towang Sector were entirely by air. Lumpu had begun to receive air-drops and a skeleton supply arrangement to the Punjabis had been organised, with staging posts at Serkhim and at the foot of Hathungla Pass. The tempo of drops increased gradually and the Punjabis were steadily built-up. By the 30th of September I was able to provide them with three first lines of ammunition and 21 days' rations. I also sent them all the available bedding, clothing and digging tools. We did not have the "luxury" items of mines and wire, elementary in normal defence stores. The Punjabis were well dug-in and reasonably well-stocked. They were exchanging fire, round for round, with the Chinese every day and getting the better of these fire-fights.

The Chinese had a healthy respect for the entrenched Punjabis. It is interesting to note that the Chinese did not attack them on the 20th of October.

9 Punjab were built-up under crippling handicaps. After the first exchange of fire, I could not use civil porters beyond Serkhim where we had organised a transhipment point, under the Rajputs. The Pioneers who completed the final carry were not a success because they could barely deliver 10 lbs. after allowing for their own rations for four days, and other survival loads. Their carrying capacity compared unfavourably with the locals, not only because the latter were able to carry heavier loads but were self-contained in every way. Some unscrupulous Pioneers were dumping their loads on the way or eating the rations meant for the forward troops. In sheer desperation Misra decided to collect vital loads with his own men, all the way to the river. It was disgusting to see two sturdy Sikhs carrying a live goat. The burden of porterage was a serious embarrassment to a battalion which was in contact with the enemy, under-strength and responsible for its own casualty clearance. We were paying for our negligence in not providing for mobility in the mountains and the right type of tinned rations.

Collection of drops was the responsibility of the Brigade and 200 men each from the Rajputs and the Gorkhas were employed daily on this chore. The primitive and improvised set-up made a deep impression on Gen. Umrao Singh, the Corps Commander, and was the primary reason which emboldened him to defy the general clamour for evicting the Chinese, regardless of the other factors. He was insistent that we should adhere to the basic principles of administration and was emphatic that there would be no concentration in the Namka Chu until the necessary administrative stock-piling had been achieved. He was deeply affected by the sight of the Sikhs carrying goats.

While the Punjabis were being stocked, we were

trying to equip the Rajputs and the Gorkhas to full scales of weapons, ammunition, wireless sets, winter clothing and other unit stores. These units should never have been sent to Lumpu without these basic items which could have been provided at a rail or roadhead, instead of being despatched by air. For days they were merely eating up valuable rations when the available airlift could have been used for building up reserves. Their precipitate induction, in pursuance of a promise to concentrate a brigade in the requisite area by a given date, enabled someone in Delhi to move yet another little pin-head on a map; but the battle-worthiness of the brigade was limited to pin-pricks.

I mention these trivia because I wish to emphasise that wars are not decided in the corridors of the Central Secretariat at Delhi. Wars are not based on wishful thinking. Wars are not based on rash promises nor improvident expectations. The Himalayan Mountains cannot be ignored on the plea of urgent political necessity.

The efforts of the troops were not appreciated. The feeling in Delhi was that the forward troops were lethargic. Later, Gen. Prasad told me that Gen. Sen had said: "If 7 Brigade do not get a move on, you know what to expect" – the classic alibi for "blaming the executors and exonerating the planners". I shall always regret that Gen. Sen had not been able to find the time to visit the forward area to see for himself whether 7 Brigade was doing its best or whether everybody in the rear was doing his best for 7 Brigade.

* * *

On the 22nd of September while the Prime Minister, Defence Minister and the Finance Minister were abroad, the officiating Defence Minister, Mr. Raghuramiah, is said to have held a war-council in his office to discuss the Thagla incident. The Army Chief estimated that the Chinese had one battalion in the area – one company near Dhola, one company north-east of Dhola and one company at Thagla Pass. He asserted that the Chinese could easily reinforce their strength opposite Dhola, retaliate elsewhere in NEFA or attack our posts in Ladakh. In spite of this it was "decided" by Government that as a matter of policy (pressure of public opinion), there was no alternative but to evict the Chinese from the Dhola area. Gen. Thapar then asked for written, formal orders as he was being forced to take action against his better judgement and because of the possible consequences of any rash action on our part.

This momentous written order was issued by a Joint Secretary, during the absence of the three senior members of the Defence Committee of the Cabinet, apparently after a trans-Atlantic telephone conversation with Menon. The unbelievable part is that the Chief was satisfied with this order and passed it on to Gen. Sen. "To be right and overruled is not forgiven to persons in responsible positions!"

Later when the Corps and Divisional Commanders, who were fully in the operational picture, protested, they were brushed aside and ordered to prepare a plan. Up to this stage Gen. Sen appeared to be a malignant shadow over the military horizon. He never visited the forward area and merely dug his spurs into the unfortunate Umrao and kept urging everyone forward. When the stark realities became apparent, Sen was in a quandary as he found it difficult to convince Government (through his Chief) to resile from its avowed declarations of evicting the Chinese.

The Government order was soon to be conveyed to me by my GOC. This was the point at which the "buck stopped". There was no one I could pass the order to. We now had the ludicrous situation where pressure of public opinion eventually became the "aim" (or mission as the Americans put it) for a military appreciation by a field commander at brigade level. This was indeed a strange manifestation of civil supremacy. The Government of India had decided to order the tide back because a mass of uninformed public opinion was allegedly ordering it to the brink. "Great things are done when men and mountains meet: This is not done by jostling in the street". (*Gnomic verses.*)

This then was the setting at the time the Army was ordered to formulate plans to evict the Chinese at the earliest. No responsible Army officer had any faith in carrying out the task, or any conception of how this task could be achieved. It fell to my lot to set out the military arguments relevant to the attainment of this object.

Chapter XII

The Final Appreciation, 23/29 September 1962

On 23rd September my Brigade Major, Major Kharbanda, joined me at Lumpu with a skeleton 'G' staff and a most welcome typewriter. I had not relished the idea of preparing comprehensive notes of my reconnaissance in longhand and without the help of a staff. I had already been separated from my staff for nine critical days.

I was determined to present as objective a military picture as I could to my GOC as I thought that my views must prevail and have a vital bearing on our future policy. The reconnaissance to the Namka Chu had made it abundantly clear that the task of clearing out the Chinese was a pipe-dream. I believed that the harsh realities of the Thagla confrontation would be conclusive and that once the magnitude of the task was appreciated we would have to modify our national policy. It appears that I miscalculated the political imperatives which were to force us into an unequal contest with the Chinese. At that time I did not know of the various Delhi war-conferences.

When Gen. Prasad arrived on the 25th he told me that he too had been evicted from his HQ and had been ordered to move on foot to Lumpu without waiting for a helicopter. The "plan" and "D-Day" for evicting the Chinese now dominated all thinking, and Prasad must move at once. Prasad was a General of the Indian Army and deserved better treatment than this. He was entitled to the normal courtesy and consideration befitting his rank, age and the state of his health. He had contracted some lung ailment just after World War II as a result of flying with the Indian Air Force.

The order to walk was not only improper but cruel to boot. He was the second key commander to wander in the blue and lose touch with everyone while trekking in the Himalayas. I had not spoken to him since the 13th. I recall this story to highlight the fact that political haste invariably infects the military command and commanders tend to forget the norms of courtesy and decorum. Gen. Prasad's arrival at Lumpu was not a pretty sight. His professional utility was limited as he had had no time to visit the Namka Chu. His advice would be confined to accepting or rejecting what I told him.

My Appreciation of September 1962 is a pivotal document. It is capable of various interpretations by different people. Gen. Kaul has used copious extracts to weave a claim of reprieval for his impatience and haste between 5th and 10th October. He has manipulated passages to insinuate that he was on occasion a helpless spectator of events which had gathered momentum before his arrival and which he could neither halt nor reverse; and that he was compelled to implement the defective plans devised at the tactical level. He has muted his role in moving 7 Brigade to the Namka Chu; and later getting it embroiled with the Chinese on 10th October. He omits the antecedents of the Appreciation and how it came into being, but quotes excerpts to achieve his ends. He has attributed some parts to Gen. Umrao and others to the Brigade Commander. In one instance he even paraphrases a portion and claims it as his own.

It is pointless to consider any battle planning critically without relating it to the precise circumstances and conditions prevailing at the time and place. This is axiomatic but it is a fact that has been conveniently overlooked in certain partisan post-mortems. A commander's line of action cannot be properly appraised unless set against the background of the exact atmosphere under which he had to function. This was especially true of the Thagla episode which to an exceptionally high degree was a mass of impossibilities which were never allowed to receive consideration due to political pressure and a compliant military command. Instead of shielding the Army from improper orders, Generals used the goad on their sceptical and reluctant subordinates.

Gen. Sen had told Gen. Umrao that Government had taken the "decision" to evict the Chinese and that the operation *had to be completed at the earliest.* Umrao, unable to resist this order, had instructed Prasad to produce an outline plan to achieve this aim. Gen. Prasad asked me to produce an Appreciation and outline plan. Although the Government order was unattainable, no one in Delhi had had the courage to say so in clear and unmistakable terms.

In a disciplined Army field commanders do not disobey orders, they try their best to implement them. It would be an evil day if overt or covert disobedience were to be encouraged. All that they can do is to point out the facts and it is for their military superiors to advise the political bosses. This is especially true when a country is not at war and military action has been ordered on the basis of certain political assumptions which local commanders have no grounds to challenge.

For the benefit of the lay reader I shall explain the procedure for making an Appreciation. The basis of an appreciation is the task given to a commander by his superior. It is well to remember that commanders do not decide to make appreciations on their own and plan attacks or offensives against a foreign country. Mr. Menon is right when he avers that such a decision can only be taken by Government. It is rather far-fetched to insinuate that plans had been drawn up at the divisional or brigade level for any form of overt action against the Chinese in a burst of misguided enthusiasm.

The tasks given to Gen. Prasad, GOC of 4 Division, were:

(*a*) You will evict the Chinese from the North Bank of the Namka Chu.

(*b*) You will contain Thagla.

(*c*) You will patrol towards Tsangle.

These were virtually the same tasks that the Chief had issued in his earlier signal and which were held in abeyance. Despite the changing situation the aims remained relentlessly constant, as Government would not budge from their declared intention to evict the Chinese. Gen. Thapar had washed his hands off the messy business by passing on the order to his subordinates and considered himself covered by written instructions from his civilian bosses. This being so he did not deem it necessary to convert the Government order into a military plan.

Before ordering a lower formation to undertake a task, the next superior is generally expected to carry out a quick preliminary appreciation to ensure that the tasks given are feasible, having regard to the resources available and also that they are within the bounds of immediate planning. A good commander thinks two down (in the case of a brigade, down to companies). This is the real art of generalship as generals are not expected to post-office impractical orders. Gen. Thapar dispensed with this requirement and so did Gen. Sen.

The next point to bear in mind is that an appreciation is valid at the time it is written and for as long as the military situation remains relatively constant. Any subsequent change nullifies an appreciation made to cope with a given military situation. On 22nd September, Gen. Thapar estimated the Chinese strength in the Thagla area to be a battalion and this was the force which he expected his subordinates to evict. On 5th October, after Gen. Kaul took over command of the NEFA operations, the Chinese strength had increased to at least a brigade. This vital change in the relative strengths was enough to render the Appreciation obsolete. A brigade does not take on a brigade without fire support, without a secure Line of Communication and without the bare essential administrative build-up. Events had superseded earlier plans and hopes. It was up to the higher commanders to restore the military balance in our favour by positioning the minimum superior force to dislodge the enemy or revoke the order.

Gen. Thapar had not laid down any relevant terms of reference for the Appreciation (except for the vague political phrase "at the earliest"); nor had he disseminated any special Intelligence summary giving his assessment of the overall Chinese intentions, concentrations, dispositions, strength and fire-power. An appreciation is not made in a military vacuum; it is a process of thought from which is derived the best course to achieve the tactical aim. The terms of reference lay down the limits within which the commander is expected to confine himself. In the absence of any high-level Intelligence Appreciation, local commanders had to rely on the information obtained from observation and what was available from the local Intelligence Bureau representative. This is a dangerous basis for plunging into a likely battle. The absence of an intelligence assessment is the ultimate proof that Thapar had not issued a military order.

The Appreciation was thus in compliance with the Chief's brief orders and was not formulated independently. GOC 4 Division and Commander 7 Brigade were in much the same predicament as Gen. Wolfe who once said: "In this situation there is such a choice of difficulties that I own myself at a loss to determine".

The local commanders were under no illusions that the task of evicting the Chinese was militarily impossible. The modest plan evolved for tackling the Chinese battalion, under duress from the Chief, was in the nature of a police action to herd out intruders; and a probe in strength to gauge the Chinese reaction. It was never envisaged that 7 Brigade would mount a set-piece attack to capture the Chinese positions.

My first reaction to the GOC's request for assistance in the preparation of a formal appreciation, for onward transmission to Delhi, for implementing these preposterous tasks, was to refuse point-blank. I exchanged some hot words with Gen. Prasad. Chief or no Chief, there was no question of evicting the Chinese. This was evident even without going through the drill of making a written appreciation, which involves a study of the relevant factors; courses open to own troops and the enemy; the course adopted with reasons for doing so and an outline plan to achieve the aim.

I had given the GOC the gist of my earlier findings and deductions which I had reduced to writing. The factors were brutally simple and it did not need a great deal of strategical or tactical percipience to deduce that it was folly to contemplate any military action to evict the Chinese and try to hold vast areas at heights of over 15,000 feet, with the Hathungla or Karpola I routes for maintenance. If anything, the Chinese build-up had made it even more improbable that the forces available in Kameng Frontier Division could ever evict the Chinese before the weather brought all military activity to a halt.

The GOC was placed in a most unenviable dilemma as he had only two alternatives. He could refuse to submit an appreciation and expose his superiors; or he could resort to covert disobedience by preparing a paper hedged with numerous, unattainable provisos in the hope that a sane decision would be forced on the higher ups. The first alternative was unthinkable in the prevailing circumstances. India and China were not at war and if the political gamble had come off, then all the 'paper-tacticians' would have been classified as cowards – or worse. Moreover, as Marshal Joffre once said: "It was not for the Generalissimo to explain but to give orders. It was not for a general to think but to carry out orders. Once a general has received his orders he should carry them out with a mind at rest, knowing it to be his duty". Only soldiers will understand these sentiments.

Given Hobson's choice, Gen. Prasad opted for the second course and asked me to prepare a first draft highlighting the maintenance and administrative problems, in addition to the awesome disparities in fire-power, so that sobriety would be induced in the planners at Delhi. The idea was that we should make it clear that even if we had any non-violent success, it would be impossible to maintain any troops in the Namka Chu Valley and Thagla Ridge areas. Nothing short of a gratuitous Chinese withdrawal would enable us to achieve the national aim of clearing the Thagla area.

I was in the same predicament as the French general who said: "I have two stars on my sleeve and he has three. How can I argue?"

The main points of the Appreciation have been given in the course of narrating my visit to the Namka Chu as also the reasons for not complying with the Chief's order tc evict the Chinese.

Briefly, the Namka Chu Valley was extremely rugged and narrow, with precipitous, thickly-wooded slopes. The river was a fast-flowing mountain stream and a considerable obstacle (as on 20th September). There was no room for manœuvre.

Terrain was the determining factor as the Thagla Slopes run from West to East. It would be suicidal to run the risk of advancing uphill from East to West. The approach from Khenzemane to Thagla was impassable even to infantry, due to sheer cliffs.

The central approach from South to North was dominated by the Chinese positions at Paitsai, a spur which juts out from Thagla and bisects the Ridge. The dvancing troops would come under cross-fire while negotiating the steep inclines and we had no artillery to neutralise them. Militarily the only possible approach was from the western end, *via* Tsangle, and the Chinese knew this.

Approach and maintenance routes to the river were long and tenuous. To avoid observation and interference from the Chinese, it would be more advisable to use the Karpola I route as the Hathungla approach ran parallel to the Chinese positions opposite Bridges I to IV. At that time I did not know that there was no direct route along the Namka Chu Valley and that a detour *via* Tsangdhar was necessary to avoid the numerous, impassable bluffs.

Relative strengths and capability to achieve a faster rate of build-up were vital factors. The outline plan was based on the presumption (foolish?) that the Chinese strength would remain constant at one battalion. We could not hope to match the Chinese in a race to build-up the forces in the Namka Chu.

It was stipulated that the minimum artillery requirements should be provided *before* moving into the Thagla Ridge area. We well knew that no artillery pieces other than the outranged para-field guns could be made available to us.

The time and space factors were set out in some detail as they would appear incredible to the planners in Delhi. Purely for the approach march we had allowed a minimum of ten days. As the snows were likely to set in by the end of October, the stipulated stock-piling would have to be achieved within a fortnight, failing which there would be no hope of undertaking any action before April 1963.

Security and surprise were considered essential. It was laid down that there was to be no movement except for controlled reconnaissances, on the North Bank of the Namka Chu, especially at the western end, to find crossing places and suitable routes and assembly areas. These reconnaissances were mandatory before committing a large force to unknown ground and against an unknown enemy. As we did not have the troops for any diversionary tactics to bemuse the enemy, the only course open was to adopt a circuitous route. This deduction also led me to suggest the western approach.

Security was deliberately compromised before Gen. Kaul took over. Our patrolling programme started on 29th September and Tsangle was the first area to be reconnoitred.

As soon as the first patrol report was received in Delhi, I was ordered to hold Tsangle without being assigned any rationale for this task. Gen. Umrao protested that "Tsangle was not a good place to hold tactically as it would give away our plans to the Chinese". He was promptly overruled. Unfortunately the Chinese were soon alerted and sent troops to contain our picquet. There was never thereafter any possibility of moving unopposed to our objectives. The Chinese could bar our way and we faced the certainty of a pitched battle for our first bound, which is in fact what happened. The third major proviso of the plan was consequently altered by an unfortunate order from Delhi.

There were many other prerequisites, viz. casualty evacuation by helicopters, the requirement of porters for the carry from Tsangdhar to Tsangle and forward, the equipping of units before any forward movement and the imperative need to acclimatise the troops before attempting the Karpola I crossing and so on. It was laid down that a minimum of three first lines of ammunition and 30 days' rations would have to be dropped and stocked at Tsangdhar before the rest of the Brigade was allowed to venture into the Namka Chu Valley. (These scales were later reduced to seven days' rations and three first lines.)

Provided all the 'ifs' and 'buts' materialised then the following limited action might be possible: (*a*) attempt an outflanking move from Bridge V at the western end of the Valley; (*b*) the move to be in three stages, i.e. Lumpu to Tsangdhar *via* Karpola I; Tsangdhar to Muksar and Muksar to Tseng Jong. Subsequent operations would depend on the Chinese reaction to our moves. No advance attack plans could be drawn up sitting in Lumpu. These would be decided only after the nature and scope of the Chinese counter-moves became clear. Our aim would be to roll down from Tseng Jong to the Chinese positions.

Even so the plan was not really a military one as it did not cater for any Chinese retaliatory action. It was more in the nature of a police action to herd out an unruly crowd. It was certainly not a rigid and inflexible course which could not be halted. There was no timed collaboration or co-ordination with other formations. The moves were for an independent formation undertaking a lone task and could readily be postponed, modified or even scrapped.

The Appreciation was the last exposition of the purely military problems posed by Government's order to evict the Chinese. It also contained the observations and conclusions of the only senior commander who had seen the Thagla area to date. Eventually the Appreciation was the joint handiwork of the Corps, Divisional and Brigade Commanders. The difficulties were brushed aside and the requirements were not made available. All that was extracted was the plan to evict the Chinese! This battered and moth-eaten Appreciation has been exhumed by Gen. Kaul, as we shall see, to exonerate himself for the defeat of 7 Brigade.

* * *

Gen. Prasad approved the draft Appreciation on 26th September after some discussion and after incorporating some alterations. He discussed it with Gen. Umrao, who came to Lumpu on 26th September. Umrao demurred at the first draft he was shown on the grounds that it was too ambitious. He wanted us to cater for more fire-power and a bigger administrative build-up. He objected to our attempt to lay down firm dates. He also insisted on a more modest tactical plan.

He accepted the revised draft. *For the second time in 16 days, Gen. Umrao counselled prudence.*

Gen. Umrao left for Lucknow on the 29th to apprise Gen. Sen of the numerous difficulties. He told us that he would insist on the irreducible minimum build-up before venturing into the Chinaman's den. He would also try to convince the Army Commander of the impossibility of evicting the Chinese without a massive build-up which was unlikely to materialise before 1st April 1963, if ever. He warned us not to expect too much from his visit as everyone was impatiently waiting for D-Day. His Brigadier General Staff left armed with the facts and figures.

Gen. Umrao Singh gave clear orders that there was to be no further concentration of troops forward of Lumpu till the bare minimum stock-piling at Tsangdhar had been achieved. He promised to pay us a second visit at the first opportunity.

Before taking off, Umrao sent for the COs of the Rajputs and the Gorkhas to wish them good-bye. Later one of them described the scene in these words: "When we met the Corps Commander we both felt as if he was saying good-bye to two gladiators about to enter the arena never to come out alive. We both assured the Corps Commander that whatever we were called upon to do we would do in the highest traditions of the Army. All we requested was a fair chance of survival and success for the men, and the minimum amount of warm clothing, supplies and ammunition".

I do not know what transpired at Lucknow but I do know that Umrao protested in writing to the Army Commander on the 30th of September. Obviously he had been unable to influence Gen. Sen to reverse the thinking at the highest levels and was forced to record his formal disagreement with the way operations were being hustled. Umrao refused to be "as a dog in obedience; and a lion in action".

Thus by the end of September there was clearly a serious divergence of opinion between the policy-makers in Delhi and the local formation Commanders. There was a rift between the "Brass" and the "Boots". Only drastic action could now resolve the stalemate if the relentless decision to evict the Chinese was still to be pursued. Government's only trump card was to change the dissident senior commander and replace him with someone who would accept responsibility for the venture. Who would accept the thankless and hopeless task?

Part IV

The End Of Make-Believe

Chapter XIII

Nehru Takes Over—2nd October 1962

After the *contretemps* between Generals Sen and Umrao there was the usual flurry of conferences and meetings at Delhi – India's panacea for solving her problems. Menon had returned from New York on the 30th of September and Nehru from Lagos, Nigeria on the 2nd of October. At last, the right people began manning the right action stations. Hitherto the higher direction of war was in the hands of a Deputy Minister whose normal functions were in the sphere of defence production and not operations.

The politico-military situation had, from Nehru's point of view, reached a climax. Goaded by a relentless Opposition for positive action and exasperated by Chinese intrusions, Nehru decided to retaliate without quite understanding what this meant in military terms. So far his only link with the gathering storm in the Himalayan border had been by telephone and telegrams and one casual meeting with Menon in London. Menon and his fire-eating civilians had given him a few hints that the time had come to halt further Chinese intrusions and had painted a rosy picture of our chances of succeeding. The Army Brass had made one or two mild protests but then Gen. Thapar did not have the force of character to influence the impulsive Prime Minister or the domineering Defence Minister. In 1962 only Kaul's advice mattered. Within a day of Nehru's return Kaul is recalled from leave. The destiny of India was now in his hands.

Undoubtedly influenced by Umrao's realism, Gen. Sen did not now exude any great deal of confidence or bellicosity. On 2nd October he told the Defence Minister that the Chinese now had a battalion at

Thagla and confirmed that three of our battalions had concentrated in the forward area. Sen also told the Minister that his logistic build-up might not be completed by the 10th of October. This was clearly on Umrao's calculations as Sen had little first-hand knowledge of what was happening in the realm of 'building-up' beyond receiving optimistic figures of air despatches to the forward areas.

Gen. Sen is also reported to have pointed out that, "This was the first time we were going to use force against the Chinese, though for good reasons (as against walking into a vacuum, without opposition, a practice followed by us so far), and that this was bound to have serious repercussions".

Menon's response to these gloomy forebodings was to issue a characteristic edict: "The Government policy is to make an impact (*sic*) on the Chinese in NEFA before they settled down for the winter". It is reasonable to assume that Sen used Umrao's appreciation as the guide-line for the advice which he rendered to his Chief and the Defence Minister. If he did not then he was guilty of an omission, which could have far-reaching consequences. If Sen agreed with Umrao, as seems more than probable, then Menon exceeded his authority in continuing to talk vaguely of making an impact. Nehru was still abroad and the Defence Committee of the Cabinet could have had no hand in such an eventful decision. In any case Government policy needs to be spelt out in more explicit terms as it is not easy to translate "making an impact" into a workable military operation order. It is even more difficult when the forward commanders keep insisting that the tasks are beyond their means. All that can be done is to refurbish and re-issue the same old slogan "Evict the Chinese".

Mr. Nehru is said to have held a meeting with Generals Thapar and Sen and found them hesitant and reluctant. The time had come to apply some soothing balm to the timid Generals and doubting Thomases. He told them that "he had good reasons to believe that the Chinese would not take any strong action against us". Was this Marshal Chen Yi's assurance in Geneva reaping its reward for China? or did Nehru still live in blissful hopes of localising the Thagla dispute? Would any nation defy world opinion and attack the Apostle of Peace? In any case such a briefing if true could hardly generate a martial spirit. It also consigned military considerations to the waste-paper basket. Armed with political optimism, we persisted with unattainable military targets, this time with the Prime Minister's imprimatur. The 'unbelievers' were silenced with assurances of Chinese good behaviour. "Don't be silly, the Chinese won't do anything" was the soporific catch-phrase that was administered every time a military objection was raised.

Even if we were compelled to display resolution we should have adhered to acknowledged principles of war and canons of military strategy. There was no need to fall helplessly into the Chinese trap against frightful odds.

Government resumed its "decision-making" role. The first decision was to 'create' a corps and to appoint Kaul as its commander. The tempo mounted. The Government's publicity machine swung into action. Kaul was given the majestic task of "evicting the Chinese from the Thagla area". Mr. Nehru undoubtedly had a hand in, if he did not actually decree, this change of command in mid-stream.

Kaul resumes duty and tries to catch up with events. He is briefed by the Officiating Chief of the General Staff, Major-General Joginder Singh Dhillon. We do not know what Dhillon told him. We can only assume that Kaul was given a thorough and lucid background of events to date. Dhillon must surely have explained the reasons for the delay in implementing Government's order to evict the Chinese. Government had been pressing the Army from 13th September. Dhillon may or may not have shown Kaul the two letters written by Umrao Singh on 12th and 30th September. All that we know is what Kaul had said: "Major-General Dhillon recounted to me what had happened during my absence in the last few weeks". This cryptic sentence conceals as much, if not more, than it reveals.

Predictably, Kaul is invited by Nehru on 3rd October and told, "We must contest by whatever means at our disposal. He (Nehru) therefore hoped that the Chinese would see reason and withdraw from Dhola but in case they did not, we would have to expel them from *our territory or at least try to do so to the best of our ability*. If we failed to take such action Government would forfeit public confidence completely".

Mr. Nehru's short-sightedness and negligence with regard to China is remarkable when judged against his far-sightedness in world affairs. It seems incredible that as late as 3rd October, when the military odds had been calculated, he was motivated by the possibility of loss of confidence in the Government whose omissions had been ruthlessly exposed by the Chinese aggression. The military defeat, and its sad aftermath, were infinitely greater disasters to the nation than the fortunes of Government or its principal members. Nehru's basis for accepting a military adventure, led by Kaul, was not in the National interest; it was the reasoning of a politician looking to his own and his Party's future. It was unworthy of a man of Nehru's stature. In the words of Alfred Vagts in his book, *The History of Militarism*, "Again and again, military men have seen themselves hurled into war by the ambitions, passions and blunders of civilian governments, almost wholly uninformed as to the limits of their military potentials and almost recklessly indifferent to the military requirements of the wars they let loose".

When the inevitable disaster came Nehru did not even have the grace or courage to admit his errors or seek a fresh mandate from the people. He did not even go through the motion of resigning; he merely presented his trusted colleagues and military appointees as sacrificial offerings. This was a great disappointment to his many admirers all over the world. President Nasser, who is not overly devoted to parliamentary democracy, made a more gracious and democratic gesture after the crushing Egyptian defeat at the hands of the Israelis, in June 1967. He accepted the blame and remained in power only when he was given a fresh mandate from his people.

* * *

The abrupt dismissal of Gen. Umrao Singh was a pivotal decision. Many devious arguments have been adduced to explain the overnight change in the command structure but none of them have the ring of truth. This, the most serious blunder on the part of the Government and the Army Chief, cannot be buried under a heap of unconvincing administrative reasons. The biggest 'if' of the NEFA War of 1962 must surely be whether there would have been an actual shooting war if Kaul had not been nominated to command, with a personal mandate from the Prime Minister. The impossible task, blithely offered to Kaul, was merrily accepted by him.

When Kaul accepted the assignment he knew that his so-called corps was a political gimmick in so far as his force bore no relation whatsoever to a corps as this term is commonly understood in modern armies. He had nothing but the two committed brigades – 5 and 7 Brigades. Kaul's own reasons for allowing himself to be associated with Government's final desperate gamble, in the face of the known odds, are: ". . . I was thus expected to perform a miracle and begin operations immediately. I could hardly start bickering (*sic*) about the obvious handicaps at a time when India found herself in a precarious situation and therefore decided to cross my fingers, make the best of my lean resources (one brigade) and face the situation as best I could". To achieve success against the Chinese, under the prevailing disparities, any commander would need more militarily sound miracles than crossed fingers and patriotic resolutions. At that stage Ground, Relative Strengths and Administration were not matters of bickering – they were overwhelmingly decisive. They could only be ignored at the risk of certain disaster. If Gen. Kaul intended to take a calculated risk in ignoring these time-honoured principles then there is little point in shifting the blame of the subsequent failure to the Army as a whole. He tried to do what others opined could not be done. He replaced Umrao who believed in "bickering" when his professional conscience told him to do so. Why was Umrao sacked?

One reason which has been suggested by Kaul is because of Umrao's differences with Gen. Sen, his immediate boss: "Gen. Thapar and Lt.-Gen. Sen decided to replace Umrao Singh as the latter and Lt.-Gen. Sen were not getting on well together". Unfortunately we are not told whether this move had the blessings of the Prime Minister or Defence Minister without whose approval such replacements cannot take place. In Menon's era this right was a jealously guarded prerogative of "Government". So the nagging question remains unanswered; was Umrao sacked before the decision to appoint Kaul or was Umrao removed to make room for Kaul? The picture between the 30th of September and the 2nd of October is blurred.

If Gen. Sen removed Umrao on grounds of professional incompetence then he should have been made to relinquish command of XXXIII Corps. Discredited Corps Commanders do not retain their ranks and appointments.

It has also been insinuated that the burden of commanding Assam, Nagaland and NEFA was too heavy for one commander. Kaul says, "Umrao had been dealing with NEFA so far. The territories under him were too vast when judged in relation to his resources". This is perhaps the most unconvincing argument of all. Kaul was the Chief of the General Staff and it was his duty to allocate the required resources to field formations. The paucity of resources was not a sudden revelation. Kaul himself had come without any resources other than his person and assorted staff officers who had been hurriedly corralled between midnight and dawn of the 3rd/4th October. He too would soon be a parasite and feed off Umrao's slender "resources". In any case the solution obviously lay in appointing another commander for the Assam and Nagaland sectors and freeing Umrao to concentrate on the NEFA operations with which he was familiar. Would Government have removed Umrao if he had agreed to have a crack at the Chinese without harping on military prudence?

The last puzzling question is why Government did not appoint Kaul to command XXXIII Corps and create a phantom corps for the dormant Assam and Nagaland Sectors. XXXIII Corps was a running organisation, had a tuned up staff under an extremely capable Brigadier and the necessary corps troops for the maintenance of troops in combat.

The unavoidable conclusion is that Delhi was afraid of making an issue of removing Umrao lest the truth about the divergence of opinions within the Army and with the politicians leaked out, thereby shattering the morale of the nation. Umrao insisted on more time and this was the one commodity Government did not have. The Indian public was breathing down its neck. There is no other explanation for the Prime Minister's personal intervention in the selection of a "corps commander" to command one brigade to evict an allegedly small, non-violent, intruding Chinese Force. Kaul was no ordinary General to be wasted on a minor assignment. I remain convinced to this day that Umrao was placed on the side-line ungracefully because he refused to collaborate with those who insisted on steering a collision course to the Chinese on the Thagla Ridge. Someone who would play the politicians' game was urgently needed and Kaul was the obvious choice as the pro-consul. He was the principal military advocate of the Forward Policy which others had resisted. When called by Government Kaul could not very well refuse to practice his theory of "positional warfare" and vindicate his strategy.

We became the laughing stock of the world when it became known that Kaul had no corps to command. The Chinese seized upon our premature disclosure of a "task force", as well as the uninformed jubilation in the Indian Press about an impending offensive, to tell the world that we had prepared for years for such an operation. We paid for ignoring the old Japanese saying that countries should "wage war silently and anonymously". It was difficult even for our friends to believe our professions of peace and that the Chinese attacked us treacherously when we ourselves announced to the world that we were determined to evict the Chinese (albeit from what we claimed was our territory) and had selected India's outstanding General to do so. Those responsible did India irreparable harm and a great disservice. History cannot be kind to them.

Before Gen. Umrao leaves the stage I would like to pay a tribute to a General whose role in the Thagla Affair has received but scant attention from observers and analysts of the Indian defeat. His wise counsel and military advice were ignored from the very inception of the tragic affair. His measured advice remained unheeded to the end.

Gen. Umrao is a tall, handsome man with an imposing personality. He hails from a famous Rajput family of Jaipur, in fabled Rajasthan — the home of generations of warriors. When I first met him during these operations, I found him calm and unruffled. His very presence was reassuring. He lived in terms of open hostility with Gen. Sen and consequently worked under severe pressure. He had had a hard time trying to resist the impracticable tasks which were being foisted on the troops. He was subjected to unjust criticism for the alleged tardiness of his command and his failure to "evict the Chinese". Despite this he remained coldly analytical of the military tasks given him. He resolutely refused to get involved in the political aspects or to allow himself to be pressurised into unsound measures to pacify the politicians. He gave his opinions fearlessly and effectively. He was one of the few senior actors in the Thagla drama who had the moral courage to record his views in writing. He proved too outspoken and had to be eliminated before the powers-that-be could complete their self-destroying policy.

In the best traditions of the warrior race from which he sprang, Umrao Singh remained conscious throughout of the men he commanded. He made one statement which I shall always remember. In discussing the first draft of the Appreciation, he clearly foresaw that there was a likelihood of a major clash without the slightest chance of achieving our national or tactical aims. He said: "This is all very well for you chaps; you will get decorated, but what about the men who will have to sacrifice their lives senselessly? Now be sensible and produce a plan that has a faint hope of success — even if we have to stall for six months". Umrao subconsciously echoed the famous words of Field-Marshal Auchinleck who once said, "Are the chaps who are going to attack going to have a reasonable chance — if not, you are just murdering them".

He sympathised with us in the difficult predicament in which we had been placed by the unreasonable orders to throw out the Chinese. He did his best to shield us, and in so doing he displayed all the qualities required of a commander in the field, the foremost being moral courage. He was the one senior officer whom I met who kept his head, poise and mental balance throughout the bitter days of September 1962.

The Indian people might have been saved much humiliation if the authorities had relied on his advice. Like many a fine soldier before him he paid the supreme price for his forthrightness. He was subjected to the most dreaded punishment of all – summary removal. In the words of the great Duke of Marlborough: "To relieve a general in the midst of a campaign, that is the mortal stroke". Those responsible for engineering and delivering the "stroke" are thrice guilty.

Chapter XIV

A Soldier Uninhibited

With the appointment of Kaul the Thagla Operation entered the third and decisive phase.

Gen. Kaul arrived at Tezpur on 4th October and amazingly was received at the airport by his Army Commander – an extraordinary reversal of military protocol. The armies of the world are usually very fussy about such matters. This is not intended to be a petty barb. It is to illustrate Kaul's power and prestige – material factors which were to gravely influence the course of events in the succeeding days. Anyone exercising authority beyond his rank is bound to stifle disagreement, discourage frank discussions and brow-beat subordinates.

The operational situation at Tezpur on 4th October was that there was a deadlock between Sen and Umrao. Gen. Sen was in a quandary. His immediate subordinate was adamant. His logistical build-up was behind schedule. He had no hope of achieving his targets even by 10th October, if ever. He was apprehensive of the Chinese reaction to any overt military move on our part. It has been said that he had had to change the promised dates for evicting the Chinese and had incurred the displeasure of the Government. Gen. Sen was rescued from his predicament by the arrival of Kaul. The heavy burden of reconciling the formidable problems posed by the Himalayas, the objections of his forward commanders and an insistent Government was taken off his weary shoulders.

Kaul was in personal command of 7 Infantry Brigade. We now had one Gen., two Lt.-Gens., one Maj.-Gen. and one Brigadier to preside over the activities of this ill-starred formation. We had five sabres in one scabbard – a suicidal command arrangement which ultimately produced utter confusion during the operations and excuses after our defeat.

Some of these officers have since been accused of direct interference and ordering the moves of units and sub-units and they have reacted violently to these strictures. If they were not commanding 7 Brigade then it is permissible to ask what were they commanding. They were certainly not confining themselves to high level strategic planning or providing the required logistic cover. All that these generals were doing was to improvidently hound, harry and hustle this one formation to achieve the unattainable.

Gens. Sen, Kaul and Umrao spent the 4th together. Kaul tells us, "I had a meeting with Lt.-Gens. Sen and Umrao soon after my arrival at Tezpur. I heard from them what had been done to concentrate 7 Infantry Brigade in the Dhola area. Lt.-Gen. Sen had said in the Defence Minister's meeting at Delhi that three of our battalions had been concentrated by the 29th, in the forward area. Actually even on 4th October, only one battalion and a bit more were in Dhola, most of the others still being in Lumpu which is 15 miles west of Dhola. The logistical build-up was far behind schedule because of lack of porters, the only means of transportation at those heights. We had grave deficiencies in the strength of porters. I commandeered about a thousand from the Border Roads Organisation and informed Government accordingly. I took other similar steps as a result of which I hoped that 7 Brigade would be concentrated in the Dhola area by 9th October".

Since there was no overall strategic concept, the second brigade at Walong did not concern Kaul immediately. He has since admitted as much when he says, "Lastly, since our Government was determined to expel the Chinese from the Dhola-Thagla area, where they had aggressed, the question of fighting them elsewhere did not arise".

Unfortunately this very cursory record of the handing and taking over of an impending clash of arms is insufficient. We are not told why the move of 7 Brigade should be accelerated, as operational moves do not just happen; there must be an executive order. What was this plan of operations? Did Gen. Sen issue any formal orders to his subordinate, Kaul? It would have been normal to do so, as the Prime Minister's and Defence Minister's general directives had to be re-interpreted in military terms. If Sen did not issue any orders, then are we at liberty to assume that Kaul did not require any from his military superior? It is no wonder that ever since 1962, Gen. Sen has steadfastly maintained that with the arrival of Kaul he had no further hand in the sordid NEFA Affair.

We are not told whether Umrao's assessment of the task figured in the discussions and whether Kaul agreed or disagreed with it. This is important to pin-point the author of the orders which were supposed to have been operative on the date Kaul assumed command, especially the order that required 7 Brigade to reach the Namka Chu by 9th October.

All that emerges from the 4th October meeting is an investigation as to what progress had been made "to concentrate 7 Brigade in the Dhola area".

After the Thagla fiasco, Kaul has sheltered behind the so-called plans that were supposed to have been drawn up before he assumed command. If he felt that he had inherited any inflexible or unalterable plans, then it was his bounden duty to have disclosed what these were and whether he discussed them with Sen and Umrao at Tezpur on 4th October; and later with GOC 4 Division and Commander 7 Infantry Brigade at a formal co-ordinating conference. This is routine procedure in the Army. Kaul was not sent by the Prime Minister of his country to supervise an operation for which others had already done the planning. From 4th October onwards it was his responsibility to assume charge of events and arrive at his own operational conclusions. As Field-Marshal Von Manstein has said: "The basic concept of a campaign plan should be born in the mind of the man who has to direct that campaign". If Kaul accepted the plans of others then they became his own. A post-mortem does not permit a plea of previous plans which were defective and which betrayed the General in actual command at the time of their implementation.

On 4th October Kaul should have known that Umrao had represented to Gen. Sen, the following facts:

(*a*) "Before the operation could be launched, 580 tons of ammunition and stores be stocked at Tsangdhar which must be accepted as the main dropping zone for the offensive operations.

(*b*) The Namka Chu Valley is extremely rugged and narrow, with thickly wooded and precipitous slopes. The river is a considerable obstacle. Room for manœuvre is extremely limited. This makes a direct assault on Thagla suicidal.

(*c*) Our non-combatant pioneers have proved useless.

(*d*) The total number of civilian porters available (far behind Dhola) is three to five hundred which is quite inadequate for our requirement. It is just not possible to stock Tsangdhar from Lumpu by the land route".

This extract (since quoted by Kaul) is a verbatim transcription of what I had written in the Appreciation of 28th September.

To add melodrama to a situation that Kaul never imagined would be anything more than "a clash of wills" he says that he, after hearing the difficulties from Umrao, decided to accelerate the concentration for the following reasons:

(*a*) If we had to expel the Chinese from our

territory near Dhola, despite our many disparities, our concentration there should take place quicker than that of the enemy.

(*b*) If we went on delaying to concentrate in the requisite area, it would soon start snowing in Dhola and the weather would then jeopardise our proposed operation.

It is permissible to infer that Kaul, having heard Umrao, decided to ignore the "difficulties", use some Irish logic and persist in his attempt to evict the Chinese.

Let us first analyse Kaul's reasons for moving 7 Brigade to the Namka Chu despite "our many disparities". Can we seriously believe these after-thoughts? The Chinese had, on 4th/5th October, already located a well-prepared, well-stocked, well entrenched and well-supported brigade in the Thagla area. They had infinitely better road communications and transport of all categories that gave them easy access to Thagla.

On our side we had literally nothing. How then did Kaul hope to achieve a "quicker" build-up, under these disparities? If a large build-up had been possible, would not Gens. Sen and Umrao have achieved more, even before Kaul's arrival? They were after all under Government orders to evict the Chinese since 13th September.

The possibility of snows retarding operations can be dismissed briefly. Umrao had highlighted that if our stipulated build-up of 580 tons was not made available, with the required porterage, before the snows set in, then the operation would have to be postponed till the spring of 1963. If the snows came, the operation would not only be jeopardised, it would be doomed. Did Kaul intend to slap the Chinese, dust his hands, and return to Lumpu before the snows threatened his stay in the Namku Chu Valley?

The reasons given for the precipitate move to the Namka Chu are not convincing, if treated as a purely military affair. The manner in which the move was ordered clearly indicates that the predominant political factors had steam-rollered the military difficulties. Kaul had the Prime Minister's appeal to do something to prevent the Government forfeiting public confidence. There was Nehru's assurance that the Chinese would not take any strong action against us. It is for these reasons that Kaul pushed everyone to the Namka Chu. That is why he took steps to concentrate 7 Brigade by 9th October, regardless.

Gen. Kaul would have been truer to himself, and would have helped the Indian people to understand the NEFA Reverses if he had admitted, in the first place, that he did not expect "a swift and catastrophic retribution" (*to use his own phrase*).

* * *

While the "big three" were holding a summit at Tezpur, Gen. Prasad visited me at Lumpu at 9.30 a.m. on the 4th of October. We had been waiting anxiously for him to give us the latest news. The silence from 29th September onwards was nerve-racking. I immediately asked him what had happened to our Appreciation. He gave me this astounding answer: "Look old boy, no one is interested in your bloody appreciation. 'They' are only interested in your D-Day for evicting the Chinese". He then stressed that the operation had to be mounted immediately for political reasons, whatever the consequences.

He then gave me the disquieting news that Gen. Kaul had been appointed GOC of a "new" corps to "speed up operations". I asked him which corps he was referring to as there was no corps within a thousand miles of NEFA. Prasad said that he had no other information than that Kaul was now Commander of "IV" Corps. Everybody knows that a corps cannot be made to materialise with a magic wand. The news was very disturbing as there was an obvious non-military angle to this development. What other rational explanation was there for this dramatic but pointless change of commanders in the midst of planning? We needed more tools not brains. The awful implication, that Umrao had forfeited the confidence of Government, dawned on me at once. We had great faith in Umrao not only because he knew the local military situation but also because he had the strength of character to stand up to brow-beating.

After giving me the news of Kaul's appointment and the rejection of our Appreciation, the GOC ordered me to leave 'at once' for the Namka Chu. He said that Kaul would be furious if he found me at Lumpu; but he could not tell me why anyone should be interested in my personal location. I was constrained to point out that I had not yet been given any orders which would have suggested the best place for my HQ or myself. I told him that there was little dignity in senior officers scurrying away like thieves in the night. Who were we afraid of, the Chinese or our own superior commanders? I told him that the time was 9.30 a.m. and too late to start and complete a day's march. In spite of this he *begged* me to leave at once and take shelter in the nearest herder's hut: all that mattered was that he should be in a position to say that the commander had gone "forward". "To hell with appreciations – to hell with porters – to hell with everything – just move to Dhola". Further orders would be issued later.

I called my COs and staff and gave them a gist of what the GOC had told me. The news was received with great misgivings as it seemed to presage something sinister and there was no longer any hope of talking in purely military terms. Prasad's order to hurry away was a clear indication that political opportunism would be the key-note of future action.

My Order Group and I left Lumpu for Dhola at about 11.30 a.m. on 4th October. I was smarting under the humiliation of having been evicted from my HQ, for the second time, without being assigned a reason or a task. There is nothing more degrading than this. I hope that never again will any senior Indian Army officer be called upon to suffer such an indignity. I was also depressed after my weird conversation with the GOC. What was the earthly use of making appreciations if they were just thrown away and the forward troops ordered to move "forward". What more can a commander do?

We camped at a herder's hut some two miles from Lumpu!

* * *

5th October 1962 is a critical day in the history of the Thagla Affair. It was the day on which Kaul moved my Brigade personally, without consulting Gen. Prasad or me. It was to prove the point of no return. Although I heard only later that Kaul had moved my Brigade, I shall narrate the manner in which he did so at this stage, in order to link Kaul's appointment with the dramatic acceleration of military activity.

Kaul had planned to meet me at Dhola on 7th October, to discuss operational plans and yet did not deem it proper to wait until then and avail himself of the two intervening days to study the ground and co-ordinate our thinking; instead of which he unbalanced the Brigade by moving it on the 5th without even its first-line loads. Kaul ignored the laid-down time-honoured customs of assuming command and exercising authority.

Instead of allowing himself time to get into the operational picture he strode into the scene like the God of War, ridiculed the tardiness of his superiors and subordinates and expressed his avowed intention to "get everyone off his arse and get him cracking!" Kaul was now reaping the fruits of the immense prestige bestowed on him by Nehru's patronage. There was no one to curb his impetuosity, or dare to challenge him. He overawed everyone, including myself, into abject and meek surrender. It is important to understand this, as it helps to re-create the atmosphere and the setting under which all subordinates had to function. I too plead guilty to lack of moral courage in not protesting when he moved my Brigade without even the courtesy of informing me.

On the 5th of October Gen. Kaul had anticipated the possibility of the Chinese overwhelming us and the possibility of a national disaster if we did not retrieve the situation rapidly. He had already informed HQ Eastern Command that the Chinese might lure us into the Tsangdhar-Dhola area with the intention of capturing Towang.

After listing all these dire prospects, Kaul nevertheless asserted that he was "taking every step to evict the Chinese from our territory despite the many difficulties, as ordered". This brash assurance was given before he had even visited the battlefield, or studied the military situation with anyone. His despatch was not that of a military man. He was not a helpless bystander of events that he could neither control nor disown. Until his arrival commanders had been stalling, on valid military grounds, and pleading that the situation was not one that could be retrieved in the foreseeable future. Kaul came and looked, but saw nothing, and became the prime motive force that ordained all activity from 5th October onwards.

Kaul flew into Lumpu on the afternoon of 5th October. His version of the visit to Lumpu is extremely ingenuous. He says, disarmingly, that he could not fly to Serkhim due to bad weather. Actually there was no helipad at Serkhim on the afternoon of 5th October but one was in fact built by my Engineers that very night. Kaul then says that, "I therefore flew to Lumpu to fill my time usefully". This unscheduled and casual visit produced the second disastrous and improper order oi the whole Thagla Episode.

Gen. Kaul goes on to say that, "I ordered the bulk of HQ 7 Brigade, 2 Rajput and 1/9 Gorkhas – awaiting porters to carry their stores – to move the next day to the Dhola area. I told them that I would hasten the despatch of their supplies and other materials forward as best I could". 7 Brigade was not only waiting for porters; it was waiting for orders. It was waiting for war-like stores at Tsangdhar.

The version of those who were at the receiving end of his orders is vastly different. According to them, the dramatic scene at the Lumpu helipad ran somewhat as follows: Kaul flew in at about 2.30 p.m. and was received by Lt.-Col. Sen, the Officer Commanding the Field Ambulance, Major Jayaraman, the Surgeon and Major Kharbanda, the Brigade Major. Kaul introduced himself as the new Corps Commander of IV Corps. After the introduction he asked Kharbanda where the GOC of 4 Division was. Kharbanda replied that he did not know as the GOC was sometimes in Towang and sometimes in Tezpur.

Kaul then asked, "Have all the troops of 7 Brigade moved to Tsangdhar?" When the Brigade Major answered, "Not yet, Sir", Kaul demanded to know the reason. "Why not? It was my definite order that the troops must be in position by the evening of 7th October". He then threatened the Brigade Major, "How dare you disobey my orders, you are the Brigade Major. I have given an assurance to the Prime Minister that I will carry out the operation. I am not a Corps Commander to sit in Shillong to conduct the operation. I intend to be present to conduct the operation myself". (This was an obvious dig at Gen. Umrao, who was based at Shillong.)

Without knowing the situation, he was openly critical of 7 Brigade's performance to date and made sarcastic remarks about its professional capability and tardiness.

Kaul then asked for the reasons why the Brigade Major had not implemented his order. Before waiting for a reply he added, "This is not Mount Everest. I now give you orders to move all the fighting elements immediately, or else I will get you dismissed". When the Brigade Major protested that he had been ordered not to move until further orders and requested that the General should refer the matter to me, Kaul refused to listen to Kharbanda's pleas. He again threatened to sack this capable officer if he made any more excuses.

When the question of the lack of porters was raised by the Brigade Major, Kaul neatly side-stepped with the assurance that "there were plenty in Towarg" and Kaul would be moving them at once. Kaul promised "to hasten the despatch of supplies and other materials forward as best I could". In the meanwhile he ordered the move to take place on "hard scales and pouch ammunition". He also emphasised that he wanted only the "bayonet strength" moved forward, a catch-phrase that did not reduce the requirement of porterage. These two battalions were under-strength – and when moving on a man-pack basis everyone is on the bayonet strength even if he is only a carrier. An intimate knowledge of the workings of an infantry battalion is a *sine qua non* for command. Slogans about "bayonet strength" and "hard scales" may impress the uninitiated and provide a convenient way of disposing of the problem of a unit's first-line loads, but are professionally unconvincing. Kaul was in a hurry to take on the world's largest land army, with the bayonet strength of two under-strength battalions, moving on hard scales!

Doubts about the shortage of rations were assuaged with the promise that these would be dropped at Tsangdhar.

Kharbanda's final desperate plea was that the move should take place on the morrow at first light, as there was little point in leaving at 3.30 p.m., halting after an hour or so and bivouacking for an extra night in the open. The odd mile or so that would be covered could be catered for by an earlier start the next day.

The story given to me by my staff, *at the time*, is a far cry from Kaul's seemingly guileless afterthoughts of how 7 Brigade came to be moved to the Namka Chu. As late as February/March 1963, there were doubts about how 7 Brigade came to be moved to and later helplessly anchored in the Namka Chu. My Brigade Major was questioned closely by the NEFA Enquiry Board, in two separate sessions. I came to know that some interested party was trying to shift the blame for the mad stampede to the Namka Chu, to others. Major Kharbanda eventually gave a verbatim account of his conversation with Kaul in the form of a playlet and vindicated 7 Brigade.

I was also told by a reliable person that an impression had been created that I was a very brave commander and that I had unhesitatingly accepted the commitment of evicting the Chinese. This story was planted and given currency when it was thought that I had been killed, and would not return to tell the truth. No doubt I would have been decorated posthumously. Unfortunately, the Chinese announced my capture on 16th November 1962, and that put the lid on this short-lived canard.

* * *

The premature move of 7 Brigade to the Namka Chu, with the vague assurance that the war-like stores would be hastened forward as best as the Corps Commander could – a pledge that was dishonoured right up to 20th October – was a military blunder.

Of what use was an infantry formation without its tools of war? 7 Brigade moved without basic winter clothing; with only three days, rations on the man; no reserves; without mortars and ammunition; without rocket launchers and ammunition; without defence stores and with only personal items of kit. This meant that the battle-worthiness of the battalions would be negligible till these caught up with them. Many of these items were not even available at Lumpu and we were awaiting drops, from the rear. Lumpu was a larger and better dropping zone for the receipt and collection of these stores than Tsangdhar.

There were no stores of any kind at Tsangdhar to issue to units on arrival. Tsangdhar was by now a proven failure as a major dropping zone, as heavy losses continued to be reported daily. Even what was dropped could not be retrieved due to the paucity of man-power. Ordinary military prudence would have suggested a staggered move based on the available porters, and after kitting up the men. The supply of the basic needs to maintain men in combat conditions, within a few days, under the circumstances, was not an inconsiderable task; nor was it a bonus.

The urgency for the move, in the face of the enormous difficulties, was not known at the time; however, they were in clear supersession of Umrao's orders. Why did Kaul disregard all military prudence? Why did Kaul decide that, in the words of Sir John French, C-in-C of the British Expeditionary Force in 1914, "We should go forward and decide destination later?" Why did Kaul disregard military protocol and issue direct orders to the Brigade Major? Kaul had come with a pre-determined D-Day and pre-conceived notions on how to tackle the Chinese. This is the only possible explanation for his moving a token brigade to ostensibly challenge a strong Chinese brigade in such a hasty, reckless, unrealistic manner.

At the time, Kaul gave the impression that he was aggressively determined that IV Corps – his first battle command – should do well; and even accomplish something spectacular. He was "keyed up to a pitch of valour and combativeness". He hoped to lead a triumphal march up the Thagla Heights, without opposition, for a spectacular Super-Galwan to silence a vociferous Indian public and save Government from forfeiting public confidence. Part of his trouble was the political foundation on which the entire strategic concept was built. His *panaché* revealed his utter belief that the Chinese would not do anything big, even if we needled them, and pranced in front of them. He may also have suffered from a feeling of professional insecurity engendered by his background and the compulsive need to silence the many enemies that he had collected as a controversial figure, in the Indian scene. He was also an incurable optimist whose temperament did not permit him to anticipate trouble. All this may provide an explanation for his intolerance of the difficulties and his reluctance to bow to infantry limitations. His readiness to classify "impossibilities" as "difficulties"; the use of phrases like "keeping my fingers crossed" and refusing to "bicker" over the impossibility of evicting the Chinese, are pointers to his attitude of mind. Of all people Kaul should have known that you "cannot make bricks without straw!"

Gen. Kaul was unfair to himself, and never gave himself a chance to get the feel of the Thagla "confrontation", without which he was doomed from the start. Admittedly it is the duty of commanders to chivvy their subordinate commanders and forestall the tendency to adopt "Fabian tactics", when speed and boldness are required. But there has to be a compromise between bold leadership and acceptance of harsh realities, especially the Himalayan terrain, the Himalayan weather, the fatigue of overworked troops and the superior Chinese force sitting on the commanding heights of Thagla. When there is no suitable compromise, speed and daring become synonymous with recklessness. It was simplicity itself to order the move of the bayonet strength of battalions, on hard scales and pouch ammunition; it was a different matter to set up a combat group to evict a superior Chinese Force.

Gen. Kaul must remain solely responsible for moving 7 Brigade, to take on a Chinese Brigade already in full battle array at Thagla, and waiting patiently for us to enter their web. It is impossible to dilute Kaul's responsibility, as there can never be two commanders in any one operation. Since he moved 7 Brigade, he must be held responsible as he would have been entitled to the glory if his gamble had come off. He was let down by the Chinese and not by his troops. His hopes were dashed by the instant and massive retaliation to the manœuvre of 10th October. It does no one any good to take refuge in so-called prior plans made by others; or blame the politicians after brashly accepting an impossible task. He learnt the "lesson by which God teaches the law to kings". Sad to say, in the process, India suffered grievously.

* * *

While we were indulging in these activities the Chinese were moving a whole division to the Thagla area. Their intentions were no longer concealed. They reasoned well that the Indian Government was now too deeply involved to retreat without loss of face, so dear to us Asians. On 3rd October they proclaimed that "The McMahon Line was null and void and has never been recognised by any Chinese Government". This official pronouncement had a vital bearing on the overall military situation as the Chinese were now free to conduct operations inside NEFA, which is precisely what they did on and after 20th October 1962. The Thagla intrusion could no longer be localised and yet there was no reaction from the Indian side. The entire military effort continued to be concentrated in the Namka Chu.

On 5th October the correspondent of *The Times*, London, wrote this excellent and incisive appreciation of the Indian Government's dilemma, "The Government's first hope was to squeeze out the Chinese intruders and to use the minimum force in doing so. It was, it is believed, only later when it appeared that the Chinese were not to be herded out that the Army was ordered to eject them with all necessary force. A complementary explanation is that the Indian Army has a sharper awareness than the civilians in the Government of the magnitude of the task".

* * *

To revert to my move to the Namka Chu; on 6th October, we made for the foot of Karpola I Pass. This route was infinitely worse than the Hathungla approach. The gradients were steeper and the temperature below freezing point. It is asking too much of unacclimatised and ill-clad troops to negotiate 16,000-foot passes cumbered with an 80-lb. load on their backs. Hounding and driving troops could not overcome human frailties and limitations.

On the 6th morning we stopped as usual to hear the 8 o'clock Delhi news, as was our wont to keep in touch with developments. The announcer gave the news of a new High Altitude Allowance that had been sanctioned by the Government. This allowance had been blocked by Finance for years on trivial issues, and we had despaired of ever getting it sanctioned during our tenure in NEFA. When the present Chief, Gen. P. P. Kumaramangalam was the Adjutant General, in April 1962, he visited Towang. He told us that he was doubtful if Finance would agree, in the immediate future, as they had raised innumerable queries about entitlement and the exact line after which men would be eligible and so on. And yet here was the allowance sanctioned within two days of Kaul's appointment. There were cynical comments about the distribution of lollipops at the last minute. The announcement did as much harm as good. Many did not live to enjoy the extra pay. It is very degrading to receive special allowances in a crisis. We did the same thing during the Indo-Pakistani War of 1965, when we announced increased pension rates after the commencement of hostilities. The modern Indian Army is not a mercenary one and does not expect special monetary inducements to do its duty.

Karpola I Pass is an awesome sight. It is practically vertical, and strewn with loose boulders. There was danger at every step of a rock being dislodged. Every foot-step is fraught with danger to the person below. It was easy to turn an ankle or stumble. It took three hours of back-breaking work to reach the top. It was especially difficult for a man burdened with something heavy like a Bren-gun or wireless set. The Pass was very narrow, barely 15 feet wide at the summit. We arrived at Tsangdhar at 4 p.m. and, for the first time, heard of the move of the Brigade to the Namka Chu. This news was received by my COs and myself with grave forebodings. The men were not clad for the march over the 16,000-foot Karpola I Pass, and for staying at Tsangdhar which is itself 14,500 feet, and bitterly cold. There were no shelters *en route* or at Tsangdhar; no firewood for cooking. No advance party could be sent to organise the reception of the main body – a routine and fundamental requirement for approach marches, and imperative in the mountains. The troops would have to bivouac in the open for two or more nights. I never dreamt that Kaul would move them to the Dhola area without consulting me as Gen. Umrao had done. Once he saw the military situation I thought that he would abandon all talk of evicting the Chinese.

Subsequently our gloom was borne out by events when reports of pulmonary disorders, chillblain and even frost-bite poured in. Many died at Tsangdhar. The battalions arrived exhausted and without the most elementary requirements for battle. They had been on hard rations and without protection against the cold for many days. Kaul himself bemoans these happenings, without realising that they were the direct result of his own orders.

We spent a cold, bleak night in another herder's hut. It was difficult to breathe. I had a severe headache and my nerves were taut. I had never felt so helpless in my life. It seemed that there was nothing I could do to control or avert the impending disaster.

* * *

After spending the night at Tsangdhar we left for Dhola Post, to meet Gens. Kaul and Prasad, who were moving on foot from Serkhim, *via* Hathungla Pass, having flown from Ziminthaung to Serkhim in a helicopter. A special helipad had been built for the Generals at Serkhim, by Major Gopal, the Commander of my Engineer field company. After leaving Lumpu, on 5th October, Gen. Kaul sent for this officer, at about 4.30 p.m., and ordered him to construct a helipad, in the marshy area near Serkhim, by 5.30 a.m. the next day. Gopal left at about 7 p.m. with Petromax and hurricane lamps. Working all night they completed the job.

Lt.-Col. Misra, CO 9 Punjab met Kaul at Serkhim on 6th October. During the march to Bridge I Kaul and Misra exchanged some light-hearted banter about the Thagla Heights. Kaul asked Misra what the height of Thagla was. On being told that it was at least 12,000 feet, Kaul said, "It can't be, take off 5,000 feet and it will be 7,000 feet". Misra was heard muttering, "Take off 12,000 feet and it will bloody well be mean sea level". When asked about the gradient of Thagla, Misra said it was about 70 degrees. Kaul said, "It cannot be. I have been told that you people are exaggerating everything as you do not want to do the job. Thagla is a plateau".

Kaul met the Punjabi detachments at Bridges I and II, and was favourably impressed with their good spirits and their excellent defensive positions. They had had 21 days to prepare these positions and had been given the entire resources of the Brigade.

The events of 7th, 8th and 9th October are best taken together, as they represent the days when Kaul was "planning" and waiting for the two battalions to reach Dhola from Lumpu.

I met Gen. Kaul at Dhola at 2.30 p.m. on 7th October. He was accompanied by his trusted staff officer, Lt.-Col. Sanjeeva Rao. Kaul met the Dhola Post Commander and the local Intelligence Bureau Officer. Without further ado, he announced that Government had specially selected him for the task of evicting the Chinese. He spent the afternoon studying the topography of the Thagla Massif, and the Chinese dispositions and strengths. I briefed both Generals about the progress of the two battalions, the various shortages, the stock position and the state of the battalions after their forced march. Strange to relate, this was our first meeting and it was held after Kaul had set the Brigade in motion. That evening Kaul signalled HQ Eastern Command as follows:

(*a*) "The bulk of our air-drops of supplies, ammunition and winter clothing were landing in inaccessible places.

(*b*) There were only three days' rations available with 2 Rajput and 1/9 Gorkhas and fifty rounds of small arms ammunition per man. Our mortars and ammunition were still in transit between Lumpu and here.

(*c*) Due to lack of winter clothing men of these two battalions were spending the night at a height of 15,000 feet in summer uniform with one blanket. (We were also short of boots.)

(*d*) There was an acute shortage of civil porters which, coupled with inaccurate drops, was slowing down the process of our logistical build-up.

(*e*) The labour I have commandeered from the Border Roads Organisation would take some days before they became available as they were spread over a distance of about 200 miles.

(*f*) Additional aircraft be placed at our disposal immediately for task of air-drops.

(*g*) I (Kaul) was taking every possible step to evict the Chinese from our territory (despite our many difficulties) as ordered.

(*h*) The Chinese with their superior resources were likely to dislodge us from any positions which we may initially capture".

This was a very encouraging signal, as I sincerely believed that Kaul was softening the Government by stating the harsh facts. Surely Government must now alter its decision about evicting the Chinese. Kaul gave me the impression that he had accepted the "impossibilities" I had listed.

Before retiring I asked Gen. Prasad, my immediate boss, what was the plan of action as the two battalions were due to arrive at Tsangdhar and I would have to give them orders. Obviously they could not survive a prolonged stay at Tsangdhar without clothes, bedding and shelters. He confessed he did not know, as the entire operational situation was under Kaul's control. GOC 4 Division obviously had no plans of his own. The General was but a passenger.

Gen. Kaul has drawn three great red herrings to cloud the activities of 7th, 8th and 9th October; and he has omitted two vital facts. In doing so he has implicated Sen, Umrao, Prasad and myself.

The first red herring is with regard to the selection of the Dhola area. He writes, "My first reactions were that the Dhola area was unsuitable from many view-points and should never have been selected for any operational purpose (defence or attack) by Lt.-Gen. Sen or Brigadier Dalvi for the following reasons:

(*a*) Its lines of approach were difficult and unsatisfactory due to poor communications and hence the inaccessibility of this place.

(*b*) Observation of mutual posts of our own and some enemy positions was not as good as it should have been. It therefore afforded indifferent fields of fire.

(*c*) Good mobility of our own troops was not possible due to poor communications.

(*d*) A raging torrent lay right in front of our positions as a difficult obstacle which was a great handicap".

He goes on to say, "Even if Government had asked Lt.-Gen. Sen to drive the Chinese from the vicinity of Dhola and take up a position in that area for this purpose, he should have represented to higher authorities the tactical, topographical and other difficulties of doing so from the area in question and should have threatened the Chinese from a more favourable position to himself".

He adds, "The enemy was located along the Thagla Ridge in an impressive array in numbers and material, which lay right under our nose and could be seen clearly. On the other hand, our troops remained short of supplies, weapons and equipment alike. Our position – *selected by others before I took command – was located in what seemed a dangerous low-lying trap*. The Chinese overlooked us everywhere".

The second red herring is drawn across so-called earlier plans that were drawn up before he assumed command. He writes, "Brigadier Dalvi, Commander 7 Infantry Brigade, had stated in an Appreciation as far back as 28th September 1962, submitted to 4 Infantry Division, that an attack was *feasible* from the left of Dhola with a firm base at Tsangley which should be secured as the first phase".

He refers to this plan a second time, "I approved the plan of Brigadier Dalvi, made by him before my arrival, of sending approximately a company, North of the River Namka Chu, in the area Tseng-Jong which lay in our territory, on the 8th and occupying this position for the following reasons:

(*a*) Our troops had gone North of the River already, *BEFORE I arrived on the scene*, when Tsangley was occupied.

(*b*) If we had not occupied Tseng-Jong when we did, the Chinese would have done so shortly afterwards (as there were indications already before we occupied it) and threatened our position at Log Bridge.

(*c*) Commander, 7 Infantry Brigade had stated in his Appreciation on 28th September, six days before I took over, that his men would cross the river and occupy Tseng-Jong (*suggestions have been wrongly made that I initiated this order*). Even if I wanted to stop this move it was too late for me to do so as when I reached there on the 8th, one company was already on the way to Tseng-Jong *under orders of the Brigade Commander*.

The third red herring concerns the alleged defective defensive positions at Bridge IV, which Kaul was "constrained" to point out to me, compared unfavourably with those of the Chinese.

These observations divert attention from the following facts which Kaul has omitted from his book, *The Untold Story*:

(*a*) He ordered 2 Rajput and 1/9 Gorkhas, on 8th and 9th October, to move from Tsangdhar to the Dhola area (having already moved them from Lumpu on 5th October).

(*b*) On 9th October, he ordered the whole of 2 Rajput to move from Dhola to Yumtsola on 10th October and sit behind the Chinese.

Why has Kaul made these observations which reflect adversely on the professional competence of his predecessors and subordinates? By criticising the Dhola position Kaul might have hoped to cover himself for using the same unsound positions as the base for his plan of action. By insinuating prior plans to the Brigade Commander he may hope to create the impression that he was forced to accept events that he could neither control nor disown, as he had been given a deadline by Government, i.e. to evict the Chinese before the snows made operations impossible, and a great deal of irreversible activity had already been initiated "before he took over".

The arguments used against the Dhola area are, ironically, my own and were well known. Gen. Umrao Singh had included them in his letter of 30th September.

Dhola was not selected for any operational purpose whatsoever. It is a matter of regret that in his hurry to reach the Namka Chu and evict the Chinese, he did not allow himself time to study the background to the operations, and the modest aims laid down initially. He also failed to avail himself of the opportunity of consulting me, before ordering the whole Brigade to this unsuitable area. Had he discussed the matter with me at Lumpu on 5th October, I could have briefed him on the unsuitability of Dhola as well as the main points of our appreciation and plan. It is inconceivable that he was not briefed by anyone on the background and that he did not know of the first limited aim, which was to relieve Dhola and to ensure that the post was not abandoned under Chinese threats. It was only for this reason that a company of regular troops had been despatched to sit near the Assam Rifles and keep the supply line open. He should have known that 7 Brigade was ordered not to allow any further encroachments into our territory and 9 Punjab had accordingly been deployed to "police" the border. Indeed 9 Punjab had been moved personally by the Army Commander who had himself been urged to do so by the Chief, after the meetings on 13th/14th September. Having lost the Thagla Heights the only other suitable tactical positions were on the Tsangdhar plateau and Hathungla; but politically it was unthinkable to give up two miles of Indian territory and abandon Dhola. The whole object of the exercise was to uphold our right to maintain posts in our territory.

The question of the tactical soundness of the Dhola area is academic and intended to evade the question of how 7 Brigade eventually allowed itself to be destroyed in the Namka Chu.

Before Kaul assumed command, the Namka Chu area had only one battalion with the rest of the Brigade at Lumpu. Even if the outline plan of 28th September had been implemented the two battalions would have by-passed Dhola and moved to Tsangle *via* Tsangdhar.

It was Gen. Kaul who himself selected the Dhola area for his plan. It was he who ordered the Rajputs and the Gorkhas to move from Lumpu to Dhola.

If the Dhola position was a wrong one, Gen. Kaul having seen it for himself, on 7th October, would surely have ordered the abandonment of this unsound position and the occupation of better positions. Why then did he permit the continued occupation of Dhola with a whole brigade, where there had been only one company?

Major S. R. Johori has this comment to offer in his book, *Chinese Invasion Of NEFA*: "Later on the Corps Commander along with the Divisional Commander was present in the Dhola sector for more than four days. As a routine the Corps Commander was critical of the Dhola defences but he did nothing to change the defended localities for a better site. Probably there was none. The 7th Brigade had to occupy Dhola and defend it. The Dhola defences could not be given up simply because they were tactically unsound. . . . In spite of the tactical unsuitability of the place there were compelling reasons for defending Dhola. One was the infiltration in the area of the Chinese which had to be stopped". How right he is!

The fact is that Kaul himself was compelled to use the Dhola approach as it was the shortest, quickest and the only one which fitted in with his plans. If he had to do something by the 10th, then the longer Tsangle-Tseng Jong approach had to be discarded on the grounds that the troops could not be moved and maintained along this route. Moreover, the approach march would have taken a minimum of 8 to 10 days and the troops would have needed an enforced rest before being committed. In other words, Kaul could not have achieved the deadline of 10th October which the Cabinet had set him, unless he chose Dhola as the assembly area of 7 Brigade. It is therefore grossly unfair to denigrate Gen. Sen and tarnish his professional reputation – at least on this score.

Now to the red herring of previous plans which were apparently binding on 8th October and which cramped Kaul's initiative, making him a passive spectator. The plan was defunct for reasons which have been amply brought out. Whatever hopes there might have been of carrying out a limited probe in strength on 28th September, there were none on 8th October. In any case, if the plan to cross the river was drawn up on 28th September why was it delayed till 8th October? And why was the route altered from Tsangle to Dhola to a frontal advance to Tseng-Jong?

The truth is that there were no plans or orders to send anyone anywhere on the night of 7th/8th October, in fact there were no plans of any kind. We were waiting for Kaul to complete his reconnaissance, arrive at his own assessment of the situation and issue fresh orders.

Equally Kaul would have known of any allegedly unilateral plan to cross the *de-facto* boundary – the Namka Chu – and occupy Tseng-Jong. He had been with us from the afternoon of the 7th. Kaul says that he "discussed till quite late various operational situations which were likely to arise during the next few days". This is delightfully vague. Is it logical to believe that the move of a company to the sensitive North bank, across the *de-facto* boundary, in the face of the massed Chinese would not have figured in the discussions? Would Kaul not have asked us for our plans, and would we not have told him? 7 Brigade was not made up of a body of fire-eaters or morons.

Major Johori has effectively demolished Kaul's references to prior plans. He writes: "The IV Corps Commander reached the sector on the 6th. He remained there from 6th to 11th October. He held many conferences with his senior commanders. He also must have formed his own views on the subject. The very presence of the Corps Commander in the field of operations was enough to confirm that he had approved the operational plan to be launched to achieve the aim of the brigade. One cannot imagine that an officer of Lt.-Gen. Kaul's calibre and influence could be an idle onlooker of historic events taking place there. Therefore it is wrong to say that it was the Brigade Commander's idea to make Tsangle a firm base for the impending operations. In arriving at this decision every senior officer present in the area had a hand in proportion to his responsibility and authority. In the first week of October 1962 Lt.-Gen. Kaul's presence in the sector makes it obligatory to him to accept full responsibility for the execution of the plan of attack against the Chinese intruders. If the plan was not to his liking he could have immediately stopped its execution. After all, he was the Corps Commander and his word at the time was law in the sector. Lt.-Gen. Kaul himself admits that he approved 'the plan of Brigadier Dalvi'. Our objection is against the association in the plan with the name of Dalvi. The moment the plan was approved by the Corps Commander, the highest authority in the area, it became the Corps Commander's plan, the Indian Army's plan".

The last lacuna in Kaul's disarming explanation for the move of the patrol which suffered so grievously, is the assertion that it was "too late" to stop it. Why was it too late? The company was in continuous wireless touch and reported its arrival by radio telephony. It could have been recalled at a moment's notice. The patrol would have returned with 'indecent alacrity'. No one relishes "sitting" in the midst of armed enemies..

The strictures about the defective preparations at Bridge IV are unwarranted and unjust. I have often wondered what could have led the General to make this observation which reflects more adversely on the junior leaders than brigade commanders. After all, Prasad and I too had arrived at the Namka Chu with the General on the 7th. On the 9th there were no defensive positions at Bridge IV, except for Major Chaudhry's company. These men belonged to the same battalion which Kaul had commended for preparing good defences at Bridges I and II, under the same CO, Lt.-Col. Misra. Why then should this company have been remiss when it was commanded by an excellent company commander? And what is the point he is making?

Major Chaudhry was a gallant and able officer who gave his life for his country during the Chinese War of 1962. He commanded one of the best companies of a first-rate battalion. Chaudhry commanded the detachment that was sent to Tseng-Jong on 10th October, and earned a gallantry award for his conspicuous bravery. It is my privilege to defend this fine young officer. I am satisfied that he and his men did all that was possible with the limited tools at their disposal, to carry out the non-military task given to them.

To complete the picture of general incompetence, inefficiency and lethargy, Kaul throws in a last shrewd observation, "Also, except for 9 Punjab, few others had good knowledge of the ground, as they had just arrived there". Who else besides 9 Punjab should have known and did not know the ground? Who were the "others" and where had they come from? And for what purpose?

These comments of Kaul were designed to create the impression that Dhola was an occupied, prepared defended area. It was not. Kaul himself moved the Gorkhas and Rajputs into the vacuum at Bridges III and IV, and on 9th October these two battalions had to occupy positions, without the normal battle drill for such an operation. Everyone just arrived at the same time, and junior commanders were virtually forced to site themselves in gross contravention of elementary infantry training and practice.

Gen. Kaul should have dismissed a Brigade Commander whose omissions ranged from a badly selected area for operations to badly prepared positions. Senior Commanders do not go round being "constrained" to point out such serious faults during operations but air their disapproval only in memoirs. Patently Kaul had no grounds to take any such action. It is intolerable that those who brought us to the sorry pass of October 1962 should dare to sit in judgement on the brave men who were never given a chance; never given the tools; never given the time, and never given the leadership to prepare for any sort of military operation of war.

Let us now turn to the climatic events that culminated in the clash of 10th October, and set up the stage without embellishments or extraneous observations. On 8th and 9th October Gen. Kaul held "operational discussions" with Gen. Prasad, Commander 7 Brigade and the three COs; the Brigade Major and sundry other officers were also in attendance. Captain Mahabir Prasad, the officer who had established Dhola Post in May 1962, was a special invitee to this august assembly, as he was supposed to know the Chinese-held area of Thagla. All this so-called planning took place without a single functioning HQ and decisions were about to be taken without benefit of staff studies, or follow-up action by staff officers. HQ IV Corps had not been established. Assorted gentlemen were fetching up at Tezpur, armed with appointment letters from the Military Secretary but not knowing where Thagla was.

Operational plans that are likely to involve the honour of the nation are not drawn up by an in-gathering of assorted commanders, without maps, without staffs and without any administrative backing. To say the least, it is most unusual to formulate plans in a soviet of leaders, after the fashion of a band of guerillas, or smugglers. Major Johori has characterised Kaul's conferences as ". . . informal and reminded one of a unit darbar though on a corps level. Here the Indian Army was making history!"

8th October was spent mostly at Bridge III, gazing at the peaks on the Thagla Massif, and showing Gen. Kaul the Chinese dispositions. He kept asking for vacant areas and the routes to them. Captain Prasad was the sole source of information, assisted by the local Intelligence Bureau representative and the Dhola Post Commander. Despite the strange nature of his queries we were not alerted as to his intentions. He discussed the possibility of various "hooks" and sending commando groups to occupy odd isolated points. There was an unnerving confusion of plans and proposals. In between, the General regaled us with stories of Rommel's turning movements, although none of us could see the relevance of the famous desert Field-Marshal's tactics at Himalayan heights of over 14,000 feet. He interspersed his "reconnaissance" with anecdotes about his experiences in Korea and his visit to China. He told us tales of Chinese bravery in the Korean War. He told us of the political background in Delhi and how Mr. Nehru was being taunted by Right-Wing elements, and pushed by pugnacious civil servants to be tough with the Chinese. I could scarcely credit that this was a serious operational conference. The whole Order Group heard these reminiscences and comments. I had never before attended anything so informal. Speaking for myself and my COs, I can say, with all responsibility, that Gen. Kaul's approach to the serious matter of evicting the Chinese did not enthuse us. In fact, on the 8th evening we thought that having seen the tactical position, he would soon be telling the Government that we should call off all attempts at ejecting them. That could be the only reason why Kaul never went into details of the various ideas with which he kept toying.

On each of the nights of 7th, 8th and 9th October, Gen. Kaul would draft signals to the highest in the land. Due to lack of a staff and an office, Col. Rao and I were turned into scribes and took down his lengthy reports in longhand. The role of amanuensis sits ill on a harassed senior brigadier. Most of them were couched in the gloomiest terms, portraying desperate shortages, predicting dire consequences and forecasting grim possibilities. And yet the General was the picture of confidence when he invariably signed off with the assurance that he would do all in his power "to fulfil the given tasks". I was quite bewildered at this apparent contradiction between the facts stated and his naive optimism.

The next day a sturdy Sikh from the Punjabis would be detailed to "run" with this vital message to Lumpu. From there, the second-in-command of the Punjabis would phone it through to Zimingthaung, where it would be enciphered and transmitted to Tezpur, Delhi and Lucknow. This "tribal" signals set-up exemplified the pre-historic arrangements that obtained in October 1962. The first such message reached Delhi after three days. Mr. Menon was extremely annoyed and demanded the dismissal of the Chief Signals Officer of HQ Eastern Command, for inefficiency. It took a great deal of tact and persuasion to convince the Honourable Minister of the primitive signals communications that existed. In those days the simple solution to every problem was to sack someone. The tragic neglect of the years, by those in the highest positions, in keeping the Army without suitable mountain equipment, was conveniently forgotten.

We now come to the fateful decision of 9th October 1962. On the morning of 9th October the Order Group assembled for the second sitting. Gen. Kaul then gave out his "appreciation". He appreciated the impossibility of physically evicting the Chinese from any of their positions because of the adverse military situation. He realised that we would not be able to hold on to any gains that we may make on the Thagla Massif.

Gen. Kaul then threw the bombshell with which he had come from Delhi. He said that in spite of the stark facts and irrefutable arguments against military action, *he had no option but to make some move on 10th October, as this was the last date acceptable to the Cabinet, whatever the cost.* He went on to say that the Army Commander (Sen) had advised Government that he would evict the Chinese on 29th September; then changed the date to 1st October; and later to 5th October. There was a feeling in Delhi, conveyed by Gen. Sen, that the forward troops were stalling and that is why he (Kaul) had been sent to speed up operations before the onset of the snows and to ensure that the Chinese were evicted immediately. He added that the Cabinet was understandably perturbed at the frequent changes of dates which the Army itself had given. He claimed that it was the Army that had misled the politicians by giving them some hopes of ejecting the Chinese.

Kaul stated, in passing, that the eviction of the Chinese was imperative in the national interest and the country was prepared to lose 20,000 lives if necessary, for the achievement of this aim. He hoped that our wills were in order! There was a macabre air about the whole business.

As a direct assault on Thagla was ruled out, he decided to do a "positional-warfare" manœuvre, and occupy Yumtsola – to the west of Thagla peak-which was not, at that time, occupied by the Chinese. Kaul said that he hoped that this action would satisfy Government that "the Army had done its best to carry out its orders". He kept emphasising that this "operation" had to be started on 10th October, as he did not have the latitude to postpone it.

The need to concentrate 7 Brigade by 9th October and the move of this ill-armed brigade, with pouch ammunition and hard scales were now clear. Now we can understand the cursory record of the operational talks at Tezpur, which were confined mainly to the progress of concentrating 7 Brigade at Dhola. Henceforth we can dispense with all talk of badly selected strategic positions; previous plans made by brigadiers; and badly sited positions. They are only intended to mitigate the miscalculation of 9th October; Kaul had decided to provide "the kind of leadership that makes of war a game of clergyman's chess" – (in the words of Corelli Barnett).

Kaul then ordered 2 Rajputs to move to Yumtsola, to sit behind the Chinese, on 10th October 1962.

This order was given when the Rajputs were still recovering from their gruelling march over Karpola I Pass. Despite the known critical shortages and the adverse tactical situation, Gen. Kaul ordered the concentration of both 2 Rajputs and 1/9 Gorkhas to the Namka Chu. The move from Tsangdhar to the Namka Chu was under direct Chinese observation and must have alerted them. The swift and vigorous Chinese riposte the next day was undoubtedly influenced by the large-scale Indian movement. Now the whole Brigade was in the same Dhola death-trap which Kaul had earlier decried.

* * *

Before recording the reactions of the recipients of this fantastic order I should like to make two military observations, one about ground and the other about battle procedures adopted by battalions to move to a defensive locality. Let us take ground first. It is necessary to understand the meaning of ground and dominating heights which have figured prominently in this narrative. It had been well said by Mr. Majdalany in his book, *Cassino–Portrait Of A Battle*, that: "Ground is the raw material of the soldier as weapons are his tools. Ground is the factor which more than any other, eventually controls the shape of a battle. This is the basis of all tactics".

Mountains pose special tactical problems. An occupied mountain is an even more difficult proposition. Mountains are dominating because they provide observation which enables one trained Artillery Observations Officer, with wireless communication to bring down the fire of all guns within range, within minutes, onto any target that he can see. The better the observation the more difficult it is for the other side to move, much less manœuvre.

The piece of ground called Thagla was a 15,000-foot mountain, was heavily garrisoned and provided excellent observation to the well-equipped Chinese Force, supported by modern artillery and mortars.

Thagla was a sensitive piece of ground which the Chinese claimed to be theirs even under the terms of the McMahon Line. Tactically it overlooked the Chinese base at Le. As of 9th October only superior military force could have regained Thagla for us. Even the most enthusiastic burst of credulity and optimism should not have induced us to imagine that the Chinese would meekly forego their many advantages – especially after we had announced to the world that we had despatched a task force, with an outstanding general, to evict them. After all, the Chinese had invented the concept of "loss of face". They would certainly not give ground without a fight.

The move of a force of battalion strength is an operation which requires meticulous planning – even when no immediate enemy opposition is anticipated. It is axiomatic that infantry units should not be committed to a task which may flare up into a battle, unless the officers and non-commissioned officers have been given an opportunity to reconnoitre the ground, formulate plans and issue detailed orders on the ground. In this case we would be dispensing with these routine procedures.

Gen. Kaul's decision, however valid in its political assumptions, would clearly involve the complete disregard of these two and other elementary precautions. He was asking the Brigade to find its own mobile echelon and secure its own base of operations along the Namka Chu, and no time was allowed for the preparation of such a base, because of political urgency. The Brigade was to arrange for its own casualty evacuation, re-supply arrangements and sundry other mundane details.

* * *

A variety of astonished gazes greeted Kaul's announcement. The reaction of the audience was one of incredulity and disbelief. Lt.-Col. Rikh looked at me with consternation clearly visible on his strong face. Gen. Prasad looked as if he was pole-axed. I was stunned and rendered speechless for a few minutes. Lt.-Col. Ahluwalia secretly thanked his lucky star that he had been spared, this time anyway. Lt.-Col. Misra murmured to me that the Chinese would wipe out anyone who tried to establish a post on the North bank of the Namku Chu. Gen. Kaul at first had the smug look of a conjuror holding the rabbit by the ears, later he had a look of defiance as if daring anyone to question his orders.

Rikh took me aside and gave vent to his anger. He told me bluntly that he could not see his way to moving his battalion into the blue without reconnaissances, without a military task and without the basic requirements. He said flatly that the order was a mad one and demanded to know what I intended to do about it. I just looked helplessly and had no answer to give him.

I had never before been placed in such an awkward predicament. Here was the Corps Commander issuing orders in front of the COs and other young officers. How was I to contradict him or argue with him in public? Kaul held an unorthodox "order group" to forestall argument. There was no question of "making plans together, appreciating each other's point of view, taking joint decisions or having interesting pow-wows" – as Kaul has since tried to make out. In any case military plans are not made after holding pow-wows. In battle there are no joint decisions. A plan devised by a million brains is still signed by one man; and that man assumes responsibility for it. Kaul was very fond of name-dropping and I am not sure whether the Cabinet did actually give him a fixed dead-line. As far as we were concerned this was the second time that we were being asked to be "Lions in action and dogs in obedience".

After a while I raised a few difficulties about moving and maintaining the Rajputs in Yumtsola, even if the Chinese permitted us to do so. When I pointed out the shortage of snow-clothing, Kaul blithely informed us that 6,000 sets had been ordered and were being flown out from Canada. Of course they could not arrive before the Rajputs left the next day. There was no solution offered for the poser of how the Rajputs were to survive at 16,000 feet till the cargo planes landed.

When the question of artillery cover was raised he first said that "Determined Infantry do not need artillery", thus topping Lord Haig's *faux pas* when he said in 1912 "Artillery only seems likely to be really effective against raw troops". When pressed he said that he would arrange to drop more para-guns. These too would arrive after the Rajputs had settled down next to our Chinese friends on Yumtsola. God knows when the gun teams would arrive from Agra.

The requirements of porters was settled by the promise to send us all the Border Roads Pioneers from

Towang. We were still waiting for our Lumpu loads to be "hastened forward".

Everything was in the future except the move of the Rajputs. There was a great deal of reluctance on our part to share Kaul's optimism and self-confidence. We could not subscribe to the curious assumption that by ignoring realities, the realities themselves will disappear. In sheer desperation I asked Kaul to have a patrol sent before committing the whole battalion. He agreed: and it was decided that a platoon under Major Chaudhry be sent, as he knew the ground. The task given was to cover the move of the Rajputs; find a crossing place and above all to ascertain the Chinese reaction to our crossing the Namka Chu.

The decision to cross the Namka Chu on 9th October was thus not based on any earlier Brigade plan. An advance patrol was sent in pursuance of Kaul's order to send the Rajputs to Yumtsola, on 10th October, to mitigate the rashness of blundering blindfolded into the Chinese defences.

Kaul has gone on record as saying that the Tseng-Jong patrol left on the 8th. In fact it left on the 9th. The true date is material. According to the Chinese: "Tseng-Jong (Chitung of the Chinese) was occupied by a batch of Indian troops on 9th October 1962" – *vide the White Paper No. VII, p. 106.*

Major Johori commenting on the variation in dates, says: "Therefore it seems logical to believe the Chinese version. If 9th October was the date of occupation of Tseng-Jong it is evident that the Corps Commander Kaul discussed the plan of operation of evicting the Chinese from the south of Thagla Ridge in the conference, otherwise it beats one's imagination why the Corps Commander was there at all for a week. Briefly, the surmise that Tseng-Jong was occupied by a company of Rajputs after the approval of the Corps Commander is correct and logical". Major Johori has arrived at the right conclusion, except that it was a

Punjabi patrol which had been sent and not a Rajput detachment.

* * *

That night 9th October Brigadiers K. K. Singh and M. R. Rajwade fetched up at Bridge IV exhausted and incapable of any constructive thinking or planning. They both flopped down and could not work up enough energy to have dinner. I do not say this with malice. It is a tribute to their grit and fitness that they did not succumb to the heights as happened in the case of the senior Corps Artillery Commander, who stayed behind.

It was the height of folly to drag them to Dhola before IV Corps had even been set up and when a battle was being hatched for the 10th. Lt.-Col. Sanjeeva Rao the GSO I had already accompanied Kaul and here was the Brigadier General Staff, thus leaving no responsible 'G' Branch officer in Tezpur. Would any commander anticipating war, or planning an "operation", permit this? The staff must be at the HQ attending to the myriad duties that are part of any battle. Instead they were swanning around when the Chinese attacked the next day. Dhola was littered with red-hatted senior officers, observers who had no role to perform, except to add "more brass than steel" to the proceedings. I cannot help feeling that they had been invited to witness the Grand Finale – the Super-Galwan.

And so we move on to the fateful day of 10th October 1962 when, for the first time in history, regular soldiers of China and India fought a pitched battle in the remote Thagla area, on an arena which was 15,000 feet above sea level. To paraphrase Sir Winston Churchill, "The days of pious words, virtuous motives and brave utterances were about to bow to the armed and resolute wickedness of the Chinese".

David had flexed his arm to throw his pebble at Goliath!

Chapter XV

The Clash At Tseng-Jong—10th October 1962

The patrol of 9 Punjab, under Major Chaudhry, reached Tseng-Jong before dusk on 9th October. Like all the place names in this area, Tseng-Jong was just a herder's hut. They had reconnoitred two suitable crossing places for the Rajputs, and had left small detachments at each place. One of these later became famous as 'Log Bridge'.

Chaudhry and his 50 odd men were heavily attacked, at 5·00 a.m. on 10th October, by some 800 Chinese supported by heavy mortars. The Punjabis stood their ground with incredible gallantry in the face of overwhelming odds. Chaudhry had sent one section to the foot of Karpola II peak (not to be confused with Karpola I Pass), from where it brought withering and accurate *enfilade* fire on the assaulting Chinese. The Chinese, caught by surprise, suffered heavy casualties. They were forced to call off the first assault, but quickly re-formed and mounted simultaneous attacks from three directions. The Punjabis, outnumbered by 20 to 1, were overwhelmed. Major Chaudhry was wounded but carried on with great determination and courage. We had six dead and eleven wounded. The Chinese admitted to 100 casualties, mostly incurred in the initial assault.

The "swift and massive retribution" for our attempt to disturb the *de-facto* boundary shook Gen. Kaul, who saw the first Chinese attack develop. His first reaction was one of disbelief, shock and disillusionment. "Oh my God", he cried, "You are right, they mean business". That is what we had been trying to tell him all along but he had preferred to believe the clap-trap prevalent in Delhi. His moment of "challenging grandeur" had turned into disaster.

He then turned to me, "This is your battle. This is a brigade battle". As soon as we got into trouble the battle became a brigade one; hitherto we had been talking of obeying Cabinet decisions, and everybody was doing the planning for and commanding this one brigade.

It was most fortunate that the Chinese attack was mounted before 2 Rajput had crossed the Namka Chu, *en route* to Yumtsola, as otherwise they would have been exterminated. They were being committed to a possible battle, at a height of 15,000/16,000 feet (after an almost vertical climb from about 10,500 feet), with only 100 rounds per man. Their move would have been observed throughout by the Chinese on Thagla Ridge, and they would have arrived completely exhausted. Even if the Chinese had consented to the occupation of Yumtsola, they could have perished in the severe cold without the Chinese firing a single round; and there was nothing that could have been done to save them. The Chinese could afford to ignore the garrison at Yumtsola. It would be helpless without the pipe-line through which it had to be maintained. The only thing the Chinese had to do was to retain their interceptor posts, close the doors and the battalion on the mountainous slope would gradually atrophy and perish of starvation. I am certain that if the Chinese had any inkling that we would do anything as unsound as sending a battalion to Yumtsola they would have waited and massacred the battalion while it was moving, in broad daylight or gradually starved it to death.

Soon after the firing started I took Gen. Prasad aside and told him to tell Gen. Kaul to stop talking of evicting the Chinese, take a realistic view of the naked military situation and pull us back. I expressed the same view to Gen. Kaul when he later asked for my opinion. I told the two Generals that we should abandon the Namka Chu at once, except for our established flag-posts. Lumpu should be restored as the main dropping zone with Tsangdhar as a minor auxiliary one for the company at Bridges III and IV. We should no longer waste valuable air effort and supply dropping equipment on Fairchild Packet drops. I reminded them that we now had only four days' rations for my Brigade. The reserve stocks with Major Chaudhry's company (about 100 men) had been whittled down to four days for a force of two battalions of about 1,000 men. The scanty drops at Tsangdhar, coupled with the lack of porters, meant that we would not be able to ensure our survival either tactically or administratively. *The Chinese were at that time estimated to be a full division.*

Both the Generals agreed with my advice.

During these discussions the position of my Brigade was grim. The Punjab patrol was being pulverised at Tseng-Jong. 2 Rajput were moving in single file towards the 'Log Bridge' *en route* to Yumtsola. Battalion HQ was passing Bridge IV when the firing started and our men were visible to the Chinese dug-in on the opposite bank. In Kaul's words, "I saw the 2 Rajput rushing towards the Log Bridge as they had been ordered the previous day to take over that position as also one at Tseng-Jong. Our men were rushing up to various positions".

Gen. Kaul saw the Tseng-Jong retribution for himself and says that he "fully understood all the implications of our predicament; and thought that the whole position in this theatre should be reconsidered". The stunning Chinese blow had chastened him and he was no longer inclined to believe that the Chinese could be bluffed out of their impregnable redoubts or that there could be peaceful co-existence on the mountain slopes of Thagla. The dynamic optimist had vanished. Kaul appreciated "the superiority of the Chinese in every respect, the untenability of our position in the Dhola area located in a hollow, the various shortages which could not be made up in a few days, the lack of fire-power, the Chinese build-up to a division and the Chinese determination to prevent the establishment of any Indian positions north of the Namka Chu".

Flying in the face of this correct diagnosis we were soon to witness a crowning act of folly. We adopted the worst possible course of action having regard to the adverse factors. Although the trial of strength had demonstrated the Chinese capability and intentions, and the perilous risks spoke only too eloquently, Kaul could not nerve himself to call off the engagement and take the tactical decision to occupy defensible ground elsewhere. He wanted to consult Mr. Nehru. He gave the impression that a decision to restore the *status quo ante* 5th October, could only be taken after he had apprised the Cabinet of the local situation and obtained fresh orders. After the failure of our ill-conceived sally, what was the point of waiting for Delhi to give clearance for a straightforward tactical decision? Perhaps Kaul did not want to be accused of withdrawing and facing the taunts of his professional enemies and unfriendly politicians. Perhaps he wanted to take shelter under "higher orders".

In the meanwhile he was content to leave 7 Brigade in a perilous position, cliff-hanging, at the mercy of the Chinese and without the tools to defend itself. Here was the most powerful General of the Indian Army, who had earlier accused others of selecting wrong positions and criticised them for being post-offices, rendered impotent. In the moment of supreme crisis he failed to accept responsibility for obligatory decisions. The senior commander was bound to extricate the Brigade from the position in which it had been placed.

Many before him have made this discovery, many after him will find out: failure to measure up to the high promise, shown in peace-time soldiering. Mrs. Barbara Tuchman has made this apt comment, in her excellent book, *The Guns Of August*: "When the moment of live ammunition approaches, the moment to which all his professional training has been directed, when the lives of the men under him, the issue of the combat, even the fate of the campaign may depend on his decision at a given moment, what happens inside the hearts and vitals of a commander? Some are made bold by the moment, some irresolute, some carefully judicious, some paralysed and powerless to act".

In which category can we place Kaul at that supreme moment of his baptism? Let Kaul's own orders tell us. Kaul told Gen. Prasad "that the instructions to drive away the enemy were to be held in abeyance till I return from Delhi. In the meantime he was to hold his present positions". Prasad had no "positions" till Kaul placed 7 Brigade in the Namka Chu! Kaul gave himself the role of a "messenger" of Prime Ministerial orders in his "moment of decision". He was powerless to act.

* * *

Kaul sincerely believes that he never gave an order personally, and no position fell because of any unsound order that he gave. He personally gave these orders before he left Dhola for Delhi, on 10th October 1962.

(*a*) The instructions to drive the enemy out were to be held in abeyance till he returned from Delhi.

(*b*) In the meanwhile we were to hold our position, i.e. the South Bank of the Namka Chu and "ensure the security of the crossings from Temporary Bridge to Bridge I at all costs."

(*c*) Our position on the North Bank (Tsangle) was to be held at the discretion of the GOC 4 Division. He stipulated, however, that there was to be no withdrawal from Tsangle until the company was actually threatened by the Chinese.

(*d*) Line of Communication *via* Lumpu will be protected.

(*e*) Hathungla will be held.

Kaul went a step further and personally gave orders to the CO of the Rajputs as well. He told Rikh not to advance any further as the situation had now changed and the enemy had reacted more violently than he had originally appreciated. He then ordered Rikh to "hold the south bank of the Namka Chu with one company each at Temporary Bridge, Bridge IV and Bridge III". Rikh pointed out that these positions would be dominated by the Thagla Ridge and in the event of a Chinese attack they could not be held. Kaul countered this by telling him that we were going into defence only temporarily and that the enemy would not attack if we remained on the south bank. Kaul emphasised to Rikh that we must not give up a single inch of territory we held.

Dhola later fell, because he ordered the holding of useless logs, in the face of a militarily hopeless situation. We could neither defend the Namka Chu nor could the Namka Chu defend us! As Napoleon once said to Marshal Berthier when he found troops deployed in linear fashion: "Is the object of these operations the prevention of contraband?" What was Kaul's object?

Had Kaul withdrawn 7 Brigade to Lumpu where he had found it in the first place and presented the Cabinet with a *fait accompli* the Brigade might not have been captive in the Namka Chu. No cabinet in the world would have dared to indicate the actual localities to be held. Kaul had taken on a grave military responsibility by bowing to the primacy of politics but he had still in no way renounced the prerogative of military leadership in his own exclusive sphere.

The decision to hold the 'Present Position' on 10th October, after the Chinese attack on our patrol, was Gen. Kaul's third blunder.

Fearing a Chinese reaction to the Tseng-Jong skirmish, I gave the two Generals an escort of one Gorkha company, under Major Pawar. I told Pawar to stay at Bridge I till he was relieved by 4 Grenadiers whom I was expecting soon, and who would be responsible for the Hathungla route. The layout of the Brigade was now chaotic. The Rajputs at Bridges III and IV had one of their companies at Bridge I under the Punjabis. I had sent this company on 25th September to relieve a Punjabi company for reconnaissance duties in the Tsangle area. The Punjabis had a company at Tsangle, about 12 miles to the west. Now the Gorkhas would have a company on the Hathungla – Bridge I approach. All this was the result of hurry and panic. It would be some days before companies could be reshuffled and a semblance of orthodox command and control restored.

* * *

After Gen. Kaul left with his *entourage* I turned to the Tseng-Jong battle which was raging furiously. I could watch the fight from Bridge IV, and had a grand-stand view of each detail of the battle. Every soldier can judge my feelings as I watched the brave Punjabis being hammered by the superior Chinese Force. To me it seemed a senseless waste of lives. I damned the pernicious theory of positional warfare and playing games of sitting behind the Chinese. Damn this non-violent kind of war!

I was soon called upon to go through the most agonising hour of my life. Major Chaudhry made a desperate appeal for mortar and machine-gun fire to extricate his force. Col. Misra relayed this request to me and added his own urgent plea for help. I was standing very near our machine-guns and mortars at Bridge IV. The crews of these weapons also begged me to allow them to open fire, and help their brethren.

I, and I alone, am responsible for the decision not to allow the mortars and machine-guns to open up. My aim was to extricate this patrol without further loss of life, and without exposing the main body to massacre. As the Commander on the spot, I had to take a broader view of the pros and cons of escalating a minor engagement into an all-out battle, along a 12-mile front. It is a cardinal principle that the security of the main body is the prime responsibility of a commander and this security must not be jeopardised for any reason whatsoever, and never to assist a small detachment.

My first and over-riding reason was that Tseng-Jong was out of range of effective fire. The range of both weapons is approximately 2,700 yards and Tseng-Jong was beyond that range. Besides, the patrol had no mobile fire controllers to engage targets. So on purely technical grounds I could not guarantee to assist the patrol by covering fire.

I could possibly have taken on, by direct observation, the Chinese reinforcements moving to Tseng-Jong, after the failure of the first Chinese assault. This movement could be clearly observed by me and the weapon crews. But in doing so I would be igniting the entire front and inviting retaliation and reprisals against my force on the south bank, without being certain that I would actually be helping the small detachment. Here are my reasons as I saw them at the time:

(*a*) The Rajputs were milling about trying to find cover and take up positions between Bridges III and IV and Log Bridge. They would have been mowed down, in the open, by the Chinese machine-guns across the narrow Namka Chu. The same fate would have befallen the Gorkhas.

(*b*) Even if I had decided to risk the consequences, I knew that I could not sustain a fire-fight for long. My weapons were sited in a small open patch directly in front of the Chinese. There were no alternative positions due to the heavy undergrowth (and hence lack of fields of fire), on the higher slopes. If I opened up I would be placed in the ridiculous position of having my mortars silenced by enemy small arms fire.

(*c*) I had two 3-inch mortars with 60 rounds per mortar; and two machine-guns with 12,000 rounds (barely sufficient for half an hour at normal rates). I would have exhausted this ammunition in a few minutes and would have been disarmed.

(*d*) The men had only 50 rounds per man, and 500 rounds per light machine-gun and were not prepared for a major engagement.

(*e*) Gen. Kaul was moving post-haste to Bridge I, on his way to Delhi. His route was, throughout, parallel to the Chinese positions along the Namka Chu, and he would have to pass Bridges I and II. I could not risk starting a widespread exchange of fire and jeopardise his chance of reaching Delhi. Kaul was on a mission that had vital bearing on the fate of my Brigade, and serious implications for India.

Looking back on events I am convinced that the Chinese were waiting for an opportunity to substantiate their claim that they counter-attacked in self-defence. They would have had an excuse if I had used my puny resources against their assembled might. Even without any overt action on our part they claimed we had attacked them first and misled even some of our friends. The over-enthusiastic Indian Press, and jubilant Government servants made much of a skirmish that was nothing more than an attempt to set up a post, in our own territory, in an area which had not been occupied by the Chinese and which was contemptuously repelled.

With a heavy heart I saw the Punjabis disengage, on my orders, to Bridge IV. The casualties came directly to Log Bridge, under the noses of the Chinese who had evidently decided to allow us to use a route which they were controlling. Very cleverly they continued to give the impression that they did not want war, but that if we crossed the Namka Chu they would resist.

Some time later I could see the Chinese burying our dead, with full military honours. It was a moving sight and certainly made an impression on the men who could also watch the proceedings. All this was part of the Chinese plan to win over the sympathy of the jawan, and suborn his will to fight.

No event of the short war caused more heated and lingering controversy, both in India and abroad and gathered more layers of dispute than the skirmish of 10th October. The Tseng-Jong action was not a battle, in the true sense. The Chinese attacked our patrol which was inside our territory. We did NOT attack first. Indeed we had no means to ward off a Chinese attack, let alone mount one ourselves. The Chinese used this incident to launch a canard that India had started the NEFA War and that the Chinese did nothing but defend themselves. Unfriendly and uninformed commentators have been inclined to swallow the Chinese line. It would be an insane commander who would even entertain a fleeting thought of launching an attack, having regard to the relative military positions of the two sides, on 10th October.

The point to be stressed is that the Tseng-Jong skirmish was not a prepared operation against the Chinese defences on Thagla Ridge. It was a hurried resumption of a weary advance to set up a post on the Thagla Ridge. Exhausted by days of marching over massive heights and appalling weather conditions, troops badly in need of a breather and the tools for war, were merely ordered to keep going to Yumtsola. A plan was devised, by Gen. Kaul, which would work only as long as the Chinese desisted from using the full military power which was available to them. Kaul himself has confessed: "We had occupied this position (Tseng-Jong) in the hope that so long as we held a particular piece of ground, it would remain ours and unchallenged — as in the past". The plan made no attempt to contend with the terrain which entirely favoured the Chinese; nor with the exceptional extremes of the Himalayan weather. The men were wet, frozen and had been continuously on the move. They had known nothing but mud, mountains and rain. They had known sickness brought on by too much exposure to wet and cold, which had taken a heavy toll of lives. But these did not matter as the men could recuperate after reaching Yumtsola and establishing themselves alongside the Chinese!

It is an indisputable fact that the action of 10th October was an *ad-hoc* affair, hastily undertaken entirely due to the alleged dead-line imposed by the Cabinet, coupled with the imperative need for some action before the impending snows. It is clear that the politico-strategical concepts erred in two respects; over-reliance on Chinese good behaviour; and under-estimating the Chinese military power to challenge our move. It was in the first place a political gamble hustled into effect by the Government, in pursuance of its belief that we had to attempt the expulsion of the Chinese "to the best of our ability". It was launched at the worst possible time, from a fighting point of view, to pacify a clamorous public. It miscalculated the Chinese mood, in its preposterous notion that a weak and unsupported battalion could boldly march up the Thagla slopes, in broad daylight and stay there without interference from the Chinese. The political move initiated by the Government, with intolerance of the military difficulties pointed out by the local commander who would have to execute the order, was pushed through by Kaul, with an immoderate degree of fanfare and publicity. The failure of the Chinese to oblige us by "seeing sense and withdrawing"; or indulging in non-violent protests, undermined the whole basis on which the venture was founded. We believed that the Chinese would not respond militarily to their eviction. In this premise everybody was wrong – politicians, civilians, soldiers, strategists, diplomats, and pandits.

Thus ended the momentous day of 10th October 1962. It was the point of no return. "David had cast his pebble – and missed!"

Part V

The Battle at the Namka Chu River

Chapter XVI

"Defend Your Present Positions"

We now enter the fourth and last phase of the ill-starred Thagla Ridge Operation. I spent the next few days with the Gorkhas as my HQ had not yet arrived (they were not on the bayonet strength of the Brigade!), and my Brigade Major and I had no protection nor messing facilities and no battle headquarters.

7 Brigade was now awaiting the results of Gen. Kaul's mission to Delhi. This was the third wait while a general officer emissary left to get fresh orders. 2 Rajput and 1/9 Gorkhas commenced preparations of such defences as were possible with the limited tools available; (the Rajputs had only 10 *dahs* and only 50 per cent of the authorised scale of digging tools): with complete lack of defence stores and in full view of the enemy. The task of securing all the so-called Bridges, resulted in tactically unsound localities. The defence of crossings is achieved by deploying three echelons. The first is the close bridge garrison, and the second a supporting detachment tactically sited, in depth. The third is a mobile column organised and prepared to counter-attack the enemy's main crossing. 7 Infantry Brigade could not even provide the men for the close bridge garrisons.

* * *

On 12th October elements of 4 Grenadiers, under the command of Lt.Col. Harihar Singh, began arriving at the Namka Chu, and took over Bridge I and the Hathungla axis. This allowed me to restore companies to their own CO's. The Grenadiers too were shabbily equipped and did not even have matchets to cut trees, for bunkers. They had only pouch ammunition. They had come straight from Delhi and were exhausted.

This was the third battalion that had been catapulated from the plains and employed without any acclimatisation. My force was now about 2,500 men.

The efforts of our troops to cut logs with entrenching tools and shovels were pathetic and openly derided by the Chinese who could see us. They had a lavish scale of mechanical saws and could build defences and bunkers at an incomparably faster rate.

On 13th October some 150 Border Roads Pioneers arrived to assist us in carrying loads and collecting air-drops at Tsangdhar. By 16th October we had a total of 450. In the event they proved an embarrassment as they had come without rations and winter clothing, forcing me to deplete my meagre stocks, to feed and clothe them. I now had barely two days rations for my command.

Kaul reached Delhi on the evening of 11th October and went straight into a conference with the Prime Minister, the Defence Minister, the Army and Air Chiefs, and the Secretaries of the Cabinet, External Affairs and Defence. At last a body resembling the Defence Committee of the Cabinet was convened to handle the grim impasse.

After explaining the situation at Dhola, Gen. Kaul claims that he pointed out that:

(*a*) If we attacked the Chinese, as things stood, then we were bound to have a reverse. We should therefore pull out of Dhola and go to a more suitable area tactically from where we could fight them better.

(*b*) The Dhola area would soon be snowbound when it would be impossible to maintain it any longer.

(*c*) Whatever build-up we might achieve opposite Thagla, the enemy with their superior resources and approach, could oust us (and in the process weaken us at our other fronts).

(*d*) The Chinese were in a better position to build a superior force due to good communications behind their forward position, an advantage we did not enjoy.

I must interpolate a comment here. Had the Chinese communications improved between 5th and 10th October? It was not necessary to have the bloodshed of 10th October to highlight the factual position that had been self-evident since mid-September.

Having belatedly analysed and portrayed the adverse military situation *vis-a-vis* China correctly, Kaul had a glorious opportunity to retrieve the position, but for some inexplicable reason he offered the august assembly three choices:

(*a*) Whether I (Kaul) should continue building up this sector and launch an attack on the Chinese despite their superiority and possibility of a reverse.

(*b*) OR to cancel the orders of an attack but hold our present positions;

(*c*) OR to hold a more advantageous position elsewhere.

Gen. Kaul tells us that, on the advice of the Army Chief and the Army Commander, Mr. Nehru agreed that, instead of attacking the Chinese under these circumstances, we should hold on to our present positions.

The three choices offered by Kaul, to the Cabinet was a capital blunder.

Kaul was ill-advised to offer three choices, at such a high-powered meeting. It was abundantly clear that there was only one choice, and that was to hold a more advantageous position elsewhere, the course recommended by Gen. Prasad and myself and accepted by him. He exceeded his brief when he talked of building up for an attack, or of holding on to our present positions. In Kaul's own words: "I was advised by my Divisional Commander that I should go to Delhi and ask the Army HQ and the Government not to press us to expel the Chinese from this area, a task which was far beyond our capacity and that we should occupy a position where we could be better placed *vis-a-vis* the enemy. Dalvi had the same view. I agreed both with the Divisional and Brigade Commanders".

Let us analyse these choices. The Chinese now had at least one strong division. It would require three divisions and at least an Army Group Artillery to dislodge them, on the basis of the minimum superiority of three to one. There was no earthly hope of any such reinforcements by air, on the pint-sized dropping zone, or across the footpaths over the Hathungla and Karpola I Passes. The build-up of the dimensions implicit in Kaul's offer was out of the question. Kaul might have misled the members of the meeting when he mentioned a continued build-up as a possible course. He also made the unwarranted assumption that there would be a great deal of inaction on the part of the Chinese, while we were furiously "building-up!"

Holding on to our present positions was an equally questionable recommendation. To hold a low-lying "death-trap" in the face of an enemy holding high ground is at all times impossible. The troops were doomed in the absence of artillery support and defence stores. A brigade in deliberate defence can hold approximately 3,000 yards: and 7 Brigade was spread-over 12 miles, or nearly 20,000 yards. Artillery is required for defensive fire to break up enemy assaults; for counter-bombardment to silence enemy guns and for neutralising infantry weapons which assist the enemy's final assault when artillery cover cannot be used due to the safety factor. How did Kaul envisage the provision of this massive support? In deliberate defence the defender lays mines and wire entanglements, with booby traps, to break up the final charge as well as to canalise his movements. Where were these vast quantities to come from?

In other words, Kaul entertained the prospect of holding a 12-mile linear defence, the so-called "present positions", without reserves, without depth and with one unsupported brigade. Kaul messed up the last chance of bringing sanity to our high-level thinking by his unfortunate offer of three alternatives. In doing so he did not display that intimate knowledge of the capability and requirements of an infantry battle that one would expect from a General, especially rated as outstanding by the Prime Minister of the Nation. The essential elements of the appreciation of the situation, on which he was bound to base his advice were virtually eliminated. Kaul had turned his back on the realities which he had fully understood, after the skirmish of 10th October. He neatly passed the onus for taking further decisions to his political bosses and military superiors.

The Indian Government was then at bay. It was committed to challenging the Chinese intrusion to pacify public opinion, and knew that an impossible military situation had been cleverly created by the Chinese. And so when a trusted and responsible senior General, who knew the ground and the military setting offered them the remote hope of continuing to maintain "a state of no victory and no defeat", they grasped the chance. We cannot blame Mr. Nehru for accepting Kaul's course of "holding our present positions!" There was by now an ominous roar from an aroused public. Government had become a prisoner of its own facile pronouncements. Perhaps it was still dominated by hopes of Chinese good behaviour if we made no further attempt to alter the *status quo* in the Thagla-Dhola area. In any case events thereafter got on to certain lines and no one could get them off again.

Mr. Nehru's now infamous, off-the-cuff verbal broadside to the Press on 12th October, while on his way to Colombo was, in my opinion influenced by the rather wooly choices presented to him. That is perhaps why he was prompted to say that the actual date for evicting the Chinese was being left to the Army. According to *The Statesman* of 13th October 1962, the text of Mr. Nehru's statements reads "For the first time since the NEFA Operations began Mr. Nehru categorically stated that the armed forces had been ordered to throw the Chinese aggressors out of NEFA. Our instructions are to free our territory". But asked how soon this would happen, he replied, "I cannot fix a date. That is entirely for the Army".

Mr. Nehru's choice of words was characteristically unhappy. It was true to his aristocratic and impulsive nature which on many occasions resulted in uninhibited statements which had unfortunate reperscussions. The plain fact is that he committed one of the great *faux-pas* of modern times. He should not have used the phrase "throw out" when referring to a major power, and especially the Chinese who are proud and sensitive. More than once I was told that they were deeply offended by Mr. Nehru's statement. One Chinese Officer said, "The Americans cannot throw us out, what can you miserable Indians do to us. How dare you talk like this about the mighty Chinese People".

It will be appreciated that we as soldiers were considerably shaken by political leadership of this kind. The decision to permit military action is, after all, the gravest that a head of State ever has to take. Gen. Sen told me many months later that he was thunderstruck when he heard Nehru's statement, especially after the briefing and the decision taken the previous night. I myself heard this amazingly casual remark over All-India Radio's 1.30 p.m. news. I called Gen. Prasad and asked him to confirm whether I was to accept operation orders from All-India Radio, or whether I shoud await his orders. Sarcasm was the only weapon I had left.

* * *

The delay between 10th and 13th October was sinister and oppressive. I was on tenterhooks to know the outcome of Kaul's meeting with the Cabinet. Alas, on 13th October Kaul sent a signal confirming the verbal orders of the 10th viz. "to hold our positions". The Namka Chu was "no longer a place but a principle". When I got this message I could no longer overcome a feeling of impending calamity. This disastrous order was sent as another slogan, as there was no Information about the enemy or Own Troops; no Method paragraph to indicate what the rest of IV Corps would be doing to achieve this task; no Administrative instructions to spell out the arrangements for our maintenance. The brief signal was a clear portent of things to come and settled the fate of 7 Brigade which was to be left to fend for itself in the remote Namka Chu Valley dependent on an erratic air supply system and at the mercy of the Chinese massed on Thagla. 7 Brigade could no longer help itself. Its thinking had been done for it. It had merely to carry out a suicidal assignment with no scope to influence its fate. Without a doubt, there had been some cardinal blundering in ordaining the task of securing the crossings over the Namka Chu, "at all costs". As Clausewitz has said: "Military plans which leave no room for the unexpected can lead to disaster". The "unexpected" in this case was the probability of a massive Chinese attack against the weak Indian garrison.

Kaul does not assume responsibility for this order as he considers that he was merely obeying the fresh directions which he had received from the Prime Minister. He affirms, "I was told to hold these places by higher authorities and they fell for causes which lay beyond my control". What may we ask was Kaul's role and function in October 1962? Why did he not demand (as did Field Marshal Manstein): "As long as I remain at this post, however, I must have a chance to use my own head"?

Chapter XVII

Feverish Activity—13th/19th October 1962

The period 13th to 19th October was one of grave anxiety and foreboding. The trap was closing. The Chinese build-up mounted in ever-increasing tempo from their 7-ton road-head at Marmang, which was only a few miles from Thagla. They used sturdy Tibetan ponies right up to their forward localities. They were industriously and methodically fortifying their positions with the thoroughness and skill which they had demonstrated to the World in the Korean War. Order groups were seen receiving orders, and artillery personnel were brazenly taking bearings on our positions for silent registration of targets. They brought guns and mortars across Thagla Ridge on ponies and positioned them opposite Bridges III and IV. They even brought a jeep type vehicle to Thagla. I saw an elderly officer, with an impressive fur hat being treated with great deference – obviously a general.

I had deployed 25 observation posts to watch the Chinese build-up and to report their activities. These posts were actually able to count the number of mortar bombs and shells dumped. On 19th October one of the observation posts above Temporary Bridge actually counted 1,978 armed Chinese soldiers concentrated at Tseng-Jong. All the Chinese traffic was duly reported in special situation reports, and was known to all concerned. We were mute witnesses of our own impending destruction.

We had to stand by helplessly, as we were out-weaponed, out-numbered and tethered to indefensible ground, with the order to defend useless logs of wood at all costs. My troops continued their feverish preparations but were handicapped by the complete lack of axes, saws, cutting tools and a total lack of defence stores, which should have been air-dropped to us. The men were growing weary of being eternally on guard, exhorted to defend what could not be defended.

During this time four para-field guns were dropped, but two were damaged beyond local repair. The gun-teams marched across Karpola I, and they too suffered grievously and had fatal casualties as they had been rushed from the heat of Agra. By 19th October 421 rounds of ammunition were collected. One troop of 4.2-inch mortars, (4 mortars), was sent to me on a man-pack basis. We managed to build up a stack of 450 bombs for this troop before the Chinese attack on 20th October. Both these weapons were out-ranged by the Chinese infantry mortar which has a range of about 7,000 yards. This is a farcical state of affairs as no one has ever heard of the Artillery Arm being out-ranged by the Infantry. There were no suitable gun sites along the Namka Chu Valley and the guns and mortars had to be deployed at Tsangdhar, further reducing their effective range. Preliminary ranging was not permitted both for political reasons, because we did not want to start a fight and because ranging in the mountains is expensive in ammunition. We had no meteorological data on which to base predicted fire, an essential requirement in the mountains where the weather is variable and unpredictable. We had only two observation parties for the whole front. This was the artillery situation, for a 12-mile front! This is the result of going to war with a token corps.

* * *

The Medical arrangements for the troops deployed in the Namka Chu Valley were primitive in the extreme. From the very outset the medical set-up was frequently rendered ineffective due to ill-thought moves and counter-moves. Although 7 Brigade started moving to the Namka Chu from 10th September onwards it was not until 25th September that the Brigade Mobile

Surgical Team (MSU) and 24 Field Ambulance (Fd Amb) were able to leave from Towang for Lumpu (which they reached on 30th September) for lack of porters. 9 Punjab had no medical cover, other than the Regimental Aid Post (RAP) from 15th to 30th September; and even this was two days march across Hathungla Pass. The Chief's initial order, of 17th September, to evict the Chinese, would have found the Punjabis fighting a battle without any life-saving medical arrangements. The rash promises to concentrate at various dates and charge at the Chinese obviously did not cater for any medical units. If true, this was not only a major breach of the canons of planning, but also extremely callous.

On arrival the HQ of the Field Ambulance (MDS) with the MSU, was established at Lumpu. One company of the same unit (ADS) had been deployed along the Line of Communication from Towang to Lumpu to act as staging posts and to render medical aid to the many transients, who were suffering grievously for lack of acclimatisation. The second Advance Dressing Station (ADS) was sent to Tsangdhar on 6th October under Captain B. B. Kolay. This detachment had a most unenviable time; and a virtually impossible assignment, as they had to function at a height of 14,000 feet without proper rations, clothing, shelters and medical supplies. They reached Tsangdhar on 7th October, on a man-pack basis, with the main body of 7 Brigade. Despite their many difficulties they did an excellent job of life-saving. Captain Kolay had to deal with an average of 30/40 serious cases every day, and placed some 8/10 men on the "dangerously ill" list. Almost all the cases were due to pulmonary oedema brought on by the lack of warm clothing, bedding and shelters.

Prompt evacuation of casualties was well nigh impossible, as the only method was by helicopter – and the only helicopter available was one two-seater Bell.

The normal channel was from the Namka Chu by unit stretcher-bearers, to Tsangdhar; thence by the Bell to Ziminthaung: and to Tezpur in a larger helicopter. Each casualty required eight men as stretcher-bearers and the men had to be found by the units themselves, as the Brigade had no stretcher bearer-units. This was a further drain on units who were under-strength and who had to find their own collecting and carrying parties for air drops. Few men were left for preparing defences, patrolling by day and night and providing personnel for observation posts. This fact is sometimes overlooked by those who have criticised the Brigade defences.

The wounded and sick had to be carried up steep and treacherous paths from about 10,500 feet to 14,500 feet, for over eight hours. This was an ordeal as the stretcher was constantly tilted or put down as the bearers tumbled, slipped or got tired. The same men would be required to carry heavy stores from the dropping zone to their units, on the return journey.

I can find no words to adequately express my praise and gratitude for the courage, humanity and devotion to duty shown by Squadron Leader Williams of the Air Force, who, under grave risks, carried out non-stop sorties from dawn to dusk. His record for one day was 23 patients – the last take-off being in pitch darkness. I salute a brave officer. I was delighted to hear that he was decorated in recognition of his gallantry, the citation for which was rightly initiated by the grateful Army Medical Corps.

The siting of the Surgical Team – the only early treatment unit within miles of the battle field, was subject to the same general confusion and interference. Initially it had been located at Lumpu to treat the casualties of 9 Punjab. On 7th October, after Gen. Kaul had reached the Dhola area, he personally ordered the unit to set up shop at Bridge I, without consulting any senior medical adviser. Thus within a week of the organisation of some sort of arrangements for surgical operations they were moved to function alongside a regimental aid post, barely 100 yards from the forward Chinese localities. Apart from the impropriety of ordering specialist units about without consulting the appropriate experts, two vital factors in the employment of this unit, were overlooked. A Mobile Surgical Team is only an operating unit and cannot function independently, since it does not have facilities to hold and nurse post-operative cases. For this reason it must invariably be sited alongside some element of the field ambulance. It is certainly wrong to locate this valuable unit with a regimental aid post, directly in the line of enemy small arms fire. The second factor overlooked was that surgical operations cannot be carried out at heights over 9,000 feet without sophisticated oxygen equipment, which we did not have. We were merely jeopardising the lives of patients. In his anxiety to provide "medical cover" for the troops which he was planning to send behind the Chinese, Kaul ignored the normal working of medical units, and gave yet more proof that he did not envisage any bloodshed.

The Surgical Team reached Bridge I, as ordered, on 10th October, and as casualties were expected from the Tseng-Jong battle that day, a 180-lb tent was put up as an operation theatre, right on the River bank. As the Tseng-Jong skirmish did not escalate into anything bigger, the Surgeon was able to treat nine casualties on the 10th and 11th.

On 12th October Major Jayaraman the Surgeon, sent a frantic signal to his departmental boss Colonel Maitra, the Assistant Director of Medical Services, of HQ 4 Division, stating that he could not function in the prevailing conditions. Colonel Maitra was not only a first rate medical officer but a man of character and moral courage. He boldly reversed Gen. Kaul's orders and instructed the unit to move to Ziminthaung and work alongside the Field Ambulance, which had since been moved there. The Team reached Zimin-thaung on 16th October and was established on 18th October, only two days before the Chinese attack.

The medical set up could barely cope with the numerous sick cases, and broke down completely when the Chinese attacked and captured Tsangdhar. It was now impossible to evacuate any casualties and that is the reason why the Chinese had so many wounded Indians on their hands. Medical aid is not a gift. It is a soldier's right. It is a prime factor in the maintenance of morale. Commanders who fail to provide proper facilities are not only guilty of negligence but of inhumanity.

* * *

The supply arrangements were equally unsatisfactory. The main base was at Tsangdhar from 8th October, Lumpu being relegated to a secondary role. The set up was again improvised at the last minute. The Deputy Assistant Quarter Master General (DAQ MG), Major Kaushik, from HQ 4 Division, was in charge of organising collection, storage and distribution to the troops on the River Bank. This *ad hoc* arrangement was forced on us by the lack of a proper air supply chain of command. We should have had a Forward Airfield Supply Organisation. The DAQMG of Division did not have any actual units or sub-units to command or assist him. He had to make do with miscellaneous bodies from other supply units who were hurriedly despatched, on foot, to Tsangdhar – again without acclimatisation. Porters and carrying parties were provided by units manning the River Line. Later they were supplemented with Border Roads Pioneers.

* * *

There was no Army Ordnance set up and no system of indenting. Equally there was no system to ensure that units received their requirements in accordance with the priority laid down by the units themselves.

Demands were unprecedently high as units had arrived without basic items, and these had to be super-imposed on the battle requirements. The creaky administrative layout could not cope with this rush. Depots and dumps in the rear were alerted and they were sending what they thought the troops would want; or whatever they could lay their hands on first. We received innumerable pairs of size 6 and size 12 boots ! For many days we could not get studs for Army boots as the item was "in short supply". If there is any one single item that condemns our production/procurement/or stocking policy it is the lack of this humble, miserable, but vital item. Anyone who has tried to walk over a moss-covered boulder, in a new pair of Army boots without studs will understand the fury of the soldier at the persons responsible. Readers will also appreciate the enormity of the crimes of those who fed the Country and the Army with tall talk of self-sufficiency in arms productions, grandiose plans to build planes and tanks, while leaving the Army short of this simple, indigenously produced item. The Generals who ordered men to move over 16,000-foot passes, in forced marches wearing these unshod boots are even more guilty of callous inhumanity.

* * *

4 Division's Signals Regiment managed to get a telephone line through from Division to 7 Brigade over the Hathungla Pass. The line ran parallel to the Chinese forward defended positions for over seven miles, in violation of every principle of laying line in the battle zone. The line was useful for conducting all the futile conversations that preceded the Chinese attack, but served no purpose whatsoever after the assault, as it was inevitably cut. This was one more feverish military activity under Chinese observation to give the illusion of feverish military preparations.

* * *

Throughout, we were in full view of the Chinese and no surprise was possible, nor hopes of purposeful camouflage. The Chinese could also be seen clearly, which fact did not do our morale any good. With their superiority and preparedness they made no attempt to conceal their movements or activities. They almost openly dared us to make the first overt move, as this would have suited their policy; and given them the excuse to carry out their famous "self-defence counter-attacks". Even when we did not oblige them they went right ahead and exercised this inalienable right!

* * *

The tempo of air drops at Tsangdhar reached a climax between 15th and 19th October. Losses due to wild drops increased in direct proportion to the number of sorties, and only 30 per cent of stores reached the troops. This was nobody's fault and certainly not the fault of the gallant pilots. It was impossible to drop supplies on so small a dropping zone from Fairchild Packet aircraft, without a large number of canisters going astray. It was infuriating to find loads landing a few feet inside the zone and then bouncing down a precipitous slope. Troops in contact were required to collect these drops. When I protested that I could not spare man-power for porters and yet prepare my defences, I was told to "retrieve or perish". The journey to Tsangdhar and back took eight hours. After returning from this duty the men had to carry out sentry duties. We had no coloured parachutes to identify loads and thus units could not concentrate on collecting those stores which they required most urgently. In one case after an arduous descent through rhododendron bushes, to a parachute, the men found broken snow-goggles. They were furious.

Nobody in the rear would appreciate the principle of saturation of drops. The greater the tempo of air-drops, the less is actually collected. This may sound paradoxical but is a fact as the dropping zone has to be cleared while aircraft are actually dropping. In other words if aircraft drop from sunrise to sunset nothing is collected that day. Someone had bullied the Air Force to drop so many tons and they were damned well going to drop them! Tsangdhar was also in full view of the Chinese positions on the Thagla slopes. I saw many pictures of our air drops in the Chinese papers. They made a big play of our having dropped paratroopers, just before "The Indian frenzied attacks" on the morning of 20th October, which was the last straw that forced the innocent Chinese to launch their massive counter-attacks!

* * *

On 16th October I was able to set up my HQ at Rongla, about 1,000 yards from Dhola post. The location was not ideal but the only one possible in the circumstances, unless I went to Tsangdhar. I rejected this idea as the men and the CO's were located near the Chinese, guarding the crossings, and could not therefore conform to the normal principles of siting battalion HQ's. I could not be the only HQ to be sited comfortably away from the River. The troops would not have understood why only Brigade HQ should adhere to normal procedures, while everyone else was being asked to violate them on the promise that the Chinese would not do anything big. I had to be near the men. Here I must express my surprise at the fact that most books written about the NEFA Operations have placed 7 Brigade HQ at Tsangdhar. This is not true.

* * *

To relieve the monotony of this litany of ineptitude, let me relate some of the lighter moments, amidst the general gloom. They were not funny at the time, but it seems incredible that we should have allowed ourselves so much bathos. As long as day to day decisions were centered at the highest levels, and there was a never-ending wait for general officer emissaries to return from Olympus with reasonable orders, the proleteriate could not be in a position to take an intelligent and constructive interest in the proceedings.

While all the hectic Chinese activity was in full swing, staff officers in the rear were blissfully unaware of the impending disasters. A young captain from Education Branch of Divisional HQ sent my HQ a most severe reprimand, and demanded an explanation for not sending our "athletes" to Tezpur, for the Sidi Barrani Celebrations of 4 Division. Needless to say, I was hard put to offer a satisfactory explanation to this irate officer, who was probably struggling to prepare a list of invitees and an outline programme for the approval of his immediate boss!

The senior staff officer on the administrative side sent me a personal rocket, on about 16th October, the gist of which was that he was very "dissatisfied" with the rate of collection by forward troops. He issued "orders" that each infantry battalion will "with immediate effect" detail 200 men each day to collect drops. He threatened disciplinary action against defaulting units. I envied this gentleman, sitting in remote Gauhati, his peace of mind and blissful ignorance of the impending pay-off for our years of neglect. He still retained unshakeable faith in the efficacy of threats, and a belief that the Indian Army Act was the magic abracadabra for getting things moving. He did not know that troops in battle require a cause and leadership and not threats. It is probable that he was not even aware that the men were facing a battle. He may have thought that we were still playing the old game of keeping track of the "progress of stocking".

When Kaul took over a non-existent corps he was faced with the unusual problem of finding somewhere to locate himself and his staff; and of scrounging some office equipment and communication facilities. He adopted the simple expedient of moving HQ 4 Division from their permanent location at Tezpur and appropriating their established resources as well as their comfortable accommodation. The Divisional Commander "went forward to Ziminthaung to control operations from nearer the front". Everybody conveniently forgot that the GOC's second brigade at Walong would now be over 300 miles away! Rear Division HQ was consigned to Gauhati to do the work of Corps and Army units. There was no perceptible dislocation of command and control as there was only one infantry brigade facing the Chinese in NEFA, which everyone was commanding verbally. Basic orders were being issued at the highest level and transmitted at an equally high military level. Administration (including air supply) was the responsibility of Army or Corps HQ's, thus rendering Divisional HQ useless and redundant. The Divisional staff was now unemployed and an embarrassment. This unprecedented situation required a novel solution. Voila! Why not send the surplus divisional staff officers to HQ 7 Infantry Brigade? As Division was not in a position to send me reasonable orders, or appreciations, or artillery or clothes or defence stores, the next best thing to demonstrate their solidarity and goodwill was to send me unemployed staff officers. In three consecutive days I found the GSO II, the DAQMG and the DAAG on my door step begging me to give them something to do. The DAQMG was killed at Tsangdhar when the Chinese attacked on 20th October: the GSO II was evacuated sick with lung trouble, within a day of his arrival: and the DAAG was returned with thanks as I did not have any problems connected with ceremonials, pay, pension, welfare or discipline.

The influx of tourist staff officers was so comic that to this day I cannot believe that this was the manner in which the Divisional Staff of 4 Division, was sought to be employed. This finally confirms the utter chaos and disorganisation that prevailed in October 1962. We cannot take refuge in political interference for this atrocious state of affairs. We are all to blame for creating the atmosphere more appropriate to a Ruritanian Army.

Chapter XVIII

The Occupation and Build-Up of Tsangle

Before venturing into the last act in the tragedy of Thagla Ridge, I must recount the unfortunate fixation on holding Tsangle. Thwarted in their endeavour to throw out the Chinese; oblivious of the Chinese build-up for an invasion; prodded by uninformed public opinion; and not knowing whether to retreat or negotiate; the higher planners at Delhi took refuge in Tsangle. The handling of the Tsangle affair typified the breakdown of the entire Indian nerve-structure for the higher direction of war and went to show how difficult it was to reconcile psychological and political inhibitions with hard military facts.

The task of guarding all the crossings over the Namka Chu was an impossible one, as we have seen, and 7 Brigade was cannon-fodder for the Chinese whenever they chose to attack. In spite of this, I was not permitted to concentrate my energies and resources towards this end. I was ordered to fritter away resources on continually building up this miserable god-forsaken herder's hut called Tsangle. It will be recalled that Tsangle was first occupied on 4th October, after a reconnaissance patrol had visited the place and reported that the place was unoccupied.

We now know that this information was a god-send to a harrassed Indian Government, clinging to straws, and seeking a loop-hole to extricate itself from the dilemma of its own making. Here was a chance to show some "gains" on the Thagla Ridge. I was ordered to hold Tsangle, despite the certainty of compromising our tactical plan. Later, I was ordered to build it up to prove to the Bhutanese that not only did we have adequate forces to handle the Chinese, but had surplus men to deploy on their borders. There are no limits to self-delusion.

From the outset Tsangle was an embarrassment because of the difficulty of maintenance. There was no direct route from Bridge IV due to impassable bluffs. This forced us to adopt the circuitous route *via* Tsangdhar. By mid-October the turn round time had increased to five days, over icy paths and slippery gradients. It was impossible to carry a worthwhile payload on this route, as the carriers themselves had to be self-contained for ten days. Men with power, but no knowledge, ignore these uncomfortable facts of life.

Most "porters" began dumping their loads *en route*, and the more stout hearted were delivering quantities that were not worth the effort of sending them there. They could have been better utilised to build-up the Namka Chu defenders.

Snow clothing at 100 per cent scales had to be provided to all porters commuting between Tsangdhar and Tsangle due to the extreme cold and the altitude of Tsangle i.e. 15,500 feet. Both the troops and the porters had to be protected against the bitter weather or else they would have perished. The only solution, lay in undressing the defenders of the Namka Chu and providing the minimal requirements for the defenders of Tsangle. This was a most unhappy solution and was deeply resented by the simple Indian jawan. It brought shame to the Officer Cadre, who are not expected to do a strip-tease with one lot of soldiers to ensure the survival of another.

I implored Gen. Prasad to permit me to abandon Tsangle and protested against the wasteful diversion of resources. My pleas were turned down on the grounds that Gen. Kaul's orders were that we could only abandon Tsangle only if directly threatened by the Chinese. Instead, I was ordered to send more reinforcements of men, mortars and machine-guns. *On 17th October I was ordered to send a company of Gorkhas* to strengthen the existing company of Punjabis. *On 19th October I was ordered to send the remainder of the Gorkhas.* Had this move taken place we would have the ridiculous situation of having five companies in one tiny locality, and ten companies spread over ten miles.

These orders were issued at a time when the Chinese were building up furiously opposite our positions along the Namka Chu, and their intentions could be ignored only by the optimistic or the foolish. The mulish determination to hold Tsangle is the final, irrefutable proof that the Civil Authority and the Army High Command did not expect, much less prepare for, a Chinese invasion, despite the open evidence.

In our trial we did not understand the significance of the fixation on Tsangle, at the expense of the task of holding "our present position". We were never given a satisfactory explanation. I pointed out that Tsangle had no tactical significance. I pleaded that I was hard put to give the troops a concrete task. I was invariably squashed by the Delphic pronouncement that "This move had been ordered at the highest level". QED! Once when I protested more vigorously than normal I was warned that my CO's and I would be court-martialled if we raised any more objections or arguments against Tsangle. After all, these moves had been ordered at the highest level.

Tsangle is a matter of vital import for an understanding of the constitutional theory of "Civil Supremacy" – a most widely misunderstood term. Gen. Umrao Singh had protested, initially on tactical grounds, that the holding of Tsangle would compromise our plans. He was overruled. Later, on 17th October, Gen. Kaul claims that he tried his best to convince the High Command to abandon this wretched place, but he failed. Kaul claims that he was unable to influence his military and political superiors to rescind this order. He argued, in vain, in the presence of his bosses, Gens. Thapar and Sen. Unfortunately he does not tell us why he did not ask for a revised task in the Namka Chu, in view of the diversion of resources to Tsangle to meet a fresh political requirement. Why did he not ask for the abandonment of the Namka Chu? Why did he not ask for the re-deployment of 7 Brigade, on higher ground? How else could he compensate for the reduction in the strength of the Namka Chu garrison? Whatever he did at the "political meetings", the fact remains that Kaul threatened and bullied his subordinates to carry out all the paper tasks. He never once visited us to explain these unreasonable and unsound orders. Indeed I never saw Kaul again after the 10th of October.

At that time I did now know who this mysterious "highest level" was. Now we are told that it was Mr. Krishna Menon himself. On 17th October, Mr. Menon is reported, by Kaul, as saying "it was politically important for us to hold on to Tsangle as it was situated near the Tri-Junction, a point where India, Bhutan and Tibet met". Menon was presumably exercising his own version of Civil Supremacy, of which he has never ceased to boast. As late as November 1967, he said, in ringing tones that, "Who else but the Government can take decisions of this nature". He apparently believes that the Tezpur meeting of 17th October, is an exercise in Civil Supremacy, in the face of the stark military and topographical facts; and the advice of his military commanders. The result was that considerations of national prestige added significantly to the probability of defeat. The reinforcement of Tsangle was achieved by depleting the Namka Chu garrison, as fresh troops could neither be inducted nor maintained. We could only reshuffle the same old pack of cards. The scope and nature of the Chinese build-up, on 17th October was well known, through the situation reports that were being sent daily; and yet Mr. Menon was laying down his own national priorities.

If Tsangle was the last symbol of misconceived Civil Supremacy, it also represented the low-water mark of the exercise of fruitful army leadership. The military Brass should have known the importance of the Selection and Maintenance of the Aim – the cardinal principle of war. The field commander reponsible for operations cannot be given a task and then have his resources diverted to a second task, without amending the first. Political pressure and futile verbal protests are poor alibis for passing orders which clearly violate principles, and interfere with primary tasks. To the officers in the Namka Chu, it appeared there was a diabolical collusion and unholy alliance, between the politician and the generalship of the day.

* * *

Before I narrate the events which rose to a crescendo on 20th October 1962, I would quote *The Times* of London. After the Tseng-Jong skirmish of 10th October, this paper commented: "There is no apparent realisation here (New Delhi) of the magnitude of the military contest which India may now have begun. Observers in a position to know better are still speaking lightly of a swift action to eject the 300/400 Chinese. Official accounts of continued strengthening of the original Chinese Force have been ignored". It is incredible that an itinerant journalist should have reached a more incisive judgement of events than those with the resources of the entire Governmental machine.

On 15th October 1962, Mr. Nehru said in Colombo that: "The attitude of the Chinese Government is to seize territory and then have talks. India is not prepared for that. China cannot be permitted to occupy Indian Territory and hold it for further bargaining". After the briefing he received, on 11th October, on the NEFA situation, was Mr. Nehru in a position to make such a statement? And what could he do about it? Prime Ministers are not expected to soliloquise in front of journalists. Mr. Nehru's views should have been confined to a Cabinet Sub-Committee, where realistic counter-measures can be formulated.

Chapter XIX

The Blinkered Command

On 16th October Gen. Prasad spoke to me on the phone from Tsangdhar. I was waiting for a sorely needed message of hope and encouragement. Instead, he told me that Gen. Kaul had not been able to convince the "higher authorities" of the impossibility of evicting the Chinese. The Defence Minister had now given the 1st of November as the last date acceptable to the Cabinet. The Defence Minister wanted to know what my requirements were for this task. At first I was too paralysed to give an answer. When I regained my composure I realised that someone had completely lost his sanity. This was the third failure of a general emissary, to convince his bosses to act in a sane and mature manner. I was practically without clothes, without rations and without artillery, and I was being asked "what I needed" to evict the Chinese. The back-log of even basic requirements was not being made up. After a bitter exchange of words, wherein I accented the prevalent lunacy, I asked Gen. Prasad to send me the Armoured Division and 200 medium artillery pieces! I gave vent to justified disillusionment as I began to realise that my troops were likely to be sacrificed through the stubbornness of others. Prasad "agreed" with me that the Defence Minister's offer had no military meaning as the movement of troops and equipment were restricted by the Himalayan terrain. There was nothing that anybody in the world could do to alter the military balance in our favour, in the prevailing circumstances.

Gen. Prasad promised to present our "joint" views to the Corps Commander. I had another wait while our views were being "represented". This was the fourth time that the military advice of forward Commanders was being represented. I was sick of this word. This time the military factors were self-evident and I could see no justification for wasting time on consulting me, or the need for any further advice or opinion. The suspense caused by these frequent representations and its effect on the officers and men facing certain destruction can easily be imagined. While we waited in the exposed valley, wet, frozen and on edge with uncertainty, we had to endure the towering Thagla Massif, the Chinese preparations for the *coup-de-grace* and abandon hopes of being rescued by our senior commanders. Visits by Senior Commanders who ask fatuous questions result in the breakdown of military protocol and breeds despair.

This vexed question of "representations" was a symptom which portrayed the demoralisation of those who should have displayed the moral courage expected of general officers. I accept my full share of blame for this fantastic procedure that passed for operational command. I should have resigned after this futile conversation.

Gen. Prasad had come to see me at Towang on 10th September and promised to represent my views to the Corps Commander, Gen. Umrao Singh. On 25th September, Gen. Prasad "agreed" that there was no hope of evicting the Chinese. On 29th September Gen. Umrao promised to go to Lucknow and represent our views to the Army Commander. On 10th October, a chastened Gen. Kaul left for Delhi to explain the desperate position at the Namka Chu to the Prime Minister. Now Gen. Prasad was going to have another crack at Gen. Kaul, and through him the Defence Minister. It is pertinent to ask who was actually supposed to take military decisions and respond to these frequent representations? Who was turning down whose advice? Where was the Army Command set up? Had they all become office-runners? Obviously the years of misplaced civilian domination were now being paid for in the remote Namka Chu Valley. The Army Brass had lost its authority and capacity to resist impracticable political orders. Civil Supremacy reigned supreme.

It was frustrating to have my views accepted and yet never found anyone who could actually decide one way or another.

There was clearly no hope of evicting the Chinese as things stood in the Namka Chu and yet this senseless pursuit of a mirage persisted.

I have often been asked why I did not resign. There were many reasons apart from the ethics of such an act. The primary one was that throughout the operation I never met a single senior officer who disagreed with me purely on the professional plane. I had, therefore, no grounds for resigning. Inept political leadership is not a valid reason for brigadiers to relinquish command or resign their commissions. One expects seniors to issue sound orders and not merely pass on orders in which they have no faith.

* * *

On 17th October I asked Gen. Prasad to withdraw my Brigade from the Namka Chu as quickly as possible as, whatever the political imperatives for my deployment, I could not maintain my troops. Again he promised to 'speak' to HQ IV Corps. Instead of acceding to my request I was asked by his staff to forward certain information 'at once'. I was ordered to find out and report data with regard to the lake near Tsangle. Army HQ wanted to know the thickness of ice in this lake during winter, as it had apparently been 'decided' at the highest level that one infantry company would be kept at Tsangle throughout the winter and that it would be maintained there by landing helicopters with floats. I replied that prior to September no one had heard of this accursed place, much less spent a winter collecting this sort of useless data. I was promptly told to liaise with the civil authorities and obtain the information. I banged the receiver down after pointing out that no Civil Authority had set up his headquarters near me at the Namka Chu; the nearest Base Superintendent lived a few yards away from Divisional HQ and it would perhaps be quicker if the Divisional Staff would get off their backsides and walk across the road for their information. It is unbelievable that this sort of wishful thinking and pursuit of delusions was going on while the Chinese were massing for an invasion. All our reports of the Chinese build up were obviously not being read, much less imbibed, by any responsible person.

On 18th October the Chinese were engaged in last minute preparations for a night advance and a dawn attack. We could see their marking parties and guides moving to forming-up places. I sent frantic messages to 4 Division but got no reaction. Everyone seemed to be deaf, dumb and blinkered.

On the night of the 18th, CO 4 Grenadiers reported that a Chinese party had infiltrated between his positions and the Punjabis, near Bridge I. We both thought that this was probably a marking party and that we should try and intercept it. I did not stop to think of how we would converse with a Chinaman, if we caught one, as the nearest interpreter was probably in Delhi! I spoke to Col. Misra and co-ordinated the attempt to bar the escape route. Unfortunately due to thick jungle, poor visibility and lack of daylight reconnaissance, the Chinese infiltrators got away. I had a small bet with Misra that we would get a 'rocket' before the morning. Sure enough, at 6.30 a.m. I was rung up and asked to explain why I was still allowing 'intruders' to enter Indian territory! By that time I was beyond being surprised at anything. The imminence of the Chinese assault and the scope of their preparations were jus-

not being comprehended at the top. The outward composure of the High Command was clearly due to a failue of imagination. There was an air of unreality and doom during the last critical days and moments of the Chinese build up.

* * *

On the evening of the 18th, Lt.-Col. K. K. Tewari, Commander Signals of 4 Division arrived at my HQ. He had been sent to check the Brigade signals communications especially the newly laid line. He was able to brief me on what was going on at the Divisional level. I was grateful as I had received no Operation Order or Intelligence Summary to date. He told me that 7 Brigade was going to be withdrawn very soon and only one battalion was being left in the Namka Chu; the rest of 7 Brigade would be located at Lumpu. One company was to stay at Tsangle for political reasons. He also told me that a Defence Operation Order was being issued by Division very soon. Needless to add that this order never fetched up.

Col. Tewari was a gentle, God-fearing man in addition to being a first rate signaller. He had worked against tremendous odds throughout the operations and had overcome difficulties which would have taxed an Army Signals Regiment. He is due much credit for providing communications with obsolete equipment and the distances involved. Instead of praise they came in for criticism for not being able to work miracles with out- dated sets and distances which were beyond the range of divisional signals.

I was once asked to sack my Brigade Signals Officer but I refused and said that I would prefer to be sacked myself. I was responsible for giving him tasks which were beyond his capability. Tewari was grateful for my intervention on behalf of an innocent young officer. I hope that young Lachhman Singh reads this small tribute from a grateful Commander, for his untiring efforts to keep me in touch.

There was a sad sequel to Tewari's visit. He asked my permission to visit 1/9 Gorkhas and I readily agreed. When the Gorkhas were attacked, Tewari found himself in the midst of an infantry battle. He was taken prisoner after the Chinese had overrun the position. Who has ever heard of a Commander Signals being sent to an infantry battalion on the night before a massive attack, if there was any anticipation of a battle? He would have been at Divisional HQ attending to the Division's communications.

Chapter XX

The Vain Fight For Decisions

And so we come to the finale in the strange drama of September-October 1962. 19th October represented the low-water mark of the post-Independence Indian Army; as 20th October was to be the day of national regeneration. Nothing short of the Thagla disaster could have exorcised the wrong notions which had crept into our ways and thinking. The years of credulity, neglect, misunderstood Civil Supremacy and the creation of a compliant High Command were to be paid for in blood and humiliation.

On the evening of 19th October, 7 Brigade was squarely in the Chinese trap and it was a matter of hours before it was sprung. Throughout the day Chinese units could be seen moving to battle locations, which they had reconnoitered during the preceding three days. All this hectic activity was passed to 4 Division in special situation reports, but there was deplorable apathy in deciphering Chinese intentions. There was neither apprehension nor the issue of military orders to counter the Chinese moves. The only response was an order from the GSO I to prepare a detailed sketch map showing Chinese concentrations. Apparently this was required by Army HQ "at once". I told him to make his own sketch on the basis of the information and grid references which I had been passing on regularly.

On the evening of 19th October, Gen. Prasad rang me up and ordered me to send the remainder of 1/9 Gorkhas to Tsangle, at dawn the next day. I protested against this senseless order. I asked him whether he had read the reports of the Chinese activities and concentrations of the last two days. One Chinese battalion had already moved to Dum Dum La, opposite Tsangle

In addition, some 2,000 Chinese soldiers were seen moving from Thagla towards Tsangle. It was plain that these moves were for a major attack, and not for defensive purposes. The Chinese had probed the defences of Tsangle, on the 18th, and suffered casualties.

I told him that the Tsangle Garrison would definitely be wiped out as it was on the north bank of the Namka Chu and the Chinese were certain to remove this sore spot. I challenged him to justify the sacrifice of more troops on a mission that had no military value. I pointed out that the Gorkhas would be under constant Chinese observation throughout the march and faced the possibility of being wiped out by Chinese fire even before reaching Tsangle. I asked him whether we had learnt any lessons from the Tseng Jong action of 10th October where we had ventured into Chinese-occupied territory, without any military preparations or support, and suffered grievously. Even if the Chinese did not attack the Gorkhas, I could not maintain them, the Punjabi Company and all the supporting arms. I was already behind in stocking the existing force there. The General's answer was the now classic – "move on hard scales and pouch ammunition".

I then took up the question of controlling or influencing any battle in which the Gorkhas might get involved. On 10th October, after the Chinese attacked our patrol, the resultant *melee* was classified as "a battalion or brigade show", although I had had no hand in precipitating the engagement. Who would handle the battle if the Gorkhas got into a fight while on the move? Would this responsibility be again handed over to me? I could not assist or reinforce Tsangle and any battle there would be an independent action. I made it clear that I was no longer prepared to be the guinea-pig for other people's futile fumbles at playing soldiers. The last time I had watched helplessly as the Punjabis were being slaughtered. The Chinese superiority was now infinitely greater and their intentions grimly unmistakable.

I demanded a written order to send the Gorkhas as I intended to take up this issue and required documentary evidence to pin-point the culprit. I was tired of verbal orders which were never confirmed in writing. My Brigade had become the sacrificial lamb to expiate everyone's sins. I reminded him that to date I had not received a single order in complete form. Everything was being done by slogans, words and signals. Prasad promised to issue formal orders which he did later in the evening.

Our heated discussion then turned to the task of 7 Brigade in the Namka Chu, where our orders had remained unchanged from 10th October, despite the massive, visible and offensive Chinese preparations and the diversion of resources to Tsangle. I told him that in view of the Chinese concentrations and their battle deployment, we must stop talking of policing our borders, or guarding every inch of our territory – as very soon we were likely to lose all our territory in this sector. There was no sense in "ensuring the security" of useless logs of wood, at all costs. The Namka Chu was no longer an obstacle and could be crossed at will at any point.

I reminded Gen. Prasad that I was already deployed non-tactically with yawning gaps between localities, in a negative, prolonged and ineffective mission in gross contravention of all military tenets. He knew that the Rajputs were holding a frontage of over 4,000 yards. The distance between Temporary Bridge and Log Bridge was 1,200 yards. That between Log Birdge and Bridge IV was 1,500 yards and between Bridge IV and Bridge III 1,500 yards. The LEFT (Western) flank was completely open as the distance between Temporary Bridge and Bridge V (Tsangle) was over six miles and it took some 18 hours to cover. Visibility from localities, at ground and bunker level was only 30-100 yards. There was no support between companies and in most cases not even between platoons.

Instead of sending more troops to Tsangle and weakening whatever defences we had along the Namka Chu, it was imperative that we pull back to Lumpu. As a first step I wanted *immediate* permission to withdraw the two Rajput Companies located in the area of Log and Temporary Bridges, and re-deploy them to give depth to the Rajput layout. I warned Gen. Prasad that unless I was permitted to occupy a more compact area, at once, the Chinese would drive a wedge between our positions and strike at our sole maintenance base at Tsangdhar, which was completely defenceless. The company that I had sent to guard the gun positions had been ordered to Tsangle on the 17th. The company I had there now would be leaving the next day, if the order to send all the Gorkhas was not rescinded. Who, in the name of heaven, was to guard the guns and dropping zone at Tsangdhar?

Prasad first gave me the grave news, that Gen. Kaul was seriously ill and had been evacuated to Delhi. He doubted whether anyone at Corps HQ would give a decision which amounted to revoking the Corps Commander's personal orders. I now understood the inaction of 17th, 18th and 19th October, and why the Gorkhas were still being forced to Tsangle, in spite of the perilous position at Thagla.

I gave Prasad my appreciation of how I thought the Chinese attack would develop:

(*a*) On 20th October the Chinese would definitely wipe out Tsangle.

(*b*) Within the next two days, the Chinese would drive a wedge between and through 2 Rajput positions and capture Tsangdhar. When this happened the whole Brigade would be in the bag.

(*c*) Due to our dispersal and lack of troops, the Chinese would have a walk-over, as they would have to contend with only two or three infantry companies, without any artillery support.

I then said words to the effect that: "I can no longer stand by and watch the massacre of my men. It is time that some senior officer took a firm stand. This is no longer a case of trying to bluff the Chinese by sitting under their noses. If a scapegoat is wanted, I am willing to offer myself and am prepared to accept the consequences, and resign my commission". I added that: "I have been palmed off all these days by senior officers, with false promises of fighting for my Brigade, and ultimately claiming helplessness in the face of political pressure. I am sick of the words 'the highest level', and other mysterious persons, who were giving orders without knowing what was happening here".

To my horror Gen. Prasad refused to assume responsibility and expressed his inability to allow any operational freedom whatever having received categoric orders to hold fast to our present positions.

Prasad promised to convey all that I had told him to HQ IV Corps and do his best to convince them to accede to my request. In the meanwhile he asked me not to do anything hasty till he rang me gain. According to a witness at Divisional HQ, who overheard this conversation, Prasad said: "I have no orders to permit you to withdraw to a place of your choice. Stay where you are. The matter had been referred to Corps but there is no reply from them yet". All my General could say to console me was that he entirely "agreed" with me.

Gen. Prasad rang me up after a while and told me that the Brigadier General Staff of IV Corps did not feel competent to agree to any retraction. The BGS (Brig. K. K. Singh) was however trying to contact Gen. Kaul in Delhi, to obtain orders. Needless to add nothing further was heard from Corps or Division. BGS is also alleged to have said that we should not worry as the Chinese were not likely to do anything big.

When I heard this, I asked Gen. Prasad to send me a helicopter the next day, to evacuate me, as I was not prepared to command 7 Brigade, under these circumstances. I then used some unparliamentary language, and accused him of deliberately hiding Kaul's illness from me. Had I known of this earlier I would have smelt something fishy about the inaction in the face of the Chinese attack plans. I then told him that I had lost faith in his (Prasad's) leadership, and the leadership of all who had had a hand in the sordid Thagla business. I had hitherto relied on my superiors, mostly against my own judgement, and they had let down my troops. They invariably agreed with my military assessment and advice and gave promises which they had flagrantly dishonoured. Finally I questioned the physical courage of all those who were willing to come and watch a *tamasha*, but who were conspicuous by their absence since the Chinese attack. Not one single general officer had visited me after 10th October. They all seemed to have time for futile conferences at Delhi and Tezpur, but no time to visit the battlefield which had now been set up as a butchery by the Chinese.

Gen. Prasad then broke down and told me that he would visit me the next morning. He said that he too had had enough and now wanted to share the fate of the Brigade. He said that he would stay and die with the Brigade, if necessary.

I could see no point in this fatalistic and supine attitude. I told him that I welcomed his proposed visit, but that I reserved my right to fly back and see anyone in India, on this subject. I told him that I would meet him at the helipad at Tsangdhar on the morning of the 20th.

These extraordinary conversations took place in the presence of my entire staff and two gunner officers, Major Balraj Singh Nijjar and Captain Talwar, creating an atmosphere of dejection and despondency. I was exhausted after this talk and depressed beyond words. I drafted a formal signal to HQ 4 Division to record my discussion with the GOC. The GOC's impotence deepened the pall of gloom hanging over my HQ.

I went back to my bunker and lay down for a few minutes. I wondered at the decline of the Indian Army which I had joined with such high hopes and with such pride. In 1941, the Indian Army was one of the finest fighting forces in the world. What had happened to us? I thought about the command set-up of the past few days. Even at this late stage, General Officers could not take obvious tactical decisions. What was even more incredible, is that they forbade others from taking them. It was not Gen. Prasad's faults, it was the fault of the system whereby the Army command chain had surrendered its authority. Here again, the years of domination and denigration of the Officer Corps, was being paid for in this desolate valley. If the Civil Authority desire obedient hacks then this is all that they can expect in a national crisis, when forthrightness and professional integrity, are called for. Government lived to rue the day for eliminating its best military talent and for meddling with Army promotions and appointments.

This is perhaps the most appropriate place to evaluate Maj.-Gen. Niranjan Prasad's role and contribution to the defeat at Thagla Ridge. Gen. Prasad suffered grievously throughout the period 8th September to 20th October. He knew what my men had been made to suffer and endure. He had first-hand knowledge of the impossibility of evicting the Chinese. He too was made to hang about while senior generals ran around in circles trying to obtain sensible orders.

I sympathise with him in the unfortunate and indeterminate role that he was called upon to play in the drama of those days. He was a General Officer, and yet his advice was neither sought nor heeded. He was too junior to influence the National Policy and yet too senior to stand by idly while one of his brigades was being led to the slaughter. Prasad was a very sensitive man and was deeply distressed at the plight of my men.

Gen. Prasad never really commanded a division. He was turned into a post-office. It was a grave injustice when attempts were made to pin the blame for the Dhola fiasco onto him. All he did was to shuttle between commanders, passing the views of his subordinates or conveying the orders of his superiors. In all honesty I cannot find it in my heart to attach any blame or guilt to his professional conduct throughout the operation. It is axiomatic that to attach blame, a person must have some freedom of action. Gen. Prasad never had the freedom to take a single decision.

My only regret is that he did not resign–certainly after 13th October, when the order to continue sitting in the Namka Chu, was received by him. He did not have to face any charge of personal cowardice as he was not in direct command, in the field. He had no command other than my brigade. He might have also acted on his own initiative on the evening of 19th October and accepted the consequences. He was the *de facto* and *de jure* Corps Commander, in the absence of Kaul.

Chapter XXI

7 Brigade Without Higher Leadership

There has been a great deal of controversy about Gen. Kaul's untimely illness on 17th/18th October: and considerable heart-burning about his recall on 29th October. Unfortunately the consequences of his illness have been clouded by the vigorously partisan approach of most commentators. There have been many unfair and improper insinuations and inuendos made. Kaul had become the *bete-noir* of some journals, and they grasped the opportunity provided by his illness to impute motives, and even imply cowardice. In the resultant mud-slinging the significance of his absence has been missed.

Gen. Kaul's illness and his evacuation from Tezpur to Delhi were calamitous to the fortunes of 7 Brigade to the extent that it was left without higher leadership during the three critical days of 18th, 19th and 20th October. There was no Corps Commander, no duly authorised deputy commander and no guide-lines for the staff of IV Corps (indeed HQ IV Corps was still in the embryonic stage) to deal with the fluid military situation which continued to be heavily infected with politics. There was no higher battle-field command to redeem the clumsiness of our so-called military plans. The already grotesque chain of command broke down completely with his sudden departure.

First let me say that commanders are human and do go sick like other mortals. When he left Tezpur Kaul was a sick man. He was disillusioned, dejected, disappointed and his belief in Chinese restraint rudely belied by events. Some have gone on record to suggest that his nerves had been affected.

Gen. Kaul's illness gave his detractors an opportunity to vilify him largely because of the timing of his evacuation and the manner in which his recall was allegedly engineered by his mentors in high places. Kaul left for Delhi soon after the crucial meeting of 17th October when Mr. Menon had invoked political necessity to force the Army to hold Tsangle and Kaul had failed to have this decision reversed. On 17th October only the blind could fail to gauge the Chinese temper and capability. The defenders of the Namka Chu were doomed if the emphasis shifted to Tsangle.

Had Kaul stayed away from NEFA the matter might have been allowed to pass into history as an unfortunate hazard of soldiering in the Himalayas. But his return to the command of IV Corps on 29th October raised many an eyebrow. Lt.-Gen. Harbaksh Singh (who later commanded Western Command against the Pakistanis in 1965) had assumed Command on 24th October, after Towang had been abandoned. He was widely credited with having restored the morale of a bewildered Indian Army and its confidence in the higher leadership. At that time the Chinese advance guards were knocking at the outer defences of Sela Pass and had paused to digest the first morsel of NEFA. Kaul's return *during the pause* gave birth to unhealthy rumours and speculations.

The first rumour was that Mr. Nehru had intervened on behalf of Kaul. The Army knew that complete recovery from a serious lung ailment, within 11 days, was a remarkable, if not a miraculous feat. The ready clearance given him by the Medical Corps to return to duty to the Himalayan Heights without the mandatory period of convalescence and sick leave was viewed with scepticism. Now the ugly rumours really gained momentum and gathered corroborative detail as circulation widened.

It was said that Kaul was not all that sick in the first place to warrant evacuation in the midst of battle.

Others said that Mr. Nehru was convinced that the Chinese had annexed all they wanted in NEFA and the lull in fighting was permanent. This view was reinforced by Government's optimistic pronouncements about the impregnability of Sela Pass. It was said that Kaul was being given the chance to restore his tarnished military image by being given the opportunity to claim the "stabilisation of the NEFA front". If the Chinese did not intend to advance, then the health of the Theatre Commander was not a critical consideration, but the rehabilitation of a favourite general was.

Mr. D. R. Mankekar has aptly summed up the repercussions of Kaul's recall in his book *The Guilty Men of 1962* in these words: "It was indeed a worse crime on the part of Government and Army HQ to have let a physically ailing Kaul to rush back to resume active command of the Corps in a grave crisis solely in order to enable him to rehabilitate his 'face' at the cost of the Country's security interests. When things were going wrong all round, we had at the helm, at the Corps Headquarters, an embittered man, mentally disturbed and physically unfit – still unrecovered from a grave ailment. . . . The Army Commander, Gen. Sen is believed to have objected to Kaul's recall but was overruled by the Army Chief, Gen. Thapar, because 'higher authorities' wanted him to be rehabilitated".

It is no secret that Kaul's authority never anchored on solid professional attainments, had been undermined by the defeats at Thagla Ridge and the fall of Towang and he was prey to all sorts of slander. Loss of confidence in a commander is a subtle, insidious and all-pervasive feeling. Mr. Mankekar says: "Further, they altogether lacked confidence in the higher military leadership. This is typified by the story told to me by Maj.-Gen. A. S. Pathania himself and confirmed by others. Pathania said that on the evening of 29th October, when the officers were clustered round the radio set and heard the announcement that Kaul was now fit and had resumed charge of IV Corps, they spontaneously exclaimed 'He has come back? Now God save us'."

There is only one remedy for this sort of demoralisation and that is to remove the Commander however unjust such action may appear to be. There are many instances in military history where this has had to be done. Indian readers need look no further than the case of their last Commander-in-Chief, Field Marshal Sir Claude Auchinleck described by the Germans in these words: "If the Auk was not the man he was–and by that I mean the best Allied General in North Africa during the war – Rommel would have finished off the 8th Army". He commanded the British Empire Forces in Egypt in 1941/42 at a time when Field Marshal Rommel, his adversary, had the edge. The Auk displayed generalship of the highest order in warding off Rommel's threat and saving the Middle East. He is also credited with drawing up the offensive plan (with the help of Gen. Dorman Smith, his Deputy Chief of Staff) which was later developed by his successor. By August 1942 the tide had turned in favour of the Empire Forces who had been built up numerically and qualitatively. They were poised to destroy the Axis Forces in North Africa.

By all norms of justice and equity the Auk should have been allowed to continue in command but the British Government of Mr. Churchill summarily replaced him and appointed Gen. Bernard Montgomery to be the new commander of the 8th Army and Gen. Alexander to be the Theatre Commander. Many in the Army were deeply grieved at the dismissal of a great general. A typical tribute paid to him was by Sir Ian Jacob, who had been sent to deliver Churchill's letter of dismissal. He said, "I felt as if I were going to murder an unsuspecting friend".

The British Government's decision was motivated by two considerations. The first was to provide fresh military leadership as the Auk had come to be associated with withdrawals and defeats. In a letter from Cairo to Mr. Attlee, the Deputy Prime Minister of the war-time Coalition Government, dated the 6th of August 1942, Mr. Churchill wrote: ". . . I have no doubt the changes will impart a new vigorous impulse to the Army and restore confidence in the Command, which I regret does not exist at the present time...". On 21st August Mr. Churchill amplified the charge: "I am sure we are heading for disaster under the former regime. The Army has been reduced to bits and pieces, and oppressed by a sense of bafflement and uncertainty".

Moreover the British Public had tired of the ding-dong desert battles and demanded evidence of Government's determination to achieve final victory in a theatre where fortunes had fluctuated for two years and no British victory was in sight despite the glib assurances of official spokesmen. The war-time Coalition Government had lately lost the Maldon Bye-election and, in July 1942, had faced and survived a censure motion. Thus the Auk had to be sacrificed on two counts. The injustice to the great Auk was of less consequence than the morale of the troops and the Public so far as the British Government was concerned. The Indian Government of October 1962 should have been as responsive to the national mood and the Army's morale.

Nirad C. Chaudhri, a noted author, and a keen student of military history, is the only commentator that I have come across who has defended Kaul's evacuation on health grounds. Reviewing Kaul's memoirs in a series of three articles in the *Times of India*, he says: "But I must make it clear that there was no impropriety in his going on leave on urgent medical advice on the eve of it. On the 18th when he left for Delhi, he could not have anticipated the massive offensive. The situation was no worse than it had been for some time, and there was no question, as will be explained presently, for any offensive on the part of our forces. If it was wrong for

Kaul to have left the front, it was even more wrong for Rommel to have gone to Germany for treatment on 23rd September 1942, just a month before the opening of the Battle of El Alamein, and three weeks after the defeat of his attack at the end of August. Like Rommel again Gen. Kaul returned to his post, even though if he wanted to avoid the stigma for an inevitable defeat he could have resigned his command. The charge of desertion of his post of duty can thus be called only a slander".

In completely exonerating Kaul, Mr. Chaudhri was undoubtedly handicapped by lack of information about the chain reaction set in motion by Kaul's untimely evacuation and abrupt recall. Whether Kaul was really sick or not is immaterial and I agree with him that it is wrong to refer to this as desertion, but the impact on the course of operations is a material issue.

There was abundant information of the Chinese build-up for a massive invasion, and the situation, on 18th October was desperate. It is a serious slur on the alertness of the forward troops to insinuate that they were sitting idly while the Chinese were openly massing in front of them: or that they failed to report Chinese moves to Gen. Kaul's headquarters. The situation, on the 18th, was critical.

Chaudhri could not have known of the break-down in the Army's command structure and therefore has missed the core of the problem.

To the professional soldiers of the world the unhappy comparison with the distinguished German Field Marshal will appear a sacrilege. If an example from history was necessary, one would have wished that Chaudhri had selected a less far-fetched, or a less misleading one.

Rommel had earned his desert sores after two years of campaigning whereas Kaul went sick after 13 days! Rommel flew back to command the dog-fight stage of the British attack at El Alamein. Kaul returned after the Battle of the Namka Chu and the evacuation of Towang, and during a lull.

When Rommel went to Germany for medical treatment he left General Stumme in full command and clear orders about the method of defending the German lines. Stumme died of heart failure on the battle-field on 24th October 1942 and General Ritter von Thoma immediately took over. Rommel, though sick, flew over to take command of his Panzerarmee; arrived on the 27th and within 24 hours of leaving his sick-bed he led his concentrated armour in a counter-attack. Thus the German Army had a commander throughout the Battle as well as carefully drawn up battle plans. There was no paralysis while reference was made to the ailing Field Marshal in Germany. This is the material point.

Field Marshal Rommel has carved a permanent *niche* in the military hall of fame as probably the greatest armour tactician of all time. At Alamein he "managed to slog it out with a gigantically superior British Force for 12 days". When forced to withdraw he fought a series of skillful rearguard actions which Corelli Barnett has described in his book *The Desert Generals*, as: "Its success must rank as a prodigious feat of arms and leadership. Rommel held his tiny Army together by force of character, by the loyalty of his veterans. In trances of exhaustion these men, the same men who had taken Tobruk and Gazala, unreinforced, unrelieved served their guns with instinctive skill, taking heart from the sight of the stocky figure of the Field Marshal as he toured the battlefield fighting his thin line of battle in person like Wellington. . . . The Panzerarmee's shield during that epic retreat was its commander's reputation. . . . It was an amazing display of military virtuosity . . .". Gen. Kaul's performance at Sela Pass and Bomdilla were hardly classics of military leadership. Kaul is reported to have completely broken down by 18th November, whereas the German Field Marshal went on to command the anti-invasion forces, along the French coast–the famous German West Wall (or Atlantic Wall).

Historical allusions apart, there are two vital lessons to be drawn from all this. The first is that commanders do fall ill, or even die, without notice. We must therefore adhere to the normal procedure of insisting on clear orders for the staff and subordinate commanders. The overall appreciation, aim and plan must be known to the key members in the chain of command and authority must be suitably delegated. Once a commander is evacuated from the battle zone he should be barred from maintaining any telephonic touch with his HQ. A remote control commander is a menace to all, besides creating conditions where the art of passing the buck flourishes.

In the political sphere, the lesson is that the selection, appointment and replacement of commanders must be made objectively. Mr. Menon and Gen. Thapar knew of Kaul's illness and his evacuation to Delhi on 18th October. This being so, the following questions arise. Were they satisfied that there was no need to appoint the next senior, Gen. Prasad, to be officiating GOC IV Corps, with full authority to take the necessary decisions? How was it that Gen. Prasad's initiative was completely curbed, and he felt impelled to consult a mere brigadier staff officer (Kaul's BGS), before taking a tactical decision? And why did this staff officer himself feel compelled to refer the matter, in turn, to Gen. Kaul in Delhi? What were the orders to HQ IV Corps that made it necessary for the senior staff officer to refer to an absent commander? And why was a "clearance" from Kaul necessary? Did the staff of IV Corps report the daily Chinese build-up to Kaul in Delhi? Was HQ IV Corps set up and functioning? If HQ IV Corps did not report to Kaul then to whom were they referring this most urgent matter? Having read the daily situation reports, did all the high personages accept that IV Corps could continue to be left without a commander and without the latitude to respond to the fluid military situation? Did anyone, at any level, read and assimilate the import of the situation reports? If Kaul's absence was accepted then would anyone in daily touch with the deteriorating situation in the Thagla area have talked about ascertaining the depth of ice in the lake near Tsangle? Are we to believe that any practical person would still harp on the possibility of staying at Tsangle, and the Namka Chu, throughout the winter? Who gave the order to send the Gorkhas to Tsangle on 19th October? Would such an order have been issued if the possibility of a Chinese attack on the Namka Chu defenders had been appreciated? The questions are infinite but unfortunately the answers are few. The vacuum created by Kaul's absence has provided an escape hatch to many of those concerned with running the war with China on 18th, 19th and 20th October. Hence all the apologias which have been served up to the Indian Public. Kaul could only commiserate with the plight of his troops, from his distant sick-bed. Gen. Sen claims that he had nothing to do with the war after Kaul's appointment. Mr. Menon claims that he never interfered with detailed army dispositions. Gen. Prasad was helpless without Corps approval. Then who, in the name of the dead of Thagla, was in higher command, on the night of 19th October 1962?

The failure to appoint a commander during Kaul's illness was a blunder of incalculable dimensions on the part of the Defence Minister and the Army Chief. While the garrote was being tied in the Namka Chu, on 19th October, Gen. Kaul was going through a complete medical check-up; the Government had no answer to the prospect of an all-out war with China; and Gen. Thapar fell between the stools of political vacillation and the Chinese arrayed might poised to annihilate an Indian brigade.

The crux of the matter is that the whole affair was handled in a typically subjective manner, by the political bosses. Kaul's appointment, in a blaze of publicity had been received with mixed feelings by the Public, and with dismay by those in the Army who knew the military situation. His sudden replacement, on the eve of the certain Chinese attack, on grounds of ill-health, however valid, would have been widely misunderstood by Kaul's many critics. Kaul himself acknowledges of the feeling against him in many quarters, and says that he preferred to risk his life than to relinquish command. This is a noble and admirable sentiment but the troops have a right to be led by generals who are 100 per cent fit and in whom they have professional confidence. The Prime Minister, the Defence Minister and the Army Chief were all party to the decision to appoint Kaul, and therefore had a personal stake in avoiding an unpleasant storm over his summary replacement on the hackneyed plea of ill-health. This one fact may have impaired their judgment. While the issue was being debated, the Chinese struck the leaderless force in Thagla. Herein lies the danger of political interference in the appointment of field commanders. There is no doubt that any other general who had fallen ill would have been replaced at once. In Mankekar's words: "Kaul lacked, at that moment, that mental poise and tranquillity essential for clear-thinking and cool decision making". An ordinary general would not have been permitted to retain a lien on his appointment. There would have been no extraneous factors introduced into a straight-forward matter. There would have no thought given to the repercussions on the General's reputation, and what others would think. In fact the change would probably have gone unnoticed by the Public. Herein lies another lesson. Generals of the Indian Army should not become controversial figures. They should serve in anonymity and should have no outside sponsorship.

* * *

Gen. Kaul is silent about the *contretemps* between Gen. Prasad and myself on 19th October. He is also silent about the order to move the rest of the Gorkhas to Tsangle, on the morning of 20th October. This silence is eloquent and bears its own testimony. Kaul was in touch with his HQ at Tezpur throughout his stay in Delhi, and Brig. K. K. Singh, his BGS, spoke to him on the morning of 20th October to inform him of the Chinese invasion. Are we to believe that the BGS did not inform him about the mounting tension of 19th October after promising GOC 4 Division that he would do so? The answer is contained in the question. Kaul's diary entries in his book "The Untold Story", for the fateful day of 19th October ramble on and on with details of his medical diagnosis; our faulty road-building policy; our failure to procure the right sort of animals for the mountains and the better Chinese road communications. What is the point of these condemnatory soliloquies about matters with which he himself had dealt as Quarter-Master General of the Army and as a permanent member of the Border Roads Committee? It can legitimately be assumed that Kaul wishes to give the impression that he was not concerned with the conduct of operations on the 19th. His absence due to illness, absolves him from responsibility. The Brigade Commander should explain the omissions which led 7 Brigade to be overrun!

Kaul's failure to ensure uninterrupted command and control after his evacuation to Delhi on 18th October, was his fifth and final blunder.

The most frequent question that I have been asked, about the Thagla Affair, is to explain how I came to be stuck at the Namku Chu specially after the Chinese build-up was an established fact. Some have even suggested that I should have walked out with my Brigade and damned the consequences. I hope that this narrative of the dismal events from 8th September onwards will enlighten them. I hope it will also alert those who may find themselves in a similar predicament.

* * *

On the evening of the 19th I had another unexpected and weary visitor in Captain Harjeet Singh Talwar, a strapping young Singh. He had lost his bearing while trying to make for Tsangle and after completing a circle had fetched up at the Rajputs, at Bridge IV. He was being sent as the Forward Observation Officer to the garrison at Tsangle, to control the fire of two light, outranged para-field guns, with 450 rounds. No one would believe me when I said that Tsangle was out of range. Planning was still based on the famous field sketch of the Assam Rifles Lance-naik, which showed Tsangle at the end of the foolscap sheet, and which appeared to be within range!

Talwar and his men were dead beat, as they too had been hurriedly rushed from Agra and had never seen a mountain in their lives. The sole reason for selecting them was the fact that their guns were the only artillery pieces which could be air-dropped at Tsangdhar. Here was the final proof of the futility of deluding ourselves by rushing troops to the Himalayas and comforting ourselves with the belief that the soldiers have been provided with artillery cover!

Talwar was to share my grim experiences of marching over the 18,000-foot Dhola Pass, and my capture by the Chinese. He was a fine young gentleman and officer. I was indeed lucky and proud to have known him, and to have had him with me during those trying days. I could not have wished for a better officer to share my ordeals. He was a silent witness to the last amazing hours of 19th October, and told me that he could hardly believe his ears when he overheard the conversation between Gen. Prasad and myself.

* * *

The last memory I have of the frustrating day of 19th October is a conversation with Lt.-Col. Rikh of the Rajputs. He gave me a clear and lucid assessment of the Chinese, in their assembly areas. He told me that he had rung up each company commander, told them to intensify patrolling and if the enemy attacked to fight to the last. His last words were, "Don't worry, sir, despite the Chinese superiority, the Rajputs will not let you or the country down. We will fight till we have nothing more to fight with. If you get back please see that the culprits who landed us in this mess get their just punishment". The Rajputs honoured their brave promise and obeyed their CO to the last letter. They fought most gallantly in the face of impossible odds.

Chapter XXII

The Ethics of Resigning A Field Command

Before dropping off to sleep I ruminated about what I might have done to avoid landing my Brigade in this mess. Up to 10th October I had been assured by all the senior officers who came to see me that they would go back to the next HQ and try to put some sense into our military thinking and political postures. I therefore had no reason to do anything more.

Every soldier will understand my wish to be released from responsibilities which I could not discharge and which were unbearable due to interminable, nerve-racking wrangles with one's own superiors. How does one command without authority, operational freedom and resources? How does a brigadier command a political battle when the highest in the land are directing the efforts of his brigade?

I was alone and lonely at this crucial stage and, for the first time, felt the full impact of the loneliness of command. The problem of resigning oppressed me particularly from 10th October onwards. I was hamstrung as I could not pick up a jeep and rush over to my superiors. I was isolated and unless senior officers chose to visit me there was no possibility of personal contact. I should not have accepted the order to defend all the bridges over the Namka Chu on the 13th of October, but then "It takes more courage to appear a coward than risk being killed".

I decided that my place was with the troops who had followed me loyally to the Namka Chu. I could not bring myself to abandon all sense of responsibility to them, desert and leave them to their fate. In all humility, I felt sure that their loyal obedience was largely due to my presence with them throughout the operation. My departure would have meant more than a change in the person of the Commander.

The first difficulty was that up to 20th October we were not at war with the Chinese. This was a vital factor. The thinking even at the Prime Minister's level was that the Chinese would not do anything big, and our entire approach was based on this fundamental political appreciation. If I left on tactical grounds, and the Chinese did not attack, I could be branded a physical coward. I did not have the moral courage to accept this stigma.

Even if I overcame my fears of being labelled a coward, what useful purpose would I serve by leaving other than to save my own skin? I knew that it would have been virtually impossible to replace me in a matter of days. The Chinese would not give us time to position a replacement. Any successor would have needed time to get acclimatised, visit the troops, study the ground and otherwise "play himself in". When every hour is vital there is no justification for a change of Commanders. The valiant troops deserved a better fate than this.

On balance I decided to stay with my Brigade and share their fate. If I had to make this decision again I would still opt to do what I did. I can only pray and hope that no Brigadier of the Indian Army is ever called upon to face such difficult options in a future "peace-time" border clash.

Field Marshal von Manstein, was possibly the ablest Commander in the German Army in World War II and of whom Capt. Lidell Hart, the noted British military historian says: ". . . he had military genius". Manstein was responsible for conducting the efforts to relieve the trapped German Sixth Army at Stalingrad in 1942. He repeatedly clashed with Hitler who refused to allow any withdrawal, creating in Manstein, that crisis of conscience which is the lot of every soldier in history who has had to face political interference or and unsympathetic superior commander – to resign or not to resign?

Field Marshal Manstein has expressed the sentiments and contradictions of all commanders, in his Memoirs: *Lost Victories*. Writing of the feelings which oppressed him when he had failed to persuade Hitler and the German High Command on the overall strategic issues he says:

"But let me make a few general remarks here on the question of a senior commander's resignation *in the field*. The first point is that a senior commander is no more able to pack up and go home than any other soldier. . . . The soldier in the field is not in the pleasant position of a politician, who is always at liberty to climb off the band-wagon when things go wrong, or the line taken by the Government does not suit him. The soldier has to fight where and when he is ordered".

He adds: "This question of resignation has another aspect, however, besides the one mentioned above. I refer to the feeling of responsibility which a senior commander must have towards the soldiers".

He concludes in these sonorous words: "To throw up my task at this moment, however justifiable the human motives might be . . . struck me as a betrayal of those brave troops who were locked in a life-and-death struggle".

---

* Italics author's.

CHAPTER XXIII

The Trap is Set

AT THE risk of being repetitious, I would briefly survey the military situation as on the night of 19th October 1962, to enable readers to appreciate the inevitability of the defeat of the scarecrow Indian Force, on the morrow. The Country and the Army should not be ashamed for the defeat at Thagla Ridge or Dhola as the odds were too grossly uneven to leave the issue in doubt. Free India had followed the same path as her feudal past. Her brave soldiers were not given the semblance of a chance to win this battle. Inept leadership and mental black-outs had set up 7 Brigade for destruction, trapped and without any escape route. The rest of the Indian Army was over 1,500 miles away. And this unhappy predicament had been accepted on the fallacious foundation of Chinese good behaviour. India's long dream of peace and progress was about to end. Nehru's long era of undisputed rule had reached its penumbra. The invasion of NEFA was to be the swansong of Nehru as a leader.

*7 Infantry Brigade was stretched along a 12-mile front along the Namka Chu River, from Bridge I to Tsangle. The marching distance from one end of the Brigade area of responsibility to the other was a minimum of five days! To grasp the true danger of the situation and the full extent to which it benefitted the Chinese, the reader should retain a clear picture of the mortal gaps between the scattered pockets of our troops. The Brigade remained ill-clad and without administrative and medical cover, and dependent on the unsatisfactory dropping zone at Tsangdhar.

The only fire support for the entire front was from

*See sketch III for layout of Indian troops on the eve of battle, 19th October 1962.

two para-field guns with 421 rounds; and four 4.2-inch mortars with 450 rounds. There were only two artillery observation parties for all the widespread localities.

The units did not have a single strand of barbed wire or a single anti-personnel mine. They had no ammunition reserves. The Rajputs had four 3-inch mortars with a total of 60 bombs and only 17 Light Machine Gun magazines filled per gun. Each man had two grenades only. There were very few 2-inch mortars bombs. The limited dumping that had been achieved between 10th and 19th October had been diverted to Tsangle.

There was no overall strategic plan or dispositions to give depth to 7 Brigade; or to provide lay-back positions to cover the withdrawal of the Namka Chu garrison. There was a blind refusal to even contemplate withdrawal. While this was valid as political bravado, it was inexcusable in military planning.

Security was completely ignored. Tsangdhar, the life-line of the Brigade and the only gun position was held by a weak infantry company. Lumpu the only other dropping zone was innocent of bayonets and rifles. There was no co-ordination between the Namka Chu and the Nyam Jang Chu sectors. The latter was directly under Divisional HQ. Hathungla Pass was held by one platoon which was also under 4 Division. A Divisional HQ commanding a rifle platoon!

(The layout of the Battalions is shown in sketch III). 1/9 Gorkhas, less two companies, were preparing to move to Tsangle. They had already sent a company on the 17th, and one company was at Tsangdhar waiting to join the main body the following day.

The Rajputs were spread out from Bridges III to Log Bridge.

9 Punjab held Bridge II, and had one company detached to Tsangle (Bridge V).

4 Grenadiers held Bridge I with a battalion less two companies. One company had been loaned to the Nyam Jang Chu Sector and was located at Khenzemane. Even on 19th October we were still 'loaning' troops from one unit to another. One company was between Hathungla and Serkhim, under Division.

There was thus no brigade defended area and no co-ordination between the forces deployed to guard the two main axes i.e. Hathungla-Lumpu and Tsangdhar-Lumpu. We violated the well-known maxim: "He who tries to hold on to everything at once, finishes up by holding nothing". There was no co-ordinated fire plan, and no worth-while defensive fire arrangements. There was no real control possible by the CO's or myself due to distances, and the vulnerability of the main tracks. (They all ran parallel to the Chinese positions on the North bank of the Namka Chu). When the Chinese attack came, all the actions were small independent company strength battles.

The command structure, which was never properly established, had disintegrated with the untimely illness of Gen. Kaul.

On the other side the Chinese, with their manifold superiority, were in their forming-up places on commanding ground. At night they lit bonfires to keep themselves warm. This disdainful and contemptuous action was the final act of humiliation against the motley force pitted against them. They knew well that we were helpless and could do nothing to forestall them or disrupt their battle-formations. If I remember right, the last time that this happened was at the Battle of Austerlitz, in 1802, when the French lit fires in front of the Russians on the night preceding the famous Battle. The close proximity of the combatants gave a quality of fantasy to the proceedings. The feelings of the men were compounded of awe and disbelief – that this surely, could not be war; it must be a show of force. Had 7 Brigade been given the normal complement of artillery support the Chinese would not have dared to form up openly in the face of the defensive fire that would have been rained on them. The Chinese Commander had a relatively easy task as he could isolate the Rajputs at Bridges III and IV and cut a way to Lumpu. To achieve his aim i.e. the destruction of 7 Brigade he had to attack but a third of it. The remainder could be encircled in subsequent phases. All this had led, with the inevitability of a Greek tragedy, to the climatic decision that awaited the morrow of 20th October.

Chapter XXIV

The Day of Reckoning — 20th October 1962

"*We were Stabbed in the Back*". — Nehru

At exactly 5 on the morning of 20th October 1962, the Chinese opposite Bridge III fired two Verey lights. This signal was followed by a cannonade of over 150 guns and heavy mortars, exposed on the forward slopes of Thagla. Our positions at Bridges III and IV; Tsangdhar; Log and Temporary Bridges and Brigade HQ, which was some 1,000 yards from the River bank came in for a heavy bombardment. The Chinese used 76 mm guns which were fed and fired automatically, and 120 mm mortars.

This was the moment of truth. Thagla Ridge was no longer, at that moment, a piece of ground. It was the crucible to test, weigh and purify India's foreign and defence policies. As the first salvoes crashed overhead there were a few minutes of petrifying shock. The contrast with the tranquillity that had obtained hitherto made it doubly impressive. The proximity of the two forces made it seem like an act of treachery. It had started. This was the end of years of miscalculations; months of suspense; days of hope and the end of a confused, nightmare week. The cataclysm broke on the dawn of a day which India will never forget. Every elementary text-book of history will carry the sad story of India's humiliation. The Battle at the Namka Chu must surely achieve the black prominence of the Battles of Panipat and Plassey.

The Chinese did not bombard the Punjabis and the Grenadiers at Bridges I and II thereby giving final proof of their plan which was to concentrate their effort on the narrow Dhola-Tsangdhar Sector. If they succeeded in reaching Lumpu the others would be trapped and dealt with while withdrawing over Hathungla Pass. No orderly or organised rearward move was possible in the circumstances, as there were no worthwhile lay-back positions, to cover the withdrawal.

The Chinese also shelled Khenzemane prior to an attack against this check-post, threatened Divisional HQ at Ziminthaung and opened the way to a second thrust towards Lumpu – along the Nyam Jang Chu Valley.

The bombardment lasted an hour and soon after massive infantry assaults followed, substantiating Nelson's famous dictum: "Only numbers can annihilate". The fate of India was now in the hands of only three weak infantry companies of the Rajput Regiment and two unbalanced companies of the 9th Gorkhas. At that time India had an Army of over 400,000 men but due to our stubborn refusal to think in strategic terms, only 600 men were engaged in the initial battle. This flimsy barrier was pierced with consummate ease by the powerful force which the Chinese had mustered, to teach India a lasting lesson.

1/9 Gorkhas were preparing to leave for Tsangle when the Chinese barrage commenced and were thus caught flat-footed through no fault of theirs. It is significant that this fact has been generally glossed over by all writers and commentators on the NEFA battles. It is a matter of shame that this fine regular Battalion of the Indian Army should have been brought to this sad pass.

1/9 Gorkhas coincidentally formed part of 4 Division in Italy and gained imperishable fame during the Third Battle of Cassino, in 1944. The Gorkhas faced troops of the First German Parachute Division which was classed by FM Lord Alexander, the Allied C-in-C, as 'The best division in the German Army'. The Battalion was given the task of capturing Hangman's Hill, a key feature in the Cassino defences. I will let Mr. F. Majdalany recount their gallantry: "For eight days and nights, this battalion of Gorkhas on Hangman's Hill occupied an exposed shoulder of the mountains, an area about 200 square yards, 250 yards from the Monastery – concealed from it only by a crag. For eight days and nights therefore they lived on an exposed cliff-face, in mid-winter, without even a coat to protect them against icy winds, the frequent rainstorms and a temperature which seldom rose above freezing point and at night, well below it".

Majdalany's final tribute to these men will warm the hearts of all those who admire and honour bravery. He sums up: "In the extraordinary ordeal of 1/9 Gorkhas on Hangman's Hill, it provided one of the genuine epics of the War".

The 1/9th were not strangers to mountain hardships nor did they lack professional skill. In the Namka Chu they were not given the semblance of a chance to fight as a battalion. Their hapless plight was the responsibility of others.

I got through to Gen. Prasad at once and reported the Chinese attacks. I told him that there was now no question of the Gorkhas leaving for Tsangle as they were embroiled in a fight with the Chinese; moreover they would walk straight into Chinese artillery fire on the way to, and at Tsangdhar itself. Prasad then told me to send at least a patrol of the Gorkhas if I could not send the whole battalion "as this move had been ordered at the highest level" . . . as if I still needed to be reminded of this. I just could not believe my ears. This was the final proof of the utter degradation and frustration that had seized us all due to pressure from and fear of 'the highest level'. We were unable at any time to think in military terms or adduce professional arguments to override military objections. In fact from the very beginning, many were merely instruments for relaying orders even when they disagreed with them. The military command set-up had never really functioned. The misuse of Civil Supremacy (so pleasant in times of peace) and the suppression of senior officers were being paid for. India's honour was about to be trampled upon and her military reputation sullied. I need hardly add that the Gorkhas did not leave for Tsangle.

* * *

*Until we have access to Chinese documents all estimates of their forces and deployment are essentially guesswork. From what I could gather, I am confident that they used a minimum of two divisions, with possibly a third in reserve – a total of 20,000 men. The Rajput and Gorkha positions in the Dhola area were assaulted simultaneously with two brigades. One brigade was used to deal with Tsangdhar – a vital objective for both sides. One brigade moved on the Khenzemane-Drokung Samba-Ziminthaung axis.

Other columns were sent to Hathungla to seal that escape route and destroy the retreating Indian force from Bridges I and II. It was obvious that these positions would be untenable once the Chinese had wiped out the Dhola defenders. One column left for Towang from the Nyam Jang Chu to threaten this vital ground from the west. A large Chinese force was poised to capture Towang from the Bumla axis, in the north.

At all events, within a few minutes of the Chinese attack, 7 Brigade lost its cohesion. There was no hope of reinforcement or influencing the battle in any way. I had no reserves and very soon no communication with my battalions as the lines were cut. Battalion commanders too could not communicate with their company commanders as all internal lines were destroyed. The unit wireless operators closed down as they had to man defences when the Chinese began physical assaults against their HQ's.

The Chinese had encircled us with one large and two small pincer movements. Before mounting frontal attacks against the Rajputs they had infiltrated one

---

*See sketch III for the direction and pattern of the Chinese attacks on 20th October 1962.

battalion behind them, and cut off the Gorkhas from the Rajputs. The Rajputs were attacked from two directions at the same time. They had no hope. They were trapped.

The Rajputs and Gorkhas put up a spirited fight against overwhelming odds for over three hours despite the demoralising lack of artillery defensive fire support.

Events took place with such bewildering swiftness that it is difficult to piece together an accurate account of the tactical battle. The Namka Chu battle-field soon became a mosaic of sprawling humans locked in mortal combat. The men fought in small sub-units under their officers and JCO'S and continued to resist even when isolated and encircled. A random sample of group and individual heroism will best throw into relief the pattern of fighting.

Let me start with that gallant soldier Lt.-Col. Rikh who was located at Bridge IV with his HQ, one rifle company and the usual specialist platoons. Within minutes of the opening Chinese salvoes, Rikh's Signals bunker was demolished, killing all the signallers including Captain Mangat. Soon after, the Mortar Platoon was wiped out – swiftly and competently.

The Bridge IV garrison repulsed two waves of Chinese attackers. Ultimately the 'big battalions' prevailed. The third attack wiped out a whole platoon of Bengalis, commanded by Jemadar Biswas, who was killed leading a gallant, but hopeless bayonet charge.

After most of the localities had been overrun, Major Gurdial Singh, the second-in-command rallied the remnants and led a personal assault. Most of this brave band were killed. Gurdial himself was overpowered and captured. He was awarded a Maha Vir Chakra, the second highest gallantry award, while in captivity.

When resistance had virtually collapsed, Rikh's command bunker was the last to hold out. It was surrounded by the Chinese who used every inducement to get Rikh to surrender, but he refused. He and those with him continued to engage the enemy. He had with him Captain Bhatia his adjutant, Lieut. Bhup Singh his Intelligence Officer and his batman. The Chinese plastered the bunker with machine-gun fire. When this failed to produce a surrender, a Chinese soldier crawled up and threw a hand-grenade. Captain Bhatia was killed and Rikh suffered multiple injuries in the jaw, left shoulder and left elbow. A final pole-charge sealed the fate of the already dazed inmates. The Chinese rushed the bunker and captured the unconscious CO and the helpless Bhup Singh.

Captain Bhatia was a very fine young officer and had been specially selected to be an instructor at the National Defence Academy at Poona. He was due to take his farewell of the men and leave on the 20th morning. Fate ruled otherwise and snuffed the life of this promising youth.

This story of gallantry beyond the call of duty was re-enacted in many platoons and companies. At Temporary Bridge Naik Roshan Singh's section clung doggedly to its position till every man was killed.

Subedar Dasrath Singh's platoon was reduced to seven men and had exhausted its ammunition in repulsing three Chinese attacks. Undeterred, the gallant men, led by Dasrath, got ready to show the Chinese what the Rajputs were made of. They charged the fourth attacking wave with the bayonet. In the ensuing hand to hand fighting four more men were killed. The three survivors, seriously wounded, were captured.

Jemadar Bose's platoon was left with only ten men after halting three Chinese attacks. He too charged with the bayonet and gave his life – as did most of his platoon.

I hope that the conduct and gallantry of Jemadars Biswas and Bose and their men will forever still the voices of those who delight in denigrating the martial prowess of our Bengali brethren. They fought with great *elan* and determination.

Major B. K. Pant's leadership and indomitable courage is a true epic. When the Chinese shelling commenced, Pant went round the locality bracing the men for the inevitable assault. He told the men that this was the day in which they would write a new chapter in the history of the battalion; and the time had come to show the Chinese the qualities which had made the name Rajput synonymous with courage and tenacity. Pant was wounded in the leg as he insisted in exposing himself during the shelling to reassure his men who had never experienced artillery fire. In spite of this he hobbled around telling the men that when the time came the fight must be to the last man and the last round.

The company held fast against three waves of Chinese attacks and suffered heavy casualties. The enemy called for heavier artillery concentrations before launching the fourth attack. Pant was wounded in the stomach and both legs. Despite his agony he continued to inspire his men, who seeing the indomitable will of this man, rose to super-human heights and broke the fourth attack. Pant losing blood rapidly was nearing his end but would not cry enough. He shouted to the men that Rajputs never give up and never die. His last stirring clarion call was to remind his jawans to fulfill their destiny and historical role as members of the martial clan from whom descend all other fighting men in India.

His last words were: "Men of the Rajput Regiment, you were born but to die for your country. God has selected this small river for which you must die. Stand up and fight as true Rajputs.

The Chinese realised that Major Pant was the main impediment in their way and the cause of their heavy casualties and directed all their attention to him. Heavy machine-gun fire was brought to bear on him and he was soon riddled with bullets. He died proudly shouting, as so many Rajput warriors have done over the centuries, the famous Rajput battle-cry: "Bajrang Bali ki Jai".

Major Pant's force of 112 men had 82 killed and wounded. What more can a country ask of its brave sons?

Space prevents me from recounting other similar deeds. I would also like to emphasise that it is not my intention to make any invidious comparisons between the Rajputs and my other Battalions who all did what was asked of them, in the highest traditions of the Indian Army. If the Rajputs hold the limelight it is only because it was their destiny to bear the full brunt of the Chinese assault of 20th October 1962.

The Chinese later admitted to one of our senior prisoners-of-war that they had suffered the maximum casualties of the NEFA fighting in the first battle – and these casualties had been inflicted mostly by 2 Rajputs.

The Gorkhas fought extremely well. Their CO, Lt.-Col. Ahluwalia was severely wounded and later captured. The Battalion's good work was recognised by the award of many gallantry medals.

The Punjabis who had borne the brunt of the fighting from 15th September and who had fought the Chinese to a standstill were out-flanked and suffered all their casualties while withdrawing over Hathungla Pass and the Dhola Massif. The same fate befell the Grenadiers.

These two famous units were sacrificed without a fight due to our faulty dispositions. The Punjabis, who were the best prepared for an attack lost many lives without being given the chance to offer a fight. The Chinese gave them a wide berth and were content to inflict casualties on stragglers.

The Tsangle Garrison of Punjabis and Gorkhas which for days was the most threatened and which had no means of defending itself, was able to escape practically unscathed. They withdrew *via* Bhutan. Such are the fortunes of war.

By 7.45 a.m. it was clear that the Chinese were about to overrun all our positions in the Dhola Sector. Brigade HQ was about to be encircled as the Gorkhas had been forced to withdraw towards Tsangdhar, thereby exposing its left flank. The Rajput resistence had been overcome and the front was also exposed.

In three short hours the flower of two regular Battalions had been hacked to pieces without a chance to do anything but die like men. I hope that their sacrifice will teach us the lessons that we must learn if we are to take our rightful place in the world community.

The full story of the ill-fated Thagla Battle, if the massacre can be dignified by such a title, may never be known as many who took part were killed in action. The others have had to submit to the shackles of active service in the Army. Under-supplied and ill-prepared, these men fought a lonely mountain battle and few in the rest of the Country, or indeed the Army knew of their ordeal and their squandered heroism, unredeemed by the faintest trace of success.

The Gorkhas, the Rajputs, the Sikhs, the Dogras, the Bengalis, the Mussalmans of the Grenadiers, the Ahirs, the South Indian Signallers and all the others from the four corners of India had nothing to sustain them but their regimental pride and traditions. They had done what they had done because they were soldiers. For no man can do more than give his life for his Country.

The heavy casualties suffered by 7 Brigade speak for themselves. The Rajputs who had 513 all ranks in the Namka Chu had the following casualties: (*a*) Killed – 282 including 4 Officers and 6 JCO's (*b*) Wounded and captured 81, including 2 Officers and 3 JCO's (*c*) Captured unwounded 90 including 3 Officers and 2 JCO's. Only 60 all ranks or about

9 per cent got away and these were mainly from rear and administrative parties left behind at Tsangdhar, Lumpu and Towang.

* * *

The Chinese shifted their attention to Tsangdhar which they had begun shelling from 5 a.m. The first attack was mounted at 9 a.m. by the Chinese force which had by-passed our positions on the River bank, between Temporary Bridge and Bridge V, on the night of 19th/20th October. Despite its being declared vital ground as early as the 10th of September, it was thinly held by an assortment of administrative personnel, a weak Gorkha company packing up to leave for Tsangle and two troops of Gunners.

Early on the morning of the 20th, our transport aircraft came to carry out drops as usual but were quickly shooed-off by Chinese fire. No one had bothered to tell the Air Force that a battle was imminent or had in fact started. We did not believe in unity of command and obviously Army-Air co-operation was not functioning smoothly.

The next unwary visitor to Tsangdhar was a helicopter carrying Major Ram Singh, second-in-command of the Divisional Signals Regiment and piloted by Flight-Lieutenant Sehgal. It was promptly shot down and all the occupants were killed. It will be recalled that Gen. Prasad was due to visit me and stay to share the fate of my Brigade. When news of the Chinese attack reached Divisional HQ and soon after communications were severed, Ram Singh prevailed upon the GOC not to fly to Tsangdhar till the tactical position cleared a bit. Prasad was adamant that he would keep his promise to me. Thereupon Ram volunteered to go first and find out what had happened. These two young men gave their lives to save their General. They were brave and deserve mention in this chronicle of the Thagla Affair.

The Divisional Signal Regiment was thus left without both its Commanding Officer who had been captured while with the Gorkhas and its second-in-command.

* * *

The Battalions could not have tried harder or fought more gallantly. It was not their fault that they were called upon to face a massive assault without the necessary fire support and defence stores; and from a tactically indefensible position. With the supply line being what it was they had no chance to stock-pile ammunition and prepare the defences required to beat-off a set-piece attack by a Chinese Force which out-numbered them by at least 20 to 1. The men had fought till exhaustion of ammunition had left them defenceless in the face of an overwhelmingly superior enemy.

Let all those who talked of our troops running away from the Chinese cut off their tongues in restitution for their slanderous statements against the men whose bravery alone could not compensate for the years of neglect, and the final inept political and military leadership which they were given. Once again in the history of India we see the heroism of her simple, tough peasantry wasted against an adversary who displayed better leadership; had better weapons and better military organisation.

* * *

At 8 a.m. I decided to move to Tsangdhar and reform there with the Gorkhas. The fate of the Rajputs was sealed as they had no escape route. I had earlier told Gen. Prasad that my intention was to move to Tsangdhar when forced to abandon the Namka Chu and he had approved. Anyway at this stage his approval was only of academic interest. No amount of political necessity or public clamour could now halt the Chinese onslaught.

I gave Major Kharbanda, my Brigade Major orders to move to Tsangdhar; The Commander's party to leave at 8.15 and the main body at 8.30 a.m. The Brigade Major needed time to burn secret papers which he personally did before leaving. Major Kharbanda and Major Pereira remained calm and unruffled throughout. The Brigade HQ was not 'overrun' at 7 a.m. or at any time. The men moved as an organised body and in an orderly manner. Let Gen. Prasad tell the story. He said, in an official report: "On 20th October 1962, Brigadier Dalvi was with his Brigade HQ at Rongla, in the Namka Chu Valley when the Chinese attacked 7 Brigade's positions in overwhelming strength. He remained at his post directing operations as best as he could. Finally when the enemy had overrun all the forward positions and had carried the fighting to the Left and the Rear of the Brigade HQ, Brigadier Dalvi asked my permission to withdraw to Tsangdhar and reorganise there. He moved only on my direct orders, but before he could get to Tsangdhar the enemy had already occupied this feature".

* * *

Thus ended the ill-fated confrontation in the Kameng Frontier Division outpost positions on the Namka Chu and Thagla Ridge. This was the tragic end to a week which had begun with Nehru's Olympian edict to 'throw out' the Chinese and had finished with the complete rout of the out-numbered and out-weaponed troops. We were not prepared to give an inch and lost thousands of square miles. The years of credulity and negligence were expiated. Bleeding from a thousand wounds, 7 Brigade expired: but India was to go on bleeding for many more years.

* * *

Were the Chinese supermen as has been made out by some uninformed commentators? I have discussed the Chinese tactics with many of my officers. The general consensus is that the Chinese used orthodox methods of fire and movement and pressed home their charges with determination. They were not afraid to close-in. Having said this, let me hasten to add that they were neither startingly original nor were they supermen.

They were well-equipped and clothed. I was amused to read the fiction about the Chinese being short of small arms weapons and how the follow-up waves of infantry had to rely on the weapons of their dead comrades. More self-delusions!

The most impressive display of Chinese training was their uncannily accurate artillery barrages despite their dependence on silent registeration. Their attacks were preceded by supporting fire of pin-point accuracy. The freedom to take close-quarter bearings paid them handsomely. They have been apt pupils and had emulated the renowned Russian aptitude for heavy and accurate artillery support.

It would be wrong to make sweeping deductions from the one-sided Thagla Battle. I will conclude by saying that the Chinese Army in Tibet is kept well-trained, physically fit and adept at night fighting.

The real Chinese success can be attributed to their High Command. They had manœuvred the Thagla incident with cunning; and the Chinese soldier had delivered the *coup-de-grace* with skill and fanaticism. This is the *epitomé* of war.

Having out-witted us they feigned to be the innocent party and added insult to injury. They received a good deal of help from our preposterous chest-thumping in the days preceding the battle.

The Chinese told the world that: "At 7 o'clock (Peking time) in the morning of 20th October the aggresive Indian forces, under cover of fierce artillery fire launched massive attacks against the Chinese Frontier Guards all along the Kachileng River and in the Khenzemane area". The poor Chinese were driven to self-defence by the fire of two out-ranged para-guns with 400 rounds of ammunition! The actual truth was well expressed by one Army Officer to the UPI Correspondent: "The Indian Army's mission was the defence of a political instead of a tactical position. The troops slaughtered along the Namka Chu River were spread out in a thin line difficult to supply and impossible to defend".

The same old story of the wolf and the lamb with a new setting, new costumes, new make-up and a new cast. Tragically, our own inept and ill-conceived bombast gave the Chinese a faint trace of plausibility to assume the role of the injured party.

* * *

I have told my story so that the Indian People should know the truth about their brave soldiers. There have been culprits who have had no compunction in directing the public wrath and chagrin to the Army's alleged ineptitude. There has also been an attempt to under-play the valour of the jawan.

It was galling to hear under-clad females of the cocktail circuits of Delhi and Bombay sidle up to me, after being told who I was, and say, "Brigadier, what happened to you chaps against the Chinese?" Their husbands usually had well paid jobs and were under-employed. The only problems these delightful and sophisticated people faced were of getting spare parts for their smuggled goods; the awkward business of finding a reliable liquor smuggler; the chronic servant problem and the awfully high taxes they paid to waste on idle and over-paid Service Officers.

The uninformed criticism of the ignorant is perhaps tolerable. Criticism from the Theatre Commander is more difficult to accept. Even the morning of 20th October is not sacred. In describing the short battle for the Namka Chu, Kaul has thrown in a last dig at some of the men who had served him faithfully then and have been silent and loyal since. While the guillotine was falling on the heads of the Namka Chu defenders, Gen. Kaul has this remark to offer: "I heard from an eye-witness that it (Brigade HQ) had not been prepared effectively. Parachutes had been put round the bushes and made into shelters against rains. Few trenches had been dug and hardly any defensive positions made".

The Brigade HQ was shelled from 5 a.m. to 8.30 a.m. mostly with heavy mortars, with a high proportion of tree bursts – the deadliest form of bombardment to endure. Fortunately there were only two fatal casualties and seven wounded, all of whom walked backed over the Karpola I route. Had the Brigade HQ not been entrenched it would have been decimated.

It is difficult to fathom the motive for this unfair, unjust, unbecoming and irrelevant remark from the military commander who was himself responsible for issuing the order which placed 7 Brigade in the plight in which it found itself; who was himself never able to provide it with the means for defending itself. He was the last person with any right to damn others for dereliction of duty. Kaul must know in his heart that even if the Brigade had been entrenched in concrete pill-boxes, behind a Maginot Line, it would still have been doomed. One thousand odd men could not have staved off 20,000 Chinese.

In his memoirs, Gen Kaul reveals a pathological impulse for self-justification. He rarely admits to major errors of generalship, though he has freely criticised others. He had accepted a thankless task in NEFA but he has not enhanced his stature or made it easier for himself by seeking to convince posterity of his guiltlessness by laying the blame on everyone else. He accepted the task of evicting the Chinese fully aware of the consequences of failure as he felt that he could not very well 'bicker' about the numerous shortcomings.

It would have been more gracious if he had not bickered after his project back-fired.

Gen. Kaul has been widely criticised in the Indian Press and by most commentators for trying to shift the blame for his failures to everyone from Mr. Nehru to the field commanders who served him. No general can claim a reprieve or vindicate his defeat in battle by claiming that he was compelled, against his better judgement, to execute an order that led to such a defeat. At the level of a Theatre Commander there are only two courses open. The first is to accept the entire responsibility for the failure, as Field Marshal Auchinleck did in 1942 when in a letter to Sir Winston Churchill, after the reverses in the Western Desert in June-July 1942, he wrote: ". . . and deeply regret the failures and set backs for the past months, for which I accept full responsibility". Noble sentiments from a noble man, which are worthy of emulation.

The second alternative is to disobey orders and be prepared to answer with one's head. As General Seydlitz said at the Battle of Zorndorf: "After the battle the King may dispose of my head as he wills but during the battle he will kindly allow me to make use of it". Gen. Kaul was neither prepared to 'use his head' nor take the blame for acquiescing in carrying out wrong orders. It is therefore unfair to burden the forward troops with guilt for obeying orders as best as they could with the resources at hand.

Gen. Kaul has not improved his case by adducing, at various stages, specious arguments to give a veneer of military thought to an episode that never had a military bias from the very outset. By doing so, he has needlessly dragged in many officers who have been unjustly in the shadows since 1962 due to their chance participation in events which they could not influence. Above all, he has given some people the opportunity to besmirch the good name of the Indian Army, as also to question its proficiency.

I bear Gen. Kaul no malice or ill-will. Indeed I bemoan the cruel downfall of a man of abundant talents and dynamism. He was destined for the highest honours. I was witness to inexplicable decisions which I knew would end his career. He needlessly gambled away his inheritance. He was a victim of a capricious fate which held out the promise of immortality and yet, in one bewildering stroke, broke him. Gen. Kaul's career, so painstakingly built over 15 years (1947 to 1962) was ruined in 15 days (3rd to 18th October 1962). It was given to me to watch him commit professional Hara-kiri, step by step. It was not an edifying sight.

It is more in sorrow than in anger that I have taken up the cudgels on behalf of the men I had the honour to command.

Chapter XXV

Captive of the Chinese Army

THE PLAY is ended and it only remains for me to tell the story of my capture by the Chinese Army of which each writer has given his own garbled version. While my HQ was moving to Tsangdhar, through a narrow re-entrant, we were subjected to incessant and accurate artillery fire. I was convinced that a Chinese Artillery Observation Officer was conducting the shoot. The deadly Chinese fire forced us to take cover every 70 to 80 seconds and in the process we lost our cohesion and formation. It was impossible to keep track of each other, with the result that the HQ split into small groups. I lost touch with the main body of my HQ.

The Chinese stopped shelling us at about 1 p.m. I do not know if they ran out of ammunition or they desisted from further bloodshed because they just got tired of hitting stragglers, without retaliation. When I took stock of the position I found myself with Major Nijjar, the Officer Commanding the Mortars, Captain Gupta, my Intelligence Officer and Captain Talwar the Officer who had strayed into my HQ the previous evening. They had started out with me as part of the Commander's party. We also had about 37 men from my HQ and the Rajputs from Bridge III. Havildar Brijpal Singh took charge of this party and was a tower of strength throughout our long ordeal.

Soon after we left Brigade HQ, I realised that it was pointless to make for Tsangdhar. I was sure that my Brigade major too would come to the same conclusion, as he too could witness the Tsangdhar Battle. I felt certain that he would make for Lumpu where we should have been in the first place.

The troops at Tsangdhar were fighting stubbornly and tenaciously. I was able to see their stout-hearted resistance, as from a grand-stand of an amphi theatre quite clearly. The Chinese were forced to reform twice before they were able to capture the dropping zone area. The battle then shifted to the Gunner positions. This troop of tough Sikhs belonged to the *élite* Parachute Brigade. They were called upon to fight a ground action and fought like seasoned infantrymen. I could see them across the valley separating Dhola from Tsangdhar, battling away with the vastly superior Chinese force. My heart swelled with pride when I saw them open fire with their guns, over open sights, to deadly effect and break up at least four charges. It was only when they had run out of ammunition (only 400 odd rounds to start with) that the Chinese were able to launch a final bayonet charge and overrun their positions.

The Gunners had given battle from mid-day to 3.30 p.m. The sound of the last crack of a bullet came at 4 p.m., from a lone straggler withdrawing from Tsangdhar. It was nothing more than a symbolic act of defiance. The Battle for Thagla Ridge was over.

My only hope now was that the Punjabis and the Grenadiers had been able to make a stand on the Hathungla axis. I fervently prayed that the Chinese had not made any spectacular gains along this route.

I was trying to fathom the Chinese intentions. As late as 19th October they were not supposed to "do anything big". How big is big? Now I had to do my own reasoning, and draw my own conclusions. As a soldier, I realised that their minimum objective must be the Tsangdhar – Hathungla – Drokung Samba Bridge Line. This would give them their version of the

McMahon Line and neutralise our dropping zone, which was the life-line of the Brigade. Quite frankly I did not credit them with the intention of invading India.

Ultimately I decided to make for Serkhim where we had a company of the Grenadiers. This was my only hope of remaining with the Brigade, an action demanded by the military code which requires officers to command to the last. To reach Serkhim we had to negotiate the massive, 18,500-foot Dhola Massif. Well, there was no alternative but to have a crack at this mountain, although I was not exactly clad for a high-altitude expedition. I was wearing a pair of ordinary rubber gum boots, a coat parka and serge trousers which had seen better days. I was lucky to have a pair of leather gloves (a gift from my father), as the woollen mittens issued were quite useless as protection against the biting Himalayan cold.

We climbed vertically and steadily till 4 p.m., when we had to stop due to the extreme cold and early darkness. The climb throughout was through thick rhododendron bushes. There is nothing more infuriating and tiring than dense, twisted, impenetrable rhododendron bushes – except perhaps bamboo clumps. The chasms and crags demanded both respect and caution. One false step or slip, at those heights, and there would be no trace of the careless one who trod unwarily in the treacherous snows.

We found a mini-cave (in modern jargon), at about 17,000 feet and decided to halt till daylight. I did not think that so many human beings would even fit into such a small space. But we did, huddling together for warmth. There was no question of trying to sleep. It was a case of not dying of the cold. The cold, at this height in October, in the Himalayas, is difficult to describe.

When we finally adjusted ourselves, we remembered that none of us had had a morsel of food since the evening of the 19th, nearly 24 hours in terms of time, and an eternity in terms of experience. For me, this last supper had consisted of two chappattis and a handful of tinned peas. The more menacing thought was that there was no prospect of finding any sustenance till we reached the Grenadiers – if we ever did achieve this feat. We had no maps, as no unfortunate lance-naik had been sent to this place to draw a sketch map, and everyone relied on my knowledge of the main features and landmarks.

Major Nijjar was not a fit man and was in great distress. He should never have been sent to the Namka Chu in the first place. I had to admire his guts and determination. He never once complained and persevered despite his visible suffering. I was touched when he insisted on carrying my brief case. When I protested that this was not the time to adhere to the niceties of military protocol, he retorted that I was his Commander and he was damn well not going to allow me to carry anything, as long as he was around and alive. I had never met this officer until he reported to my HQ on or about the 17th of October.

During one of the halts, a jawan came up to me diffidently and said, "Sahib, I have been watching you. You smoke a lot. I have a few cigarettes that I would like you to have. Please forgive me because they are cheap ones". Again, I can only say that I was deeply touched. Another jawan offered me his box of matches. These little gestures, in moments of great stress and danger made me feel proud of belonging to such a wonderful Army. Despite the harrowing time we had been through and the mortal dangers we had faced, the Officers and the men retained their natural and traditional sense of discipline; their mutual regard and respect.

We left the cave at 3.30 a.m., on 21st October and headed for the formidable, 18,500-foot Dhola Peak. We climbed over treacherous rocks and deep crevices. Halts were necessary at frequent intervals as I could see that the men were getting more and more listless – a dangerous sign in the mountains. Gradually I began to lose the odd man who could not keep up with the party. Speed was essential if we were to forestall the Chinese.

By midday, Major Nijjar had difficulty in breathing: Captain Gupta who had contracted chill-blains could not walk: and Talwar's stomach was giving him trouble in spite of the tablets that he kept swallowing to alleviate the pains. It was ironic that the only officer who seemed to be free of any physical infirmity was the oldest member of the party. Soon it was evident that we would have to split into two parties if we were to have any hopes of reaching our destination in time.

The summit of the Dhola feature was a mass of sprawling false crests. There were no clearly defined peaks and we kept plodding along in the optimistic hope of eventually reaching the Hathungla-Lumpu track, somewhere near Serkhim.

To our relief, we hit the Lumpu-Karpola I track at about 1.30 p.m. My party was now down to a dozen men. My unofficial batman had got left behind. Despite his suffering he refused to jettison my transistor radio. After 8 days he proudly fetched up in the Brigade collecting point, saluted the Brigade Major and said: "Where is my Brigadier Sahib? I want to give him his radio set". It is now a cherished memento and a further reminder of the affection of the Indian soldier for his officer. Major Nijjar and Captain Gupta could not proceed any further that day. The lack of food and water added to their discomfort and increasing weakness. I told them to rest and follow us when they felt better. I left a few men to look after them. Captain Talwar volunteered to accompany me. He refused to stay behind despite his own ailment. He said that he was not going to allow his Commander to wander in the blue without an officer escort. This young man had an iron will.

I left Major Nijjar and Gupta with mixed feelings. I was sorry for them as I thought that they may get captured, or even die in the cold or of starvation. The last laugh was on me. They moved along the Karpola I-Lumpu track, not realising that the Chinese were ahead of them. When they reached Lumpu they found the Chinese in occupation. After some incredibly narrow escapes they got through the Chinese lines and reached Bhutan.

Talwar and I resumed our march, accompanied by seven stout volunteers led by Havildar Brijpal Singh, straight down a water-course which I reckoned would lead us to Serkhim. We slid on our bottoms in some places; and had to retrace our steps frequently to by-pass sheer cliffs. The water-course had to be crossed and re-crossed to negotiate bluffs. The boulders in this stream were moss-covered and slippery. One slip and the unfortunate one would have to be left behind to perish, as it was impossible to carry an injured person. Even if we had the will to save a comrade, none of us had the strength to hazard a long carry. We were weak and famished. I once slipped and fell about 30 feet and was surprised to find myself in one piece. I thanked my Dehra Dun Military Academy Physical Training Instructor for teaching me how to break a fall.

It was soon dark and we could proceed no further. I reluctantly decided to halt where we were, on the mossy, cold, damp bank of the stream, under an overhanging rock. I had torn my trousers while negotiating the thorny slopes and it was impossible to sit without discomfort. We lit a fire with wet wood for warmth but it was difficult to keep it going.

This was the second full day without food. We had found water but it was freezing cold and hard to swallow. We were all suffering from dehydration. We left this inhospitable shelter at 4 a.m. on the morning of 22nd October sore, frozen and tired, and continued the cross-country march towards Serkhim. Progress remained very slow. I was again assailed by doubts about my navigation and was certain that we had lost our way. The penalty for this was death. I did not know how much longer the men and I could go without any nourishment, as we had already been without food and without sleep for 60 hours.

We kept descending steadily. At about 6 a.m. we halted for a rest and while we were sitting we saw a long line of armed Chinese moving on the track below us. I watched mesmerised as I saw a seemingly endless column of infantry weapons. I counted at least one battalion passing, and for the first time I knew that the Chinese had launched an invasion and had crossed their version of the McMahon Line. Mr. Chou En Lai had made good his threat. I was sure, from my position, that they had crossed Hathungla Pass and were on the way to Serkhim and Lumpu. Their target now must be the dropping zone at Lumpu, the loss of which would force us to vacate the Nyam Jang Chu Valley, forward of Towang. There was no other maintenance base. I knew that the Lumpu-Choksen defile was not held and Lumpu was defenceless. We were now in real trouble. I was worried about the fate of the Punjabis and the Grenadiers. Were they in the bag? There was now no chance of re-organising at Serkhim or Lumpu. The Grenadiers detachment (of less than one company) would be brushed aside by the Chinese Force that I had myself seen moving towards Lumpu.

I immediately decided to head for Ziminthaung to reach Division HQ. The last hope was that the Nyam Jang Chu Force was holding out at the Drokung Samba Bridge which was a formidable obstacle that could not be easily by-passed. If the Bridge had been demolished then the Chinese could not resume their advance till a new bridge was built. This would be our last chance of slipping through the fast closing Chinese net.

I did not know then that Divisional HQ had already been abandoned on 21st October. The Chinese advance from Khenzemane on 20th October threatened the HQ which was virtually undefended. The medical units there were called upon to man the perimeters. On the night of 20th October the Chinese were barely two miles from Ziminthaung.

The Army Commander was expected at Divisional HQ on 20th and 21st October to give on-the-spot decisions in the absence of Gen. Kaul regarding the withdrawal from the Nyam Jang Chu axis, but he never arrived. Perhaps he had classified the Chinese attack as a "divisional" or "corps" battle!

On 21st October GOC 4 Division decided to withdraw to Towang. One large helicopter landed to evacuate the casulties that were at the Main Dressing Station – these were earlier casualties. Everyone from the General downwards left for Towang on foot. The Indian Army did not have a spare helicopter for the Major-General who was still responsible for the Towang sector and who was the *de-facto* Corps Commander. The Towang Sector disintegrated while the General was on the move. Towang was abandoned and most stragglers were forced to withdraw *via* Bhutan.

The Chinese reached Lumpu on the 21st on the heels of the departing HQ. On the Nyam Jang Chu they had made significant gains and were well on their way to Lumpu *via* Drokung Samba Bridge of 1959 fame. This time there was no pushing, prodding and protest notes. The world of words had come to an end. This time it was an invasion. The Indian flag had been pulled down. It could be re-hoisted only by an act of force or when Mr. Chou-en Lai consented and permitted us to do so!

The Chinese raced to the Brahmaputra Valley which they reached on 20th November.

* * *

I estimated our observation point to be at a height of 10,000 feet; a drop of 8,000 feet from Dhola Pass. It was absolutely impossible to attempt the climb back, in our state of near starvation and exhaustion. Besides there was no point in doing this as the Chinese had control of the Karpola I-Lumpu track. There was only one course open, and that was to make for the Nyam Jang Chu Valley.

We started walking after the tail of the Chinese column had passed, and soon reached the track. For a moment I allowed myself the indulgence of congratulating myself on my navigational skill. The years as the Intelligence Officer of 5 Baluch Regiment (now in the Pakistan Army) had seen us through – so far. We hit the Hathungla-Serkhim track barely half a mile from Serkhim, as I found out later when walking back with the Chinese, as a prisoner.

After crossing the track we made a dash for the Nyam Jang Chu Valley, straight down a steep hill-side. Immediately we did this we found ourselves in the middle of a thick primary jungle. We slid and slithered for a while till we hit a precipice. Navigation was now impossible as we could not see any features or landmarks. I had no option but to retrace my steps and try all over again from the track we had left. We climbed through the thick jungle hoping that we would not get lost. I directed myself more by instinct than judgement.

After some hours we came to what looked like a clearing, round a bend. I was in the lead, followed by my party of seven men. As I stepped into this narrow open space I found myself in the midst of a Chinese infantry company, which had selected this spot to rest. I immediately found myself staring into a dozen assorted weapons and barrels and heard some sharp grunts. I am still not sure as to who was more surprised, the Chinese or myself.

I glanced at my watch. It was exactly 9.22 a.m. of the 22nd of October 1962. I was a prisoner of the Chinese People's Liberation Army.

At this time I had been without food for 66 hours; had climbed from 10,500 to 18,500 feet and then descended down a water-course to 10,500 feet. I was exhausted, hungry, unshaven and despondent. My mouth was full of sores due to dehydration. My clothes were in tatters due to walking through bushes and sliding down thorny slopes.

This was the end to the bizarre and unbelievable events of September-October 1962. The incredible sequence of events had come to an end in a small clearing on the Hathungla-Serkhim-Lumpu track, which was once my domain. I was now at the mercy of the tough, pock-marked Chinese Captain whose company I had stumbled into. At such moments the will to live is stilled, and all initiative is lost. It is difficult for a person who has exercised command for 20 years to fully grasp the fact that his fate and future lie in the hands of another and possibly hostile person. The ignominy of captivity is, for the soldier, a fate worse than death.

It was a miracle that I was alive. So far I had not thought of my good fortune in being alive and free of sickness and injury. I would now live to tell the tale of the Thagla Battle some day. The human body is indeed God's most amazing creation. The mind and the body had overcome the most grievous hardships and dangers; and made light of starvation, intense cold, lack of sleep and super-human exertions at heights where it is difficult to even breathe under normal conditions. These physical hardships were accompanied by mental depression, humiliation and anger at the culprits, mingled with sorrow for all those who gave their lives.

The Indian Army had some of the toughest, bravest men in the world. In all humility I can say that few armies in the world would have endured the incredible hardships and shown the steadfastness of the jawan during the days of September-October 1962. Given the right leadership and equipment he is more than a match for anyone who casts covetous eyes on our soil. Why then did we not harness these great qualities in the service of India instead of dissipating them on a futile show of force?

The death struggle of 7 Infantry Brigade is a tale of indescribable suffering. It was marked by despair and justifiable bitterness of the men who had been deceived in their trust. And yet they displayed steadfastness in the face of an undeserved but inexorable fate. They came to terms with the cruelty of their lot only because of their sterling heritage.

The sufferings of the men who were able to escape death or evade capture will always haunt those who were responsible for their predicament. Many died from exposure to the severe cold and a large number from pitiless hunger. In those days the Indian Army did not even have an emergency ration when the children of the affluent could walk into any confectionery shop and buy chocolates. All of us must accept the guilt for this outrageous state of affairs.

Innumerable dead bodies could not be identified by the Chinese as many of our men did not have 'identity discs' (dog-tags)!

Our mistakes and shortcomings must now be recorded so that in future we do not blunder into a Himalayan military operation and create for ourselves the conditions for inevitable disaster and humiliation. From 8th September to 20th October 1962, the mistakes were wholly and solely due to faulty Higher Direction of War. Government "decided in haste and ignorance and repented at leisure and in desolation".

I do sincerely believe that there is no call for despair and despondency. The Army is good and the reverses at Thagla do not call for any sweeping condemnation of the officers and men, who behaved in the highest traditions of the Indian Army. Unfortunately we had adopted some strange and inexcusable notions on the higher direction of war and based our National Aims on invalid premises.

By their self-less immolation the defenders of the Namka Chu converted this remote Valley into a grim reminder to the Indian People of their duties and responsibilities as a sovereign Nation. We learnt that nations do not exercise power and influence, or have real independence unless they have the force to defend their rights. The Battle in the desolate Thagla Ridge area was the cremation ground for the triple tragedies of negligence, credulity, and the national disinterestedness in defence matters. We learnt that war is an act of force and not a verbal debate: it is a test of skill as well as a test of fortitude. We learnt that bravery alone is not enough. We learnt that the Politician, the Civil Servant and the military High Command must adhere to the accepted Principles of War and exercise circumspection and method. We learnt that we cannot leave our defence in the hands of a few.

For the Indian Army, particularly for the jawan, it was a tribute to his endurance and tenacity. Looking back on events I marvel at the valour, loyalty and simplicity of the Indian Sepoy. He had implicit faith in his leaders and followed them without hesitation or doubt. Throughout he lived on hard scales and fought with pouch ammunition. He never flinched when ordered to Thagla, nor later when the Chinese were preparing for their assault.

It is a tragedy that the impeccable behaviour of these men has not received due recognition. They are entitled to praise. Above all, we have denied them the homage that is their due, for largely by their sacrifice and debacle was wrought the awareness of our weaknesses and our defence problems.

I hope that this book which is my tribute to them will partially redress the wrong done them.

Part VI

The Reason Why

Chapter XXVI

Faulty Higher Direction of War

The story of the events that culminated in the Thagla Battle makes it amply clear that the main faults lay in the sphere of what is known as the Higher Direction of war — a term which embraces the entire process of the formulation of the National Policy, and the readiness of the Nation and Armed Forces for war.

In his statement on the NEFA Enquiry, Mr. Chavan told the Lok Sabha, on 2nd September 1963: "This brings me to the next point which is called the Higher Direction of War/Operations. Even the largest and best equipped armies need to be given proper policy guidance and major directives by the Government, whose instrument it is. These must bear a reasonable relation to the size of the Army and state of its equipment from time to time. An increase in the size or improving the equipment of the Army costs not only money but also needs time". This is a courageous but singularly revealing admission by Mr. Menon's successor, about the Government's failure to issue proper policy guidance and major directives i.e. Government failed to exercise what is known as 'Civil Supremacy'.

Lt.-General P. S. Bhagat, VC, whom I have known for many years, was kind enough to autograph my copy of his book *Forging The Shield*. He wrote, "John, I know you have suffered for want of proper Higher Direction of War. May this book, though inadequately, give a line of thought. May no one ever be placed in the predicament you were in, in 1962 . . . Prem Bhagat". General Bhagat was a member of the two-man Enquiry Board held to study the causes of the NEFA Reverses. Despite the obvious handicaps under which this Board had to carry out its investigations, it showed remarkable percipience in arriving at the basic causes of the setbacks in the short war with China in 1962. I shall be quoting extensively from the report of this team.

There is no gainsaying the fact that there was something amiss in the manner and methods we had adopted to arrive at the National Aims and implement them in peace and war. On paper we had a sound enough system which was largely copied from the British. Unfortunately, the system was not allowed to function in the recognised way. Even during the years preceding the Chinese Aggression, the enunciation of the National Policy had become the prerogative of a few people, whose views prevailed even when there was unmistakable evidence that the Policy was faulty. There was no harmonious fusion of civil and military thinking. The politician, soldier and civil servant had not evolved a smooth working arrangement whereby each could have his say, and each could get a respectful hearing.

The reasons are partly historical and partly due to the strong personalities of Mr. Nehru and Mr. Menon. India got off to a bad start in 1947. From the very outset there was a lack of *rapport* between the politician and the Service Officer. Indian Independence had been achieved peacefully and constitutionally, without a war of independence and without the need of a military force, as in the case of Algeria and Indonesia. There was thus no contact between the Congressman and the Armed Forces. The leading figures of the freedom fight were household names and when the British left, they were given the entire credit for this remarkable feat. Mahatma Gandhi, Pandit Jawaharlal Nehru and Sardar Vallabhbhai Patel were not mere political leaders – they were treated as demi-gods. This was natural and this adulation was later to be repeated in the case of Dr. Soekarno of Indonesia; President Nasser of Egypt and Dr. Nkhruma of Ghana.

On the other hand, the soldier and civil servant had reached his specialised eminence in comparative obscurity. On 15th August 1947 the British Government transferred power to the Indian and Pakistani peoples in a peaceful, orderly and cordial manner bequeathing all British Indian institutions, organisations and Services to the new Indian and Pakistani Governments. The Indian Freedom fighters, as the Congressmen fondly called themselves, assumed the highest posts in a sovereign State. The Civil Service and the Indian Armed Forces were rapidly 'Indianised' and on 15th January 1949 the last British Commander-in-Chief was replaced by the first Indian, General K. M. Cariappa. Promotions were rapid and relatively inexperienced men assumed the highest posts in all spheres of activity. Few Indian Officers had any experience of command or staff work at the highest level; and in the early days we had the spectacle of senior officers playing musical chairs to give an illusion of varied experience and a sound military background. The Civil Servant was equally new to defence work in a sovereign country. The average politician had little knowledge of administration at the national level; and barring a few notable exceptions, little understanding of international affairs, which soon became the special domain of Mr. Nehru.

The British Indian Army had been kept aloof from politics and had been raised primarily to fulfil an Imperial role. Recruitment to both officer ranks and the soldiery was restricted to a few so-called martial classes, who were rewarded handsomely for their services to the British *Raj*. Officers were carefully screened for their loyalty; and were forced to refrain from showing any interest, much less sympathy, for the freedom struggle lest they incurred the displeasure of their superiors and jeopardised their prospects in the Army. Some, of course, were beneficiaries under the British connection and had a vested interest in maintaining it. Most of the Officers had imbibed Western ideas, culture, dress and social habits, further widening the gap between them and the average politician.

The Indian Independence movement was conceived and led by the middle-class intelligentsia, spearheaded by lawyers and other professional men, and financed by merchants. Most of them were drawn from the ranks of those who did not directly benefit from the British presence in India. They made immense sacrifices in the national interest. Many suffered financial loss and some were subjected to physical beatings and long periods of incarceration in British jails. In 1930, the Congress Working Committee was as inspired, patriotic and talented a group of men as in any liberation movement in history. Each man was a giant in his own way; and the top leaders will assuredly find a permanent place in the history of modern India.

It was sad but true that when India attained Independence, there was no meeting ground or contact between the Politician, the Civil Servant and the Soldier – there was in fact more than a little distrust. The Congressman claimed a monopoly on patriotism and "Indianness" – a dangerous assumption as the technical and professional men who had served the British Regime could not be summarily displaced. Instead of getting together to thrash out a *modus vivendi*, a marriage of convenience was contracted.

This compromise soon affected the civil servant who now had to please his new political bosses, as well as to safeguard his exaggerated position in the Indian administrative set-up. Friction between the civil servant and the soldier was a natural and inevitable outcome. Rapid promotions, immaturity and a false sense of dignity further contributed to the incipient disharmony. There was a good deal of wrangling about who was senior, the 'equation' between civil ranks *vis-a-vis* Army ranks, and who should go to see whom in official matters; there were petty squabbles about who was entitled to an office carpet and air-conditioners.

Many are the stories which I can recount about the infantile behaviour of officials who should have known better. The culprits came from all categories of officialdom, but I shall refrain from quoting instances that are within my knowledge and which took place in my time at Army HQ, from 1954 to 1959. The stories are unworthy of mature persons.

The Order of Precedence was frequently changed and each time the Army General was down-graded. On the surface these might appear to be petty pinpricks and trivial; but in fact they were early warnings of a deep and latent malaise. We have seen how, in 1962, Generals had lost their authority to resist improper orders or to influence the course of events. We have seen how so serious an order as the one to evict the Chinese was conveyed to the Chief of Army Staff by a mere Joint Secretary. We have seen how the advice of the General Staff to re-equip and reorganise the Army was summarily brushed aside by ministers, civil servants and financial experts without any formal protest from the military authorities.

Our political philosophies contributed to the lackadaisical attitude to defence matters. We did not fear war. We did not seek war to settle any of our problems. We believed that our non-aligned policy and our inflated international prestige would ensure us friends in a crisis. The Indian Government would gladly have disbanded the Army in 1949/50 if the Kashmir problem had been solved.

The attainment of Independence was followed by an intense desire to eradicate poverty and provide the people with the minimum amenities in the way of medical services, education, housing, clothing and food. We gave priority to development, and launched the First Five-Year Plan as early as 1950.

As the first and most important colonial country to be liberated after World War II, we were the vanguard for the independence movements all over the Asian and

African Continents. We became engrossed and involved in the affairs of the world and soon attained an honoured place in the World Community. Unfortunately, in the process we tended to neglect our own domestic problems.

Given the background of our Independence movement, the lack of fear of war, the priority allotted to development and the preoccupation with world affairs, it was inevitable that there could be no sense of urgency in keeping the Armed Forces in good shape and ready for War, if thrust upon us. Everybody could delay, obstruct and theorise over defence issues, on every conceivable count and with impunity.

On paper our procedures for the Higher Direction of War followed logically from the parliamentary democratic system which we had given ourselves in the 1950 Constitution. The Government of India, formed by the majority party of the elected Legislature is responsible for all aspects of the Higher Direction of War, and no other body can usurp or dilute this function. This is the quintessence of "Civil Supremacy" or "civil control" of the Armed Forces. Government functions through the Cabinet, which is thus supreme. The Cabinet is assisted by the Ministry of Defence and the Service Chiefs, both in formulating the National Policy and when prosecuting war. The Cabinet is vested with unfettered political and military authority, and is in fact the only level at which the overall political and military considerations of the National Aims converge.

The Defence Committee of the Cabinet (DCC) is a handy working group of the Cabinet which is responsible for handling the Nation's defence problems both in peace and war, and consists of the key Cabinet members viz. the Prime Minister and the Foreign, Home, Finance and Defence Ministers. Other ministers are co-opted whenever their special subjects are under consideration. Service Chiefs and Civil Servants are in attendance.

The DCC is required to assess the military threat to the Nation and decide on how the threat is to be met; whether by raising the necessary defence forces or seeking allies, or a combination of the two. Such a decision must be based on an objective, realistic and hard-headed appraisal of all the politico-military factors. There is no room for wishful thinking and extravagant hopes. In arriving at a sound National Aim, it is necessary to pose the following questions, from time to time, and deduce replies with the impersonality of a computer:

(*a*) What are the Nation's fundamental interests now and for the foreseeable future? Forward planning of foreign policy must be closely related to the long term military consequences. There is little wisdom in pretending to go-it-alone and then screaming for help in a crisis.

(*b*) What countries can effect our interests by economic or military means?

(*c*) Which countries have identical interests and can be relied upon to help?

(*d*) Which countries can oppose us and what is the extent of the threat?

(*e*) If more than one country can become hostile, can we take them on simultaneously? If not, what needs to be done to isolate one while dealing with the others?

(*f*) How long can we sustain hostilities single-handed?

(*g*) How much money can be diverted to defence without hurting the economy of the Nation?

The National Aims must be tailored to the capacity of the Armed Forces and the resources of the country. Conversely, the required forces must be raised and maintained, if diplomatic means are considered to be uncertain or inadequate to sustain our fundamental interests. No nation can afford to be deflected, by extraneous factors, from its paramount duty to defend itself.

Having assessed the threat, the DCC must give clear and feasible instructions to the Armed Forces to meet the anticipated threat, and must allot the necessary funds in time for the money to be converted into the required battle-field units. It is for the experts at Service HQs to assess this requirement and they must not be subjected to a cross-examination by amateur civilians. There is no question of making every available rupee go as far as possible as Menon has since averred. All the rupees must be found or the National Policy recast. Sudden political imperatives cannot be allowed to spark off a war for which there has been no preparation. The Army was first sent to man the borders in 1959/60 without the basic requirements for mountain warfare. Later we embarked on a "limited" programme to make up a few of our deficiencies; while our political postures were not enforceable by arms. Again in 1962, the Army was bludgeoned into attempting the impossible task of evicting the Chinese although we did not have the troops, fire power or other minimum resources.

From 1947 to 1962, the DCC was called upon to take decisions on at least the following occasions i.e. (*i*) when the Kashmir issue was not settled at the UN during the period 1949 to 1954; (*ii*) when the Chinese annexed Tibet in 1950 and we faced a long border with a powerful neighbour; (*iii*) when the United States and Pakistan signed the Mutual Aid Pact which gave Pakistan substantial arms during 1954 to 1957; (*iv*) when the Chinese began nibbling at our territory in Ladakh and built their highway through our Aksai Chin Plateau; (*v*) when the Dalai Lama was given asylum after he had fled from Lhasa in 1959; (*vi*) and lastly in 1960 after the failure of the talks between officials of India and China, which were held in the wake of the three major border clashes in 1959.

It is not unfair to say that the DCC never approached the serious matter of defending ourselves, or of solving the political issues which could lead to war, with the determination and thoroughness demanded. Despite being bounded by two hostile neighbours, the role of the Army was laid down (by the DCC) as: "To be prepared to defend ourselves against a second class power". Financial appropriations were restricted to this modest aim. When the Pakistani threat agitated the public and military planners in 1956, Government reluctantly permitted some inescapable reorganisations and a few new raisings to meet the challenge of Pakistan's American aided mobile corps – and even so there was to be no arms race. In 1961, when the Chinese threat was no longer a hypothetical question, but merely a matter of time, Government embarked on a "limited" programme for improving our defences. At this time, Mr. Nehru is quoted as saying that any additional defence expenditure would cause a major economic setback. He thought that we should rely on indigenous production rather than "waste" valuable foreign exchange on purchases from abroad. There can be little purposeful military planning if the DCC wavers and displays a split personality over the issue of defence expenditure.

The nature of the twin Chinese and Pakistani threats were never really analysed in a hard-headed manner. To comfort ourselves and lend respectability to our half-hearted actions, we created imaginary problems for our potential enemies. It is said that Mr. Nehru told Mr. B. K. Nehru and Gen. Kaul that, apart from creating tension, neither China nor Pakistan was in a position to provoke a war with us as they had their own problems. At another time, Mr. Nehru is quoted as saying that the Chinese were not really strong, as they had their own troubles and internal disorders due to food shortages and an unpopular dictatorial regime. He thought that they faced a revolt in Tibet and the morale of the Chinese People and the Chinese Armed Forces was cracking up; and if we dealt with them firmly we should get the better of them. This particular view was relayed to the Army by Gen. Kaul during the Infantry Commanders' Conference in 1962.

On yet another occasion when asked for money to buy the minimum requirements of the Army, Nehru is reported to have held the view that there would be no war with China, and all the scare the Army High Command were making was a military miscalculation. He thought that the military was over-stressing the point and putting up extravagant demands which were not quite necessary. This view was belied when we presented our shopping list to the Anglo-American Military Missions which flew to our rescue after the Chinese invasion. The American *Time* Magazine put it aptly. The paper wrote: "The Indian Army needs almost everything except courage".

Gen. Kaul has summed up the Government's approach to policy-making neatly. He told a Press Conference at Delhi on 3rd April 1967: "The Army was never given any charter or directives from the Civil Administration. The Army had never been asked to prepare itself against any threat from China. In fact our leaders and civil servants and service officials did not have the impression that there was a possibility of war with China". He added: "The fact was that due attention had not been paid to defence matters until 1962. There was no policy-making body for defence matters at the highest level. Decisions were taken from day to day". (*Times of India* correspondent in a despatch from New Delhi dated 3rd April 1967). These words from a former Chief of the General Staff reveal a very strange state of affairs. What had become of the DCC?

Apart from the domination of Mr. Nehru's personality, the DCC was rendered more ineffective due to irreconcilable differences within the Cabinet. It is well known that the Indian Cabinet of the Congress Party contained diverse elements, and was riven with personal and ideological contradictions. The Indian Cabinet was not designed to harness the best talent, but to accommodate aspirants from the various regions of the country; to fit-in the various political hues and shades; and to recognise the seniority of the leading members of this huge, amorphous Party.

Everybody knows of the clash between Mr. Desai the Finance Minister and Mr. Menon the Defence Minister – a clash which is alleged to have resulted in the Armed Forces being starved of urgently needed funds, particularly foreign exchange, for vital military equipment. This state of affairs, if true, is inexplicable if the DCC had functioned in a constitutional manner.

If the DCC had laid down the National Aims, then both these august gentlemen were party to the deliberations and the decisions taken, as the Indian Cabinet works on the basis of "collective" responsibility. The financial implications of the National Aim would have figured prominently in the discussions which preceded the decision. It is the very essence of high level planning that a judicious balance be struck between the minimum requirements of defence and the maximum that can be spared without retarding the development of the Nation (the residual requirements being secured by arranging allies). No country can afford to think in terms of war and be too proud to accept help; and be too poor to find its own resources. To approach the life and death matter of national defence in any other way is to indulge in pipe-dreams. The allotment of inadequate or "available" funds is wasteful as this does not provide security and yet handicaps development. A poor country like India cannot live in a perpetual state of semi-readiness for war.

If the above theses are accepted, as they must be, then the financial implications of the National Policy arise naturally, and the Finance Minister (and his experts) cannot exercise any further, independent judgement of what is to be bought, from what source and with what currency. If a disagreement had arisen, then the Prime Minister was duty bound to intervene and adjudicate; either the Finance or Defence Ministers moving the DCC to reconvene to discuss the details arising out of the basic policy decision. To accept a deadlock which affects the honour of the Nation is unacceptable.

The inescapable deduction is that one of three things happened: (*a*) the Government did not have a clear National Policy; or (*b*) the DCC did not keep a watching brief on defence preparations which it had decreed in the first place; or (*c*) Mr. Nehru avoided the unpleasant chore of intervening between two senior ministers – especially as they were the leading spokesmen of the so-called Rightist and Leftist Groups. Some unkind commentators have suggested that Mr. Nehru allowed his senior colleagues to be at loggerheads to consolidate his own position and power as well as to leave the race for the succession to his seat open. Both Menon and Desai were front rank aspirants for the Prime Ministerial *gaddi*, after Mr. Nehru.

The DCC had never really functioned from the very earliest days after we became a free, sovereign nation. Mr. Nehru became the sole arbiter of the National Policy, and his views and ideas became dominant. The rest of the country was content to let the matter rest at that; and we were content to allow Mr. Nehru to play the vital defence problem "by ear", intuition and instinct. The DCC was never the free forum for formulating the National Policy that it was designed to be. All failure in war is directly attributable to this key body in the Indian constitutional set-up, and every member from 1947 onwards must share responsibility, with the Prime Minister for the disasters of 1962. When the Chinese defeated us, we descended on Mr. Nehru, in the manner of crows who proceed to cannibalise a dead comrade, when we were all to blame. People get the Government they deserve and the foreign policy they desire. It is preposterous to claim that Mr. Nehru forced any views on the Nation. All that can be said is that he succumbed to adulation and resented advice which was contrary to his views; but this could have been put right by a knowledgeable public, an alert Press and a forceful Lok Sabha headed by a fearless and dedicated Cabinet.

Perhaps the most tragic manifestation of the impotence of the DCC was shown during September 1962, when it was virtually defunct as the Prime Minister, the Finance Minister and the Defence Minister were mostly abroad at crucial stages of the Sino-Indian confrontation. National decisions were formulated under pressure of events, on a day-to-day basis. Orders were being obtained by trans-Atlantic cables; and minor functionaries were gaily relaying war orders to the Chief of Army Staff.

The DCC of 1962 was overhauled after the debacles in NEFA when Mr. Menon was removed and Mr. Desai was Kamaraj-ed (to remove dissidents and opponents as well as to restore the balance between the Right and Left Wings of the Congress). The Prime Minister carried on as if he had been let down by erring subordinates, and he himself had nothing to do with the military shambles in which the country found itself. It is amazing that everyone was satisfied that an enquiry was being held into "the causes of the NEFA Reverses" under the authority of the Nehru Government which was itself primarily responsible for the politico-military unreadiness of the Army and the Nation. To get down to the root-causes, we needed a Presidential Enquiry which would have spared no one, and made every one liable to answer for his conduct of national affairs from 1947 onwards.

The Ministry of Defence

The Ministry of Defence is the main organisation at the command of the Defence Minister to fulfil his responsibilities as the political head of the Armed Forces, and ensure that they are capable of implementing the directives of the DCC. Without a firm hand on the rein of National Policy, and without clear-cut instructions, the Ministry could not be the effective organ that was needed to handle our perennial defence problems. The officials too were forced to react on a day-to-day basis, as best as they could.

The Ministry of Defence grew from humble beginnings in 1947 to a giant organisation in 1962. With Independence, a political head took over the Services and real authority passed to the new Defence Ministry. Prior to 1947, the Commander-in-Chief India was the 'Number Two' after the Viceroy, and Head of all three Services. As a member of the Viceroy's Executive Council, he was *de-facto* and *de-jure* Defence Minister and exercised Governmental powers, in addition to his powers as the C-in-C. These powers would henceforth be shared between the Indian Defence Minister and the Chiefs of the three Services.

The civil servants of the erstwhile Defence Department had gained experience mainly in non-operational matters. The Indian Army was part of the Imperial Forces and major policy decisions were taken in Whitehall and the War Office. Military equipment was entirely British and the Indian Defence Department was only required to place the necessary indents, and process the necessary financial appropriations. They were also concerned with the Law and Order situation in India – a vital matter for the colonial rulers. There were no research cells and only a rudimentary ordnance establishment, mainly for small arms. There was little need for liaison with the other Ministries for procuring the many items required for the Services, both in peace and war. Above all, the primary interest in maintaining the brightest jewel of the British Empire, and the unfettered authority of the Viceroy obviated all personal or departmental jealousies, rivalries or friction. The aim for all Britishers was very clear.

Whereas other Government departments were able to carry on from where the British had left, there was an unavoidable need for a major overhaul of the Defence Ministry, conceived and implemented by a dynamic team of civil servants and Service Officers, led by an imaginative and knowledgeable defence minister. It is a matter of regret that this vital portfolio was never given the ministerial talent required till Mr. Menon was appointed in 1957. He too failed, but for his failures we have to look for reasons other than his undoubted brilliance.

The first critical decision required of India's new rulers was with regard to the organisation of the Defence Ministry. There were only two options. The first was to create an entirely separate ministry of civilian officials and place the three Services under this organisation. The Services HQs then became cells of this ministry and could exercise no Government authority. The second was to create an integrated set-up of both civil and military officials on the lines of the British War Office in London. In either case, the ultimate responsibility rests with the Defence Minister.

In 1947 we opted for the full-fledged civilian ministry for personal and political reasons. The proliferation of sections and rapid expansion produced a crop of promotions. Parkinson had a field day in the first years of our Independence. Civil officers with a few years of service found themselves at par with military officers with twice their seniority; office superintendents of the British era found themselves suddenly equated with majors. A good time was had by all.

Changes and transfers were frequent as the Indian Civil Service brains evolved schemes to expand and multiply into a plethora of ministries and directorates. Congress ministers, still recovering from the glamour of their new positions of power and privilege were not able to provide any purposeful political leadership; it would have been unfair to expect them to master the intricacies of the Government machine in a few months.

The Ministry of Defence gradually duplicated Army HQ: started their own filing system. Duplicate cells cropped up to "scrutinise" the correctness and validity of the Army's proposals and recommendations. The expansion was unplanned, often redundant and mostly induced by self-generated work. The Indian's love of power without responsibility was given full rein.

The Ministry eventually became a super military HQ, and their "approval" to everything except the times for reveille and retreat was required. They took "decisions" or accorded "sanction" on every conceivable occasion. The members of the renowned Indian Civil Service (ICS), who headed the early Ministry saw nothing incongruous in this system. They, and their more humble successors of the Indian Administrative Service, were firmly convinced of their omniscience. They had a deeply ingrained belief that every sphere of Indian activity was merely a matter of good administration – and administration was their special *forte*. Soldiers, engineers, irrigation experts etc. were mere advisers to the administrator. ICS arrogance was a material factor in the sequence of events that found India unprepared for war in 1962.

Both the politician and the civil servant found it convenient to keep the soldier in his place, and devise a system whereby the Army was always asking, begging, pleading and justifying. I know that over the years this method wore down the Army, and many officers were content to let cases drop through sheer exhaustion. The role of perpetual appellant can be very frustrating.

The standard *modus operandi* was somewhat as follows. After endless notings, futile correspondence and some pathetic informal pleading, the Ministry would "accept" a proposal, then "sponsor" the "case" with Finance. The Ministry of Defence thus had all the executive authority but no responsibility. Everybody magnanimously promised to do his best as if he was a disinterested and benign spectator of events, instead of acting as a member of a key link in the system which was created to ensure India's security. The Indian People thought that the Military Establishment had a free hand in the direction of military affairs, as it would never have occurred to anyone that professional advice would have to run the gauntlet of civilian scrutiny. It is a fact that promotions, postings in the higher ranks, policy of introduction of new weapons, equipment, conditions of service, future plans and operations, all required "acceptance" by the Ministry. In 1962, few responsible civil officials were brought to book, as they had already passed to the oblivion that they should have been consigned to in the first place. The Indian Public believed that the Army was primarily responsible for the military disasters of 1962; and this belief was confirmed when the NEFA Enquiry confined itself largely to the "military causes" of the defeats, presumably in pursuance of the charter given to the members. The accused wrote their own charge-sheets.

The civil service have a vital role to play, not as benevolent intermediaries or super military HQ, but alongside the military experts. They can never be substitutes for military experts who spend a life-time studying the subjects that civilians cannot learn in a short "spell" in the Ministry of Defence on their way to bigger things in some other Ministry e.g. Housing or Food.

Another major disadvantage of our present system is that the Minister often gets unbalanced views put up to him for a final decision. The Ministry, although a separate and superior HQ, does not bear any executive responsibility. The Minister is often influenced by civil officials whom he meets frequently and who soon gain his confidence. Let us say that the Chiefs of Staff put up a proposal to Government. This proposal represents the considered views of the three senior-most advisers to Government on Service matters. These proposals are then "examined" by the Ministry, perhaps at the level of a Joint Secretary. The latter is entitled to "note" to the Secretary and through him to the Minister. The note is recorded on a Ministry of Defence file, which is never seen by any Service Officer. I know of one case where a relatively junior civil servant had the audacity and impertinence to start his note by saying that, "I do not entirely agree with the proposals of the Chiefs of Staff", and then went on to suggest a modification of the proposal. The Minister agreed with the civil servant, but the Chiefs were never told why the Minister's final orders differed from their original recommendation. They never saw the relevant file to find out who was the genius who knew better than them.

In the early years of our Independence it may have been necessary to quarantine the Defence Minister from the Services. The first Ministers had no military knowledge and may have required someone to help them understand the matters on which they were suddenly called upon to give decisions, without exposing their ignorance. It is time that the political head of the Defence Ministry dealt more intimately with the Services, who are in the final analysis responsible for the execution of our war plans. This is even more necessary because we are living in a perpetual state of war readiness. We have had 20 years to earmark and train political talent for expert appointments. All advanced democracies train their bright junior legislators to hold highly technical cabinet posts. It should no longer be necessary to "find" someone for defence.

There is no longer any justification for superimposing a senior HQ composed of civilians, or asking the civilian to be an intermediary on behalf of the Defence Forces. We have to get together and further the National Aim by carrying out the duties that we have been trained for, and which we understand. Unless this is done, we shall go on passing the buck.

Parallel to, but not under the Ministry of Defence, is the Ministry of Defence (Finance). This is a cell from the Finance Ministry and is headed by the Financial Adviser who holds a rank "equivalent to" an army general. This cell has to serve two masters. It has to spend to satisfy Defence, and exercise parsimony to please Finance. This is a highly unsatisfactory state of affairs and was partly responsible for the delays in arming and equipping the Forces in 1962. If we are to believe that Mr. Desai and Mr. Menon were involved in a personal feud, then I pity the finance officials, and commiserate with them in the plight in which they found themselves. No one can function efficiently in the midst of contradictions.

Gen. Kaul was in an excellent position to appreciate the damage done to our preparedness by the amazing goings-on in the corridors of the Ministry of Defence, when the Chinese were sitting inside our territory, and it was our openly declared policy that we would fight to defend our borders – indeed that we shall open up more posts, and eventually force the Chinese to vacate their intrusions.

He writes: "The Finance Ministry at various levels – with rare exceptions – split hairs over our urgent proposals and sanctioned only a fraction of what we had put up for approval. They indulged in academic and infructuous arguments in prolonged inconclusive meetings and notings on files. They carried out unrealistic scrutiny of our cases, raising many fresh points each time the file went backwards and forwards. This caused inordinate delays (effecting the defences of our country). Without being experts, these financial pundits dabbled in technical matters and harped on the financial angle. The operational angle appeared to them the least important of all considerations. Shortage of foreign exchange was used as an argument for not sanctioning the import of essential equipment. Many cases were rejected even when no foreign exchange was involved. When practical reasons were given by us to these experts, they usually remained unconvinced and looked at our cases with deplorable apathy. . . . Their attitude amounted to block, hinder and delay so that eventually most cases fell by the wayside".

The blame for this sorry state of affairs again lies with the DCC. Finance officials could not hinder, much less veto, proposals which were put up to fulfil the National Aim. They would have been (or should have been) briefed by the Finance Minister – a key member of the DCC – on the broader aspects of national defence and preparedness. When the DCC decisions are couched in such vague terms as "to fight a second class power", or carry out "limited defence preparations" etc., then finance officials can be pardoned for concentrating their efforts on "saving the tax-payers' money".

Finance officials enjoy their extraordinary discretionary powers partly due to our out-moded, colonial financial and audit control system. Under our fiscal policy, funds are allotted for a year at a time and they automatically lapse on the 31st of March each year. If Finance hindered and blocked proposals, then they saved all the lapsed funds. This was treated as an achievement on the part of the official who had saved the tax-payer and a favourable note made in his dossier. The tax-payer's honour was but a secondary consideration.

The second reason is our budgetary control system. The annual budget of the Services is carefully forecast with the advice of financial advisers, at all levels. A great deal of haggling goes on before a firm figure is sent to the Ministry of Finance for inclusion in the annual budget proposals to the Lok Sabha. These figures are worked out under various heads e.g., recurring, non-recurring expenditure and capital projects and so on. But this is not the end. When the time comes to spend some of the allotted funds, Finance again enter the fray and start raising questions about why we want this, or can we not make do with less and so on *ad nauseam*. Every minor expenditure requires financial "approval". Financial experts are positioned at all levels, and this sort of scrutiny goes on down to the humble Engineer Officer who tries to put up a hutment – he has to "justify" his expert engineering specifications!

If a Service recommends a saving at one point, to find the money to introduce a new idea, the saving is gratefully snatched but the new idea is squashed. If the Army recommends a change in organisation, it is asked why the French Army has not got what we are asking for. The explanation that the French Army is not deployed in the Himalayas sometimes makes Finance relent and other times is not considered sufficient. When we ask for something and say that the British Army has it, we are told that as a poor country we cannot afford everything the British Army has! The same arguments are used to deny changes and improvements. It is all very frustrating.

The eventual solution undoubtedly lies in having some sort of contract budget system. Under this system, the Defence Ministry would be granted a sum of money, after due pre-budget scrutiny, and thereafter it will be given a fairly free hand in details. The only stipulation is that the budget must not be exceeded in whole or under each head. Financial advisers would then really be advisers and book-keepers instead of arbiters of India's defence destiny. A thorough spring-cleaning of our methods and procedures is urgently called for, and it is heartening to note that the Administrative Reforms

Committee has given this matter due attention and has recommended changes on these lines.

Our present system makes it impossible to pin-point responsibility. Who is to blame? The Services for faulty recommendations; or the Ministry of Defence for delay; or Finance for financial stringency? There must be one authority responsible, and this authority can only be an integrated HQ of civilians, military officers and financial experts, under the Defence Minister. No future culprits should be given the loop-hole to evade responsibility by blaming Finance. Equally let us do away with financial experts whose main aim is "to effect savings in the defence budget". Year after year the Defence Ministry has been surrendering funds, and such surrenders have been greeted with thunderous applause in the Lok Sabha and in the Press. There is something wrong somewhere.

Chiefs of Staff Committee

So far we have dealt with the Cabinet and the Ministries of Defence and Finance. We now come to the highest military body in the country viz. The Chiefs of Staff Committee comprising the three Service Chiefs. Under the present system, the Chairman is the Chief who has held office longest. In a well regulated democratic set-up this expert body renders advice to the political bosses – advice which under most circumstances is treated with the respect that must be accorded to the best military talent that a nation can muster. The reader will have noted that this Committee played but an insignificant part in the deliberations that preceded the larger defence decisions from time to time.

Many major military powers have adopted the system of appointing a permanent Chairman, the post going to the most competent officer, irrespective of his parent Service. He is generally designated as the Chief of Defence Staff; or Chairman Chiefs of Staff. He is responsible for overall policy and co-ordination of all three Services. Unified co-ordination of the defence effort, at the professional level, under a military expert has many transparent advantages; and *prima facie*, is better than having the Defence Minister dealing with the three Services separately. This is especially so in our case, as we are living under a semi-war state of readiness, and shall have to so live in the foreseeable future.

A well-chosen Chief of Defence Staff would not owe allegiance to any Service. He would be required to take the broadest possible view of the National Strategy; the requirements of each Service; the size and composition of the various Services and the financial appropriations. He would of course not act arbitrarily but be guided by the advice of the heads of each Service, although the statutory responsibility would be his.

The present Chiefs of Staff system encourages a good deal of parochialism, friction and horse-trading. The *ex-officio* Chairman has not the authority or standing to speak for all three Services in the Higher Direction of War. This role is filled by the Defence Minister and his civilian advisers. The Chiefs of Staff are sometimes reduced to a mere formality. Is it fair and proper to expect a Minister to take on the duty of being a titular Chairman of an expert body?

Our foreign policy up to 1962 primarily required us to be prepared to defend ourselves in Kashmir and the Himalayan Sino-Indian borders; and possibly in the plains of the Punjab. We had no ambitions or desire to fight outside our territorial limits, or to organise an Expeditionary Force. In view of this, ground forces had the predominant role and the other Services the subsidiary roles. This must be so for many years to come until we have built-up our industrial base and have maritime interests which we can safeguard with our own industrial backing. Even if we have to take over the mantle of the departing British in the Indian Ocean, it will be many years before we can afford a sizeable

Navy. Equally, it will take a decade or more to develope a Strategic Air Force. Of course it is right and proper that we keep alive the technique of naval warfare and strategic air warfare, for the day when we are ready to become a major military power, but not at the expense of the deployed field army.

The point that I wish to make is that the organisation and armament of a nation's defence forces is dictated by the nation's fundamental interests and foreign policy. It is militarily unsound to deny the Infantry an automatic rifle and a modern mortar on financial grounds, while we spend millions on an outdated aircraft carrier and expanding dockyard facilities. We had no money to buy helicopters and mules, and yet found money for other items which could not be of any use in the event of a Sino-Indian border war. This is a straightforward matter of getting our priorities right, in the larger National interests. No Indian worth his salt would look at this problem in any other way. I am certain that if we had a Naval Chief of Defence Staff in the years preceding the Sino-Indian conflict of 1962, he would have pressed for better equipment for the ground forces, even at the expense of the Navy. As a responsible Indian, he would have had no other option.

The main obstacle to the adoption of the Defence Chief system is the fear of the Army by the other two Services. The Army is by far the largest Service and will remain so for many years to come. The Chief would probably have to be found from the Army – a possibility that would not be relished by the Air Force and Navy. They might prefer to be independent and have the right to represent their requirements to the Defence Minister directly. They would argue, with some justification, that they would stand a better chance of getting a larger slice of the cake. We can only hope that patriotism and realism will prevail over narrow parochialism; and we see the day when the vital link of the Chiefs of Staff will be reformed to serve the larger interests of the Country more effectively.

The second hurdle to the adoption of a unified Services' command set-up could well be put up by the politician and the civil servant. The Civil Authority relish the present loose arrangements as this gives them the power and opportunity to adjudicate in purely Service matters, and on professional issues. The Civil Authority remains undiluted; and there is no delegation of power to any Serviceman.

It is to be hoped that with increasing maturity at all levels Government will take an objective view of this very vital organisational matter. The National interests demand a unified command structure of the three Services, to utilise our meagre resources to the best advantage, to ward off the Pakistani and Chinese threats.

The present Chiefs of Staff system eventually finds expression in the loose command and control arrangements in the field. We have already noted that air transport support Squadrons functioned independently and there was no co-ordination between the tasks given to the Army and the resources or capability of the Air Force. Despite the clear lessons of World War II, we have not evolved the task force method, whereby an integrated team of the Army and Air Force is set up to prosecute a particular campaign. Conferences and Liaison Officers are no substitutes for unity of command. Unity of command is fundamental and more suited to the Indian temperament. Only the British are able to work the committee system and "co-operate" successfully. The Americans and the French believe in the principle of unity of command – in fact this was one of Napoleon's most established precepts.

The lack of co-ordination beween the Army and Air Force in the matter of air drops at Tsangdhar, between 10th and 20th October 1962, was the primary cause of the misplaced hopes of building-up and maintaining a force in the Namka Chu Valley. The Army and Air Force received separate orders from Government, and when the air drops were ineffective there was no single military voice to protest to the Government. The Air Force had dropped the tonnages ordered – it did not matter that they were dropped beyond retrieval.

The Air Force was short of helicopters in 1962. Who was to blame? The Army or the Air Force or the Defence Minister? Who was to enunciate the requirement of helicopters, the only source of mobility in the mountains? This is but one example where a unified command would have ensured the disposal of the necessary air effort, having regard to the prevailing conditions and the terrain.

The Cabinet Secretariat (Military Wing)

The Chiefs of Staff are assisted by a high-powered secretariat, forming part of the Cabinet Secretariat. At the top we have the Joint Planning Committee, (JPC) made up of the Director of Military Operations, the Air Force Director of Policy and Plans and the Director of Naval Plans. This Committee is assisted by a permanent Joint Planning Staff, an inter-Service staff of hand-picked officers. All these professional experts are required to prepare operational plans for the Chiefs, or to carry out inter-Service staff studies of subjects referred to them by the Chiefs. These officers are not burdened with routine chores and can concentrate on the larger planning issues. It is a matter of conjecture whether the JPC had any hand in the formulation of the Forward Policy. It is certain that they were not consulted, nor did they function in September-October 1962, due to the haste of our actions and the invalid assumptions on which we based our decision to have a military show-down with the Chinese, whatever the cost.

Parallel to the JPC, we have the Joint Intelligence Committee (JIC) consisting of the Directors of Intelligence of the three Services and representatives of certain ministries which are concerned with these matters. This Committee also appears to have been placed on the side-line in 1962. It would be pertinent to enquire whether this body received any appreciation from the Intelligence Bureau and advised the Chiefs of Staff and through them the DCC, of the Chinese intentions and the magnitude of their build-up. If they did not, we must know the reason. If they did produce an appreciation, then what happened to it? Was it doctored to conform to the political assumptions? Or was it ignored under political pressure? Had we mesmerised ourselves into believing that there were only two or three hundred Chinese soldiers in the Thagla-Dhola area? Did the Intelligence Bureau know that two Chinese divisions were massed opposite NEFA? Who was responsible for the 1961 assessment that the Chinese were cracking up? Does the 'hunch' of a Prime Minister supersede the calculated deductions of such an expert body, which has the necessary resources and information? Did this expert body function during the Nehru-Menon era?

After we had allowed ourselves to be irretrievably enmeshed in the Chinese web, we discounted the eye-witness reports of the front-line troops. The Chinese build-up was obvious even to newspaper correspondents. Let me quote the *Times of London* of 11th October 1962: "There is no apparent realisation here (New Delhi) of the magnitude of the military contest that India may now have begun. Observers in a position to know better are still speaking lightly of a swift action to eject the 300 to 400 Chinese. Official accounts of continual strengthening of the original Chinese Force have been ignored". Comment is superfluous.

There are other inter-service and inter-ministry committees and expert bodies to assist the Government and the Chiefs of Staff in their duties. They too were not called upon to function in 1962. The moral of all this is that wars cannot be planned by one or two people meeting informally in someone's office.

Chief of Army Staff

The Chief of Army Staff exercises command over the Army and discharges his responsibility to his political boss through Army HQ. Although he must operate within the frame-work of the policy laid down by the Defence Minister, **he** is the final authority for issuing executive and operational orders to HQ's Command. He must never be by-passed by politicians issuing orders direct to subordinate commanders. An equally important responsibility is to render advice to the Minister. The relationship between the political head and the Service Chief depends on their personalities and there are no hard and fast rules or precedents. But there is nothing more fatal to the destiny of a nation than to have a strong and wilful Defence Minister and a compliant Chief as we had in 1962. A Chief must have the confidence of his political bosses and should have unquestioned prestige in the Country and the military community. In a country like India, beset with the constant threat of war and lack of funds, the Chief carries an awesome burden. Denigrating and downgrading the status of the Chief carries within itself the seeds of disaster in war. He should never be treated as inferior to any civilian on defence matters and his authority should never be eroded by according exaggerated importance to any junior general as in the case of Kaul. The Chief is subordinate to, but not inferior, to the political personalities of the time.

In both World Wars Britain had powerful and self-willed Prime Ministers in Mr. Lloyd George and Sir Winston Churchill. It is to their credit that they selected equally powerful and capable Army Chiefs in Generals Robertson and Lord Alanbrooke. Alanbrooke is the *beau-ideal* of a great Chief of Staff and is the type of man and officer required to shield the Army from any misuse of the temporary power bestowed on the political head, or to resist the imposition of impossible military tasks. Churchill and Alanbrooke worked that most misused term Civil Supremacy in the correct and healthy way, although their personal relations were not always cordial. They led Britain from the despondency of Dunkirk in 1940 to the final Allied victories in 1945.

The prime duty of the Chief is to ensure that the Army has a clear objective from Government and that the Army is fully geared to fulfil this objective. It is almost unbelievable that for many years Chiefs had tried to function in a vacuum without proper directives. Nehru's vague directions were accepted as Government orders. Gen. Thimayya was the only vocal dissident and we know how he was silenced.

A Chief must act fearlessly both in peace and war, especially if he is being hustled into a military course which he feels may land the nation in disaster. To put it mildly, Gen. Thapar's tenure was notable only for his conformity with the prevailing mood of Government. He foresaw the impending doom but was too helpless to influence events. The Nehru-Menon-Thimayya episode of 1959 had far-reaching effects on the authority and role of the Service Chiefs. Seeing how Thimayya was silenced and sensing that popular opinion generally favoured the politician on the grounds of the sanctity of civil supremacy, Gen. Thapar probably thought discretion was the better part of valour, and confined himself to verbal and occasional written representations. It is said that he and his CGS appreciated the shortcomings of the Army and had represented these to Government but they failed to get any response to their urgent pleas for equipment and other requirements. There are many stories of backroom battles being waged at the secretarial level, with the benevolent help of influential Secretaries from other ministries and how these attempts proved abortive. The reader may well ask what was the earthly use of letting matters rest at an exchange of pieces of paper. Why did the Chief not threaten to resign or refuse to implement the Forward Policy if he felt that the Army was not prepared for such a role? Why did he order the Army Commanders to establish more posts without giving them the military capability to administer and protect these posts? The answer is plain and simple. By 1962 the fangs of the Army Brass had been skilfully removed and they feared a confrontation with the politician, especially those of the power and eminence of Nehru and Menon. They feared that their loyalty, patriotism and integrity would be questioned by a hostile public and Press who tend to side with the Civil Authority. Besides, Thapar had been selected to conform and not to argue.

An enlightened public and a strong, independent Press must maintain strict impartiality in judging a major policy crisis arising out of a disagreement between the professional and political heads of the Armed Forces. The intrusion of fallacious concepts of Civil Supremacy will only stifle argument and still the professional voice till the time comes for rude awakening–as in 1962. In a serious divergence of opinion, which forces a Chief to submit his resignation, both the Service Chief and the politician must get a fair hearing at the bar of public opinion and during Parliamentary scrutiny. The high standards of the Western armies is largely due to this healthy and time-honoured custom. Any attempt to brow-beat a Service Chief or to pick one who is likely to conform is a self-defeating arrangement. The elimination of outspoken generals is unfair both to the Army as well as the Nation. In the Nation's highest planning bodies discussion and disagreement are prerequisites for the formulation of sound policies.

Had Gen. Thapar followed the dictates of his conscience and shaped his actions according to his military judgement, the course of events in Thagla may have been quite different. Up to 20th October, he acquiesced meekly and was party to many questionable decisions notably the decision to evict the Chinese; the appointment of Kaul to command a new "corps" and not replacing Kaul when he fell ill and was evacuated to Delhi.

Let us first analyse the controversial decision to evict the Chinese. We know that Thapar ordered the local unit in NEFA to evict the Chinese on the authority of a written instruction from "Government" despite his qualms about the proposed operation. Although his advice and warnings were overruled, he accepted the impossible task, and considered himself covered by the scrap of paper given to him by a minor dignitary.

Mr. Nirad C. Chaudhuri tells us the fantastic story. He writes: "There was no written directive when the attack was first authorised. Instead, the local commanders were given verbal instructions by the Eastern Command at Lucknow to throw out the Chinese. They represented that they had no resources to carry out such a task. At this stage, the Defence Minister left for New York to give his performance before the UN. Everything was thus left in the air by the man who was responsible for the task". He goes on to add that the Army had qualms about carrying out the task: "On 22nd September, Thapar refused to authorise an attack without a written directive from Government. There was consternation and the Deputy Defence Minister, Mr. Raghuramaiah, telephoned his chief in New York for instructions and was airily told to give the order. In the afternoon of 22nd September Gen. Thapar got a letter from the Defence Department signed by H. C. Sarin, a Joint Secretary, which ran as follows (for obvious reasons the citation is not verbatim): "With reference to our discussions this morning, the Government have decided that the Chinese should be evicted from the Thagla-Dhola area. The Chief of Army Staff should take necessary action".

Chaudhuri concludes: "Thapar did not have the

boldness to throw away this scrap of paper into the waste-paper basket. But at all events the General wrote back to the Joint Secretary to say that the order involved great risks. There was no reply to that letter from the august civilian, nor even an acknowledgement". The authority and status of the Chief of Army Staff had been so eroded over the years that he was on a par with a mere Joint Secretary even in the matter of going to war. This was a scandalous misuse of purely political and executive authority which the Cabinet derived from Parliament and which it could not delegate to assorted civil officials. Only the Cabinet was authorised to take such a momentous decision and the order should have been issued by the DCC to the Chiefs of Staff Committee – but then this Committee had also been downgraded by the Menon regime.

The reader will recall that this "scrap of paper" became the "Aim" for the Appreciation which the Chief ordered the local commander to prepare during 23rd-28th September. In spite of his misgivings about the risks involved, Thapar did not recall the Chief of the General Staff, Gen. Kaul, from leave. Thapar did not visit the front to personally explain the facts. He merely issued slogans from Dehli.

Many of the omissions which resulted in the tragedy of 1962 can legitimately and fairly be attributed to Gen. Thapar. He had achieved little in preparing the Army for a war with China; and gave it no leadership after 8th September 1962. He was content to cover himself and let the forward troops be committed to impossible tasks. He is said to have got tough after the Chinese were hundreds of miles inside Indian territory, but then it was too late for dramatic gestures. Had he stood his ground on 22nd September 1962 and insisted on a Cabinet meeting, he might have forced the return of Nehru and Menon from abroad. The Government may have been forced to a realistic approach to the Chinese incursion instead of being committed to a hard posture from which there was no retreat.

Army Headquarters

The Chief of Army Staff is assisted by and functions through Army HQ, a vast and complex organisation of numerous cells. It took me fully one year to find out who deals with what subject. By 1962, Army HQ had ceased to be the solid professional, independent and objective organ which it was designed to be. The cumulative effects of the lack of rapport between the politician, soldier and civilian and the domination of Nehru and Menon had rendered Army HQ impotent. Most of the senior officers at Army HQ were cowed down by Kaul whose authority was unquestioned and whose views prevailed.

Army HQ is divided into four main branches each headed by a Principal Staff Officer (PSO) of the rank of Lt.-General. Each branch has a number of directorates under Lt.-Generals, Maj.-Generals and a few under brigadiers. It goes without saying that the Chief must be the unquestioned boss and the politicians should never deal with any other officer, on major policy matters. Equally, the Chief must have faith and trust in his PSO's. Any friction at the highest level impedes the smooth running of the whole Army.

The real art of being a successful Chief is to co-ordinate and control the working of all Branches. Army HQ can be compared to a train in that it cannot be stopped suddenly; it cannot be reversed without first bringing it to a halt; and it cannot leave its track and move in a new direction. The fountain-head of real, effective co-ordination is the issue of clear, long-term orders to enable the numerous cells to work to a common purpose. This may appear to be self-evident and yet we know that for years Army HQ functioned without clear Government notions of what was expected of the Army. In the absence of firm, unambiguous Cabinet orders, the links in the defence chain had no clear objectives. This is the crux of the matter. Over the years, Army HQ had been reduced to an administrative HQ instead of General Headquarters controlling field armies.

The primary duty of Army HQ is to prepare the operational plans and gear up the Army for war. All other functions are subordinate to this. Even the truncated NEFA Enquiry Board had a few harsh words to say about the manner in which Army HQ carried out its forward planning. Talking of staff work, Mr. Chavan said: "Now about our staff work and procedures. There are clear procedures of staff work laid down at all levels. The inquiry has, however, revealed that much more attention will have to be given than was done in the past, in the work and procedures of the General Staff at Service HQ's, as well as the Command and below, to long-term planning, including logistics as well as the problem of co-ordination among various Service HQ's. So one major lesson learnt is that the quality of General Staff work and the depth of its prior planning in time is going to be one of the most crucial factors in future preparedness".

This statement by a politician cleverly lets his colleagues off the hook because no General Staff can plan without clear Government orders. Surely the Army did not need a slap in the face to learn the first lesson, of the first primer, of military science? What depth of planning did we need for what Government thought was a non-existent threat? What plans can the General Staff draw up if the Prime Minister says that the enemy is cracking up, and he refuses to allot additional funds? Mr. Chavan's statement gives the impression that if someone had "polished up" our paper plans, we may have done better. That is not so. Let us follow the various stages which go into real, deep, long-term planning.

The Army is not capable of responding instantly to a fundamentally new situation which a vocal public opinion may force on the Government in power. It certainly could not produce the military power to cope with the massive Chinese invasion which Government had not foreseen and for which it had not geared up the nation.

Before 8th September 1962, there were no General Staff plans for dealing with Chinese incursions or for repelling a full-scale invasion. Such plans as were drawn up were more in the nature of a political compromise. The border deployment of troops was designed to stake our claims. The misgivings of the forward commanders were dismissed with the observation that there was no prospect of a war with China in the foreseeable future. As Government did not anticipate a war, it did not bother to issue any directives to the Army. Had there been any apprehension of war with China, we would have gone about our business somewhat on these lines.

Military Intelligence would have been ordered to prepare an objective study of the Chinese threat in all its aspects, a study without which there can be no purposeful military response. Military Operations would then have made a formal appreciation of the situation and drawn up an outline plan, indicating the troops required, the specialised equipment and weapons needed and so on. Other directorates of the General Staff go into the question of new raisings, gearing up domestic production and making a shopping list for purchases from abroad where vital items are not likely to be available locally in time. The General Staff is assisted by experts from the administrative branches with whom there will be a series of conferences to arrive at the required logistic cover to sustain the projected operations. The Quarter-Master General's Branch is a vital one in war as logistics is a Principle of War. The importance of administration had been emphasised by every captain of war in history, and has not been underrated by any. The Quarter-Master General has to plan the layout of depots, forward dumps, movement control, veterinary cover, postal and canteen cover.

The Services must ensure an uninterrupted flow of the 'Q' requirements of the forward troops who must never be asked to look back for their needs. 'Q' control all forms of transport from heavy transport aircraft down through heavy lorries to jeeps, mules and porters.

In 1962, we virtually had nothing at the right time and place. The force sent to the Namka Chu was made to fend for itself. We hoped to undo the lack of forward planning, the years of neglect and the shortage of funds, by driving unacclimatised troops on "hard scales and pouch ammunition". We dropped vast tonnages by air and ordered the front line troops to "retrieve or perish". To regain mobility, we commandeered the local Border Roads Pioneers who were spread over 200 miles. This was a strange breach of all the canons of military administration. Could all this have been put right by better staff work?

The Master General of Ordnance Branch is responsible for the procurement and distribution of war-like stores based on the General Staff estimates. They are responsible for repair, maintenance and replacement of all major items. Ordnance ensures regular replacements by the setting up of forward dumps. In 1962 we were short of most ordnance items and tried to rush stores from rear depots and even fly out snow-clothing from Canada.

Where are the civil servants and finance officials who "blocked, hindered and delayed" the setting up of the required pipeline for feeding the fighting formations in NEFA and Ladakh? Why have they not been called to account? In fairness to the civil officials, it must be said however that they are handicapped in carrying out their duties due to the vagueness of Government's intentions. Their initial confusion is compounded when politicians go around making such off-the-cuff remarks as "there will be no war in the near future" or "there is no money for defence" or "the Chinese are cracking up". The situation is irretrievable when the Finance and Defence Ministers are barely on talking terms. If only the politicians will appreciate how damaging their casual utterances can be to officialdom they may learn the virtues of silence. There is one more factor which breeds delays. Civilian officials are denied access to Top-Secret operational plans and it is grossly unfair to expect them to use wisdom and act with urgency when they do not know what all the hurry is about. It is amazing that officials who cannot be trusted with secrets have the last word about whether the Army shall have something or not.

The result of all these inter-Branch and Ministry confabulations should result in the production of a draft operation order to HQ Commands which is sent to them for comments, to ensure that no unreasonable task is thrust upon them as was done in 1962. Once the order is approved, with such modifications as have been mutually agreed upon, a final Army HQ Operation Order is made out under the signature of the Chief himself. A copy is given to the Defence Minister to obtain political clearance as well as to confirm that the Army is ready, willing and able to implement the Aims of the Nation. It is only at *this* stage that politicians can take a decision which may lead to war.

This process is inevitably slow and laborious, but then nations do not drift into war. There is usually a decade or more of warning and we in India did have a long warning period which we wasted on wrong theories.

Once the Operation Order has been issued, all energies will be devoted to training the Army for its role. Training for operations is a pre-requisite for success in war—a self-explanatory fact which is not always appreciated by the layman. An important and influential civilian official once asked me at a large formal conference, at Army HQ, why was it that the Army needed large sums of money annually to train. He said: "Tell me Colonel, am I to understand that the Army is untrained"? I was hard put to give him a diplomatic answer.

There is an old Japanese Army saying that "In peace an army trains for war, in war it trains for operations". Training had been completely neglected in the years preceding 1962 and the Army was found wanting when the Chinese attacked. Let Mr. Chavan reveal the findings of the NEFA Enquiry Board: "The inquiry has revealed that our basic training was sound and soldiers adapted themselves to the mountains adequately. It is admitted that the training of our troops did not have orientation towards operations *vis-a-vis* the particular terrain in which the troops had to operate. Our training of troops did not have a slant for war being launched by China. Thus our troops had no requisite knowledge of the Chinese tactics and ways of war, their weapons, equipment and capabilities. Knowledge of the enemy helps to build up the confidence and morale, so essential for the jawan on the front". The last sentence must surely be the understatement of the century.

He went on to add: "The inquiry has revealed that there is certainly a need for toughening and battle inoculation. It is therefore essential that battle schools are opened at training centres and formations, so that gradual toughening and battle inoculation can be carried out".

He ended by saying: "It has also been revealed that the main aspect of training as well as the higher commanders' concept of mountain warfare requires to be put right. Training alone, however, without correct leadership will pay little dividends. Thus the need at the moment, above all else, is training in leadership".

What can one add to this dismal picture of what passed for training in the years when politicians were making bombastic and reassuring statements to the Lok Sabha? And is there any doubt that the blame lies at the door of the General Staff? Once we had accepted the possibility of war and had moved to the Indo-Tibetan Border, it was imperative to re-orientate the training of the Army for operations in the Himalayan Mountains. We had moved to NEFA in 1959 and yet up to 1962 we had not got down to training to fight the Chinese, at those heights. Why is it then that we did not do anything? The answer is simple. We did not have any clear and feasible operational plans on the basis of which the troops would have been required to organise and plan their training programmes. The main emphasis was on survival and we used our troops to carry logs, build helipads and otherwise aet as labourers to ensure their survival in the Himalayas.

Formations were deployed for years without being relieved for periodic training camps. The Army Order of Battle did not cater for additional formations to man the borders whilst the front-line troops were training for mobile operations. In April 1962, a half-hearted attempt was made to hold an "exercise with troops" but nothing came of it.

When war came in 1962, 7 Infantry Brigade had NEVER carried out a single manoeuvre since it had been exercised in the plains of the Punjab, in early 1959.

We already know that the infantry battalions had not had a chance to fire their weapons. Under these circumstances, no formation has the slightest chance of survival in war, against a first-class land power. The troops we rushed from the Punjab were largely ineffective as they were lost in the mountains.

The blame for this state of affairs lies with the General Staff, the Army Commander and the formation commanders, including myself, who accepted command of troops who were not ready, and who were not allowed to get ready for war. Senior commanders were content to accept an "operational role" without any theoretical or practical experience of operating against the Chinese!

It is astonishing that Gen. Kaul who was the Chief of the General Staff should now ask his subordinate formation commanders to offer an explanation if their troops and units were not "professionally up to the mark".

* * *

Before leaving the General Staff, let us take a look at the state of weapons and equipment of the Army in 1962. We have already enumerated the crippling shortages of all items and the lack of mobility of the troops rushed to Thagla. Speaking of this, Mr. Chavan said "The second question was about our equipment. The inquiry has confirmed that there was indeed an overall shortage of equipment both for training and during the operations. But it was not always the case that particular equipment was not available at all with the armed forces anywhere in the country. The crucial difficulty in many cases was that, while the equipment could be reached to the last point in the plains or even beyond them, it was another matter to reach it in time, mostly by air or by animal or human transport, to the forward formations, who took the brunt of the fighting. The position of logistics was aggravated by two factors: (*i*) the fast rate at which troops had to be inducted, mostly from the plains to high mountain areas; and (*ii*) lack of a properly built roads and other means of communications. The situation was aggravated and made worse because of an overall shortage as far as vehicles were concerned, and our fleet was too old and its efficiency not adequate for operating on steep gradients and mountain terrain. . . . The inquiry has pin-pointed the need to make up the deficiency in equipment particularly suited for mountain warfare, but more so to provide means and modes of communication to make it available to the troops at the right place at the right time . . .".

The discerning reader will at once note the implied criticism of the Government, the Ministry of Defence and Finance and the General Staff who are equally to blame for allowing this unhappy state to exist, and what is more to try and bluff the Chinese with all these transparent weaknesses. It is pertinent to ask whether Mr. Nehru was aware of all this. It must remain a matter of speculation whether the Prime Minister and the Cabinet had received any assurance from the Defence Minister of the operational readiness of the Army, before everyone started making brave and bombastic statements to Parliament and the Press. Had Mr. Menon carried out periodic objective studies of our defence readiness, as he was bound to do as the political head of the Armed Forces, he could not have rested after deploying the Army along the Indo-Tibetan Border. There could have been no clash with Finance if he had alerted Mr. Nehru; nor would he have had to stretch every available rupee to the utmost. He would have been given the rupees or the National Aim would have been tailored to our resources.

* * *

The Adjutant General's Branch is responsible for all personnel and disciplinary matters. Their work is not spectacular in peace-time. Nevertheless, terms and conditions of service, welfare and other morale factors play an important part in the fighting efficiency of any army, and more so in a volunteer one. A neglected Army is not a good fighting force. Finance hamper and veto all efforts to ameliorate the conditions of service in an Army which is largely deployed in hardship areas, for prolonged periods. Nothing is more galling than to be constantly compared with the "civil counterpart". The reader will recall the announcement of the grant of a "High Altitude Allowance" on 6th October, after Finance had blocked the proposal for years. This was not very edifying.

* * *

The Penalty for Hustling

It is axiomatic that no nation should allow itself to fight a war for which it is not prepared. It is for the politician to prevent the political issues which could lead to war reaching the stage where hostilities become inevitable. There are many ways in which canny politicians play for time. September 1962 was about the worst possible time in which to get involved in a war. We had established a string of half-baked outposts which the Chinese had not openly challenged. During the preceding three years little had been done to train and equip the Army for a war.

When the Chinese entered Indian territory in strength on 8th September 1962, the Government was flabbergasted. It could not very well take the affront lying down, and decided on a policy of bluff. Bluffing the Indian people was easy; it was not so easy to bluff the Chinese. The Government lost the initiative in the early stages. Without waiting for a senior commander to reach the Namka Chu and assess the Chinese threat, Government took the "decision" to evict the Chinese. The Defence Minister pushed the Chief; the Chief pushed the Army Commander; and the Army Commander pushed the nearest brigade to the River. The Government was now squarely enmeshed in a web of its own words. Thereafter it was compelled to act as best as it could. Government's decision has since been characterised as "a plain act of political opportunism in the face of the ignorant clamour of the Opposition and the uninformed public". According to Mr. Nirad C. Chaudhuri "The political authorities had asked the soldiers to open an offensive without giving them a chance to win. The contemplated offensive was never approached as a military measure. It was insisted upon in the most frivolous manner out of a sense of political expediency".

The Government made another serious mistake in the early stages. It donned blinkers and refused to consider the wider repercussions in Ladakh in the event that the Thagla incident could not be localised. The Chinese were known to have concentrated a large force there and our defences were woefully weak. Both Gens. Daulet Singh (Western Army) and Sen (Eastern Army) had expressed their inability to cope with any escalation of the Sino-Indian confrontation. Despite this expert advice, Government remained adamant that we had to "do our best" or Government would forfeit public confidence. Mr. Chaudhuri has lambasted Government in his inimitable style: "The Government thought as if they (Chinese) were a number of importunate beggars at their door and asked the durwan (watchman) to drive the noisy fellows away, or even it appeared to them that the problem was like shooting birds from a garden, and it was enough to employ a sprightly boy. But the Chinese were not sparrows".

In this sort of setting of political hustling and bravado, the General Staff and local field commanders became superfluous. Army HQ became the agency for passing on Government orders which were being freely issued at the frequent high-powered conferences with politicians and civilians. There was no chance to draw up fresh strategic plans for the entire border. There was no time to organise defence in depth, secure bases or assured supply lines. Every principle of war was violated.

The Government's "orders" were never processed at Army HQ before being passed down the line. The key directors at Army HQ did not seem to know what was happening. The Director of Military Operations was still blissfully hoping to let his 9th Gorkhas spend Dussehra in Yol. The Director of Staff Duties was compelled to resort to the extraordinary expedient of commandeering the nearest troops in Assam "to make up a brigade" to throw out the Chinese. As troops were collected they were thrown into the same battle.

No formal orders were issued by anyone to anyone. No written orders were given to Gen. Sen and he in turn gave none to Kaul. Kaul issued one verbal order which he confirmed in a brief cryptic signal. The mental reservations of the Army Chief found expression in the vague signals sent – generally a paraphrase of the political order. From time to time, these orders were issued: (1) Establish contact with Dhola; (2) Evict the Chinese from the Namka Chu (as if the Chinese had no say in the matter!) (3) Ensure no further Chinese incursion south of Thagla; (4) Clear all Chinese south of Thagla; and (5) Ensure the security of all crossings over the Namka Chu.

Since Government did not deem it fit to issue formal orders through the correct channels, no one else was prepared to stick his neck out and sign anything. It is startling to remember that throughout the operation, I was not given a single operation order in writing. I was not given a single intelligence appreciation and I was never issued a single administrative instruction. My immediate superior, GOC 4 Division, did not give me a single order on his own initiative or based on his own assessment of the military task. In the case of 7 Brigade, the operation lasted for 42 days from 8th September to 20th October, enough time for the most dim-witted staff officer to produce a written confirmatory order.

* * *

The curious way of issuing orders and getting things moving played havoc with the established chain of command and control. Let us hear Mr. Chavan again: "The third question is regarding our system of command within the armed forces. The inquiry has revealed that there is nothing basically wrong with the system and chain of command, provided it is exercised in the accepted manner at various levels. There is however a need for the realisation of responsibilities at various levels which must work with trust and confidence with one another. It has also been revealed that during the operations, difficulties arose only when there was a departure from the accepted chain of command. There again, such departures occurred mainly owing to haste and lack of prior planning". The Inquiry Board then goes on to record this severe censure: "The inquiry has revealed the practice that has crept into the higher army formations of interfering in tactical details even to the extent of detailing troops for specific tasks. It is the duty of commanders in the field to make on-the-spot decisions when so required, and details of operations must be left to them".

Mr. Chavan has again skilfully extricated his political colleagues. The impression he gives is that only the Army Brass interfered with local commanders. The criticism is applicable to the political figures as well. It was Government which pressed the panic buttons thereby forcing everyone to command every unit within sight. Interference from above is a clear indication that the forward troops have no faith in the mission and no confidence in the leadership. Here we must blame everyone at Delhi who was pounding, prodding and pushing the local troops to do the impossible. If plans are correctly devised and are accepted at all levels, then the actual tactical details can be left to the field commanders in the chain of command. Army HQ and Government can rest content with watching, assisting and providing moral and logistic support. There would be no need to use the goad on reluctant subordinates.

Politicians and commanders who had no idea of the battle-field started issuing orders for the move of units and sub-units without appreciating the other relevant factors. When a military order cannot be justified with professional arguments, it will be resisted by the recipient. The only way to get any action is to order units and sub-units directly, threaten juniors and forget all about the normal battle procedures.

Interference started at the level of Mr. Menon himself. He and his deputies held almost daily conferences and required the presence of those who should have been with the troops. Since we had no pre-plans and had no idea of how we were going to achieve the miracle of evicting the Chinese, daily confabulations became unavoidable. Gen. Sen was summoned to Delhi every other day. It is amazing that his presence in Delhi was more important than with the troops that he had ordered to halt the Chinese incursion. Not once was he able to visit me although I was at the end of a helipad.

Another key factor in the breakdown of the command set-up was interference with the location of commanders. I was evicted from my HQ on 13th September and a second time on 4th October. I was never really able to set up a working HQ till 16th October. Except for my meeting with Gen. Prasad between 23rd and 28th September, I could not contact him. Gen. Prasad was himself evicted from his HQ. Gen. Kaul had no HQ or staff. Gen. Sen functioned from Delhi, Lucknow and Tezpur. How could there be any orthodox command arrangement? The difficulties were multiplied by the pernicious habit of issuing verbal orders on matters of national importance – orders which the initiator would have hesitated to give if he was later forced to confirm them in writing. That explains why so many rash and hasty orders were issued, sometimes based on temper, anger or faulty assumptions.

The most blatant disregard for the normal channels was shown by Kaul, after he assumed command. He found the forward troops stalling and he had to assume personal command to "intensify operations". That is why he ordered 7 Brigade forward and thereafter gave orders for the guarding of all the bridges personally to the Rajput Commanding Officer. Later he and the politicians decided to hold all the crossings and to build up Tsangle against the advice of the local commanders and he had to issue personal orders to achieve this end.

* * *

The order to move 7 Brigade to the Namka Chu was a compulsive reaction ordered without thought, without warning and without preparation. We thus became party to a policy of bluff without assessing the Chinese strength, preparations and intentions. When the first riposte failed, we indulged in political gimmickery. We took the spurious decision to raise a "corps" overnight, a hoax which raised extravagant hopes among Indians. Obviously it was never intended to raise a corps as Kaul's command would consist of the same two brigades which were already committed and which had no supporting arms or a functioning HQ. A corps normally consists of three Divisions of three Brigades each, with a full complement of supporting arms.

What right then had anyone to expect an *ad hoc* formation, ill-equipped, out-numbered, out-gunned and without administrative backing to challenge an infinitely superior Chinese Force? Why did we professionals allow ourselves to get embroiled under the most disadvantageous conditions in an all-out war with the Chinese, at the time and place of their choosing? Why did we allow ourselves to be lured into a trap? Mr. Nehru, in a moment of rare introspection gave the correct answer. Speaking in the Rajya Sabha on 3rd September 1963, he said: "The reverses in NEFA were entirely due to the compulsion of events, and no other Government would have been able to do anything vastly different". This honest statement was a welcome change from his earlier attitude. After accepting the Thagla Confrontation as a political measure and knowing fully well that it may end in disaster, Nehru feigned surprise. He sacked politicians and generals. He talked of being stabbed in the back. His *protegé* talked of being out-numbered and out-weaponed.

I fear that posterity will not forgive Mr. Nehru for his credulity and negligence before 8th September 1962 and his inept handling of the politico-military situation thereafter. Posterity will not forgive the senior Army Officers, including myself, for our ignominious roles, although we may try to still our consciences by putting the entire blame on the politicians and/or Generals Thapar and Kaul.

Kaul certainly shares the greater responsibility. He had been Quarter-Master General from 1959 to 1961, and Chief of the General Staff from April 1961 to October 1962. He was a permanent member of the Border Roads Organisation from its inception. He was therefore the one General in the Army who should have had no illusions about the operational unreadiness and indeed the pathetic state of the Army *vis-a-vis* the Chinese in Tibet. How are we to understand his ready acceptance of the Forward Policy? How are we to excuse his ready acceptance of the task of evicting the Chinese when his predecessor thought that he needed a build-up of six months? Was he justified in trying to bale-out cornered politicians?

The breakdown of Army HQ as the fountainhead of professional thinking was the most damaging factor perpetrated by the Nehru-Menon-Kaul regime. Let us be frank and admit that Army HQ in 1962 had been reduced to the status of messengers of political orders which could not be resisted and in which they had no faith. If this is the net result of forceful political leadership, by a dynamic Defence Minister, then we had better have a re-think.

It is a fact that few Army officers feel a personal sense of involvement in the events which culminated in the defeat in NEFA. They feel that those tragic events concern Government and Gen. Kaul. When I returned from my imprisonment in China, I met many senior officers who had served in key posts during the critical days of September-October 1962. They were in fact keen to meet me and to impress on me that they were in no way associated with the chaos of those days. They were anxious to find out what had happened and what I proposed to write in my report to Government. One and all they disclaimed any responsibility for the decisions that were being taken in that hectic month. They went to great lengths to explain to me how they had tried to put sense into someone's head but no one would listen to their sound military advice. They obviously wanted me to exonerate them and their departments for their part in the decisions which had led to the massacre of my troops. Many of them abused Kaul. I found this particularly amusing as most of them were indebted to Kaul for their positions and had fallen-in readily with his ideas. How the mighty had fallen! And how the mice roared!

I was so amazed that I wondered what had happened to Army HQ and the Army's time-honoured ways of functioning. Had it broken down and ceased to function? Was it so emasculated by the towering personalities of Menon and Kaul? Had the Chief ignored the Army HQ machine with whose help he is supposed to carry out his statutory functions? Did he have any staff studies carried out; or else how could key persons claim that they did not know what was happening? Did the Chief issue orders through the normal channels? No Army expects its Chief to merely pass on the impracticable orders of his political bosses. Had policy-making been confined to a select band of politicians, Civil Servants and one or two army officers? Had the Chief held any conferences with his Principal Staff Officers before issuing the order to evict the Chinese; or when he agreed to create a new corps? If he had, I am sure there would have been a hue and cry.

In September 1962, the advice of PSO's was redundant once Government had taken the "decision" to throw out the Chinese. There was no time for them to take the necessary steps to implement this decision even if they had had the resources (which they did not have.)

Every disaster produces its own crop of wits. I heard this funny story in 1963. One PSO is reported to have expressed surprise that "there was some sort of flap on in NEFA". Apparently, he had gathered this information from his daily paper! This story could well be true judging by the way decisions to evict the Chinese were being taken, and the forward troops hustled in those black days in the history of Army HQ.

Chapter XXVII

India's Defence Ministers 1947/62

What then went wrong in 1962? We cannot blame the organisational set-up for the Higher Direction of War. We had the right system. We had the talent. We had the brave soldiery without which there can be no victory in war. The blame lies in the ineffective incumbants who allowed the system to atrophy. Even before 1962, the Prime Minister and the Defence Minister appeared to take vital decisions on their own. Expert committees were ignored and expert advice not sought – and there was not a murmur from anyone. Persons holding high office were content to watch events helplessly, after futile efforts to "put up papers".

War is not a game for giant geniuses who rely on hunches. It is a game with many humble players, each contributing his mite to the over-all effort. No single individual however great or highly placed should ever again be allowed to dictate the National Policy, or be expected to carry the burden of implementing it on his own.

How did the dominance of Nehru and Menon come about? The British system we had adopted did not envisage the sort of ascendency of one or two persons over matters that affect the National interests. The erosion of the authority of the Armed Forces began soon after the attainment of freedom in 1947. The Defence Ministry had been singularly unfortunate in its ministers and till Menon came none had the talent and ability to enforce a healthy working arrangement with the Prime Minister or to project the needs of the Armed Forces. The gradual ascendancy of Mr. Nehru, after the death of Sardar Patel in 1950, led to the down grading of the Ministry of Defence till it had little voice in policy-making. The unhealthy practices started as early as the tenure of the first Indian Defence Minister, Sardar Baldev Singh. The pay-off was a long time a-comin' but it did have to come; and it came on 20th October 1962. The era of "Papa knows best" was shattered in a shower of shame and humiliation.

The first Indian Defence Minister was Sardar Baldev Singh, the Sikh leader of the pre-Partition talks with the British Government. He probably found a place in the Interim Cabinet of 1946 as a compromise Sikh representative; he was later confirmed as Defence Minister in India's first Cabinet probably because no other senior Congressman wanted this chair which offered little scope for power and patronage. Mr. Nehru did not look beyond the Congress benches and by-passed such eminent people as Mr. H. N. Kunzru who had achieved some fame as a defence expert in pre-Partition days. In any case, Sardar Baldev Singh's talents did not merit the important Defence portfolio. He was a wealthy man, easy-going and disliked handling awkward or troublesome problems. He understood little about National Strategy and had not specialised in defence subjects. He left everything to his Defence Secretary, Mr. H. M. Patel, an outstanding Indian Civil Service Officer of the old school. Mr. Patel was a proud and ambitious man and was bent on establishing control in his own hands.

Gen. K. M. Cariappa, the first Indian C-in-C was an equally proud man; and the temperamental and official clashes between them are now part of the history of the Defence Ministry. In the event, India's defence organisations got off to a bad and unhealthy start. Sardar Baldev was fully aware of these differences but did nothing effective to iron them out. He did not devise fresh guide lines for the smooth functioning of his ministry, nor did he draw a clear line of demarcation between civil and military powers and responsibility. He should have ordered changes to fit in with the new constitutional changes. Much of the confusion, mistrust, overlapping of responsibility and out-moded procedures had their genesis in those early days and had got unmanageable by September 1962. 1947 was not the time for a Defence Minister to coast along with old, colonial and obsolete ways. Sharing the spoils of the authority bequeathed by the Viceroy and the British C-in-C could not be left to the civil servant and the soldier to sort out, as each would attempt to usurp a major share. Sardar Baldev Singh did not have the necessary background, force of character and essential harshness to provide forceful political leadership to effect the necessary changes and modifications. He did not have the personality to influence or restrain Mr. Nehru and gradually allowed himself and the Ministry of Defence to be overshadowed. The dominance of Cabinet proceedings by the Prime Minister began during his tenure. He was also not equipped to take long-term steps to visualise and anticipate the Chinese threat which started in his time, when China annexed Tibet in 1950. He was a good simple man, in the wrong place, at the wrong time of India's defence history.

Sardar Baldev Singh was succeeded by Mr. Gopalaswami Ayyangar, an ex-ICS officer, with a cold analytical, brilliant brain and unexcelled administrative experience. His tragic death after only a few months in the chair was an irreperable loss. He was well-equipped to organise a healthy working arrangement between the Civil Service and the Army. He would not have allowed himself to be over-awed by the famed ICS Cadre.

Mr. Ayyangar's permanent successor was Dr. Kailash Nath Katju, an old Congress war-horse. He was a Doctor of Law and practised with conspicuous success before joining the pre-war United Provinces (now Uttar Pradesh) Ministry as Minister of Jusice, Industries and Development in 1937. Thereafter, he had done his stint of "jail-going". He was again appointed a minister in 1946. Later he was a member of the Constituent Assembly. In 1947, he was appointed Governor of Orissa and in 1948 Governor of West Bengal. He became a Central Government minister in 1951 and was allotted the Home Affairs and Law portfolio. After Mr. Ayyangar's sudden death, he was shifted over to Defence and remained there till 1957. In January 1957, he was sent post-haste to be the Chief Minister of Madhya Pradesh to bale-out the strife-riven State Congress Party.

His undoubted talents, ability and wide humanity were misplaced in Defence. His *forté* lay elsewhere. In 1952 he was 65 years old, tired and deaf when he assumed office. It was grossly unfair to expect him to master the intricacies of the Higher Direction of War. I say this with no malice. Dr. Katju's forensic ability and political skill were of immense value to newly-independent India, and he filled many high posts with distinction. But there was no valid reason for shifting him to Defence purely on the grounds of seniority or because Mr. Nehru continued to fill the key ministries with Congressmen only. Mr. Nehru himself held the Defence portfolio in addition to his many other posts during any *inter-regnum* while he searched for a permanent incumbent. It was an injustice to an otherwise able man and fatal to the Armed Forces, at a time when vigorous lobbying was called for to match Pakistan and forestall China. Dr. Katju did nothing that was wrong but he also did nothing that was right. He merely completed an uneventful tenure. There was very little that he knew about Defence matters having spent most of his life in the domestic political spheres.

Towards the end, he had become a standard politician who would not voluntarily retire. In 1962, at the age of 75, he still aspired to be the Chief Minister of Madhya Pradesh, but he was defeated in the General Elections of 1962. Although he was later returned in a bye-election, he did not hold office again. In this respect, he was the typical Congressman. Although he had reaped a rich harvest for his "sacrifices" in the Independence movement, he insisted on "serving the people" to the bitter end!

The Army skid to its lowest depths during his term. Nothing was initiated by him and everything was left to the ICS and the Army to sort out. All efforts to make a purposeful response to Pakistan's re-armament floundered due to apathy and inertia. This then was the man on whom India relied to take suitable counter-measures to face Pakistan's American-aided strike force, which began and was completed in his time. He was the second misfit, at another critical juncture in India's defence history.

Mr. Mahavir Tyagi was associated with Defence for a number of years under various titles specially created for him. He was a well-known Congress heckler who had to be eventually silenced with some sort of ministerial appointment to protect ministers from being nettled and subjected to awkward questions. What better place than the unimportant Ministry of Defence? He too knew nothing about defence despite his boasts that he had served in the Army in World War I in some humble capacity. His most notable contributions were the introduction of khadi items in the Army (such as cottage industry blankets weighing a few pounds each); and his Hindi notings which no one could read. He loved to be surrounded by "his" generals, visit foreign countries on purchasing missions; and to address troops with senior officers in attendance. He gave the impression that he could not get over his good fortune in achieving such eminence. After an uneventful stint he was shunted out when Mr. Menon took over in 1957. After a few years in the wilderness during which he returned to his favourite pastime of prodding Congress ministers, he was rehabilitated in the Ministry of Rehabilitation!

Mr. Tyagi was the third misfit. He held office at a time when the Army had to be re-equipped and the old World War II weapons discarded. As Minister of Defence Production, this onerous duty fell on his shoulders. He did little to either gear up domestic production or to influence the Cabinet to allot the necessary funds for purchases from abroad. When he left the equipment state of the Army was most unsatisfactory.

* * *

The reader will now appreciate the elation of the Army at the news of the appointment of Mr. V. K. Krishna Menon as the Defence Minister in 1957. The news coincided with the news of the appointment of Gen. K. S. Thimayya as the new Chief. For the first time since Independence, we would have a brilliant, alert and powerful Defence Minister to work with an equally brilliant General. I was serving at Army HQ at the time and I can vouch for the thrill and exhilaration felt by all. Now the Army could hope to get things moving, and Mr. Nehru would get the truth about our weaknesses, and the dangers posed by Pakistan's increasing strength, from two men he respected and admired. Menon was on the threshold of his political career in India, in contrast with his predecessors who were ineffective party men past their prime. Gen. Thimayya was the first Indian Chief with a military career which would stand comparison with Army Chiefs anywhere in the world. This team induced a feeling of great expectations which were unfortunately to be belied in the next five years.

Menon was an international figure and had played a notable, if somewhat unspectacular, part in India's struggle for independence. He had spent the best part of his adult years in England i.e. from 1924 to 1952. He was one of the few Indian politicians who was in tune with Nehru, their friendship and mutual admiration dating back to the 1930's.

Menon had studied at the London School of Economics from where he had graduated with a B.Sc. Degree. He obtained his Master's Degree from London University and his Doctorate of Laws from Glasgow University. He thus had an unimpeachable educational background as well as a sound foundation to international problems, in marked contrast to the average Congressman's narrow and limited outlook.

In 1929 Menon took over the moribund India League and transformed it into one of the most effective lobbies in English history. He served without pay and often had to pay bills from his own limited and casual income. He lived abstemiously and sometimes on the verge of poverty in the poor district of Camden Town in London. He entered British politics and had aspirations of becoming a Labour Member of Parliament.

Menon made a notable contribution to India's cause from England, enlisting the sympathy and understanding of powerful and influential men in the British socialist movement like Mr. Harold Laski and Bertrand Russell. He is entitled to a great deal of credit for his work in pre-Independence days. His spadework helped to convince the Labour leaders of the justice of India's cause. Unfortunately, his long absence abroad made him lose touch with the Indian people and India's leaders.

Menon worked briefly with a British publishing house and was thus able to act as Mr. Nehru's literary agent thereby earning the gratitude of India's future Prime Minister. Nehru and Menon had toured the Spanish battlefields during the Civil War, in 1938, and had found much in common. Nehru was delighted to find someone who differed from his conservative Congress colleagues. Both believed that each had the necessary radical socialist approach to the solution of the gigantic economic problems of India. Both men had at that time faith in Fabian Socialist doctrines. Both were mentally foreigners in contrast to the average grass-roots, parochial Congressman; and both were impatient with the established order in India.

Soon after Independence, Nehru appointed Menon High Comissioner in the United Kingdom to project the image of free India; as well as to reward an old friend. Menon had then travelled a long way from Camden Town to the Court of St. James. His long stay in England was at once an advantage and a disadvantage but we are not concerned with his achievements as a High Commissioner. He survived a few crises arising out of alleged indiscretions in the procurement of military stores, the most notable being with regard to the purchase of jeeps for the Army. This particular incident was the subject of bitter acrimony in Parliament and the matter was also the subject of adverse comments from the Public Accounts Committee of Parliament. A lesser mortal who did not command the patronage of the Prime Minister might well have blighted his future. The Committee had noted that: "It is not possible to hold that the lapses were merely procedural or due to defects in the rules".

In 1957, with his reputation providentially untarnished, his political stock was at its zenith. After his tenure as High Commissioner, he was appointed the Deputy Chief of the Indian Delegation to the United Nations, thus enabling him to enter the international arena and take an active part in world debates and problems of the troubled fifties. India's contribution was then material and this gave Menon many opportunities. Mr. A. M. Rosenthal of the *New York Times* said at the time: "Menon made a name for himself but lost it for his country". The peak of his international standing was reached during the negotiations which preceded the 1954 Geneva Conference which was expected to settle the Indo-China problem.

He was the only man in Nehru's orbit who understood world politics and who could present India's non-aligned viewpoint. By the mid-fifties, Nehru had parted company with most of his pre-Independence colleagues with any independence of mind. Mr. Ram Manohar Lohia had been the Congress Party's shadow foreign minister in pre-war days and much was expected from this able man. He fell out with Nehru and in his last years became a bitter critic of Nehru's policies.

Menon gave many virtuoso performances in UN debates, especially when defending India's Kashmir policy. He was greatly loved and admired by the literate people of India who got a vicarious thrill when they read of the verbal lambastings which he heaped on the Anglo-Saxons. He won many verbal duels but he did not succeed in convincing the majority of India's case; in fact it has been said that he hardened the views of many against India by his unnecessarily brusque manner.

His critics harp on his apparently contradictory stands during the Hungarian and Suez episodes of October-November 1956.

The exposure to international affairs did not give him the necessary suavity and urbanity so essential in a diplomat. It is a matter of regret that his personality and methods had an abrasive effect on Western diplomats. His overbearing manner did little to endear him to his political critics or advance the cause of his country.

I have dwelt at some length on Menon's background prior to 1957 as this has a material bearing on his performance as Defence Minister. The first point is that Menon got permanently involved in India's foreign affairs and became *de-facto* Deputy Foreign Minister, often to the detriment of his primary duties. The second result was that he became a confidant of Nehru and wielded more influence on India's policy than would have been the case if he was an ordinary man, say like Dr. Katju. In the process, he got his two portfolios mixed up, and he could not differentiate between his duties as Defence Minister and his role as unofficial foreign policy adviser. The last adverse effect was on his personal behaviour. Having got away with being rude and overbearing to the diplomats and newspapermen of the world, he was unlikely to show any restraint with ordinary generals and civil servants in India. He was to become insufferable.

Even his best friends do not really know his political affiliations. He has been variously described as Leftist, Socialist and even Communist. He certainly attracts followers of leftist leanings and was considered to be the leading Left leader of the Cabinet, before his downfall. It is also a fact that during the 1962 Elections, he was backed and actively helped by the Communist Party which even forsook its leader, Mr. Dange, who lost from another constituency in Greater Bombay. It is also a fact that he has an unreasonable and outdated phobia against the Private Sector of Industry in India. However, sensing the contradictions and struggles within the Congress Party, he submitted loyally to the mild brand of Congress socialism, which has so far defied any definition. He carried out his ideological fights within the inner councils of the Congress High Command and by using his personal influence with Nehru.

He had many enemies both within and outside the Congress, inspired by powerful business interests. All but a few members of parliament hated or feared him. Menon was in the line of succession to Nehru and vested interests wanted to eliminate him before he reached the top. To senior Congressmen, he was a threat to their own prospects and they resented his close personal relationship with Nehru. Some thought that Mr. Nehru meticulously avoided giving any indication of his preference for a successor, or thwarted attempts by Mr. Desai, merely to give Menon time and a chance to build up a following in the country. Initially Menon's political advancement and indeed survival depended on Nehru's patronage. Nehru invariably backed him against his other Cabinet colleagues. Later Menon did acquire personal stature as a result of his thumping electoral victory in 1962, in a bitterly contested fight against a powerful coalition of the Right, and against the redoubtable Acharya Kripalani. He became even more ambitious, ruthless and insufferable. Throughout his career as a Minister, he never practised the virtue of humility. In his moment of humiliation, when Mr. Nehru was forced to sack him, he was friendless. He left unsung and unmourned; his achievements forgotten.

The appointment of this able confidant of Mr. Nehru was hailed as a harbinger of greater defence awareness in the Cabinet. It was hoped that the stalemate in the functioning of the Ministry of Defence and Finance would be broken. It was also hoped that our defence preparations would be dove-tailed with our foreign policy and bear a reasonable relation to our commitments.

There was some speculation as to why Defence was being honoured by the appointment of such a high powered minister. Surely Menon's *forte* was foreign affairs. After the Elections of 1957, many thought that Mr. Nehru would shed this portfolio to concentrate on the larger issues facing the country. The routine affairs of a ministry were unnecessary and burdensome to a busy and ageing Prime Minister. Many theories were advanced. The most charitable interpretation was that Mr. Nehru was at last beginning to appreciate the mortal danger from a hostile, revengeful and well-armed Pakistan. It will be recalled that Pakistan was expected to be ready with her new-look Army and Air Force by about June 1957. The United States may not be able to restrain her from attempting a military adventure in Kashmir. China had occupied thousands of square miles of Indian territory in Ladakh and had laid claim to NEFA. Nehru was aware of this and was said to have had serious doubts of whether friendship alone would suffice to fend off an expansionist neighbour, and had decided to get his powder dry. Therefore, Defence would require one of his ablest colleagues.

The uncharitable view was that Menon was recalled to India and made Defence Minister to act as a counterpoise to Gen. K. S. Thimayya who was due to take over from Gen. S. M. Shrinagesh in March 1957. There had been a spate of military *coups* in neighbouring countries and Nehru did not want to risk being shunted to the side-line and treated as a benevolent elder. His fears were not entirely unfounded as we know what happened to other Afro-Asian leaders who were virtually worshipped by their peoples.

In any case, with his experience and ability, Menon would have had to be accommodated in a senior Cabinet post. The Home Ministry would have found him out of his depth as he was out of touch with domestic politics. Moreover he was unknown to, and possibly unacceptable to, some powerful State Chief Ministers, without whose tacit approval Menon would have been stymied. The Home portfolio is a coveted one and is sought after by senior Congressmen as it represents real political power. It is also a useful base for expanding the incumbent's political stature and prospects by a judicious blend of fear and favour. Menon was a tyro in the Congress hierarchy and was therefore ineligible for this chair.

Since Mr. Nehru would not give up the External Affairs Ministry, the choice lay between Finance and Defence. Mr. Morarji Desai coveted the Finance portfolio to control the purse-strings of the Nation. It is possible therefore that Mr. Nehru appointed Menon in all innocence and for the good of the country. Little did he realise that the Ministry of Defence would be the most controversial organisation of Government generating heat at every turn and polarising the Nation into pro-Menon and anti-Menon forces. In the debris, the Armed Forces suffered till they were subjected to a humiliating defeat by the Chinese in 1962.

Mr. Menon was a complete failure as Defence Minister despite his abundant talents. He was a victim of his own brilliance and over-confidence. He brought to Defence ideas, theories and methods which were inappropriate to this office and caused his own downfall.

At the politico-strategic level, it can be said that he failed to appreciate the Chinese threat in its true dimensions. He was always harping on the Pakistani threat as being the major one, and for this reason he was complacent about the equipment of the Forces which he had deployed in the Himalayas, till it was too late. Despite mounting and irrefutable evidence of China's aggressive intentions, he lulled the Nation into a false sense of confidence and security. In the immediate pre-1962 period, he made nebulous and sometimes contradictory statements which sowed the seeds of doubt in the minds of the public and perhaps the Army as well.

On 10th January 1960, Mr. Menon said at Tezpur (Assam): "The India-China border dispute was not of such magnitude as could precipitate war". Tezpur was the HQ of the local military command in charge of NEFA and was about the worst place in the world to propound such a theory. It did incalculable harm and created a phoney-war atmosphere.

On 18th January 1960, Menon said: "While nobody could say what would happen in a conflict of physical forces, it is reasonable to suppose that another square inch of our territory will not be occupied by anybody". Perhaps this pronouncement was a reaction to the statement he had made a few days earlier at Bangalore when he had said: "No Army can protect the Himalayan heights". The Indian border in NEFA runs along the Himalayan watershed i.e. along the Himalayan heights. Thus in two days he made two diametrically opposite statements. This sort of ambivalence was not calculated to produce clear thinking and resolute action from the Army.

His personal traits had a material bearing on the functioning of India's defence apparatus. His brilliant brain, acid wit and extraordinary memory were negatived by his conceit, arrogance, vanity and his inability to suffer whomsoever he chose to consider a fool. He was extremely rude in his personal behaviour – a failing which is fatal in a politician or diplomat and disastrous in a Defence Minister who has to deal with proud and successful men who have reached the top on their own merits. Such conduct is even more reprehensible since these senior Officers cannot fight back due to the shackles of Service protocol and their own code of conduct. His rudeness and arrogance antagonised his professional advisers and made a mockery of the committee system which is the bed-rock of the democratic system. In some cases, there was an unbridgeable chasm which precluded free and frank discussions and the evolution of joint solutions. He was recently (November 1967) quoted as saying: "Of course neither the Army nor the Civil Service is a mere office-boy running up and down". It is most unfortunate for India's destiny that he did not adhere to this belief when he held high office. By eliminating or attempting to eliminate tough generals and choosing tractable ones, he reduced key commanders to the role of office boys, as we have seen in the story of Thagla. Senior generals were forced to justify the issue of impossible and impracticable orders on the grounds that they themselves had received orders from "the highest level". Menon is reported to have once told Gen. Thapar that Service Chiefs could not be expected to understand everything that he was doing as Defence Minister, but they need not worry as it was all for the best!

With his arrogance and near-contempt of senior officers (of which Gen. Kaul recounts numerous unhappy instances), Menon began to depend on his chosen coterie of advisers and his own judgment. He by-passed the duly constituted committees of the Government and the Service Chiefs. He handled border disputes, the Naga problem and ultimately the NEFA crisis on his own, till it was too late to reverse the trend of events. Some of his civil advisers became "defence experts" and military tacticians as a result of sitting in on discussions about handling border disputes. They became experts in moving infantry platoons and companies. When a military argument was adduced to suggest a different course, they would use the solid sledge-hammer of "political necessity" or "Government has decided", to force the Army to be embroiled at a disadvantage. In September 1962, it was difficult to resist or refuse to obey orders which were clearly impracticable and unwise. The natural sense of duty and discipline of the officer corps was mistaken for servility and weakness. For politicians who had spent the best part of their lives in humble circumstances and even obscurity, political supremacy was a heady wine.

Despite his outward image of bluster and fearlessness, Menon was unable or unwilling to face up to Mr. Nehru whom he feared or wished to placate at all costs, to safeguard his position. He must have realised that he owed everything to Nehru for his exalted place in Indian politics. This may be one of the reasons why he did not bring his differences with Mr. Desai to the surface and face an open debate with Mr. Nehru and the other members of the Defence Committee of the Cabinet as referees. It may also explain the allegation that he was forced to go along with Nehru and Kaul, against his own judgment, when they decided to adopt the Forward Policy. Possibly he was not strong enough to stave off accusations of being pro-Communist if he did not agree to some counter-measures against the Chinese intrusions and provocations.

Since the reverses of 1962, many Menon apologists have attempted to take the pressure off Menon and spread the blame to Mr. Desai for starving the Services of vital funds, particularly foreign exchange. There is little doubt that there were serious ideological and personal differences, and a feud between Menon and Desai; and that these differences concern our study of the defence preparations of India prior to the Chinese invasion of 1962. Mr. Welles Hangen sums up the situation astutely: "If India had anything approaching Cabinet Government the conflict between Menon and Desai and their respective ministerial supporters would long ago have become unmanageable. But important decisions are rarely made by the full Cabinet. At best they are made in Cabinet Committees; and they are usually made by Nehru in consultation with one or two ministers chiefly concerned with a particular problem. Desai is consulted on strictly financial problems. In foreign affairs only Menon's advice is usually sought".

Mr. Morarji Desai had been a minister in the Union Cabinet since he was hustled out of Bombay State in November 1956, as he had become anathema to both the Maharati and Gujerati communities as a result of his stand on the reorganisation of the erstwhile undivided State of Bombay. Desai's career in the Centre soon brought him into the Sino-Indian problem when he took over the Finance portfolio from Mr. T. T. Krishnamachari, who had been forced to resign as a result of a scandal concerning the investment policy of the nationalised Life Insurance Corporation of India. Indian readers will know that Desai is reputed to be an austere man, dedicated to a puritan outlook and a fanatic prohibitionist. His admirers like to canvass the impression that he is tough, incorruptible and unafraid to court unpopularity for his principles. He is considered to be a conservative and the leading Right Wing Spokesman of the Congress Party. He has no phobia against the Private Sector whose excesses he believes can be controlled by legislation and not by curbs on initiative and expansion. He was therefore a foil to Menon and Nehru's brand of socialism and faith in the public ownership of most new heavy industrial projects. Desai is considered to be a good administrator having served in Bombay's Provincial Civil Service at one time and by virtue of his executive experience from 1937.

As the leading spokesman for the Congress Right, Mr. Desai has always considered himself to be a potential prime minister. In 1961, he made a bid to have himself elected the Deputy Leader of the Congress Parliamentary Party but was forestalled by Nehru. Desai was opposed by Menon and his allies who backed Mr. Jagjivan Ram on the basis of the latter's seniority in the Cabinet, as he had been a minister since 1947. Mr. Nehru, the consummate politician, changed the Congress constitution and provided for two deputy leaders. This was a major reverse for Desai. In early 1962, after the General Elections, Menon is alleged to have tried to get Desai removed as Finance Minister and bring back Mr. Krishnamachari. Desai refused to leave Finance for any other post.

Mr. Desai is quoted as saying that Menon was a rootless anarchist who could just as well be extreme Right as extreme Left. He is also reported to have characterised Menon as a "political non-entity with no following of his own and no ability to attract one".

When Menon's career was blighted by the Chinese invasion, Desai's stock rose correspondingly and he became the most likely contender for Mr. Nehru's throne. Sensing this, Mr. Nehru *Kamaraj-ed* him in August 1963 as by then Nehru was too feeble and disillusioned to stand up to internal Cabinet rifts. Desai remained in the wilderness, making an abortive move to succeed Mr. Shastri in 1966, and staging his come-back as Finance Minister and Deputy Prime Minister after the General Elections of 1967. His lode-star remains the Prime Ministership of India.

India's destiny and Higher Direction of War were in the hands of the Prime Minister, Finance Minister and the Defence Minister. Two of these three key persons had a natural antipathy towards each other and this was fanned by Nehru's inaction. India paid for allowing two adversaries to conduct their private feuds at the expense of India's defence preparation. There is no point in trying to find out who is to blame. The Prime Minister must accept responsibility for this unfortunate fact of history.

Menon's ideological beliefs affected our defence preparations. His antipathy to private enterprise in India made him refuse their help in providing urgently needed items for the Army. He tried to produce everything in existing Ordnance factories or the new ones which he built. The Finance Ministry under Desai was equally obdurate and refused funds for the purchase of items which it believed could be produced indigenously. The resultant stalemate meant that the Army remained short of everything including bare necessities like boots and clothing, not to mention parachutes, tinned-food and many others which could have been produced in the country. Battle formations were short of snow clothing, grenades, ammunition, general stores, woollen underwear and even studs for boots! During Menon's era most unit indents were returned by ordnance overstamped "Not Available".

The ideological clash was carried over to the import of vital and urgently needed military equipment and aircraft. We set about looking for rupee payment sources (Communist countries) and bought what was available rather than what was required. In the process, we may have broken the monopoly of Western countries on the supply of arms, but we also broke our own backs. Menon rejected the idea of purchasing a modern American Rifle, and ignored offers of testing the American C-130 turboprop transport aircraft which, ironically, came to our rescue in November 1962, and was used by the American Air Force to supply our battered Ladakh Garrisons, after the Chinese withdrawal. Despite ordering the Army to be deployed along the Indo-Tibetan Border, Menon could never provide the required number of aircraft and supply dropping equipment. The Air Force could never meet the minimum tonnages of the Army and the Border Roads Organisation.

Menon has since claimed that he made every available rupee go as far as it could. He asserts that "The Army was better in 1962 than in 1957. If it was not any more capable than it was, the shortcomings were related to the resources of the country and also the position inside the country and the Government". How does he explain the purchase of an out-dated Aircraft Carrier for the Navy and the concentration of effort on producing tanks and aircraft while starving the Infantry of basic weapons and equipment? This was a serious error of judgment and showed poor notions of the correct priorities. In September 1962, we had no automatic rifle and no suitable Artillery or Infantry mortar. We had no animals and no helicopters. Our World War II mortar was out-ranged by the Chinese Infantry mortar – an outrageous state of affairs. The Army had frequently represented the need for replacing our obsolete weapons but our pleas were ignored.

Let me prove this point by recalling the vexed question of providing the Army with a modern automatic rifle. Every Army Officer appreciated the need for replacing the 1904 Model British Lee-Enfield Rifle. Various proposals for purchasing these were turned down. This subject found a place in the agenda of every Infantry Commanders' Conference and the professional organ of the Basic Arm, *The Infantry Journal*. It is doubtful whether Menon or his civilian "military experts" ever considered it necessary to glance through any professional publications. At that time *The Infantry Journal* was edited by Lt.-Col. (then Major)

C. L. Proudfoot, an able and forthright military writer. Two editorials of the time are worth quoting verbatim:

Vol. X, October 1959, No. 2, Page 4. "The Self-loading Rifle.

"Whilst the modernisation of the Air Force and the Navy are without doubt of the utmost importance to the country's security, it is hard for the Infantryman who, on and off since Independence, has been continually and actively engaged in border defence and internal security duties, to understand why he is still armed with the bolt loading rifle of World War I which has long since become a museum piece in most modern armies. In the type of defensive war this country may be called upon to wage, the brunt of the fighting will unquestionably be borne by the Infantry, and it will be grossly unfair to ask them to match their antiquated rifles against automatic weapons in a type of warfare which will be fought and decided principally by ground troops".

The Infantry Journal returned to the attack after the clashes of 1959 to which we have referred in this narrative, and which brought urgency to the problem. In Vol. XI, April 1960, No. I, Page 2, the editorial said:

"The recent Chinese incursions across our Northern borders and their possible future implications have suddenly stirred the Nation into a greater awareness of the importance of the country's Armed Forces, an awareness which tends to be absent in nations which maintain strictly professional armies as against those in which conscription exists; and this is but natural, since nobody thinks of the doctor when there is no illness about. What is urgently required in the present contingency in addition to our present weapons, is a significant increase in automatic weapons strength of the Infantry Battalion with special reference to a self-loading rifle. We have stressed this point in the last issue of *The Infantry Journal* and are in duty bound to reiterate it, *lest we be accused by posterity of having allowed our case to go by default.* For it should be clearly apparent to all that any war into which this country is likely to be forced will be a limited war fought principally by ground troops and in the kind of fighting that is envisaged, the full weight of heavy weapons support that will be denied to the Infantry by extreme difficulties of terrain, can only be compensated by an increased volume of small arms automatic fire".

I hope that the Corps of Infantry, to which I had the honour to belong throughout my Army career, will be vindicated, and that posterity will lay the blame at the correct door-step. Let Mr. Menon and his defence and financial pundits not say that they were misled by the Army as a whole. Had Mr. Menon taken some time off to read military journals, or to meet officers who were manning the borders, he might have been more enlightened as to his duties and he would have got his priorities right. The country would have been in better shape if he had concentrated on defence matters instead of reading External Affairs files on international problems, and UN affairs for his secondary role as India's Ambassador-at-large.

Mr. Menon's duty was crystal clear. He was bound to obtain all the funds needed to implement the National Aims or to insist on having the National Aims recast to suit our modest means. He should not have misled the country about our preparations or mouthed brave words like "not giving up an inch of territory" or making an impact on the Chinese, or evicting the Chinese from Thagla; or putting up a brave front by sending troops to the Bhutan border (Tsangle) for the benefit of the doubting Bhutanese.

Prior to the showdown of September 1962, he indulged his craze for personal publicity and availed of every opportunity to project his image to the Indian public, to whom he was largely unknown and with whom he could not readily communicate in any Indian tongue. There was seldom a day without Menon being in the news. To achieve this, he accepted any and every invitation – official, social or personal. Some of his projects and ideas were publicised more to glorify him than to be of any use in the impending war with China. He loved being photographed opening border roads in a remote area or landing in Ladakh wearing an oxygen mask. He raised and created a large research and development organisation to produce weapons and equipment indigenously. As a long term measure, this was a laudable idea, but was untenable in the context of the imminent Chinese threat. Perhaps he never really believed that the Chinese would actually attack in force. Who knows?

Gen. Kaul has revealed that Gen. Thapar and he had put up the shortages and the urgent requirements of the Army to Government but Menon did not even bother to reply to these communications. If true, and we have no grounds to disbelieve this forthright assertion, Menon must accept the blame for the Army's shortages. The years of neglect could not be put right in one month, after the Chinese had intruded in strength and were bent on war. It was sad to hear Gen. Kaul telling me that "Government had agreed to purchase and fly out 6,000 sets of snow clothing from Canada" at a time when men were dying of the severe cold. Where did the foreign exchange suddenly come from? Why were these vital items not available in stock? Did the Army General Staff miscalculate the requirements? Or did Mr. Menon hope to produce these in his factories? Or did Mr. Desai deny the foreign exchange just to "fix" Menon? Who was the mystic "Government" who needed actual deaths to make it relent and accord "administrative and financial sanction"?

No amount of white-washing can absolve Menon of his direct contribution to the failure of 1962. He was a dominant personality and had free access to

Nehru. He did not do enough to prepare the Army for a major showdown with the Chinese and therefore must be allotted the major portion of the blame. If his military advisers failed him, then the blame is still his as he selected them himself.

Despite his immense prestige and acumen, Mr. Menon did not evolve a smooth running apparatus at the Ministry – Army HQ level. There were acrimonious debates in Parliament about his alleged interference in Army promotions. It has been said that he sometimes exceeded his authority in the matter of appointments, creating jobs and upgrading the appointments of his favourites. His critics say that he sought to create a personal following in the Armed Forces.

After allowing for the inevitable exaggeration in such matters, it is undoubtedly true that there was a good deal of ill-feeling in the Army. Every subaltern knew that there were rifts and rivalries among the top generals and an altogether unhealthy atmosphere prevailed. Menon succeeded in pushing out a number of senior officers who were supposed to have resisted his dictation or disagreed with his handling of the China problem. He is accused of promoting Kaul against the bitter opposition of the older generals. The appointment of Rear-Admiral B. S. Soman to Naval Chief caused a rumpus and Rear-Admiral A. Chakravarti resigned as he felt that his seniority and greater sea experience had been ignored.

Unquestionably the most unsavoury episode during Menon's tenure was the attempted plot to arraign Major-General (now Lt.-Gen.) S. H. F. J. Manekshaw with Menon's approval and with the help of Gen. Kaul. There was a persistent rumour in the Army that some officers were influenced to "bring up trumped-up accusations" against Gen. Manekshaw after his promotion to Lt.-Gen. had been announced but not yet sealed with an appointment. The Army was horrified at this naked attempt to eliminate one of the best officers of the Army. Apart from his military reputation, Manekshaw had been Commandant of the Infantry School as well as the Staff College and so was personally known to thousands of officers. In the end a Court of Inquiry composed of three generals of high integrity and commendable force of character dismissed the charges and recommended that those who gave evidence be asked to answer for their conduct. India was lucky that one of her ablest generals was saved to help rehabilitate the Army after the fiasco of 1962, and unless fate intervenes Gen. Manekshaw should be the next Chief of the Indian Army.

To round off Menon's role in the Sino-Indian War of 1962, it is necessary to study his methods and behaviour during the crisis-ridden days of September-October 1962.

On 8th September 1962, when Menon was first informed of the Chinese incursion into the Thagla Ridge area, he was inclined to dismiss the affair as just another border incident. He tried to handle the situation on his own assisted by the usual *ad hoc* set-up of assorted officials. Day to day decisions were taken based on inadequate or doctored information and this procedure replaced overall Government policy. Despite the absence of Mr. Nehru and Mr. Desai, decisions which could involve the nation in an all-out war were taken by a small group of officials. Had Menon given some sober thought to the politico-military consequences of his earlier rashness in demanding the eviction of the Chinese, he may have saved his political future and India's reputation. He preferred to ignore the inalterable factors of geography, terrain, time and space and the relative build-up of the two forces, at a place and time chosen by the Chinese. To him the Thagla incident was just another border incident. At one stage, he left for New York as planned. This was an unbelievably casual approach to a situation that could explode into war.

Mr. Menon held the centre of the stage throughout. His main war-like activity was his penchant for holding frequent conferences in his Delhi office or at the "field HQ" at Tezpur. Mr. Menon became a sort of field commander and was reported to be holding regular briefing conferences and being informed of the latest moves and dispositions. This is not the constitutional duty of a Defence Minister. By all means, a Minister should be kept informed of what is happening, but the level must be appropriate to his position. His job was to formulate Government policy with the help of his Service Advisers and communicate formal orders to the Army Chief. He did not formulate any overall policy and he did not give any formal orders. He did not allow any minutes to be kept of his numerous conferences. As late as 17th October when the military situation was unfavourable for a tough posture, and he well knew the weaknesses of the Army, he kept harping on "political necessity".

Eventually, he came to be known as the "highest level", a mysterious title that emasculated most of the Army Brass. Menon has since been accused of ordering the moves of troops and ignoring military advice. He has used a variety of alibis. Sometimes he blames pressure of public opinion and would have us believe that he was but an emissary of the street mobs or their senior cheer leaders. At other times, he trumpets loudly (as in the NEFA debate in August-September 1963): "It has been said the other day that political decisions have been taken to resist the Chinese in NEFA. I beg with great respect to you Mr. Deputy Speaker, and to the House, to ask who else could make a decision to fight against a country except those who can make political decisions . . . and for myself and I feel the Government will make no apologies for the assertion of civilian control over the Army". Apparently in Mr. Menon's vocabulary a mob or something called "public opinion" can also make political decisions which can humiliate the nation.

Menon has made other ringing assertions. He disclaims that he or Government "Ever told the operational commanders what positions they should take, what formations they should have, what military moves they should make. . . ." On the positive side, he has said "Whether we should defend a particular area, whether we should repel the Chinese invasion of our territories are political decisions, and on political issues Government must decide. . . ." He concludes emphatically: ". . . entirely wrong to say we took anything but political decisions. . . ."

These words are unexceptional. It is a pity that Menon did not enlighten the House about his definition of political decisions; how they are arrived at; and how civilian control is exercised in a working democracy.

This narrative brings out many decisions which have been attributed to him, or for which he shares responsibility as the Defence Minister. He decided to challenge the Chinese intrusion and insisted on a speedy eviction of the Chinese intruders. He hustled the Army Command and forced unwise tactical decisions. He insisted that there would be no further violation of Indian territory. He *de-facto* dictated the disposition of troops. By agreeing to the D-Day of 10th October 1962 (as claimed by Kaul), he forced Kaul to plan operations with the only troops available viz. 7 Infantry Brigade, whatever the professional assessment of "troops to tasks" appreciated by the local commanders.

To repel the Chinese invasion is admittedly a political decision; but can any responsible person claim that the issue of impossible tasks should be condoned purely on the grounds that the politician has a right to issue political decisions? Mr. Menon would have been on firmer ground had he anticipated and prepared for the final die-hard stand which he was forced to adopt in the face of a vocal public opinion. Does he wish us to believe that the whims, future or fortunes of politicians can override hard military facts and the advice and judgment of experts? The due processes of planning at all levels cannot be ignored; and no Defence Minister however exalted can be equated with the entire Cabinet and the chain of civil authority viz. Parliament, the Cabinet and the Service Chiefs. Some of his political decisions will not stand the scrutiny of time.

Mr. Menon would have been more credible if he had told us what the National Aim was and what steps he took to ensure that the Army was prepared to implement this Aim. Mr. Menon and the Cabinet are admittedly the proper authorities to take political decisions at this primary stage – indeed this is their constitutional duty. It is wrong to classify panicky *ad-hoc* conferences as exercising civil control; the issue of casual random orders is even more reprehensible.

The truth was told when, in his moment of agony, Menon said: "We have been outnumbered and out-weaponed". This phrase concedes the ineffectiveness of the policy-makers of the nation.

The Indian people have given their verdict. Menon continues to live in the wilderness despite the sad lack of talent in the Congress Party. His silence, which his friends label as a virtue, is his own indictment. Who was it who said, 3,000 years ago "When he is silent he shouts"? One noted Indian political commentator has this to say about Menon's silence: ". . . nor is Mr. Menon ever unready to take up a polemical challenge and give back in vituperation more than what he receives, but he has been discreetly silent". Is it any wonder?

Menon remained a Member of Parliament for his full term and occasionally reminded the Indian public of his existence but he no longer exercised power, although the Leftist Press played up his occasional breakfast sessions with Mr. Nehru. Over the years

I am sure he must remember Acharya Kripalani's classic indictment. On 11th April 1962 the veteran Indian statesman had this to say: "I charge him with wasting the money of a poor and starving nation. I charge him with having created cliques in the Army. I charge him with having lowered the morale of the Armed Forces. I charge him with the neglect of the defences of the country against the aggression of Communist China. . . ." These majestic and prophetic words reflect the views of the vast majority of the people who suffered the great sense of humiliation at the summary chastisement meted out to India by China.

The price paid in 1962 was by all counts a heavy one, but it was worth it, as a defeat at the hands of Pakistan in 1965 would have been a frightful catastrophy for India. Sooner or later India had to learn that its security and honour are not matters which can be left to one or two brilliant people, even when they are of the calibre of Nehru and Menon. These serious matters are the concern of the People, the Press, Parliament, the Cabinet, the Civil Servant, the Defence Services and all Government agencies. Co-ordination is the responsibility of the Minister of Defence, with the accent on co-ordination. There is no room for domination.

I hope that by understanding the machinery for the evolution of the National Policy and its implementation in war, the People will keep a watching brief on Government and will see through the sort of opiate that was dished out in the years preceding the Chinese attack.

The lessons of 1962 were well learnt. In August 1965, Pakistan launched a well-planned and well-organised guerilla movement against the Indian State of Jammu and Kashmir. Regular Pakistani officers and men were infiltrated into the State to disrupt communications, cause panic and eventually to take over the administration with the help of local sympathisers. The Cabinet could not evade the issue of retaliating with maximum force and accept the consequences. Mr. Shastri and his able Defence Minister, Mr. Y. B. Chavan, took two momentous decisions without hesitation. When told by the Army leaders that the situation in Kashmir could not be restored without violating the Cease-Fire Line established after the termination of hostilities in January 1949, the Cabinet permitted the Army to take whatever action they deemed necessary. Indian forces captured the strategic Haji Pir Pass and an important height overlooking the major base at Kargil. They also crossed the Line in the Tithwal Sector and cut off the major infiltration routes.

Frustrated and humiliated by the swift Indian riposte, Pakistan launched a massive attack with tanks against Indian positions at Chhamb-Jaurian in Jammu, and in doing so crossed the International Boundary at the point where it joins the Cease-Fire Line and threatened India's supply lines. The Army requested Government for air strikes. The request was granted in a few minutes and aircraft were over the target area within an hour. By 3rd September it was obvious that, for strategic and other reasons, Pakistan could not be held in Jammu. Mr. Shastri took the second momentous decision to move the Indian Army against West Pakistan to forestall the strangulation of our forces in Kashmir. Pakistan's bluff was called and she had to pull out of Jammu and concentrate on defending herself against the full weight of the Indian Army. Kashmir was saved.

The actual fighting was left to the Service Chiefs. The political chiefs courted no publicity and indulged in no heroics. The Army was grateful for this correct behaviour. Mr. Shastri and Mr. Chavan did their duty which was to take timely political decisions firmly, issue unambiguous orders and carry on with their proper constitutional duties. They gave the Defence

Forces all the moral and material support within their power.

The smooth functioning of the higher planning bodies was largely due to the background and personality of the Defence Minister. Mr. Chavan came to the Defence Ministry after the dismissal of Mr. Menon. His appointment was a welcome change from the rule of brilliant and unpredictable men. A spell of normalcy, orthodoxy and hard work was what was needed by the country and the Defence Ministry, and Chavan was the ideal choice. Mr. Chavan set about repairing the cracks of Menon's regime. He trusted and respected his new Chief, Gen. J. N. Chaudhuri. The two had become personal friends when Gen. Chaudhuri commanded Southern Command with his HQ in Poona, in Maharashtra. This was most fortuitous.

Mr. Chavan was instrumental in restoring the confidence of the Army and bringing a calm orderliness to the functioning of the Ministry and the Service HQ's. Gone were the days of grandiose plans, flashy meetings and acid words. Mr. Chavan's outward meekness and lack of flamboyance soothed the nerves of a ruffled officer corps, still smarting under the accusation that they had let the country down. He had true Indian humility. He was fortunate in that the crisis of 1962 had loosened the purse-strings of Government and friendly powers had opened their arsenals to us. He did not interfere with, nor allow Civilians to interfere with the Army's plans to remodel and re-equip the Armed Forces. By 1963, the Civilian was a thoroughly chastened man and had begun to understand his enormous responsibilities, as well as the limits of his authority. Mr. Chavan led a purposeful assault on old ideas and organisations. Within a few months the Army had been reorganised, mountain divisions raised and modern equipment and weapons issued to the troops. He did not seek scapegoats and exhorted everyone to forget the past and prepare for the second round, if it came.

The proof of his success came in the short war with Pakistan. He gave firm leadership and stayed in the background. He acted constitutionally and based his decisions on professional advice. He restored the proper functioning of the various organs of Government in the formulation and implementation of war plans.

A brief look at Mr. Chavan's background and character may give us a clue to the reasons for his success where a more talented man failed. By Congress standards, Chavan was a young man. He was only 48 years old when he joined the Union Cabinet. He is a member of the martial Maharatta clan and many in his constituency are soldiers. Soldiering is the major profession of the people and almost every home has a serving or retired soldier. The people of Satara District, situated in a rugged hilly area, have a reputation of cherishing freedom above all else. During the final stages of British Rule, the people formed a parallel Government, called the *Patri-Sarkar*, and the British writ was barely discernible in the area. Mr. Chavan took an active part in the revolutionary movement and did in fact go underground in 1942, till he was captured by the British Police and imprisoned.

It is not surprising therefore to find the following qualities in Mr. Chavan. He respected the profession of arms unlike some of his predecessors. He had a personal interest in the welfare of soldiers; if he did not, his voters would soon have reminded him of his obligations. He was not a slave to the hypocritical pretensions of non-violence.

EPILOGUE

The Political Aftermath

THE SINO-INDIAN conflict of 1962 was restricted to a small fraction of the opposing armies; was fought in a small, remote corner of the border and lasted a mere month – with only ten actual days of fighting and yet it is a fact that it did initiate profound changes in our international standing, domestic politics and economic progress.

The world was shocked at India's political ineptness and military collapse. India startled her friends by her panicky reaction and the unceremonious *volte-face* with regard to non-alignment. She refused to break off diplomatic relations with a country that had unleashed a war on her. The poor performance of the respected Indian Army made many wonder at what had happened to reduce one of the finest professional armies of World War II to such depths of incompetence.

Non-alignment, India's post-war contribution to international political philosophy, was hurriedly scuttled despite contrary professions. According to Mr. D. R. Mankekar: "New Delhi now feverishly negotiated with Washington and London for arms aid in order to meet adequately the impending Chinese threat. On 26th October, New Delhi made an urgent appeal to the United States and United Kingdom for military supplies. Indeed the first consignment of United States arms arrived on 3rd November, even though the formal pact between the two countries was signed only on 14th November". He adds: "On 19th November, New Delhi made an urgent and specific request for American fighting air support. . . . According to one British observer, Nehru asked the U.S.A. and UK for 15 bomber squadrons to interdict the advancing Chinese troops in NEFA".

Mr. Nehru's last unqualified appeal on 19th November, after the fall of Sela Pass, made every Indian share the anguish of this proud man. He admitted: "We shall require more help because it is a matter of survival for us. We have asked for every kind of help. There is no inhibition about it". This was a sad admission for a man who had allegedly disdained Mr. Eisenhower's offer of military aid without strings in 1953. Circumstances of his own creation compelled him to accept the presence of foreign military personnel on Indian soil, a short 15 years after we had rid ourselves of the British Army. Once we sought Western aid we could no longer pretend to be non-aligned where China and the United States were concerned. It may well be that we employed the face-saving formula of seeking help from all our friends, but we knew that only the United States and the United Kingdom had the will, the resources, the desire and above all the means to ensure timely delivery of vital war-like stores. The other major power Russia was a confused and unhappy spectator. She was just recovering from the tension of the Cuban Confrontation which had brought the world to the brink of a dreaded thermo-nuclear war. She also faced the unenviable dilemma of antagonising either 'fraternal China or friendly India'.

The sad truth was that, in November 1962, India's defence capability was heavily dependant on the generosity and identity of interests of the Western Powers. President Kennedy assumed the role of 'big brother' – a role which sat lightly on this true friend of India. Speaking with the immense authority of the President of the United States, he promised: . . . "to help India maintain herself against an attack if such an attack should come again". Not content with generalisations, Mr. Kennedy gave this unmistakable warning to China: "If China advanced any further they would be forcing the hand of the President of the United States". Significantly the Chinese withdrew two days later.

The Western Powers responded generously and war material was flown in with remarkable speed and efficiency. Up to the time of the Cease-Fire on 19th November there was no limit placed on the types or quantities required.

With the Chinese withdrawal the short-lived Indo-United States detente first came to a grinding halt and soon came to an end. When the urgency for re-arming the Indian Forces was removed, the Western Powers could afford to take a closer look at the long term implications of giving India further unfettered aid, without a re-definition of her foreign policy. Nations do not work on the basis of altruism or vague notions of friendship and it was inevitable that we would have to justify their faith in us. We would also have to give evidence of a more permanent identity with the donors' interests. The United States and United Kingdom were obviously not prepared to underwrite and arm a nation which had frequently opposed them.

The first obstacle in the way of a more permanent Indo-United States relationship was the tension between India and Pakistan. The Western Powers were deeply committed to maintaining a balance of power between the two neighbours. Additionally, the United States had a vested interest in retaining her bases in Pakistan. We were asked to 'renew efforts to settle the Kashmir issue'. Our desperate need for arms forced us to offer concessions and even to countenance mediation. Fortunately Pakistan over-played her hand and the series of 'talks' were called off in August 1963. It had been a close shave.

The second prerequisite was a statement of our long-term relationship with China with particular reference to our non-aligned policy. We would obviously have to be a little more non-aligned towards the

Western Powers if we were to qualify for continued massive aid. In the event we did not steer a fresh course and fell back on the stale and sterile policies of non-alignment, self-reliance and a facade of independence. Mr. Nehru's authority had waned and he had to resort to tight-rope walking to pacify and placate the many diverse political elements in his Party and in Parliament. In the difficult circumstances of 1962/63 it was not easy to alter course. Nehru's precipitate decline left a power vacuum which has yet to be filled and which has denied India purposeful leadership and a fresh outlook regarding our long-term interests.

Mr. Nehru's downfall was an undiluted tragedy for India. He was a universally admired and respected elder statesman. The facile Chinese victory brutally exposed his failure in anticipating and preparing for a military showdown with China. Whereas he had displayed remarkable adroitness in handling world affairs he had been disastrously myopic in a sphere of vital import to India. His international stature suffered a severe set-back.

More tragic from India's point of view was his fall from grace in the minds of his countrymen. Mr. Nehru, the pride of India's masses, was humiliated and lost his immense self-confidence. Never again was he to have a charismatic hold on the Indian People. He was tolerated only because of his past achievements and the Indian's traditional loyalty to elders and leaders. He retained his post because of sentiment and the lack of a second line of leadership, which he himself had not nurtured. By and large, the intelligentsia was disillusioned with him. His health deteriorated and he suffered a stroke in January 1964. The Chinese perfidy and betrayal, as he saw it, accelerated his end. He died within 20 months of the episode.

Without a Nehru India ceased to be the moral leader of the non-aligned world. Whereas prior to 1962 she wielded immense power and influence despite her poverty and lack of military power, after the Chinese attack she was 'cut to size' in the words of one unfriendly critic of Nehru.

The rude awakening to the realities of life was just the kind of shock-therapy required to prod India to formulate and pursue a more realistic foreign policy based on her own national interests. Over the years, public opinion had been trained to look upon India's special place in the world community as proof of her success and re-awakening from imperial subjugation. Mr. Nehru's glittering international conquests were an opiate to a people weighed down by poverty and backwardness. His international perigrinations and the tumultuous receptions given him were a source of pride to the Indian people who did not appreciate the fatal consequences of neglecting domestic problems. Tragically for India, up to 1962, the Government was more concerned with the Cold War, Korea, Hungary, Indo-China, Gaza, the Congo and other world problems.

After the painful lesson of 1962 we have come to realise that the world role of a nation is related to its power. We have realised that there is no place for policies based on flimsy notions of fellowship with coloured ex-colonial countries. The Afro-Asian concept is at best a tenuous link. The reaction of the so-called non-aligned Afro-Asian group initially shocked us and later was a major sobering factor in the post-China War reappraisal. Only Emperor Hailie Selassie of Ethiopia and Tunku Abdul Rehman of Malaysia came out openly in our favour and condemned the Chinese attack unequivocally.

It has been brought home to us that it is unwise to adopt a self-righteous attitude on every world crisis. We trod on many sensitive corns and made enemies who, quite understandably, gloated over our discomfiture in 1962. It is good to note that Indian spokesmen now do not express opinions on each and every international issue and gratuitously offer a solution, or mediation, or a peace-keeping contingent. We have learnt what has been common knowledge for over 2,500 years ago when a Greek sage said: "You know as well as we do that right as the world goes, is only in question for equals in power: the strong do what they can, the weak suffer what they must".

* * *

The domestic Indian scene was radically altered. The Congress Party had enjoyed absolute hegemony in the political field and a complete monopoly of power. Without a restraining Opposition, it was clear that our set-backs were entirely due to the wrong policies of the Congress. The Party became the prime target for the wrath of the people. It soon lost its *élan* and confidence. The decline of Mr. Nehru's authority and his demise in 1964 spelt the death-knell of this once-great organisation. In the General Elections of 1967 the voter expressed his disillusionment and the Party was rejected in 9 out of the 17 States of the Indian Union. Its majority in the Lok Sabha has been drastically reduced. India has no All-India Party which is capable of providing an alternative, stable Government and this central fact has had major repercussions, as India required another decade of stability and order to enable the economy to reach what the economists call the 'take-off' stage. The decline of the Congress has brought together coalitions of unlike-minded parties who have no common political or economic aims. Their main motive is to oust the Congress and rule themselves. Many of the leaders of these small political groups are disgruntled ex-Congressmen who were not given Party tickets or a share in the Congress ministerial appointments. Firm, decisive and when necessary, unpopular action, is not always possible for uneasy coalitions, with precarious majorities. We have witnessed the unseemly spectacle of members crossing the floors of State Legislative Assemblies; changing allegiances; last minute defections and outright trading of votes. In some cases the number of ministers is inflated to accommodate as many members as possible and forc-stall defections. The tax-payer is called upon to bear the cost of these strange machinations.

Recently the Congress has moved in to the counter-attack and at the time of writing three such Governments have been toppled and replaced by Congress sponsored governments – the Party lending its majority to an acceptable chief minister. Presidential Rule has been imposed in some other States, barely a year after a General Election. Apart from doubts about the constitutional and ethical propriety of such manœuvres, the people are denied good government.*

The fact is that there is more instability and uncertainty that does not augur well for the Indian People; and it is also a fact that the Chinese aggression, which heralded the premature decline of the Congress has been largely responsible for the dramatic change in the Indian political scene.

The situation in the Central Union Government has undergone a major change from the palmy days of pre-1962. The Congress has a much reduced majority; it is faced by hostile non-Congress State Governments, it does not have an unquestioned leader like Mr. Nehru and is troubled by rivalries in the top echelons. This being so, it is not easy to take timely and firm decisions on vital matters. Evasion and compromise are the order of the day. We have yet to take a wise, long-term and acceptable decision on the explosive language issue. A compromise formula was pushed through the Lok Sabha, in December 1967, but this has not satisfied the contending parties. There have been language riots in the northern provinces as well as the southern states.

Minority groups are clamouring for separate statehood and while we have acceded to the wishes of some we have yet to decide on whether to agree to the others or devise more formulas to satisfy irreconcilable factions.

* Presidential Rule was imposed on the States of Bengal, Bihar, Punjab and Uttar Pradesh. In February 1969 mid-term Elections in these States resulted in the utter rout of Congress in Punjab and Bengal. No clear majority party emerged in Bihar and Uttar Pradesh.

Any statement by a Minister is likely to spark off disturbances and palace squabbles.

We have yet to evolve a sound food policy, the most vital matter for the masses. We appear afraid to antagonise powerful Chief Ministers, the peasantry (the bulk of the voters), landlords and grain merchants. Disturbances over rising food prices were endemic in 1967/68. Despite an unprecedentally bountiful harvest in 1968 there are still pockets of shortages and statutory rationing alongside a flourishing black market.

The dismal list can be extended to include inter-State border 'disputes', economic policy and others. There is a feeling that the Government is more concerned with survival than governance. Unless wiser counsel prevails we may see our Government qualify for Sir Winston Churchill's terrible indictment of a certain British Government: "The Government cannot make up its mind or they cannot get the Prime Minister to make up his mind. So they go on in strange paradox, decided only to be undecided, resolved to be irresolute, adamant for drift, solid for fluidity, all powerful to be impotent". (Quoted by Lord Moran from G. M. Stanley's *Stanley Baldwin.*)

The changes in the economic field have been just as significant as in the military and political fields. Both China and India had started their new era of freedom with approximately the same economic base, with India holding the advantage, if anything. India had not been subjected to a debilitating and prolonged civil war as was China. In 1947 India was a creditor country with substantial sterling balances, a sound industrial base and an impressive net-work of rail and road communications. We had a reservoir of skilled technical and professional men and one of the world's most efficient civil services. There was a great upsurge of nationalism and an intense desire to succeed as an independent nation. There was a sense of unity.

The lightning Chinese victory appeared, superficially, to be a victory for China's authoritarian regime and economic system over India's mixed economy where the Public and Private Sectors were allotted complementary roles. India's planned economy, launched with great gusto and which had the blessings of the people came in for some rude soul-searching. Some questioned India's ability to match China in the economic sphere. China had exploded a hydrogen bomb and pays in gold for her food purchases, while we continue to need loans and grants for our grain requirements. The confidence of 1950 was replaced by the uncertainty of 1967/68. The Chinese attack blasted the comforting theory of a planned, leisurely development programme which would cause the minimum dislocation to the existing order of things. In our democratic system, the support of the masses and the intelligentsia is a prerequisite for the success of a planned economy and the temporary hardships that go with it. The loss of faith in planning is a momentous development.

India's economy was strained in 1962/63 and now in 1968 remains in the doldrums despite the administration of artificial respiration in the forms of loans and grants. The Budget of 1963 levied additional taxes to meet the increased defence expenditure, which rose from Rs. 350 crores to Rs. 900 crores in four years. The immediate spurt in expenditure was perforce met by deficit financing. The cascade of printed money has been the bane of the Indian economy and was perhaps the most damaging consequence of the fleeting Chinese War. Deficit financing has been the most potent factor in raising the price level, in creating conditions for inflation, increasing unemployment, lowering the purchasing value of the poor man's hard-earned rupee and the grave hardships to the middle-classes and other fixed income groups.

In the international economic field we have been forced to devalue the rupee, allegedly under foreign pressure and beg for rescheduling of our debt repayments. We need grants or loans to buy raw materials for the factories we have set up. We cannot make up our minds about the size and content of the Fourth Five-Year Plan, as it no longer possible to find nations to subsidise us. Our viability is questioned more closely than was the case in the early fifties. For food we have to rely on the bounty of the United States. Our debts have now, according to many experts, reached unmanageable proportions. Dependence of foreign aid and food makes us economically and politically vulnerable. There is little point in pursuing this litany of economic woes. The point that I have tried to bring out is that the Chinese Aggression has had far-reaching consequences and there is no sense in blinding ourselves to these harsh facts.

We have paid a heavy price for our China Policy and our military unpreparedness. In the ultimate analysis the blame is attributable to every thinking Indian. We elect Members of Parliament who in turn endorse policies, accept the military appropriations and confirm the political decisions which govern the National Aims. "We need not expect a better State until we have better men; till then all changes will leave every essential thing unchanged".

We are still faced by two hostile neighbours with whom we have fundamental differences and we still spend a sizeable portion of our national budget on defence. We maintain a large standing Army of volunteers. But this is not enough. As Corelli Barnett, the British military historian has said: "It is generally true that the Army is an extension of society; military disaster is often national decline exposed in the violence of battle". The National Will is the key factor in the military performance of a nation but this was sadly lacking in 1962.

Many of us frittered away our energies on linguism, parochialism, casteism and other petty issues. By and large we were apathetic and indifferent to national problems which we left to a few chosen leaders. The unity and fervour unleashed by Independence were soon dissipated. The financial and commercial opportunities opened up as a result of freedom from British domination were soon utilised to selfish ends. Moral standards deteriorated and we became used to reading of tax evasion, black money, concentration of wealth and nepotism.

Gradually we became *efféte* and looked upon the Army as a drain on the public exchequer instead of the instrument for enforcing our interests. We preferred terelyn shirts to parachutes; chocolates to emergency rations and transistors instead of vital Army communications equipment.

This outline of the events from 1950 to 1962 should stimulate wide public interest in national defence. India with her resources and skilled man-power is more than capable of ensuring her legitimate interests. It is only necessary for us to exercise vigilance on our leaders and to resolve never to allow ourselves to be pacified by words.

Let us resolve now never again to be credulous and negligent.

Appendix I

Sardar Placed China 18 Years Ago

My Dear Jawaharlal,

Ever since my return from Ahmedabad and after the Cabinet meeting the same day which I had to attend at practically fifteen minutes' notice and for which I regret I was not able to read all the papers, I have been anxiously thinking over the problem of Tibet and I thought I should share with you what is passing through my mind.

I have carefully gone through the correspondence between the External Affairs Ministry and our Ambassador in Peking and through him the Chinese Government. I have tried to peruse this correspondence as favourably to our Ambassador and the Chinese Government as possible, but I regret to say that neither of them comes out well as a result of this study.

The Chinese Government have tried to delude us by professions of peaceful intentions. My own feeling is that at a crucial period they managed to instil into our Ambassador a false sense of confidence in their so-called desire to settle the Tibetan problem by peaceful means.

There can be no doubt that, during the period covered by this correspondence, the Chinese must have been concentrating for an onslaught on Tibet. The final action of the Chinese, in my judgement, is little short of perfidy.

The tragedy of it is that the Tibetans put faith in us; they chose to be guided by us; and we have been unable to get them out of the meshes of Chinese diplomacy or Chinese malevolence. From the latest position, it appears that we shall not be able to rescue the Dalai Lama.

SUSPICION OF INDIA

Our Ambassador has been at great pains to find an explanation or justification for Chinese policy and actions. As the External Affairs Ministry remarked in one of their telegrams, there was a lack of firmness and unnecessary apology in one or two representations that he made to the Chinese Government on our behalf. It is impossible to imagine any sensible person believing in the so-called threat to China from Anglo-American machinations in Tibet. Therefore, if the Chinese put faith in this, they must have distrusted us so completely as to have taken us as tools or stooges of Anglo-American diplomacy or strategy. This feeling, if genuinely entertained by the Chinese in spite of your direct approaches to them, indicates that, even though we regard ourselves as the friends of China, the Chinese do not regard us as their friends. With the Communist mentality of "Whoever is not with them being against them", this is a significant pointer, of which we have to take due note.

LONE CHAMPION

During the last several months, outside the Russian camp, we have practically been alone in championing the cause of Chinese entry into the UNO and in securing from the Americans assurances on the question of Formosa. We have done everything we could to assuage Chinese feelings, to allay their apprehensions and to defend their legitimate claims, in our discussions and correspondence with America and Britain and in the UNO. In spite of this, China is not convinced about our disinterestedness; it continues to regard us with suspicion and the whole psychology is one, at least outwardly, of scepticism perhaps mixed with a little hostility.

I doubt if we can go any further than we have done already to convince China of our good intentions, friendliness and goodwill. In Peking we have an Ambassador who is eminently suitable for putting across the friendly point of view. Even he seems to have failed to convert the Chinese. Their last telegram to us is an act of gross discourtesy not only in the summary way it disposes of our protest against the entry of Chinese forces into Tibet but also in the wild insinuation that our attitude is determined by foreign influences.

It looks as though it is not a friend speaking in that language but a potential enemy.

In the background of this, we have to consider what new situation now faces us as a result of the disappearance of Tibet, as we know it, and the expansion of China almost up to our gates. *Throughout history, we have seldom been worried about our north-east frontier.* The Himalayas have been regarded as an impenetrable barrier against any threat from the north. We had a friendly Tibet which gave us no trouble. The Chinese were divided. They had their own domestic problems and never bothered us about our frontiers.

MELTING POT

In 1914, we entered into a convention with Tibet which was not endorsed by the Chinese. We seem to have regarded Tibetan autonomy as extending to independent treaty relationship. Presumably, all that we required was Chinese counter-signature. The Chinese interpretation of suzerainty seems to be different. We can, therefore, safely assume that very soon they will disown all the stipulations which Tibet has entered into with us in the past. That throws into the melting pot all frontier and commercial settlements with Tibet on which we have been functioning and acting during the last half a century.

China is no longer divided. It is united and strong. All along the Himalayas in the north and north-east, we have, on our side of the frontier, a population ethnologically and culturally not different from Tibetans or Mongoloids.

The undefined state of the frontier and the existence on our side of population with its affinities to Tibetans or Chinese have all the elements of potential trouble between China and ourselves. Recent and bitter history also tells us that Communism is no shield against imperialism and that Communists are as good or as bad as imperialists as any other. Chinese ambitions in this respect not only cover the Himalayan slopes on our side but also include important parts of Assam.

They have their ambitions in Burma also. Burma has the added difficulty that it has no McMahon line round which to build up even the semblance of an agreement.

IDEOLOGICAL CLOAK

Chinese irredentism and Communist imperialism are different from the expansionism or imperialism of the Western powers. The former has a cloak of ideology which makes it ten times more dangerous. In the guise of ideological expansion lie concealed racial, national and historical claims.

The danger from the north and north-east, therefore, becomes both communist and imperialist. While our western and north-western threats to security are still as prominent as before, a new threat has developed from the north and north-east. *Thus, for the first time, after centuries, India's defence has to concentrate itself on two fronts simultaneously.* Our defence measures have so far been based on the calculations of a superiority over Pakistan.

In our calculations we shall now have to reckon with Communist China in the north and north-east – a Communist China which has definite ambitions and aims and which does not, in any way, seem friendly disposed towards us.

Let me also consider the political considerations on this potentially troublesome frontier. Our northern or north-eastern approaches consist of Nepal, Bhutan, Sikkim, Darjeeling and the tribal areas in Assam. From the point of view of communications they are weak spots. Continuous defensive lines do not exist. There is almost an unlimited scope for infiltration. Police protection is limited to a very small number of passes. There too, our outposts do not seem to be fully manned.

TENUOUS LOYALTY

The contact of these areas with us, is, by no means close and intimate. The people inhabiting these portions have no established loyalty or devotion to India. Even Darjeeling and Kalimpong areas are not free from pro-Mongoloid prejudices. During the last three years, we have not been able to make any appreciable approaches to the Nagas and other hill tribes in Assam. European missionaries and other visitors had been in touch with them, but their influence was, in no way, friendly to India or Indians. In Sikkim, there was political ferment some time ago. It is quite possible that discontent is smouldering there. Bhutan is comparatively quiet, but its affinity with Tibetans would be a handicap. Nepal has a weak oligarchic regime based almost entirely on force; it is in conflict with a turbulent element of the population as well as with enlightened ideas of the modern age.

DIFFICULT TASK

In these circumstances, to make people alive to the new danger or to make them defensively strong is a very difficult task indeed and that difficulty can be got over only by enlightened firmness, strength and a clear line of policy. I am sure the Chinese and their source of inspiration, Soviet Russia, would not miss any opportunity of exploiting these weak spots, partly in support of their ideology and partly in support of their ambitions.

IN MY JUDGEMENT, THEREFORE, THE SITUATION IS ONE IN WHICH WE CANNOT AFFORD EITHER TO BE COMPLACENT OR TO BE VACILLATING. WE MUST HAVE A CLEAR IDEA OF WHAT WE WISH TO ACHIEVE AND ALSO OF THE METHODS BY WHICH WE SHOULD ACHIEVE IT. ANY FALTERING OR LACK OF DECISIVENESS IN FORMULATING OUR OBJECTIVES OR IN PURSUING OUR POLICY TO ATTAIN THOSE OBJECTIVES IS BOUND TO WEAKEN US AND INCREASE THE THREATS WHICH ARE SO EVIDENT.

Side by side with these external dangers we shall now have to face serious internal problems as well. I have already asked Iengar to send to the External Affairs Ministry a copy of the Intelligence Bureau's appreciation of these matters. Hitherto, the Communist Party of India has found some difficulty in contacting Communist abroad, or in getting supplies of arms, literature, etc. from them. They had to contend with difficult Burmese and Pakistan frontiers on the east or with the long seaboard.

EASIER ACCESS

They will now have a comparatively easy means of access to Chinese Communists and through them to other foreign Communists. Infiltration of spies, fifth columnists and communists would now be easier. Instead of having to deal with isolated Communist pockets in Telengana and Warangal we may have to deal with Communist threats to our security along our northern and north-eastern frontiers where, for supplies of arms and ammunition, they can safely depend on Communist arsenals in China.

The whole situation thus raises a number of problems on which we must come to an early decision so that we can, as said earlier, formulate the objectives of our policy and decide the methods by which those actions will have to be fairly comprehensive involving not only our defence strategy and state of preparation but also problems of internal security to deal with which we have not a moment to lose. We shall also have to deal with administrative and political problems in the weak spots along the frontier to which I have already referred.

URGENT PROBLEMS

It is, of course, impossible for me to be exhaustive in setting out all these problems. I am however giving below some of the problems, which, in my opinion, require early solution and round which we have to build our administrative or military policies and measures to implement them.

(*a*) A military and intelligence appreciation of the Chinese threat to India both on the frontier and to internal security.

(*b*) An examination of our military position and such redisposition of our forces as might be necessary, particularly with the idea of guarding important routes or areas which are likely to be the subject of dispute.

(*c*) An appraisement of the strength of our forces and, if necessary, reconsideration of our retrenchment plans for the Army in the light of these new threats.

(*d*) A LONG-TERM CONSIDERATION OF OUR DEFENCE NEEDS. MY OWN FEELING IS THAT UNLESS WE ASSURE OUR SUPPLIES OF ARMS, AMMUNITION AND ARMOUR, WE WOULD BE MAKING OUR DEFENCE POSITION PERPETUALLY WEAK AND WE WOULD NOT BE ABLE TO STAND UP TO THE DOUBLE THREAT OF DIFFICULTIES BOTH FROM THE WEST AND NORTH-WEST AND NORTH AND NORTHEAST.

(*e*) The question of Chinese entry into the UNO. In view of the rebuff which China has given us and the method which it has followed in dealing with Tibet, I am doubtful whether we can advocate its claims any longer. There would probably be a threat in the UNO virtually to outlaw China, in view of its active participation in the Korean war. We must determine our attitude on this question also.

(*f*) The political and administrative steps which we should take to strengthen our northern and north-eastern frontiers. This would include the whole of the border i.e. Nepal, Bhutan, Sikkim, Darjeeling and the tribal territory in Assam.

(*g*) Measures of internal security in the border areas as well as the States flanking those areas such as Uttar Pradesh, Bihar, Bengal and Assam.

(*h*) Improvement of our communications, road, rail, air and wireless, in these areas, and with the frontier outposts.

(*i*) Policing and intelligence of frontier posts.

(*j*) The future of our mission at Lhasa and the trade posts at Gyangtse and Yatung and the forces which we have in operation in Tibet to guard the trade routes.

(*k*) The policy in regard to McMahon Line.

RELATIONS WITH BURMA

These are some of the questions which occur to my mind. It is possible that a consideration of these matters may lead us into wider questions of our relationship with China, Russia, America, Britain and Burma. This, however, would be of a general nature, though some might be basically very important, e.g., we might have to consider whether we should not enter into closer association with Burma in order to strengthen the latter in the dealings with China. I do not rule out the possibility that, before applying pressure on us, China might apply pressure on Burma. With Burma, the frontier is entirely undefined and the Chinese territorial claims are more substantial. In its present position, Burma might offer an easier problem for China and, therefore, might claim its first attention.

I suggest that we meet early to have a general discussion on these problems and decide on such steps as we might think to be immediately necessary and direct quick examination of other problems with a view to taking early measures to deal with them.

Appendix II

Author's Career and Credentials

Brigadier John Parashram Dalvi's genealogy can be traced to a long line of military forebears. He is proud to claim numerous blood relatives serving in the ranks of the Indian Army and especially in his 'Family Regiment' the Maratha Light Infantry.

He was born in Basra (Iraq) on 3rd July 1920, where his father was serving with the British Administration. Returning to India in 1929 he studied at St. Mary's High School, Bombay, from where he graduated in December 1937. He continued his studies under the Jesuits at St. Xavier's College, Bombay. At the outbreak of World War II he decided to discontinue his studies and join the Army. He took the Entrance Examination for admission to the Indian Military Academy, Dehra Dun, in March, 1940, and secured a vacancy. On completion of his training he was commissioned into the Baluch Regiment.

Dalvi served with the 5th Battalion of the Baluchis almost throughout the War. During his service with the Battalion he took part in Field-Marshal Sir William Slim's pursuit of the Japanese Army, from October 1944 to March 1945 and saw fighting, with 19 Indian Division, notably at the crossing of the Irrawady, in January-February 1945. He was mentioned in despatches for gallant and distinguished service.

In March 1945 he was selected to join the staff of General Sir Montague (Monty) Stopford, General Officer Commanding XXXIII Corps and later General Officer Commanding-in-Chief 12th Army, in Burma. He was one of a handful of Indian Officers fortunate enough to serve on the General Staff of a senior military formation, in action, during World War II

During his post-War career, he held a variety of regimental and staff appointments. In 1947 he was posted as instructor to the Indian Military Academy, Dehra Dun. From the Academy he returned to Infantry as the second-in-command of the 5th

Royal Gorkha Rifles (Frontier Force), the Baluch Regiment having been allotted to Pakistan.

In 1949, Dalvi was detailed to the newly raised Brigade of Guards, the Indian Army's first experiment in organising all-class infantry units. In 1950 he appeared for, and obtained a competitive vacancy, to the Staff College, at Wellington. On graduation in 1951, he was posted to the Lorried Brigade of the Armoured Division as Brigade Major.

In January 1952 Dalvi was promoted Lieutenent Colonel to command the 4th Battalion of the Guards.

On completion of his command tenure he was posted to Army Headquarters as General Staff Officer Grade I to Military Operations Directorate of the General Staff. This Directorate which deals with operational planning at the highest level gave Dalvi his first insight into our decline, which eventually led to the Thagla Episode and our ignominious defeat at the hands of the Chinese.

After a brief spell in a second tenure of Command (1st Guards), Dalvi was promoted Full Colonel in January 1960 and appointed Deputy Commandant of the Military Academy. In October 1960, he was given accelerated promotion and made Brigadier-in-Charge Administration to Headquarters XV Corps. In this appointment, his area of responsibility extended to Ladakh and Jammu and Kashmir. His experiences in this vital assignment are narrated in his book and make very depressing reading indeed.

In January 1962 he volunteered to command 7 Infantry Brigade in the North-East Frontier Agency Sector of Towang, on the Indo-Tibetan Border. His lucid and gripping narrative of his command describe the events leading to the 20th of October which resulted in his Brigade being pushed, prodded and finally presented to the Chinese on a plate.

Whilst endeavouring to rejoin the remnants of his command, he was captured on 22nd October 1962. He was repatriated in May 1963. During the months of his incarceration Dalvi formed the general outline of this book and resolved that the Indian People should hear the truth from the only senior officer who was there throughout; who has no axe to grind; no reputation to save and is too junior to worry about a place in history.

Index

Abdullah, Sheikh, 89-90
Administrative Reforms Committee, 417
Afghanistan, 5
Agra, 289, 315, 355
Ahmedabad, 489
Ahluwalia, Lt.-Col. Balwant Singh, 118, 126, 129-130, 137, 371
Akhnur, 108
Aksai Chin, 18, 28, 31, 36, 38, 146, 404
Alanbrook, Field-Marshal Lord, 424-425
Alexander Field-Marshal Sir Harold, 201, 347, 365
Algeria, 398
All-India Radio, 270, 312
Ambans (Chinese Residents in Tibet), 8-9
America (see United States)
Amrik Singh, Maj.-Gen., 108, 139
Anglo-Chinese Treaty (1906), 9-10
Anglo-Tibetan Treaty (1904), 9, 20
Appreciation, 23/29 Sept. 1962, 231-232, 235, 240, 253, 260-261, 428
Arakan, 49, 91
Arnim, Gen. von, 191
Assam, 1, 4, 30, 41, 44, 56, 60, 64, 155, 250-251, 439, 459, 491-492, 495
Assam Rifles, 40-41, 57-58, 70, 72, 114, 118, 121, 124-125, 128, 130-131, 134, 136-137, 139, 143, 166-167, 169, 177-179, 185, 188-189, 198, 209, 216, 224, 277, 355
Attlee, Clement, 348
Auchinleck, Field-Marshal Sir Claude, 253, 347-348, 379
Austerlitz, Battle of, 362
Ayyangar, Gopalaswami, 449-450
Azad Kashmir (Forces), 26

Baldev Singh, Sardar, 448-449
Bara Hoti, 21
Bandung Conference (1955), 21
Bangalore, 459
Barnett, Corelli, 286, 350, 487
Battalions
- 1st Bn. The Guards (Punjab), 497
- 4th Bn. The Guards (1 Rajput), 497
- 9 Punjab, 107-108, 112, 121, 132, 144, 170, 177-178, 181, 183, 185-186, 188-189, 193-194, 197-198, 202-203, 205-209, 211-213, 215-216, 220-221, 226-227, 272, 277, 281, 284, 291-292, 294, 300, 316-317, 327, 333, 337, 361, 364, 371, 382, 387
- 4 Grenadiers, 183, 297, 307, 333 362, 364, 371, 382-384, 387
- 2 Rajput, 178, 222-225, 227-228, 241, 263, 272-274, 276, 278, 282, 286, 288-290, 292-294, 298-299, 307, 338-339, 355-356, 361, 363, 365, 367-372, 374, 381
- 2 Jat, 56
- 5 Baluch, 92, 389, 496-497
- 1 Sikh, 71, 110-111, 121, 137, 144, 178, 183, 226
- 6 Kumaon, 224
- 5th Gorkhas, 181, 497
- 1/8 Gorkha Rifles, 150-151
- 1/9 Gorkha Rifles, 56, 58, 120-121, 126, 128-129, 144, 165, 178, 222-223, 225, 227-228, 241, 263, 272-273, 276, 278, 282, 286, 297-299, 307, 326-327, 335-339, 352, 354, 361, 365-368, 371-374, 439

Bengal, 450, 495
Berthier, Marshal, 297
Bewoor, Lt.-Gen. G. G., 91-92
Bewoor, Sir Gurunath, 92
Bhagat, Lt.-Gen. P. S., 397
Bharat Electronics, 185
Bhargava, G. S., 67, 69, 74
Bhatia, Capt., 369
Bhup Singh, 369
Bhutan, 11, 14, 108, 372, 492, 495
Bhutan Tri-Junction, 57, 71, 133, 206, 208, 328, 467
Bihar, 23, 495
Bikram Singh, Lt.-Gen., 107
B'swas, Jemadar, 368-369
Bleting, 208
Bombay, 377, 462
Bomdilla, 1, 58, 60-61, 67, 72, 113, 144, 184, 190, 350
Border Roads Organisation, 61, 75, 79, 110, 113, 115, 119-120, 122, 127, 149, 256, 273, 289, 308, 319, 354, 432, 444, 465
Bose, Jemadar, 369
Bose, Subhas Chandra, 92
Boucher, Gen. Sir Roy, 24
Bowles, Chester, 142
Brahmaputra River (Valley), 1, 57, 389

Bridges
Bridge I, 204-206, 209, 211, 213, 216, 219, 221, 238, 272, 281, 296-298, 300, 307, 317-318, 360, 362, 364, 367
Bridge II, 204, 208-209, 213-214, 219-221, 238, 272, 281, 300, 361, 364, 367
Bridge III, 209, 213, 216, 221, 238, 282-283, 294, 296, 298-299, 314, 338, 361, 363-364, 381
Bridge IV, 209, 213, 221, 238, 276, 281, 282, 294, 296, 298-300, 314, 326, 338, 355, 363-364, 368
Bridge V, 239, 338, 361, 373
Log Bridge, 276, 292, 294, 299-300, 338-339, 364
Temporary Bridge, 296, 314, 338-339, 364, 369, 373
Brigades
Parachute, 382
5 Brigade, 249
7 Brigade, 99, 103, 107, 109-110, 113, 121-124, 132, 139-141, 144-145, 158, 170-171, 173-174, 176, 178, 181-183, 185, 189, 193, 222-224, 226, 228, 232, 236, 240, 249, 255-257, 259-260, 262-264, 266, 268-269, 271, 273, 275-280, 286-288, 294-298, 300, 307, 313, 315, 317, 320, 322, 324-325, 328, 334, 336, 338-341, 344, 354, 360-363, 367, 372, 375, 378, 391, 435, 440, 442-443, 472, 497
11 Brigade, 110, 144, 174
Brijpal Singh, Havildar, 381, 386
Britain (see United Kingdom)
Bulganin, Marshal, 33
Bumla, 58, 132, 178, 367
Burma, 11, 16, 38, 57, 64, 97, 491, 495-496

Cairo, 348
Canada, 289, 468
Cariappa, Gen. K. M., 399, 448
Cassino, 121, 190, 201-202, 365
(CENTO) Central Treaty Organisation, 25
Ceylon, 38, 156
Chacko camp, 110
Chakravarti, Rear-Admiral A., 469
Chamberlain, Neville, 161
Charduar, 224
Chang Chenmo Valley, 46
Chaudhry, Major, 216, 280, 290, 292, 294, 298
Chaudhuri, Gen. J. N., 96, 108, 212, 476
Chaudhri, Nirad. C., 348, 427-428, 438-439
Chavan, Y. B., 29, 60, 158, 191, 397, 430, 434, 436, 440-441, 475-477
Chen Yi, Marshall, 150-151, 157, 247
Chhad Bet, 30
Chhamb, 27, 475
Chiefs of Staff Committee, 69, 100, 187, 192, 414, 418-419, 421-423, 428
Chien Lung, Emperor, 9
China, 2-4, 6-16, 18-23, 27-29, 31, 33-38, 41-43, 48-49, 51, 53, 60-62, 65, 67-68, 74, 90, 94-95, 101, 113, 117, 133, 135, 138, 142-143, 146-150, 153, 159-160, 165, 169, 184, 201, 212, 216, 221, 236, 247-248, 291, 329, 398, 404-406, 428, 431, 434, 444, 449-450, 457, 459, 468-469, 474, 479-481, 485-487, 490-492, 494-495
Chindit Operation (1944), 16
Chindwin River, 64
Chinese Communist Party, 8
Chinese Frontier Guards, 45, 208, 210, 376
Chinese Peoples' Congress, 38
Chinese Peoples' Liberation Army, 6, 8, 12, 36, 97, 199, 208, 390, 406
Chinese Peoples' Republic, 9
Chinese Revolution (1911), 10
Choksen, 131, 172, 387
Churchill, Sir Winston, 291, 347-348, 379, 424-425, 485
Chusul, 85, 103
Chutangmu, 39
Chou En-Lai, 21, 31, 38, 66, 77, 148, 387, 389
Clausewitz, von, 184, 313
Colombo, 156, 312, 329
Commonwealth Prime Ministers' Conference (1962), 156-157
Congo, 482
Congress Party, 27, 35, 42, 52, 95, 407, 456, 462, 473, 477, 483
Corps
IV, 5, 260, 264, 267, 280, 282, 291, 313, 332, 340, 344-345, 347, 351
XV, 77, 80, 82, 84, 497
XXXIII, 69, 140, 155, 168-169, 178, 214, 222, 250
Cromwell, Oliver, 161
Cuban Confrontation (Oct. 1962), 479
Curzon, Lord, 9, 135
Czarist Russia, 9

Dagshai, 56
Daily Telegraph, 64

Dalai Lama, 9-10, 12, 18, 37-38, 116, 151, 404, 489
Dalvi, Brig. J. P., 223, 274-276, 280, 310, 375, 496-497
Dange, S. A., 456
Darjeeling, 492, 495
Dasrath Singh, Subedar, 369
Daulet Singh, Lt.-Gen., 87, 199, 439
Defence Committee of the Cabinet, 57, 69-70, 96, 101, 156-157, 187, 200, 229, 246, 308, 402-410, 416, 423, 428, 461
Defence Services Staff College, 15-16, 110, 120, 470, 497
Delhi, 25, 36, 53, 57, 77, 86, 99-100, 103, 107, 111, 117, 122, 145, 149, 151-152, 157, 167-168, 171, 173, 181, 183, 186, 188, 194, 198-200, 212, 215, 225, 228, 231, 233, 236-239, 242, 245, 251, 270, 283-285, 292, 295-296, 300, 307-208, 310, 325, 329, 331, 333, 339-341, 344-345, 348, 351, 354, 377, 406, 423, 427-428, 441-442, 471, 478
Desai, Morarji, 157, 407-409, 415, 456, 458, 461-464, 468, 470
Dhillon, Maj.-Gen. J. S., 247-248
Dhola Post (also area), 44-45, 71, 125, 133-139, 143-144, 166, 169, 171-173, 177-178, 180-182, 185-189, 192-194-198, 201-203, 207, 209, 211-212, 216, 218, 220-221, 228-229, 248, 256-259 261-264, 271-279, 281-283, 286, 291, 294, 296, 308, 317, 322, 360, 364, 367, 372, 382, 423, 427
Dhola Massif (also Peak), 355, 371, 383, 385, 389
Digboi (Oilfields), 4
Dimapur, 64
Dirang, 58, 110-111, 113, 121-122

Divisions

7th British Armoured, 190
4th Indian Division (Red Eagle), 56-57, 59, 70-71, 109-110, 121-122, 137, 139, 141-145, 158, 167-168, 181, 190-191, 203, 210, 214, 275, 318, 323-324, 333, 336, 342, 361, 365, 388

Dorman Smith, Maj.-Gen. E., 347
Drokung Samba Bridge, 39, 43, 130, 367, 382, 388-389
Dulles, John Foster, 25
Dum Dum La, 336
Dunkirk, 425

Eagles' Nest, 113
Eastern Command, 60, 82, 140, 155, 168, 177-178, 182, 186, 192-193, 214, 222, 263, 273, 284, 427
Eden, Sir Anthony (Lord Avon), 161
Egypt, 190
Eisenhower, President D. D., 25, 27, 479
El Alamein, 349-350
Eritrea, 190

Ferozepore, 30
First Five-Year Plan, 19, 401
Foothills, 56, 110, 112-113, 174, 190
Forward Policy, 38, 44, 67, 69-74, 97, 109, 133, 135-136, 143, 167, 217, 252, 422, 426, 444, 461
Fourth Five-Year Plan, 487
France, 33, 161
French, Field Marshal Sir John, 267

Galwan (Valley), 148, 150-151, 155, 267, 291
Gandhi, Mahatma, 398
Gauhati, 69-70, 99, 122, 323-324
Gauhati Officials' Meeting (Feb. 1962), 69-72, 109
Gaza, 482
Gazala, 350
Geneva, 149-150, 247
Geneva Conference on Indo-China (1954), 454
Geneva Conference on Laos (1962), 150
Gilgit, 27
Goa, 156
Gopal, Major, 272
Gracey, Gen. Sir Douglas, 24
Gupta, Capt. T. K., 171, 196, 210-211, 381, 385
Gurdial Singh, Major, 368
Gyantse, 20, 495
Gyspu, 129

Haig, Field Marshal Sir Douglas, 289
Hailie Selassie, Emperor, 482
Haji Pir Pass, 475
Hangen, Welles, 43, 54, 69, 90-91, 462
Hangman's Hill, 365-366
Harbaksh Singh, Lt.-Gen., 345
Harihar Singh, Lt.-Col. 307
Hart, Capt. Lidell, 358
Hathungla Pass, 63, 138, 172, 177, 181, 204, 208, 214, 217, 226, 236-238, 270, 272, 277, 296, 298, 307, 310, 316, 320, 361, 362, 365, 367, 371, 382, 385, 387, 389-390
Hazra, Capt. P. K., 129
Hindi-Chini Bhai Bhai, 19, 21, 31
Hooja, 71
Hitler, Adolf, 63, 161, 358-359

Hungary, 32, 455, 482
Husseiniwala, 30

India League, 453
Indian Delegation to UN, 89, 454
Indian Military Academy, Dehra Dun, 219, 386, 496-497
Indian National Army (INA), 92
Indo-China, 19, 454, 482
Indo-Pak War, (1965,) 27, 32, 62, 108, 270, 474
Indo-Tibetan Border, 2, 19, 35-36, 97, 435, 437, 465, 497
Indo-Tibetan Border Force, 22
Indonesia, 8, 398
Infantry Commanders' Conference (1962), 210, 406
Infantry Journal, 465-467
Infantry School, Mhow, 158, 171, 470
Inspector-General of Assam Rifles (IGAR), 124, 134, 188-189
Instrument of Accession, 23
Interim Cabinet of (1946,) 448
International Control Commission, Korea, 50
Irrawady Crossing, Battle of, 92, 496
Israeli-Arab War (June 1967), 249
Italy, 121, 180, 190, 365

Jacob, Gen. Sir Ian, 347
Jagjivan Ram, 463
Jaipur, 252
Jammu and Kashmir, 26-27, 30, 108, 474, 497
Jammu and Kashmir Militia, 89, 475
Jang, 112-113
Jayaraman, Major, 114-115, 264, 318
Joffre, Marshal, 212, 236
Johnson, President Lyndon, 27
Johori, Major S. R., 278, 280, 283, 290
Joint Intelligence Committee, 124, 187, 422
Joint Planning Committee, 422
Joint Planning Staff, 422

Kalimpong, 492
Kalyan Singh, Brig., 189-191, 193, 226
Kameng Frontier Division, 1, 39, 60, 110, 118, 127, 129, 144, 158, 168-169, 171, 192, 197, 236, 375
Kamraj Plan, 409, 463
Karam Singh, Havildar, 46, 55, 78
Kargil, 475
Karpola I Pass, 172, 177, 205, 217, 236-237, 239-240, 270-271, 286, 291, 310, 315, 378, 385-386, 389
Karpola II (Peak), 211-212, 292
Kashmir (Issue/War of 1948), 7, 15, 22-24, 26-27, 29-30, 33, 49-50, 78, 89, 121, 125, 183, 401, 404, 419, 457, 475, 480
Katju, Dr. Kailash Nath, 449-450, 455
Kaul, Lt.-Gen. Brij. Mohan, 5, 53-54, 67-75, 82-84, 88-94, 96, 109, 113, 132, 136, 142, 156-157, 185, 191, 201, 210-213, 223, 232, 234, 239-240, 245, 247-252, 255-274, 276, 278-286, 288-298, 300-302, 307-311, 313, 317-318, 323, 326-328, 330-331, 339, 341, 343-346, 348-354, 362, 377-380, 388, 405-406, 415, 424, 427-429, 436, 440, 442-445, 460-461, 468-469, 472
Kaushik, Major, 319
Kennedy, President John F., 142, 479
Keren, 190
Kesselring, Field Marshal, 180
Khampas, 18, 40, 49
Kharbanda, Major R. O. (Rex), 171, 231, 264-266, 375
Khempo (of Towang Monastery), 116
Khenzemane, 39, 43, 47, 58, 125, 130-131, 148, 151, 208, 216-217, 237, 362, 365, 367, 376, 388
Khruschev, Nikita, 33, 150
K. K. Singh, Brig., 291, 340, 354
Kohima, 64
Kolay, Capt. B. B. 316
Kongka Pass, 46
Korean War, (1950/53), 6, 8, 14-15, 19, 152, 283, 314, 482, 495
Kripalani, Acharya, 88, 457, 474
Krishnamachari, T. T., 462-463
Kulwant Singh, Lt.-Gen., 22
Kumaramangalam, Gen. P. P., 270
Kunzru, Dr. H. N., 448

Lachhman Singh, Capt., 334
Ladakh, 14, 31, 35-36, 42, 46-47, 69, 73, 76-79, 81, 83-86, 96, 102-103, 107, 109, 142, 146-147, 149-150, 199-200, 229, 404, 432, 439, 457, 465, 468, 497
Lagos (Nigeria), 156, 245
Laski, Harold, 453
Le, 66, 134, 153, 287
Leh, 84, 85
Lentaigne, Maj.-Gen. W. D. A. (Joe) 15, 16, 17
Lhasa, 9-12, 18, 36-37, 142, 152, 158, 404, 495
Lloyd George, David, 424
Limeking, 40
Lio Po-Chang, Gen., 8
Lohia, Dr. Ram Manohar, 455
Lohit Frontier Division (NEFA), 224

Lok Sabha (also Parliament), 14, 25, 27, 28, 35-36, 38, 40-43, 48, 51-52, 55, 57, 63, 68, 86, 88, 96-97, 191, 397, 409, 417-418, 428, 434, 437, 454, 469, 471-474, 481, 483-484, 487
London, 156, 245, 411, 453, 478
Longju, 39-40, 43-45, 47, 148, 151, 208, 216
Lucknow, 122, 145, 168, 186, 241, 284, 427, 442
Lumla, 128, 175-176, 186, 188, 197, 331
Lumpu, 130-131, 144, 166-167, 170, 175, 177-178, 181, 185-186, 188-189, 194, 197-198, 202-203, 205, 214, 216-219, 223, 225-226, 228, 231-232, 240-241, 256, 258-264, 266, 267, 272, 276-278, 284, 290, 293, 296-297, 316-317, 319, 334, 339, 361-362 365, 373, 381, 385-390

Maginot Line, 378
Maitra, Col. A. K., 115, 318
Majdalany, F., 180, 190, 287, 365-366
Maldon (Bye Election), 348
Malhotra, Inder, 61, 135
Mallick, Major, 115
Manchu (Dynasty), 10
Manekshaw, Lt.-Gen. S. H. F. J., 96, 469-470
Mangat, Capt., 368
Mani, Brig. O. M., 120
Mankekar, D. R., 346, 353, 478
Manohar Singh, Lt.-Col., 109, 158
Manstein, Field-Marshal Eric von, 313, 358-359
Mao Tse Tung: 46, 258
Marlborough, Duke of, 254
Marmang, 66, 152, 154, 173, 314
Master, Lt.-Col. Byram F., 108, 110, 118, 171
Mathura, 224
McMahon Line, 11, 18, 43-44, 57, 60-61, 63, 66, 77, 102, 105, 118, 125, 131, 133, 136, 140, 143, 148, 165, 206, 209, 287, 383, 387, 495
Meerut, 215
Mehta, Lt.-Col. B. N. ("Baij"), 16, 110, 171
Menon, V. K. K., 3-4, 42-43, 46-48, 51-55, 61-62, 68-69, 75, 81, 88, 93, 111, 135-136, 139, 150, 156-157, 159, 161, 198, 200, 212, 228, 233, 245-246, 250, 284, 328, 345, 351-352, 397-398, 407-409, 411, 415, 423, 425-426, 428-429, 437, 442, 444-445, 447, 451-465, 467-474, 476
Migytun, 39-40
Military aid to Pakistan, 25
Ministry of External Affairs, 6-7, 16, 41, 43, 57, 63, 71, 124, 134, 136, 151, 222, 458, 467, 489-490, 493
Ministry of Defence, 51, 55, 63, 96, 136, 157, 222, 402, 410-415, 417-418, 447-449, 451, 457, 458, 476
Ministry of Finance, 80, 96, 415, 417-418, 437
Ministry of Home Affairs, 22, 136, 458
Misamari, 56, 65, 108-110, 113, 121-123, 155, 170, 176, 179, 214, 220, 226
Misra, Lt.-Col. R. N., 171, 179, 189, 206, 208-209, 214, 218-219, 227, 272, 281, 288, 298, 333
Mongia, V. V., 177, 219
Monpas, 115-116, 127-128, 202, 210-211, 223
Montgomery, Field-Marshal Lord, 347
Mookerjee, Shyama Prasad, 6
Moran, Lord, 485
Moti Sagar, Lt.-Gen., 93, 103
Muksar, 240
Mullick, B. N., 71
Mutaguchi, Gen., 64
Mutual Aid Treaty, 25, 404

Naga, 461, 492
Nagaland, 110, 144, 174, 190, 192, 200, 251
Namka Chu River, 1, 44, 98, 101, 138, 145, 152, 172, 174, 182-183, 185, 188, 194-195, 198, 204-209, 213-215, 218-219, 221-222, 227, 231-232, 234, 237-239, 257-261, 266, 269-271, 275, 277-279, 281, 286, 288, 290, 293, 295-297, 299-301, 307, 313, 315, 317-319, 322, 325-329, 331-334, 337-339, 343, 345, 350, 352, 354, 357, 360-362, 364, 366, 368, 373-375, 377-378, 384, 392, 421, 432, 438, 443
Napoleon, Bonaparte, 63, 297, 421
Narayan, Jayaprakash, 12
Nasser, President Abdul Gamal, 249, 398
Nathu La (Pass), 63
National Defence Academy, Poona, 369
National Defence Council, 48
Nayar Kuldip, 4
Nehru, B. K., 405
Nehru, Pandit Jawaharlal, 2, 4, 5, 7-8, 13-14, 17, 20-21, 23, 25-28, 30-32, 34-41, 43-45, 47-52, 67-72, 74, 76-77, 79, 86, 88-90, 92-96, 136, 150, 155-156, 201, 245-249, 260, 262-283, 295, 209, 311-312, 329, 345-346, 360, 364, 379, 398-399, 405-

406, 408-409, 423, 425-426, 428-429, 437, 443-444, 447-450, 452-454, 456-458, 461, 463-464, 469-470, 473-474, 479 481-484, 489
Nelson, Lord, 365
Nepal, 14, 492-493, 495
New China News Agency, 8
New York, 245, 427, 470
New York Times, 74, 454
Nijjar, Major Balraj Singh, 341, 381, 384-385
Nkrumah, Dr., 398
North East Frontier Agency Administration, 57-59, 72, 114, 127-128, 134, 143, 211, 223, 497
North East Frontier Agency (NEFA), 1, 14, 18, 30, 35-36, 40, 42, 45, 47, 55-57, 60-61, 65-66, 69-71, 76, 78-79, 84, 94, 109, 112, 114, 129, 133, 136, 150, 152, 168, 171, 184, 190, 199-200, 212, 216, 224, 229, 234, 246, 250-251, 257, 260, 269-270, 312, 322, 324, 329, 345-346, 360, 365, 371, 378, 397, 409, 423, 407, 432, 435, 443-444, 446, 457, 459, 461, 471, 479
NEFA Enquiry Board, 191, 266, 397, 413, 430, 434, 441
Nuranaung, 111-112
Nyam Jang Chu River, 126-127, 131, 172, 206, 208, 361-362, 365, 367, 387-389

Operation ONKAR, 109, 121, 133, 134, 141

Paintal, Lt.-Gen. R. S., 108
Paitsai Spur, 218, 237
Pakistan, 23-34, 41, 47, 51, 53-54, 169, 171, 404-405, 450-452, 457, 459, 474, 480, 492-493
Palit, Brig. D. K., 107, 118, 130, 165
Panch Sheel, 20-21
Pangong Lake, 149
Panipat, Battle of, 364
Pankentang, 58-59, 120, 132
Pannikar, Sardar K. M., 7, 489-490
Pant, Major B. K., 370-371
Parliament (see Lok Sabha)
Partap Singh, Subedar, 24
Patel, H. M., 448
Patel, Sardar Vallabhbhai, 7, 17, 95, 398, 447
Pathania, Maj.-Gen. A. S., 346
Patharia Reserve Forest, 30
Patri Sarkar (1942), 477
Pawar, Major, 297
Pearl Harbour, 167
Peking, 12-13, 77, 221
Pereira, Major C. L. (Bertie), 166-167, 171, 375
Peshawar, 25
Press Trust of India, 62
Pinto, Air Vice-Marshal Erhlich, 102-103
Plassey, Battle of, 364
Poona, 476
Poonch, 93, 121
Prasad, Capt. Mahabir, 71, 137, 282-283
Prasad, Maj.-Gen. Niranjan, 139, 141, 165, 177, 181, 192-195, 228, 231-234, 236-237, 240, 260-262, 264, 272, 274, 281-282, 288, 293, 296, 209, 312, 326, 330-332, 336, 338-343, 351-352, 354-355, 366, 373-375, 442
Proudfoot, Lt.-Col. C. L., 466
Punjab, 1, 23-24, 26-28, 30, 56, 125, 155, 165, 170, 419, 435
Punjab Boundary Force, 49

Radhakrishnan, Dr. S., 2
Raghuramiah, K., 228, 427
Rajasthan, 252
Rajwade, Brig. M. R., 291
Rajya Sabha, 443
Ram Singh, Major, 373
Ranbir Singh, Brig., 59, 118, 132
Ranga, Prof. N. G., 16
Rangiya Station, 108
Rangoon, 64, 77
Rann of Kutch, 27, 30
Richardson, Hugh, 11-12
Rikh, Lt.-Col. Maha Singh, 223-224, 288, 297, 355, 368-369
Robertson, Field-Marshal Sir William, 424
Rommel, Field-Marshal Erwin, 283, 347, 349-350
Rongla, 322, 375
Rosenthal, A. M., 74, 454
Roshan Singh, Naik, 369
Rudok, 18
Russell, Bertrand, 453
Russia (see Soviet Union), 479, 495

Sandhu, Lt.-Col. P. S., 110, 111
Sanjeeva Rao, Lt.-Col., 273, 284, 291
Sarin, H. C., 427
Satara District, 477

Second Five-Year Plan, 33
Sehgal, Flt.-Lt., 373
Sela Pass, 1, 65, 111, 113, 114, 122, 144, 170, 174, 184, 190, 225, 345, 346, 350, 479
Sen, Lt.-Gen. L. P., 82-83, 87, 186-188, 191-195, 198, 200, 212, 228-229, 233-234, 241, 245-246, 250, 253, 255-259, 274-275, 279, 285, 312, 327, 346, 352, 439-440, 442
Sen, Lt.-Col. K. B., 115, 264
Senge, 111, 224
Senger, Gen von, 202
Serkhim, 204, 220, 226-227, 268, 272, 362, 383, 385, 386, 387, 389, 390
Seventeen-Point Agreement, 12, 18
Seydlitz, Gen., 379
Shakti, 58, 128-131, 144, 170, 172, 186, 197
Shaiza, W., 115, 126, 177
Shastri, Lal Bahadur, 4, 200, 463, 475
Shillong, 124, 134, 168, 264
Shrinagesh, Gen. S. M., 458
Sidi Barrani, Battle of (Day), 145, 158, 323
Sikkim, 14, 492, 495
Simla Conference 1913/14, 10, 206
Simla Convention (Agreement), 11, 12, 43
Sinkiang Province, 18
Sinkiang Highway, 28, 31, 36, 38
Sino-Indian Agreement on Trade and Intercourse 1954, 19, 20, 22, 31
Sino-Indian Border, 38, 42-43, 48, 74, 150, 159, 168, 419, 420
Sino-Indian Officials' Talks (1960), 43, 151
Slim, Field-Marshal Sir William, 64, 496
Soekarno, Dr., 398
Soman, Rear-Admiral B. S., 469
South-East Asia Treaty Organisation (SEATO), 25
Soviet-Pakistan Arms Deal, 27
Soviet Union (also Russia and USSR), 25-27, 33, 34, 63, 64, 479, 493, 495
Spanggur, 39
Spanish Civil War, 453
Srinagar, 90, 157
Stalingrad, 358
Statesman (Calcutta), 61, 63, 72, 135, 312
Stopford, Gen. Sir Montague, 496
Stumme, Gen. 350
Subansiri Frontier Division, 39
Suez, 32, 161, 455
Sweden, 33
Taiwan (Formosa), 148, 490
Talwar, Capt. Harjeet Singh: 341, 355, 381, 385, 386
Telengana, 19, 493
Tenga Valley, 58
Tewari, Lt.-Col. K. K., 334
Tezpur, 4, 72, 141, 158, 165-166, 168, 171, 181-182, 189, 192, 198, 201, 255-257, 260, 264, 282, 284, 286, 291, 317, 323, 328, 335, 341, 344, 354, 442, 459, 471
Thagla Affair (also Operation/Episode) 152, 157, 159, 161, 167, 169-170, 179, 184, 198-199, 202, 219, 221, 228, 231, 233, 247, 252-253, 255, 262-263, 268-269, 336, 341, 352 354, 372-373, 376, 390, 397, 426, 439, 443, 460, 497
Thagla Ridge (also area/heights/massif/slopes), 1, 43, 63, 77, 125, 130-133, 136, 138, 143, 152, 154, 156, 158-160, 165-166, 168, 170-176, 182-185, 187, 192, 198-199, 207-209, 211-213, 217-222, 226, 229, 234, 237, 240, 246-247, 252, 256, 258-259, 267-269, 272-273, 275, 277, 282-283, 285, 287, 290-291, 293-294, 297, 301-302, 307-308, 311, 313-314, 322-323, 325, 331, 337, 339, 342, 346, 352-353, 360, 364, 375, 382, 392-393, 423, 427, 460, 470
Thapar, Gen. Pran Nath, 4, 68-69, 73, 86-87, 93, 96, 113, 132, 191, 198-199, 211, 213, 229, 234-235, 245-246, 250, 327, 346, 351-352, 425-428, 444, 460, 468
Thimayya, Gen. K. S., 46-55, 61, 67, 73-74, 87-89, 425, 452, 458
Third Five-Year Plan, 77
Thoma, Gen. Ritter von, 350
Thompson, Brig., 64-65
Thonglen, 126, 128
Thorat, Lt.-Gen. S. P. P., 60-61, 67, 73-74
Tibet, 6-18, 20-21, 36-37, 40, 43, 49, 64-66, 77, 96, 116, 132, 150, 152-153, 210, 376, 404, 444, 449, 489, 490, 491
Tibet (Inner), 10-11
Tibet (Outer), 10-11, 147
Times of India, 50, 348, 406
Times of London, 269, 329, 423
Time Magazine, 406
Tithwal, 475
Tobruk, 350
Towang, 1, 44, 56, 58-59, 61, 65-66, 72, 98, 103, 107, 110-119, 121-123,

125-126, 128-129, 132-134, 139-140, 144, 154, 160, 165-168, 173-176, 178, 181-184, 186, 189-192, 195-198, 201, 203, 214, 224-226, 263-265, 270, 290, 316, 345-346, 367, 373, 387-388, 497
Towang Monastery, 116
Tsangdhar, 138, 172, 208-209, 219, 239-241, 258, 263-265, 267, 271-272, 274, 276-278, 286, 294, 308, 315-317, 319, 321-322, 324, 326, 330, 339, 341, 355, 361-362, 364, 366-367, 372-375, 381-382, 421
Tsangle, 207, 234, 238-239, 275, 278-280, 296, 298, 325-328, 332, 334, 336-339, 345, 352, 354-355, 360-361 365-367, 371, 373, 443, 467
Tseng-Jong, 185, 240, 275, 276, 278-279, 287, 290, 291, 294, 297-299, 301, 314, 318, 329, 337
Tsona Dzong, 66, 153
Tuchman, Mrs. Barbara, 295
Tunis, 191
Tunku Abdul Rehman, 482
Tyagi, Mahavir, 451-452

Umrao Singh, Lt.-Gen., 69, 137, 170, 177, 181, 185, 192-193, 195, 227-228, 232-233, 239-242, 245-246, 248-256, 258-259, 261, 264, 267, 271, 274, 277, 327, 331
United Kingdom (also Britain), 9, 32-33, 87, 452, 454, 478, 479, 480, 490, 495
United Nations, 7, 13-14, 21, 23, 26, 30, 157, 404, 427, 467, 494, 495
United Nations General Assembly, 13, 157
United Nations Peace Force, Cyprus, 53
United Nations Security Council 30. 33
United States of America (also America) 25-27, 32-34, 404, 478-480, 487, 490, 495
U.S.S.R. (see Soviet Union)
Uttar Pradesh, 21, 224, 449, 495

Vagts, Alfred, 248
Verma, Lt.-Gen. S. D., 73-74, 83, 86-88, 96, 102
Viet Minh, 19
Vietinghoff, Gen., 202

Walong, 36, 145, 224, 256, 324
Warangal, 19, 493
War Office (London), 410-411
Washington, 89, 478
Wellington, Duke of, 225
Wellington (South India), 15
Whitehall, 410
Williams, Sqn.-Leader, 317
Wingate, Gen. Orde, 16
Wolfe, Gen., 206, 235
Wuje (Bara Hoti), 21

Yatung, 20, 495
Yol, 165, 178, 439
Younghusband, Col. 9
Younghusband Expedition, 9
Yumtsola, 211-212, 276, 285-286, 28 290, 293-294, 301-302

Ziminthaung, 130-131, 272, 284, 31 319, 324, 365, 367, 388
Zorndorf, Battle of, 379